Religious Zionism, Jewish Law, and The Morality of War

How Five Rabbis Confronted One of Modern Judaism's Greatest Challenges

—————— ⌒⌒⌒ ——————

Robert Eisen

OXFORD
UNIVERSITY PRESS

OXFORD
UNIVERSITY PRESS

Oxford University Press is a department of the University of Oxford. It furthers the University's objective of excellence in research, scholarship, and education by publishing worldwide. Oxford is a registered trade mark of Oxford University Press in the UK and certain other countries.

Published in the United States of America by Oxford University Press
198 Madison Avenue, New York, NY 10016, United States of America.

Library of Congress Cataloging-in-Publication Data
Name: Eisen, Robert, 1960– author.
Title: Religious Zionism, Jewish law, and The Morality of War:
how five rabbis confronted one of modern Judaism's
greatest challenges / Robert Eisen.
Description: New York: Oxford University Press, [2017]
Identifiers: LCCN 2016059264| ISBN 9780190687090 (alk. paper) |
ISBN 9780190687120 (online content) | ISBN: 9780190687106 (UPDF)|
ISBN: 9780190687113 (EPUB)
Subjects: LCSH: War—Religious aspects—Judaism. | Religious Zionism—Israel. |
Religious Zionists—Attitudes. | Jewish ethics. | Kook, Abraham Isaac,
1865–1935—Philosophy. | Herzog, Isaac, 1888–1959—Philosophy. |
Valdenberg, Eliezer Yehudah—Philosophy. | Yisraeli, Shaul R.—
Philosophy. | Goren, Shlomo, 1917–1994—Philosophy.
Classification: LCC BM538.P3 E375 2017 | DDC 296.3/827—dc23
LC record available at https://lccn.loc.gov/2016059264

1 3 5 7 9 8 6 4 2
Printed by Sheridan Books, Inc., United States of America

To all Israeli soldiers who have ever wrestled
with the moral implications of war

CONTENTS

PREFACE

The inspiration for this project came from a conversation I had with Stuart Cohen a number of years ago over lunch at a café in Silver Spring, Maryland, a short walk from my home. I had just completed the manuscript for my last book, *The Peace and Violence of Judaism: From the Bible to Modern Zionism* (Oxford Univeristy Press, 2011), and Stuart, a distinguished Israeli academic in the field of political science, was taking a sabbatical in the area at the time and had graciously agreed to read the manuscript. Stuart's feedback was generously positive, and when he and I went to lunch that day, we discussed a number of items pertaining the book. At one point in the conversation, Stuart recommended that I consider extending my research on peace and violence in Judaism into the realm of Halakhah, an area that had not been dealt with in my book in any depth; I had focused primarily on how peace and violence had been treated in the realm of Jewish thought. What Stuart had in mind was the voluminous material on war in Halakhah that had been produced in recent years by rabbis in Israel, primarily in the religious Zionist camp. Stuart himself had written a number of pioneering articles on this material, which up to that point had not attracted much interest from academics.

I decided to take up Stuart's suggestion, for even though Halakhah was not really my area of expertise, the treatment of war in Halakhah dealt with matters that were certainly relevant to my work on Jewish approaches to peace and violence, and I figured that I should have at least some acquaintance with it. As I began my exploration, I was struck by how interesting the literature was that Stuart had spoken about. The rabbis in the religious Zionist camp who had written on war in Halakhah had created a large body of work in a relatively short period of time on a topic about which little had been written beforehand, and they had done so with great creativity and ingenuity. The lack of prior material was due to the fact that the issue of war had not been relevant for halakhic authorities before the creation of the state of Israel. During the many centuries in which Halakhah evolved, Jews did not have their own state and therefore had no army. However, with the creation of the state of Israel, that issue was now not only relevant but of pressing importance, and the rabbis were forced to address it. The result was a fascinating body of writings on the subject.

It was not long before I resolved to make this material the focus of my next book. Initially, I had wanted to write a comprehensive study analyzing how halakhic authorities in the religious Zionist camp have dealt with war in Halakhah since the establishment of the state of Israel, but it soon became clear to me that I could not possibly cover that topic in a single volume. I therefore decided to limit my focus to five rabbis in this camp who were highly influential figures in formulating halakhic positions on war. I also decided to restrict the focus further by dwelling on a number key moral issues that they grappled with.

The present study represents the outcome of these plans, and the first person who deserves my thanks for its publication is, of course, Stuart Cohen, who planted the idea for this project in the first place. The distance between the United States and Israel has made it difficult for us to be in regular contact since his stay in Silver Spring during his sabbatical year. Nonetheless, with the help of electronic communication, I have been priviledged to have Stuart as a source of help and encouragement in the past several years as I have pursued this project.

The full manuscript was read by a number of colleagues: Motti Inbari, Reuven Kimelman, Alan Mittleman, David Shatz, and Dov Zakheim. Each brought a unique set of skills to their reading, and their comments greatly improved the final product. I must also acknowledge a number of colleagues who read portions of the manuscript. Yitzchak Roness provided excellent feedback on my chapter on R. Isaac Halevi Herzog, and Aviad Hollander provided extremely helpful suggestions on my chapter on R. Shlomo Goren. Shifra Mishlov is also to be thanked for sending me her dissertation on R. Goren to read. Needless, to say any errors that remain in this book are entirely my own responsibility.

Thanks also go to my parents. Both of them have read every book manuscript I have written, and each time, the manuscript has benefited greatly from their suggestions. The present project is no exception. My father, a retired historian, is one of the most insightful readers I have ever consulted. Even though he is not a specialist in Judaism, he always manages to provide feedback that is just as valuable as that given by the best experts in the field. My mother has copyediting skills that are better than most professionals I have worked with. Few mistakes escape her eagle eye.

It has been wonderful to work again with the team at Oxford. Cynthia Read, who by now is a legend among scholars of religion in the U.S., sheparded the project with her usual blend of professionalism and common-sense. Her assistant Hannah Campeanu was also a pleasure to work with.

I am grateful for the permission granted to me by several journals to reproduce material in this book that was previously published. Chapter 3 includes material from "R. Abraham Isaac Kook on War in Jewish Law," *Modern Judaism* 33, no. 1 (2013): 23–44. Chapter 5 includes material from "Rabbi Eliezer Yehudah Waldenberg on the Justification of War." *Torah U-Madda Journal* (forthcoming). Chapter 6 includes material from "War, Revenge, and Jewish Ethics: Rabbi Shaul Yisraeli's Essay on Kibiyeh Revisited." *AJS Review* 36, no.1 (April 2012): 141–163.

The last person I must thank is by far the most important: my wife Naomi. At this point in life, any praise I would give her could only be an understatement. Suffice it to say that this book would not have been possible without her—nor, for that matter, would anything else that I have produced in the past two decades in which we have shared our lives.

NOTE ON STYLE, TRANSLATION, AND TRANSLITERATION

Throughout this book, I use male pronouns as a default. That is not because of any bias on my part. It is just that gender-neutral pronouns—"he/she" or "they"—sound completely out of place when analyzing the work of halakhic authorities who subscribe to a highly traditional worldview. The translations of all texts are my own, unless otherwise noted. My transliterations follow that of *Encyclopedia Judaica*, except that "h" is used for ח, and "ts" is used for צ. Proper names are transliterated except when they have a form commonly used in English, in which case, that form is used.

ABBREVIATIONS

BT   Babylonian Talmud
HM   *Hilkhot Medinah* (of R. Eliezer Yehudah Waldenberg)
HRL   Human Rights Law
JT   Jerusalem Talmud
LOAC Law of Armed Conflict
M   Mishnah
MK   *Mishpat Kohen* (of R. Abraham Isaac Kook)
MT   *Mishneh Torah*
PKOH *Peskaim u-Khetavim be-Diney Orah Hayim* (edited writings of R. Isaac
        Halevi Herzog)
T   Tosefta
TsE   *Tsits Eli'ezer* (of R. Eliezer Waldenberg)

CHAPTER 1

༄

Introduction

It has often been noted that the very notion of "war ethics" seems paradoxical, perhaps absurdly so. It conjoins two terms that, at least superficially, appear to be at odds with each other. War gives expression to the basest and most destructive instincts in human nature. It allows human beings to engage in brutality and killing on the grandest scale. Ethics, by contrast, is a discipline instructing human beings in how to live in accordance with their highest ideals. It focuses on what it means for people to be "moral" and "good" in their interactions with each other. What, then, does it mean to speak of "war ethics?" Is the phrase not an oxymoron?[1]

And yet, there is such a discipline as war ethics, and, in fact, it has been around as long as war has. All major cultures have developed a set of rules and guidelines to regulate this activity. And upon reflection, one can see why such a discipline must exist. The institution of war has been a regular feature of human culture throughout its entire history, and however much we may want to wish it away, it is unlikely to disappear any time soon. Even in the age in which we now live, when war is frowned upon more than at any time in history, when we have a United Nations that was created in large part to make war a thing of the past—war remains an all too common occurrence in our global community. And so, the thinking goes, if we are

---

1. This observation has been made by those who engage in war ethics from a philosophical standpoint, as well as by those who do so from a legal standpoint. For an example of the former, see Michael Walzer, *Just and Unjust Wars: A Moral Argument with Historical Illustrations*, 4th ed. (New York: Basic Books, 2006), 3. For an example of the latter, see Gary D. Solis, *The Law of Armed Conflict: International Humanitarian Law in War* (New York: Cambridge University Press, 2010), 8.

stuck with this scourge, we may as well try to limit the harm it causes. We may as well do our best to minimize its mayhem. Viewed in this light, the phrase "war ethics" is not as problematic as it may seem. It represents an acknowledgment that violence will always be a means for human collectives to settle their differences, while holding out hope that we can, at least, curtail its worst effects.[2]

Few modern nations have had to reflect on these matters as much as the state of Israel. Israel was thrust into war from the moment that the United Nations voted for the establishment of a Jewish state in 1947. Palestinian Arabs and the surrounding Arab nations rejected the founding by the United Nations of a Jewish state in their midst, and they immediately set out to destroy it. And even though Israel decisively won its first war against its enemies, there were many more to follow. In fact, Israel has never known a time when it has been entirely free of war. Even when not engaged in actual war, Israel has always had to prepare for the next war on the presumption that it is not likely to be far off.

Israeli writers in a wide range of disciplines have reflected deeply on the moral dilemmas associated with war, including legal specialists, philosophers, literary figures, and academics. Among these writers, one finds a wide range of political orientations: those who are hawkish, those are dovish, and everything in between. These orientations, in turn, reflect deep divisions within the larger Israeli society to which they belong. Israel has always been torn by disagreement over how to make sense of the violence it had to perpetrate at its creation and must still perpetrate to remain in existence.[3]

Israelis in the religious Zionist camp have faced a unique set of challenges in dealing with war because of their need to seek guidance from the sacred texts of Judaism regarding all aspects of life. As Orthodox Jews, religious Zionists adhere to the view that all their beliefs and actions have to be determined by the Bible and the literature of the rabbis that interprets it. These texts are believed to embody God's wisdom about the world, and His will as to how human beings should live. And even though religious Zionists understand that Israel is a mostly secular state in which the biblical and rabbinic

---

2. Walzer, *Just and Unjust Wars*, 4–20; Solis, *Law of Armed Conflict*, 8–10.

3. Ehud Luz analyzes how Zionists have grappled with the moral dilemmas that have arisen because of the need to use violence in implementing their goals, in *Wrestling with an Angel: Power, Morality, and Jewish Identity*, trans. Michael Swirsky (New Haven, Conn.: Yale University Press, 2003). Yosef Gorny deals with this issue as well, but he focuses on Zionism prior to the establishment of Israel, in *Zionism and the Arabs, 1882–1948: A Study of Ideology* (Oxford: Oxford University Press, 1987). Anita Shapira narrows the focus even further in her study *Land and Power: The Zionist Resort to Force, 1881–1948*, trans. by William Templer (New York: Oxford University Press, 1992). Shapira, like Gorny, examines how Zionism dealt with this issue before the founding of the state, but her analysis deals exclusively with Labor Zionism.

tradition does not dictate policy, they feel that this tradition must guide their lives as Israeli citizens.[4]

When it comes to the waging of war, here too, religious Zionists have looked to the sacred literature of the past for guidance on what they should believe and how they should act. Moreover, because war is such a serious matter, religious Zionists have usually turned to their leading rabbis for such instruction. On a matter of such gravity, it is generally assumed that only the most respected religious authorities have the right to speak for the religious Zionist community.

Secular Zionists have not had this burden. They have never entirely discarded the sacred texts of Judaism. After all, it is the Bible that provides them with the basic claim that the land of Israel is the homeland of the Jewish people. However, secular Zionists treat these texts as historical artifacts, not as revelations from God, and they therefore can afford to ignore them when they offer opinions with which they disagree.[5]

If religious Zionists have had to come to terms with war in the spheres of both belief and action, each of these realms has raised its own set of questions. In the sphere of belief, the leading spokesmen in the religious Zionist community have had to grapple with the theological meaning of war. The rabbis in this community have had to ask why God has required Jews to engage in violence in order to return to their homeland. This question has in turn been connected to the larger issue of God's plan for history and the role of the state of Israel in that plan. Does the establishment of Israel have messianic significance, and if so, what role does violence play in that enterprise? For questions of this kind, religious Zionist rabbis have turned to Jewish texts that are usually consulted by Orthodox Jews on theological matters: rabbinic aggadah, medieval Jewish philosophy, and Kabbalah.[6]

4. Basic introductions to religious Zionism can be found in Gideon Shimoni, *The Zionist Ideology* (Waltham, Mass.: Brandeis University Press, 1995), chapter 4; and Dov Schwartz, *Religious Zionism*, 2nd ed. (Brighton, Mass.: Academic Studies Press, 2012).

5. See Luz, introduction to *Wrestling with an Angel*; and Yosef Salmon, *Im Ta'iru ve-Im Tit'oreru: Ortodoxiyah be-Metsarey ha-Le'umiyut* (Jerusalem: Zalman Shazar Center, 2006), pp. 11–15, and chapters 13–15. See also Anita Shapira, "The Religious Motifs of the Labor Movement," *Zionism and Religion*, eds. Shmuel Almog, Jehuda Reinharz, and Anita Shapira (Hanover, N.H.: University of New England Press, 1998), 251–72; Shlomo Avineri, "Zionism and Jewish Religious Tradition: The Dialectics of Redemption and Secularization," in Almog, Reinharz, and Shapira, *Zionism and Religion*, 1–9.

6. Both Gorny and Luz deal with the attitudes of religious Zionists to violence as part of their more general studies on Zionism and its approaches to violence. A more detailed treatment of how religious Zionism has dealt with this issue can be found in Aviezer Ravitzky, *Messianism, Zionism, and Jewish Religious Radicalism*, trans. Michael Swirsky and Jonathan Chipman (Chicago: University of Chicago Press, 1996). Ravitzky's book is devoted to examining how Orthodox Jews of all stripes reacted to the rise of Zionism and the moral and religious questions it raised, and his book therefore includes material on ultra-Orthodox Jews, whose attitudes to this issue were markedly different from those of religious Zionists. We will discuss the views

In grappling with the issue of war in the realm of action, the same rabbis have had to explore the sources of Jewish religious law, or Halakhah, in order to deal with another series of questions. Does Halakhah, in fact, support the use of war by the state of Israel, and if so, under what circumstances? And once war has been waged, how should Jewish soldiers conduct themselves in battle? There have also been multiple questions about how religiously observant soldiers are supposed to fulfill their ritual obligations while serving in the army or going to war. For instance, what does one do when one's military duties require the violation of the Sabbath or do not allow one to fulfill one's obligation to pray three times a day?

The challenges that religious Zionist rabbis have faced in dealing with war in the sphere of Halakhah have perhaps been more daunting than those in the area of theology. First, the halakhic questions have been more consequential than the theological ones. In issuing halakhic rulings on war, the rabbis have engaged not merely in speculations about theoretical matters but in judgments about life-and-death issues for the individual and the state alike. Second, it was not clear from the outset that Halakhah was up to the task of dealing with wars waged by a modern Jewish state. When the state of Israel was created, Jews had not had political power, or the capacity to wage war as a nation, since the first century of the Common Era, when the Jewish commonwealth was destroyed by Rome. In the many centuries that passed between that event and the creation of the state of Israel, most Jews lived as minorities in Christian Europe and in Muslim lands, and it was during this extended duration of time that Halakhah evolved and became consolidated as the law system guiding all aspects of Jewish life. Therefore, when the state of Israel came into existence, there was very little material in Halakhah about political matters in general, and war in particular. These topics were simply not relevant to Jewish life in the medieval and early modern periods, and thus halakhic authorities throughout the centuries had not said much about them.

Yet the fledgling Jewish state was immediately at war upon its founding, and rabbis in the religious Zionist camp therefore had to quickly formulate positions on war that were both true to the halakhic tradition and able to deal with the dire situation at hand. It was not an easy task. The rabbis had to wring as much as they could out of the little material on war that existed in Halakhah in order to apply it to their circumstances. They also had to make use of halakhic sources that did not directly address war but could be stretched and interpreted to give guidance on war.

of ultra-Orthodox Judaism on this matter later in the chapter. Eli Holtser focuses on religious Zionism and its attitude to militarism in general in *Herev Pipiyot be-Yadam: Activizm Tseva'i be-Hagutah shel ha-Tsiyonut ha-Datit* (Jerusalem: Hartman Institute, 2009). More recently, Reuven Firestone has analyzed the attitudes of religious Zionism to war in *Holy War in Judaism: The Fall and Rise of a Controversial Idea* (New York: Oxford University Press, 2012), part 4.

In subsequent years, the halakhic literature on war would grow. The rabbis who composed the first pioneering treatments on war in Halakhah produced more literature on the subject as they refined their views on war and probed various aspects of it that had not received attention. Their students added to this literature as they matured into respected halakhic authorities in their own right and had new insights to offer about war. Furthermore, there was never a shortage of new questions about the topic. Fresh issues kept cropping up, as they always do in any area of law, and these issues elicited more insights and more literature. And the nature of warfare itself changed as the Jewish state matured, making it necessary for halakhic authorities to address these developments as well. The result of all this reflection and writing has been a large and complex body of halakhic literature on the subject of war that has appeared in the form of numerous books and scores of articles published in Israeli journals catering to the interests of the religious Zionist community.[7]

Academics have only just begun to appreciate the significance of this literature. In recent years, a number of important articles have appeared in academic journals mapping out the field and exploring various elements of it.[8] However, there has yet to be a book-length treatment of this literature by a single author writing from an academic perspective. The present volume hopes to provide the first treatment of this kind.[9] Yet I must emphasize that

7. Stuart A. Cohen and Aryeh Edrei have done pioneering work in mapping out this literature. See S. Cohen, "*Sifra ve-Sayfa u-mah she-Beinehem: 'Itsuv Hilkhot Tsava u-Milhamah be-Yisra'el*," *'Iyunim bi-Tekumat Yisra'el* 15 (2005): 237–49; idem, "The Quest for a Corpus of Jewish Military Ethics," *Journal of Israeli History* 26, no.1 (2007): 35–66; idem, "The Re-Discovery of Orthodox Jewish Laws Relating to the Military and War (*Hilkhot Tzavah U-Milchamah*) in Contemporary Israel: Trends and Implications," *Israel Studies* 12, no. 2 (2007): 1–28; Aryeh Edrei, "Law, Interpretation, and Ideology: The Renewal of the Jewish Laws of War in the State of Israel," *Cardozo Law Review* 28 (October 2006): 187–227; idem, "*Mi-Kibiyeh 'ad Beirut: Tehiyatan shel Diney ha-Milhamah ha-Hilkhatiyim be-Medinat Yisra'el*," *Yosef Da'at: Mehkarim be-Historiyah Yehudit Modernit Mugashim le-Prof. Yosef Salmon le-Hag Yovlo*, ed. Yossi Goldshtein (Be'er Sheva: Ben Gurion University Press, 2010), 95–127.

8. See the references to S. Cohen and Edrei in the previous note.

9. Holtser and Firestone have both written academic books devoted to the history of war ethics in religious Zionism, but their studies are focused primarily on the theological dimension of the topic, not its halakhic aspects. Recently, 'Ido Rekhnits and El'azar Goldshtein have published a study on war ethics in Halakhah as it pertains to the state of Israel entitled *Etikah Tseva'it Yehudit* (Tel Aviv: Yedi'ot Sefarim, 2013). However, Rekhnits and Goldshtein write as committed religious Zionists, and therefore their work is not academic in orientation but is instead an exercise in constructive ethics. As I note at the end of the chapter, many Jewish writers who write about war ethics in Halakhah deal with the subject from this perspective, and I have no objection to this approach. In fact, I believe that engaging the subject from this standpoint is vital for Jews in our era. It is just that an academic approach offers another way of examining war ethics in Halakhah, one that can yield valuable insights into the topic, and thus far, there have been no book-length studies on the subject written from this viewpoint.

this study will not be comprehensive. A thorough examination of the halakhic literature on war since the creation of the state of Israel is well beyond the scope of a single volume. I have therefore focused my study on five of the leading rabbinic figures in religious Zionism who wrote on war in Halakhah. I have also concentrated my efforts on a limited number of problems that these rabbis had to address in the moral sphere.

RELIGIOUS ZIONISM: AN OVERVIEW

While the description of my project up to this point provides a fairly good idea of what it intends to accomplish, there is a good deal more that needs to be said for my reader to have a clear picture of its goals, and it is to that end that the rest of this chapter is devoted. Let us begin by giving some background to the phenomenon of religious Zionism.

This brand of Zionism has never claimed the allegiance of more than a small fraction of Jews who identify themselves as Zionists. When Zionism first emerged in Jewish communities in Europe in the 1880s, most Orthodox Jews viewed it with suspicion or outright hostility because it was a staunchly secular movement. It rejected the traditional Jewish belief that the only way Jews would return to their ancient homeland was by observing God's commandments and patiently waiting for Him to reward them by sending His messiah to bring an end to the exile. In fact, many early Zionists did not believe in God at all, or if they did, they did not see Him as the type of deity who willfully intervened in history. Their view was that Jews would return to their homeland only if they took matters into their own hands. That meant emigrating to the land and settling it while organizing politically to convince the international community that the Jewish people were the land's rightful owners. Moreover, the political state that secular Zionism wanted to create was one in which religion would not play a central role. Religion had been critical for Jews during the centuries of exile because it gave them a strong sense of identity that in turn allowed them to bear their suffering, but it would no longer be needed in a modern state. Nationalism, not religion, would be the anchor of Jewish identity. Orthodox Jews, therefore, had two major problems with Zionism. It supported the active return of the Jewish people to its homeland prior to messianic times without looking to God for help, and the vast majority of its adherents were secular and intended to build a state reflecting that way of thinking.[10]

10. General histories of Zionist thought can be found in Shlomo Avineri, *The Making of Modern Zionism: The Intellectual Origins of the Jewish State* (New York: Basic Books, 1981); Shimoni, *Zionist Ideology*; Arthur Hertzberg, *The Zionist Idea: A Historical Analysis and Reader* (Philadelphia: Jewish Publication Society of America, 1997).

However, a small number of Orthodox Jews supported the Zionist enterprise despite these problems, and thus religious Zionism was born.[11] Two versions of it soon emerged. One was initiated by R. Isaac Jacob Reines (1839–1915) who took a pragmatic approach to Zionism. He believed that Orthodox Jews should support the Zionist enterprise because they needed their own state as a refuge from the physical and spiritual dangers that threatened them. A Jewish state would protect Jews from the anti-Semitism that, despite their emancipation, had remained a persistent problem in European culture. It would also help Jews stem the tide of assimilation into non-Jewish society, which was also plaguing the European Jewish community, by allowing Jews to build a state of their own based on Jewish culture and values.[12]

Far more influential was another approach to religious Zionism that was spearheaded by R. Abraham Isaac Kook (1865–1935) and was more dramatic in its thinking. According to R. Kook, Zionism was not only compatible with Judaism in its traditional form, it was, in some sense, its fulfillment. The founding of the Zionist movement and its project of settling the land of Israel represented nothing less than the beginning of the messianic redemption. Most Orthodox Jews subscribed to a passive form of messianism according to which the messianic era would come about through God's sudden and willful intervention into history. It was this conception of messianism that was represented in most traditional Jewish sources addressing the subject. But R. Kook was inspired by a number of other sources in rabbinic literature espousing a more active type of messianism in which human initiative would play a significant role in bringing about the redemption, and he therefore believed that Zionism was the embodiment of messianic aspirations.[13] The fact that Zionism was a mostly secular movement was not an issue for him. R. Kook argued that secular Zionists were being compelled by the divine spirit to settle the holy land for messianic purposes, even though they were not aware of it, and eventually, they would return to religion when they understood the significance of their actions. Underlying this way of thinking was the view that

---

11. The beginnings of religious Zionism are analyzed in Ehud Luz, *Religion and Nationalism in Early Zionist Thought (1882–1904)*, trans. Lenn J. Schram (Philadelphia: Jewish Publication Society of America, 1988), and Yosef Salmon, *Dat ve-Tsiyonut: 'Imutim Rishonim* (Jerusalem: Magnes Press, 2001).

12. R. Reines's approach to Zionism is analyzed in Joseph Wanefsky, *Rabbi Isaac Jacob Reines: His Life and Thought* (New York: Philosophical Library, 1970); and Yosef Shapira, *Hagut, Halakhah, ve-Tsiyonut: 'Al 'Olamo ha-Ruhani shel ha-Rav Yitshak Ya'akov Reines* (Tel Aviv: Ha-Kibuts ha-Me'uhad, 2002).

13. The distinction between active messianism and passive messianism and their influence on Zionist thinking are discussed in Jody Myers, "The Messianic Idea and Zionist Ideologies," *Studies in Contemporary Jewry VII: Jews and Messianism in the Modern Era: Metaphor and Meaning*, ed. Jonathan Frankel (New York: Oxford University Press, 1991), 4–7.

the messianic process was a gradual one. It would evolve slowly through the progress of normal historical events.[14]

R. Kook's teachings were further developed by his son, Rabbi Tsevi Yehudah Kook (1891–1982), who applied his father's ideas to the momentous events his father did not live to see: the Holocaust, the establishment of the State of Israel, and its struggle for survival in the face of several wars with its Arab neighbors. The younger Kook also cultivated a loyal band of disciples who had great success in disseminating his teachings in the religious Zionist community. During his lifetime, the elder Kook's views did not win large numbers of adherents, but his thinking, reshaped and popularized by his son, became dominant among religious Zionists in the decades after the Six Day War in 1967. Most important, the younger Kook radicalized his father's teachings, and in their new form they inspired the aggressive settlement activity in the territories captured by Israel in the Six Day War.[15]

The younger Kook followed his father's lead in believing that secular Zionism was unwittingly motivated by a divine impulse and was a vehicle for bringing about the messianic redemption, but he extended these ideas to the political reality of the state of Israel. Thus, the secular political state was now holy, as was its army. The wars waged by the state were also holy. Their purpose was to establish Jewish sovereignty over the geographical area that God had promised to Abraham in the Bible and that later became the territory of the ancient Jewish kingdom, for according to rabbinic tradition, this land would be possessed by the Jewish people once again in the messianic period.[16]

14. There is a vast literature on R. Kook's life and thought. Some general academic treatments include Benjamin Ish Shalom and Shalom Rosenberg, eds., *The World of Rav Kook's Thought*, trans. Shalom Carmy and Bernard Casper (Avi Chai Foundation, 1991); Ezra Gellman, ed., *Essays on the Thought and Philosophy of Rabbi Kook* (Rutherford, N.J.: Fairleigh Dickinson University Press, 1991); Benjamin Ish-Shalom, *Rav Avraham Itzhak HaCohen Kook: Between Rationalism and Mysticism*, trans. Ora Wiskind-Elper (Albany: State University of New York Press, 1993); Lawrence J. Kaplan and David Shatz, eds., *Rabbi Abraham Isaac Kook and Jewish Spirituality* (New York: New York University Press, 1995); Avinoam Rosenak, *A. I. Kook* (Jerusalem: Merkaz Zalman Shazar, 2006); Yehudah Mirsky, *Rav Kook: Mystic in a Time of Revolution* (New Haven, Conn.: Yale University Press, 2014). More sources on R. Kook's thought will be cited in chapter 3, which is devoted to his views on war.

15. The impact of R. Kook's thought on religious Zionism after his lifetime, including the key role played by his son in shaping his father's thinking, is analyzed in Ravitzky, *Messianism, Zionism*, chapter 3. The most prolific author on this subject is Dov Schwartz who has addressed the legacy of R. Kook in a series of studies, including *Erets Mamashut ve-Dimyon: Ma'amdah shel Erets Yisra'el be-Hagut ha-Tsiyonut ha-Datit* (Tel Aviv: 'Am 'Oved Publishers, 1997); *Ha-Tsiyonut ha-Datit: Bein Higayon le-Meshihiyut* (Tel Aviv: 'Am 'Oved Publishers, 1999); *Etgar u-Mashber be-Hug ha-Rav Kuk* (Tel Aviv: 'Am 'Oved Publishers, 2001); *Faith at the Crossroads: A Theological Profile of Religious Zionism*, trans. by Batya Stein (Leiden: E. J. Brill, 2002).

16. Ravitzky, *Messianism, Zionism*, 86, 122–23; Luz, *Wrestling with an Angel*, 223–24.

While the basic elements of R. Tsevi Yehudah Kook's thinking took shape after the 1948 War of Independence, his views were further consolidated in the wake of the 1967 war. Israelis were stunned by their seemingly miraculous victory. For the younger Kook, the victory was nothing short of a miracle in the literal sense of the term. Israel now controlled a much larger portion of the territories that were part of the land promised to Abraham, and this seemed to be proof that the messianic era was indeed unfolding. Moreover, the victory inspired the younger Kook and his followers to lobby the Israeli government for settlement of the captured territories in order to secure Jewish sovereignty over them, to block attempts on the part of the government to trade land for peace, and to ensure that the messianic process continue.[17] Gush Emunim (the Bloc of the Faithful), an organization formed in 1974, became the leading force for this cause and was soon taken over by elite students of R. Tsevi Yehudah Kook, who used it as a vehicle to implement their messianic program. This organization was remarkably successful. It raised the profile of religious Zionism from a relatively marginal phenomenon in Israeli society and politics to one that had strong influence on the entire national agenda. It was extremely effective in lobbying successive Israeli governments to support and implement its plans. Since the founding of Gush Emunim, scores of settlements have been established throughout the territories captured in 1967, and they are populated by hundreds of thousands of Israelis.[18]

Yet since the 1970s when R. Tsevi Yehudah Kook's thinking was enormously influential, religious Zionism has faced a number of challenges, and it has become increasingly diverse as its followers have adopted different approaches to deal with these challenges. The idea that the founding of the state of Israel is the beginning of the messianic redemption has not been easy to uphold. A number of events have raised doubts about whether the messianic redemption is indeed in process, and if so, what stage it is in. Since the victory

17. Ehud Sprinzak, *The Ascendance of Israel's Radical Right* (New York: Oxford University Press, 1991), 43–46.

18. Sprinzak, *Ascendance*, 46–55, 67–69; Ravitzky, *Messianism, Zionism*, 129, 131–33; Gideon Aran assumes that from the very outset the leaders of Gush Emunim were disciples of the elder and younger Kook and therefore saw the settlement of lands captured in the '67 war as an expression of their messianic Zionism. See Aran's discussion in "Bein Halutsiyut le-Limud Torah: Ha-Reka' le-Ge'ut ha-Datit Le'umit," in *Me'ah Shanot Tsiyonut Datit: Heibetim Ra'ayoniyim*, eds. Avi Sagi and Dov Schwartz (Ramat Gan: Bar-Ilan University Press, 2004), 3:31–72. However, Avi Sagi and Dov Schwartz reject Aran's view and contend that Gush Emunim began as an organization inspired by classical religious Zionist philosophy that was not messianic. Only later did Gush Emunim attract the followers of the two Kooks who brought with them their messianic Zionism. Yet, even if Schwartz and Sagi are correct, there is no question that the settlement movement eventually received much of its energy from the supporters of Kookian theology. See Avi Sagi and Dov Schwartz, "Bein Halutsiyut le-Limud Torah: Zavit Aheret," in *Me'ah Shanot Tsiyonut Datit: Heibetim Ra'ayoniyim*, eds. Avi Sagi and Dov Schwartz (Ramat Gan: Bar-Ilan University Press, 2004), 3:73–76.

in the Six Day War, Israel has fought several more wars, some of which have been unsuccessful or have been won at a high cost, and it has witnessed two intifadas. Israel also willingly gave land back to the Palestinians with the Gaza disengagement in 2005, which seemed to reverse the progress of the messianic process. Social realities have also soured the messianic expectations of some religious Zionists. The secular population in Israel has shown no greater interest in adopting Orthodox religious observance than it did at the time of the founding of the state, an indication that progress toward messianic times has been halted or was an illusion to begin with. And many Israelis of secular orientation have consistently supported the notion of trading land for peace that would allow for the creation of a Palestinian state on the West Bank and in Gaza, a plan, that, if successful, would constitute an enormous setback for the messianic process in the eyes of most religious Zionists. The Oslo Accords, which were signed in the 1990s, embodied this way of thinking among secular Israelis, and even though the accords ultimately failed, they were evidence that a substantial number of Israelis could be swayed to support territorial concessions in return for a peace agreement with the Palestinians. To complicate matters even more for religious Zionists, some in their own camp backed the Oslo Accords.

These factors have caused the religious Zionist community to splinter. Some have become disillusioned with R. Tsevi Yehudah Kook's vision. Others have held fast to it and continue to believe that the messianic process is on track, despite the setbacks outlined here. A fringe element has also developed within religious Zionism that has adopted violent views regarding Arabs and vilifies secular Israelis. The religious Zionist community, at present, is therefore divided about its agenda.[19]

Now that we have reviewed the major developments in the history of religious Zionism and the theology that underpins it, let us now turn to its treatment of religious practice. As Aryeh Fishman points out, the greatest challenge for religious Zionism in its early years was not in making sense of Zionism from a theological standpoint, but in dealing with a series of halakhic problems that cropped up as religious Zionists began to settle in Palestine. For instance, a good number of religious Zionists became farmers, just as their secular counterparts did, but this way of life brought with it many halakhic difficulties because Jews in Europe had not owned their own farms for centuries, and there were halakhic issues with farming that rabbinic authorities rarely had to address. Thus, as one example, cows had to be milked every day, and the question therefore arose whether Jews could perform this activity on the Sabbath, or whether non-Jews had to be hired for that purpose. There was

19. This latest phase in the development of religious Zionism has been analyzed by Motti Inbari in *Messianic Religious Zionism Confronts Territorial Compromises* (Cambridge: Cambridge University Press, 2012).

also a host of halakhic regulations with respect to farming that were unique to the land of Israel and had to be dealt with as well. For example, what was one to do about the rules of biblical origin according to which farmers in the land of Israel had to allow their fields to lie fallow every seventh year? Another conundrum that arose for religious farmers and city dwellers alike had to do with voting rights for women. The institutions of the Jewish community in Palestine were organized democratically, and in the secular sector of the community, women had the right to vote. Yet, it is not clear that Halakhah allows women this privilege, and arguments were brought that would deny the privilege to them. All these halakhic challenges elicited much debate among the rabbis in Palestine, and solutions were proposed, though there was not always consensus on which solutions should be implemented.[20]

Once the state of Israel was created, there were even more halakhic challenges to deal with. Jews now had jurisdiction over a substantial population of non-Jews. What was the status of this population from the standpoint of Halakhah? Most important for our concerns were the military questions. What approach should the Orthodox Jewish citizens of Israel take to army service or the waging of war? Underlying these questions was the more basic challenge of what attitude halakhically committed Jews should have to the laws of the state in general. Were they binding, and if so, were they binding on all matters even if they conflicted with Halakhah? Rabbinic authorities in the medieval and early modern periods had had to deal with such questions in the non-Jewish countries in which they lived, and they managed to find reasonable ways to accommodate Halakhah to the laws of the state. However, matters were different in a state that was Jewish but not halakhic. In this situation, what should the precise relationship be between Halakhah and the laws of the state?[21]

Asher Cohen has shown how, in the early years of the Jewish state, religious Zionists attempted to deal with this dilemma by promoting the notion of *medinat ha-torah*, "a state according to Torah." This phrase represented the belief that harmony could be found between the position that political matters in Israel should be guided by the teachings of the Torah and the view that such matters should be decided by a democratically elected government. The program to promote this ideal, however, would fail within the first few years of the state because Israel's secular public had no interest in it. The religious Zionist political parties banded together into a single party, which ran in the first election of the Israeli parliament on the platform of *medinat ha-torah* but won only a small percentage of the vote. The failure of the program was also due to the fact that the religious Zionist camp did not have a clear idea of

20. Aryeh Fishman, *Bein Dat le-Idiologiyah: Yahadut ve-Modernizatsyah be-Kibutz ha-Dati* (Jerusalem: Yad Yitshak ben Tsevi, 1990), 55–77.
21. Edrei, "Law," 189–92.

what *medinat ha-torah* meant. There was a wide variety of opinions among religious Zionists about how Halakhah should be brought into harmony with the laws of the state. Those on the traditional end of the spectrum wanted to see the state's laws conform to Halakhah as it developed prior to Zionism. Those on the more liberal end of the spectrum had the opposite view. They wanted Halakhah to undergo significant change, even reconstruction, to conform to the demands of the state. And there were, of course, a variety of approaches between these two poles. Because of the failure of the program to promote the notion of *medinat ha-torah*, the religious Zionist parties decided to shelve this initiative and devote themselves to more pragmatic matters. Their interest now was in ensuring that halakhically observant Jews living in Israel had their religious needs taken care of in day-to-day life.[22]

But the abandonment of the notion of *medinat ha-torah* did not mean that the religious Zionist community in Israel ceased to think about political matters and their halakhic ramifications. Religious Zionists were still Orthodox Jews whose lives were guided by Halakhah, and they therefore continued to seek counsel from their rabbis about what their obligations should be to the society of which they were a part, and what to do if these obligations were in conflict with the demands imposed on them by the state. Some religious Zionist rabbis also probed political issues from a halakhic standpoint because they believed in R. Kook's vision that the state of Israel had a role to play in the messianic process, and they therefore thought it necessary to create a body of Halakhah about political matters to prepare for the time when the state was ready to fulfill that vision.[23] The result of these reflections on political matters was the emergence of a large body of halakhic literature dealing with multiple aspects of this topic, and as one might expect, that literature contained a wide variety of viewpoints on such issues.

The great challenge that religious Zionism has always faced and that explains many of its dilemmas, both in the realm of theology and Halakhah, is that it has consistently tried to bring together two worlds that do not easily mix. On the one hand, this movement has identified with mainstream Zionism. But this form of Zionism has been primarily secular, and many of its adherents have been in rebellion against the traditional Judaism that religious Zionists regard as the basis of their lives. On the other hand, religious Zionists have had common cause with the ultra-Orthodox community and its firm commitment to traditional Judaism. However, the ultra-Orthodox community has largely rejected Zionism in any form because of its secular orientation.[24]

---

22. Asher Cohen's study, *Ha-Talit ve-ha-Degel: Ha-Tsiyonut ha-Datit ve-Hazon Medinat ha-Torah Bi-Yemey Reshit ha-Medinah* (Jerusalem: Yad Yitshak ben-Tsevi, 1998), is devoted to analyzing the process by which the concept of *medinat ha-torah* was formulated and eventually abandoned.

23. As we shall see later on in our study, R. Sha'ul Yisraeli was one such rabbi.

24. Asher Cohen, *Ha-Talit ve-ha-Degel*, 15; Schwartz, *Faith at the Crossroads*.

RELIGIOUS ZIONISM AND WAR

Our interest in this study is in how rabbis in the religious Zionist camp dealt with the specific topic of war, and so let us now focus on this issue. We will proceed in the same manner here that we did in the preceding sketch of the general history of religious Zionism. We will first look at the theological dimension of the topic, and then proceed to an examination of its halakhic dimension.

The Theological Dimension

Before we look at how religious Zionism has viewed war from a theological standpoint, we should first say something about how war was viewed in Jewish thought prior to Zionism. There is one word that characterizes all of Jewish thought leading up to Zionism when it comes to this issue: ambiguity. As I have shown in a previous study, in every period and in every major school of Judaism, there were sources that looked positively on violence and war in general, and sources that looked on them negatively. Moreover, there were a good many sources in every one of these schools that could be interpreted both ways. This assessment applies to the literature of the Bible, rabbinic Judaism, medieval Jewish philosophy, and Kabbalah.[25]

Many Jewish scholars have argued that Judaism underwent a major transformation in its attitude to war in the transition from the Bible to rabbinic Judaism in the first centuries of the Common Era. While the Bible often saw virtue in the waging of war, the rabbis consistently exhibited an aversion to it.[26] Yet, as I have demonstrated in my study, this judgment is flawed. A careful analysis of rabbinic literature demonstrates that rabbinic Judaism was just as ambiguous on this matter as the Bible.[27]

25. Robert Eisen, *The Peace and Violence of Judaism: From the Bible to Modern Zionism* (New York: Oxford University Press, 2011). Scholarly treatments of how war has been viewed in Judaism in a variety of literatures can be found in Yigal Levin and Amnon Shapira, eds., *War and Peace in the Jewish Tradition: From the Biblical World to the Present* (London: Routledge, 2012).

26. Firestone's study is predicated on this approach. He argues that the notion of holy war figured prominently in the Bible, was rejected by the rabbis in the medieval and early modern periods, and was then resurrected in religious Zionism. For a similar perspective on rabbinic Judaism prior to Zionism, see Luz, *Wrestling with an Angel*, 21–24; Edrei, "Law," 193–96; S. Cohen, "Quest," 35–36; Michael S. Berger, "Taming the Beast: Rabbinic Pacification of Second-Century Jewish Nationalism," *Belief and Bloodshed: Religion and Violence across Time and Tradition*, ed. James K. Wellman Jr. (Lanham, Md.: Rowman and Littlefield, 2007), 47–62.

27. Eisen, *Peace and Violence*, chapter 3.

It is therefore no surprise that Zionism itself would also exhibit ambiguity in its approach to war. Throughout its history, some in this movement have taken a bellicose stance on war, while others have adopted positions that are far more circumspect. Still others take positions between these extremes. The views of Zionists on this issue therefore reflect the same diversity one sees in prior Jewish tradition.[28]

There are, however, some nuances in the attitudes of Zionism to violence and war that should be mentioned. Anita Shapira has shown that in the first few decades of Jewish settlement in Palestine, when Jews were confronted with Palestinians who were hostile to their presence, they tended to adopt a "defensive ethos" when it came to the issue of violence. That is, these Jews believed that violent force could be used against Israel's Arab enemies, but only for defensive purposes. Yet during the years of the Arab rebellion in 1936–1939, when Palestinians rose up *en masse* to protest the growth of the Jewish community and engaged in violence against Jews that was more widespread and intense than ever before, the defensive ethos of the Zionist community began to give way to a more aggressive ethos characterized by militarism and nativism. Of course, all of this was prior to 1948, and therefore the violence here could not be called "war" in the formal sense, seeing as neither Jews nor Palestinians had a state or an army. Still, one cannot draw a sharp line between the violence involving Jews and Arabs before 1948 and that which occurred afterward. By the time the Arab rebellion broke out in the late 1930s, the conflict between the two groups was gradually looking like a war.[29]

Yet, what Shapira writes about is Labor Zionism, the brand of Zionism to which most Jews in Palestine adhered and which was secular in its orientation. Religious Zionism went through a somewhat different evolution in its attitudes to violence and war. This sector of the Zionist community held on to the defensive ethos longer than the Labor Zionists did. Thus, when the Arab rebellion broke out, most of the leading rabbis in the religious Zionist camp pleaded for Jews to exercise restraint, and they rejected calls for revenge that were coming from the secular Zionist community.[30]

But religious Zionism eventually adopted an aggressive ethos, and the transition to this way of thinking has already been alluded to earlier in this chapter. When Israel achieved victory in the Six Day War in 1967 and R. Tsevi Yehudah Kook's views became popular in the religious Zionist community, this community began to look upon war as a holy endeavor. War not only served the purpose of defending the state from its enemies, it also allowed the state to dramatically increase the amount of territory under its control, territory

28. Ibid., chapter 6.
29. Shapira, *Land and Power*.
30. Gorny, *Zionism and the Arabs*, 242, 275; Luz, *Wrestling with an Angel*: 205–7; Eliezer Don-Yehiya, "Dat ve-Teror Politi: Ha-Yahadut ha-Datit u-Pe'ulot ha-Gemul be-Tekufat 'Ha-Me'ora'ot,'" *Ha-Tsiyonut* 17 (1993): 155–90.

that had been promised by God to the Jews and would therefore be part of the future messianic kingdom. There was also more land destined for Jewish sovereignty in messianic times that remained in the hands of the neighboring Arab countries, and therefore some rabbis in the Zionist camp began to speak about the need for war to bring this land under Jewish control as well. These views were accompanied by highly negative views of Palestinians and Arabs, who were seen as enemies of the Jewish people aligned with the forces of evil and therefore out to thwart the messianic process.[31]

These views are still popular in some sectors of the religious Zionist community. Yet, as discussed earlier, religious Zionism has, in recent years, experienced a number of setbacks, such as the Gaza disengagement, and its following has therefore become more diverse in its thinking. Its views on the role of violence in general and war in particular in achieving its aims have therefore become similarly diverse.[32]

The Halakhic Dimension

Now that we have some understanding of how religious Zionism has treated war from a theological perspective, we are ready to look at how it has dealt with this topic from the standpoint of Halakhah, which gets us to the central concerns of this study. We have already noted that one of the major challenges that rabbis in the religious Zionist camp have faced in formulating halakhic positions on war is that there is a paucity of material on this topic in Halakhah prior to Zionism. But it behooves us to say something about this material, for even though these rabbis have not had a large body of earlier halakhic sources to work with when attempting to formulate positions on war, they have not had to work in a complete vacuum.

The Bible, of course, contains a good deal of material on war, including laws about how war should be conducted. Particularly important is Deuteronomy 20, which provides instructions about exempting certain sectors of the population from military duty and negotiating peace with the enemy, and about whom to kill among the enemy population when victory is achieved. The Bible also includes multiple narratives about war that could be used as sources of guidance for how war should be conducted.

In early rabbinic and medieval Halakhah, we have far less material on the subject of war because, as we have mentioned, rabbinic literature was composed in the years of exile when Jews did not have political power, nor an

31. Above, pp. 8–9.
32. Above, pp. 9–10. Yoel Finkelman, "On the Irrelevance of Religious Zionism," *Tradition* 39, no. 1 (2005): 21–44; Chaim Isaac Waxman, ed., *Religious Zionism Post-Disengagement: Future Directions* (New York: Yeshiva University Press, 2008).

army. Still, there is some discussion of the laws of war in this literature. By far the most significant is Maimonides' systematic presentation of these laws in the *Mishneh Torah*, his massive code of Halakhah composed in the twelfth century, which organizes all of Halakhah up to his time, including laws that were in abeyance because of the exile.[33]

Halakhic authorities in Europe in the nineteenth century took more interest in the laws of war than their predecessors did because in this period the movement throughout Europe to emancipate the Jews brought with it the obligation of Jews to serve in the armies of their respective countries. For many Jews, this was an obligation that they assumed most reluctantly, though some Jews were glad to take it on in order to demonstrate their loyalty to the countries in which they lived. Orthodox rabbis therefore had to address how halakhically observant Jews should conduct themselves while fulfilling their military duties.[34] This issue would continue to preocuppy halakhic authorities in the twentieth century as well, as Jews became increasingly integrated into European society and continued to be called up for army duty.[35]

With the establishment of the state of Israel, a whole new chapter was opened up on the subject of war in Halakhah, and we have already seen a general outline of what that new chapter looked like. For the first time in almost two millennia, Jews had a sovereign state in their ancient homeland, and its survival depended on its ability to wage war, and yet Halakhah gave preciously little guidance on how war should be conducted by a Jewish state. The rabbis in the religious Zionist community therefore had to exert immense effort in order to formulate halakhic regulations on this topic. This enterprise began when Israel was founded, it has continued to the present day, and it has produced a substantial body of literature.[36]

33. MT *Melakhim*, chapters 5–8.
34. R. Israel Meir Kagan (1838–1933), better known as the *Hafets Hayim*, composed an entire treatise dealing with this topic, entitled *Sefer Mahaneh Yisra'el* (Beney Berak, Israel: Torah va-Da'at, 1967).
35. See Derek Penslar, *Jews and the Military: A History* (Princeton, N.J.: Princeton University Press, 2013), especially chapters 2–6.
36. Above, pp. 4–5. Mention may also be made here of the literature on war in Halakhah produced by American Jewish scholars and rabbis. As Stuart A. Cohen notes ("Quest," 39–40), this group of thinkers began to engage this issue in the 1960s in the period of the Vietnam War when public debate was raging in American society about the war. Cohen also observes that American Jewish scholars and rabbis have produced literature on Jewish attitudes to nuclear war, a topic that has not been dealt with much by Israeli scholars and rabbis (ibid.). See, for instance, Daniel Landes, ed., *Omnicide: Jewish Reflections on Weapons of Mass Destruction* (Northvale, N.J.: Jason Aronson Press, 1991). Special note should be made here of Bradley Shavit Artson's *Love Peace and Pursue Peace: A Jewish Response to War and Nuclear Annihilation* (New York: United Synagogue of America, 1988). Arston is an American rabbi, and his book traces the history attitudes to war in Judaism in order to formulate a Jewish position on the nuclear arms race.

We should note, however, that there was another sector of the Orthodox community in the state of Israel that has refused to serve in its military, has opposed the wars that Israel has fought, and has remained steadfast in these positions up to the present day. The views of this group will be a factor in our study, and therefore a few words about its positions on war are in order here.

We have already noted that when the Zionist movement was founded, a large portion of the Orthodox community in Europe greeted it with suspicion or outright hostility, because it advocated that Jews should return to their homeland prior to messianic times and without divine assistance and because it was primarily secular in its orientation. This view of Zionism was particularly strong in the ultra-Orthodox communities in Eastern Europe, where the forces of Enlightenment had not penetrated the Jewish community as much as they had elsewhere in Europe. But even more important for our purposes is that the same outlook on Zionism was held by ultra-Orthodox communities in Palestine itself, communities that long predated the Zionist settlements, and the Jews in these communities were not inclined to change their positions when the state of Israel was established.[37]

The views of ultra-Orthodox Jews on military matters followed from their overall perspective on Zionism. The leading rabbis in this community believed that if Halakhah prior to Zionism had not developed laws of war, it was because war had no place in Judaism until the coming of the messiah. The only activity that Jews should engage in was the observance of God's commandments and the study of His Torah. Only religious piety would bring about the longed-awaited redemption.[38]

These opinions continue to be expressed in the ultra-Orthodox community in Israel. R. Eliezer Shakh, a prominent rabbinic authority in the ultra-Orthodox community in Israel in the 1980s and 1990s, argued that the Jew is required to survive in today's world without waging war, and if Jews go to war, they are no different from the other nations of the world, and they therefore betray their mission as God's chosen people. He also claimed that Israel was constantly at war because God was punishing its people for their reliance on military power for survival rather than religious faith.[39]

Since the creation of the state of Israel, the Israeli government and the ultra-Orthodox community have found a modus vivendi. The vast majority of

37. An analysis of ultra-Orthodox viewpoints on Zionism can be found in Ravitzky, *Messianism, Zionism*, pp. 13–26, chapters 2, 4, and 5.

38. Ravitzky, pp. 13–26, chapters 2, 4, and 5.

39. Edrei, "Law," 200–202; R. El'azar Menahem Man Shakh, *Be-Zot Ani Boteah: Igrot u-Ma'amarim 'al Tekufat ha-Yamim u-Me'ora'oteha* (Bney Berak, 1998). Perhaps the best-known opponent of Zionism in the ultra-Orthodox community was R. Yoel Teitelbaum (1887–1979), the first Satmar rebbe, who presented his views on this matter in *Va-Yo'el Moshe* (Brooklyn, NY: Jerusalem Publishing, 1961) and in *'Al ha-Ge'ulah ve-'al ha-Temurah* (Brooklyn, NY: Sander Deitsh, 1967).

ultra-Orthodox Jewish men do not have to serve in the Israeli army. As long as they are registered as students in a yeshiva, they can avoid enlistment. That arrangement has come under attack in recent years from the rest of the Israeli population, and attempts have been made to require more ultra-Orthodox Jews to perform military service. A growing number of ultra-Orthodox Jews, in fact, have been joining the army willingly in order to reap the benefits that come with it. Service in the army is an entry to Israeli society on a number of levels, including employment, and ultra-Orthodox Jews have increasingly begun to appreciate its value. But thus far the original arrangement in which these Jews avoid army service has remained largely intact.[40]

I have digressed here to discuss the views of the ultra-Orthodox community because in this study they have to be kept in mind. Even though religious Zionists deeply disagree with this community about fundamental issues and have often expressed hostility toward it, they have felt a certain affinity with ultra-Orthodox Jews, as we noted earlier. The commitment of ultra-Orthodox Jews to religious observance provides common ground with religious Zionists that is lacking among Israel's secular population. Religious Zionists have also had to acknowledge that many leading rabbis in the ultra-Orthodox community are great Torah scholars whose halakhic decisions carry significant weight. The views of ultra-Orthodox Jews will therefore come into play in our study.

ISRAEL AND THE WAGING OF WAR: THE HALAKHIC OBSTACLES

We can carry our discussion a critical step further by noting that the rabbis in the religious Zionist camp not only had to come up with laws on war where none had existed before; they also had to contend with several serious obstacles in Halakhah that seemed to preclude the possibility of a modern Jewish state waging war. It was not clear from a halakhic standpoint that such a state could go to war at all, even for defensive purposes. Some of the halakhic challenges that the rabbis had to consider were alluded to at the beginning of the chapter, and we will now look at them in greater detail.[41]

Mandatory War, Discretionary War, and Legitimate Authority

Early rabbinic and medieval Halakhah spoke of two categories of wars that Jews could wage when they had sovereignty prior to the exile: mandatory war

---

40. S. Cohen, "Quest," 40–41.
41. A full treatment of this issues, however, will be given in chapter 2.

(*milhemet mitsvah*) and discretionary war (*milhemet ha-reshut*). A full description of these categories need not concern us now. At this point, it is sufficient for our present purposes to note that wars of self-defense belonged to the first category, while the second category included wars of a more aggressive variety, such as wars waged to expand territory or for economic benefit.[42] We should also mention that, according to one prominent medieval halakhic authority, the commandment for Jews to wage war in order to conquer the land of Israel was an eternal one that did not expire once they had vanquished the Canaanites in the time of Joshua.[43] Therefore that commandment was still theoretically in force when the state of Israel was created. In light of all this, the question for modern halakhic authorities was whether the state of Israel was permitted to wage war, and if so, whether that permission went beyond the right to conduct wars of self-defense and included wars initiated for more aggressive purposes.

The answers to these questions were dependent in part on whether, according to Halakhah, the Israeli government had legitimate authority to initiate a war. It was not clear that it did. Medieval halakhic sources specified that mandatory war could be conducted only by a king in the line of King David, an office that no longer existed, while discretionary wars required both a Davidic king and a Sanhedrin, a rabbinic Supreme Court of seventy-one rabbis that also had not existed for centuries.[44] How then could the state of Israel wage war without these institutions? Would Halakhah regard the government of Israel, or various components therein, as appropriate substitutes? And if the answer to that question was a positive one, there was still the question of which types of war were then permissible: were only wars for defensive purposes allowed or wars of the more aggressive variety as well? And what of the international community of which Israel was a part? Did the government of Israel have to heed the fact that international law no longer allowed wars to be waged for aggressive purposes?

Conscription

Another halakhic challenge was the issue of conscription. In biblical and rabbinic literature, it was assumed that the king could draft soldiers into his army. However, it was not clear to the rabbis in the religious Zionist camp why conscription was permitted, even for wars of self-defense. According to rabbinic and medieval halakhic sources, no individual may be forced to risk his

---

42. MT *Melakhim* 5:1; BT *Sanhedrin* 16a–b.
43. R. Moses ben Nahman, or Nahmanides (1194–1270), "Addenda to Positive Commandments," in Maimonides' *Sefer ha-Mitsvot*, addendum #4.
44. MT *Melakhim* 5:1–2.

life to save others from harm.[45] Yet that is precisely what soldiers are asked to do when they are drafted into an army to fight a war to defend their country. How, then, was it permissible for a king to draft soldiers for this purpose? The problem with conscription was, of course, even greater for discretionary wars that were overtly aggressive. How could a king ask a Jewish soldier to give his life for a war that had no defensive value whatsoever?

It was not that the rabbis in the religious Zionist movement were retroactively challenging the right of Jewish kings to draft soldiers. Sources in the Bible and rabbinic literature assumed that the kings had that privilege. It is just that the practice of conscription did not make sense from a halakhic standpoint, and the rabbis had to explain how that practice was permitted before considering whether a modern Jewish state could engage in it as well. The root of the problem was that while medieval Halakhah developed a large and complex body of laws governing individual behavior, it had much less to say about the topic of war, and, in this instance, one law pertaining to individuals seemed inconsistent with the demands of waging war. This inconsistency was noticed by some halakhic authorities prior to Zionism, but it was not a major concern until the creation of Israel, when the problem had to be confronted and resolved. In general, rabbinic authorities do not tolerate inconsistencies in Halakhah. God's law is perfect and it cannot contain any contradictions.

Dealing with this issue was, of course, crucial for the rabbis in the religious Zionist movement, for without a clear position on why conscription was permitted, they could not advise their followers to serve in the Israeli army; and if they could not do so, the rabbis were effectively removing themselves and their followers from the Zionist project that they passionately supported. Moreover, it was obvious to all that the state of Israel would not survive without the power to conscript soldiers. An understanding of why and under what circumstances conscription was halakhically acceptable was therefore imperative.

Civilian Casualties

Perhaps the greatest moral difficulty with war is that it almost always claims the lives of innocent people. Civilians, who are not engaged in combat and may not even be supportive of war, often die when wars are waged because armies are not always able to achieve victory without fighting in areas in which civilians are located. Therefore, even when armies do their best to spare civilian lives, casualties among them are common. This problem has increased dramatically in the past century as weapons have become more powerful and more indiscriminate in the damage they cause.

45. BT *Bava Metis'a* 62a.

Western ethicists have dealt with this issue in a number of ways. But we are, of course, interested in how the rabbis in the religious Zionist camp have handled it, and here as well, medieval Halakhah has presented them with serious difficulties. According to Halakhah, one is allowed to kill an individual in self-defense, but if there is any chance that killing one's attacker will also claim the life of an innocent bystander, one is forbidden to take action. One must accept death at the hands of the assailant rather than kill anyone innocent.[46] The rabbis in the religious Zionist camp have therefore had to explain, as they did with the issue of conscription, how a Jewish army can ever go to war even for defensive purposes, for it would seem that no war should be halakhically permissible unless one can guarantee that no innocent individual in the enemy population will be killed, and that is a condition that is virtually impossible to fulfill, especially in modern warfare. And here again, the halakhic problem is even greater with discretionary wars, which do not necessarily serve a defensive purpose. Why should innocent civilians die in wars waged for the expansion of territory or economic benefit?

We should note once again that despite the halakhic problem being raised here, the rabbis in the religious Zionist movement were not questioning the right of Jewish kings in biblical times to wage war. It is just that these rabbis had to explain, from a halakhic standpoint, why war could be waged if it resulted in the loss of innocent life. And here, too, the source of the problem was that the laws in Halakhah governing individual behavior were developed without the issue of war in mind, and an inconsistency between these laws and the demands of war had gone mostly unnoticed until the creation of the state of Israel, when it suddenly became relevant.

Ritual Observances

As was pointed out at the beginning of this chapter, numerous halakhic obstacles to the waging of war had to be confronted in the area of ritual, because there were any number of obligations in this realm of Halakhah that could not easily be fulfilled in war. The obligations that were perhaps most vexing in this regard were those that pertained to the Sabbath. The laws of the Sabbath include a multitude of restrictions on one's activity for one full day of every week, restrictions that, if observed by soldiers, would make the waging of war impossible. No army at war can win if its soldiers are, in effect, required to take a day off from military duties every seven days. Thus clarification was needed on the extent to which laws of the Sabbath applied in military life. Was the Sabbath effectively canceled when one was engaged in war? Or did some restrictions still apply? What about the status of Sabbath restrictions

46. BT *Sanhedrin* 74a; *Yoma* 82b; *Pesahim* 25a.

for soldiers who were not at war but were in training or performing other critical military functions that were not directly connected to war? Were Sabbath
restrictions overridden for soldiers in these situations as well?

We should also mention in this context the question of whether, according
to Halakhah, men engaged in full-time Torah study were required to serve in
the army. This activity is a much revered ritual in Orthodox life. Orthodox
men often devote a number of years to the study of Torah in a yeshiva just
around the time that they are eligible for army duty. The question, then, was
whether these men were required to serve in the army, or whether they should
attempt to defer their service on the premise that others who were engaged in
less worthy pursuits could take their places.

The Three Oaths

One final obstacle to war that rabbis in religious Zionism had to contend with
straddles the boundary between theology and Halakhah. In early rabbinic literature, a number of passages report a mythical conversation between God and
the Jewish people in which the Jewish people make an oath to God promising
that they will not attempt to take the land of Israel by force until the messianic
period.[47] These sources were likely an attempt on the part of the early rabbis
to quell the desire of Jews in Palestine to mount violent insurrections against
their Roman overlords, because such action had resulted in terrible destruction
and had convinced the rabbis that accommodation with Rome was preferred.
Yet ultra-Orthodox rabbis in the modern period took these sources as providing instruction that transcended historical context. They read them as specify-
ing a divine imperative that military force must not be used to conquer the land
of Israel until God sends His messiah, a reading that provided one more reason
not to cooperate with the Zionist enterprise.[48] Rabbis in the religious Zionist
movement took these sources no less seriously, and they therefore had to find a
way to interpret them to allow for Zionism to accomplish its goals. Otherwise,
the entire Zionist agenda was in jeopardy from a religious standpoint.

THE GOALS OF THIS STUDY

The halakhic obstacles to the waging of war by the state Israel that have just
been described are the focus of the present study. We will analyze how a number of leading rabbis in the religious Zionist community justified the practice of

47. BT *Ketubot* 110b–111a; *Shir ha-Shirim Rabbah* 2:1, 2:18, 8:11.
48. Chief among the proponents of this view was R. Yoel Teitelbaum, mentioned
in note 39.

war despite these difficulties. The emphasis of this study will therefore be on *jus ad bellum*, in the terminology of Western war ethics, which refers to guidelines governing when a nation is permitted to go to war, as opposed to *jus in bello*, which refers to norms instructing soldiers how they should behave in the course of battle.[49]

This study will touch on all the halakhic difficulties just described, but our interest will be primarily in the first three, which are concerned with moral issues. My preference in concentrating on these matters has several reasons. First, there is more than enough material on these issues for a book-length study.[50] Second, my scholarly interests are primarily in the field of Jewish ethics, and therefore I prefer to deal with matters in this area. Finally, an examination of how modern halakhic authorities deal with moral issues in war will allow for a comparison between Halakhah and international law, and at the end of this study, I plan to conduct a comparison of this kind. Such a comparison is possible only with respect to moral norms in Halakhah, as opposed to those that concern ritual. The rituals that Jews practice are unique to Judaism and have no analogue in international law. Comparing the two bodies of law on the moral aspects of war is valuable because it will give insight into where the religious Zionist community stands on issues of war in relation to the international community of which Israel is a part.

Alongside the specific halakhic challenges that rabbinic authorities in religious Zionism had to confront with respect to war, they had to deal with a basic question that underlay all their discussions about these challenges: Does Halakhah treat the laws of war as somehow separate and different from the laws that govern everyday life?

A similar question has often been posed by Western ethicists and legal scholars, for they, too, have had to grapple with the question of how the rules of war are related to those that govern day-to-day life. Western ethicists and legal scholars often argue that the rules of war are different from those that regulate ordinary life, but they also acknowledge that the two groups of norms must share some common ground. In war, one must be permitted to kill in a way that would normally be forbidden, but one's conduct in war cannot be so different from that of ordinary life that there are no limitations on what one may do to achieve victory. Without some connection to the morality that governs our everyday lives, war becomes barbaric.[51]

We will ask the same questions in this study but within a halakhic framework. Have halakhic authorities in religious Zionism treated wartime

---

49. As we shall see, however, it is difficult to entirely separate the two categories in Halakhah, because the questions about whether a Jewish state should go to war are intimately tied to questions about what then happens on the battlefield.

50. The same could be said about the halakhic challenges that war presents in the realm of ritual, which are referred to in the fourth point above.

51. Solis, *Law of Armed Conflict*, 24–26.

Halakhah merely as an extension of everyday Halakhah? Or have they viewed the two spheres as separate and, if so, to what degree?

Our study will be delimited not only by its focus on select issues but also by its concentration on select halakhic authorities. I had initially wanted to compose a comprehensive study about how the moral issues of war have been treated by halakhic authorities in the religious Zionist camp, but I soon came to realize that such a study would be impossible to do in one volume. The body of material on this subject is large and complex, and very little has been written about it from an academic standpoint. I therefore chose to explore the views of five rabbis in the religious Zionist movement who have been selected in accordance with three criteria: their level of influence on halakhic discussions of war, the volume of work they produced on this subject, and their degree of originality. The rabbis chosen are not all equal with regard to the three criteria. Some are more accomplished than others with respect to one or another of these standards. But each of them is distinguished to some degree with regard to each of the standards. My study should therefore be viewed as an initial step into an enormous topic.

The first rabbi we will explore is R. Abraham Isaac Kook, who has already been mentioned in this chapter. R. Kook died before the creation of the state of Israel, and his writings contain relatively little material on war in Halakhah. However, he is perhaps the most significant rabbinic figure in the history of religious Zionism, and the little that he did say about war in Halakhah had immense influence on subsequent halakhic authorities in the religious Zionist movement. Therefore, no study on the treatment of war in Halakhah in religious Zionism can begin without him.

We will then move on to R. Isaac Halevi Herzog (1888–1959) who was the first Ashkenazi Chief Rabbi of Israel. He was one of the first halakhic authorities in the religious Zionist camp to deal with the war as an actual reality because Israel's War of Independence broke out during his tenure. During this war, he composed a series of important responsa dealing with various aspects of war from a halakhic standpoint.

R. Eliezer Yehudah Waldenberg (1915–2006) is the next figure to whom we will turn. R. Waldenberg is perhaps the least distinguished among the rabbinic figures in our study when it comes to issues pertaining to war in Halakhah. However, he was a leading halakhic authority on many other issues, and his contributions on the subject of war in Halakhah were significant as well. He produced one of the first book-length studies that dealt with the topic, as well as a number of important responsa on the subject.

The next figure we will examine is R. Sha'ul Yisraeli (1910–1995), a highly respected halakhic authority in the religious Zionist community who composed perhaps the most influential work on war in Halakhah. It was an essay on the Kibiyeh raid in 1953, a military operation in which Israeli soldiers attacked a village in Jordan in retaliation for several incidents of terrorism perpetrated by individuals who, the Israelis believed, had launched the attacks from that village. In dealing with this incident, R. Yisraeli provided insights on war in Halakhah that were both provocative and original. We will devote an entire chapter to this essay. We will also dedicate a second chapter to R. Yisraeli's later writings on war, which have received far less attention than the essay on Kibiyeh but are nonetheless important.

Finally, we will analyze the halakhic writings of R. Shlomo Goren (1918–1994), who was the first Chief Rabbi of the Israeli army and served in that post for twenty-three years before becoming Ashkenazi Chief Rabbi of Israel. He produced the largest body of writings on war in Halakhah of any of our rabbinic figures. He is also the only one of our rabbinic figures to have actually served in the Israeli army and engaged in combat.

There are a couple of major drawbacks to my choice of rabbinic figures that I must fully acknowledge. First, my study effectively ends in the early 1990s, when the most recent of these figures, R. Yisraeli and R. Goren, produced their last writings. That means that my analysis will not deal with the moral questions of war that Israeli rabbis have had to grapple with since then. Some of my readers will be disappointed by this. In recent years, Israelis have had to confront some of the most difficult moral challenges regarding war they have ever faced. From the late 1980s to the present, Israelis have dealt with two intifadas and several wars in Gaza and Lebanon in which enemy civilian casualties have dramatically increased compared to previous military campaigns. That is because more than ever before, Israelis have had to engage in irregular warfare against terrorist organizations, such as Hamas and Hezbollah, which are based in civilian centers. There have been sharp debates in Israeli society about this problem, and rabbis in the religious Zionist camp have had a lot to say about it in their halakhic writings. It is therefore understandable that my readers would be curious to know about how halakhic authorities have dealt with this issue. However, as I explained earlier, there were limitations on what I could cover in this study. I had initially intended to examine how religious Zionism has dealt with the morality of war in Halakhah up to the present, but I discovered that an exploration of this kind was not feasible in a single volume, and I therefore chose to focus on five of the most important rabbis who have dealt with this subject in the history of religious Zionism, and these rabbis happened to have lived before the most recent moral challenges regarding Israeli warfare arose. Yet I hope that the richness of the material that I examine and the insights I bring to it will justify my choices. The present study will also lay the groundwork for a separate treatment of the more recent moral challenges that halakhic authorities in religious Zionism have faced regarding war. These authorities have been greatly influenced in their thinking about war by the rabbis examined in the coming pages.

One other major drawback with my choice of rabbinic figures is that all of them are Ashkenazic; none are Sefardic. That is, they all belong to communities that have roots in Europe, as opposed to those that originated in Islamic lands. The reason I chose to focus on Ashkenazic figures is not that Sefardic rabbis have been any less important or interesting when it comes to war in Halakhah. For instance, Rabbi 'Ovadyah Yosef (1920–2013), who served as Sefardic Chief Rabbi of Israel from 1973 to 1983, was a figure of immense stature who produced a significant amount of material on war in Halakhah, and his writings remain highly influential in Orthodox circles in Israel today. The reason for my not including Sefardic rabbis is that little work has been done by academics on their halakhic writings, and virtually nothing has been written about their views on war. Including these figures in the present study would have therefore presented formidable challenges. It would have required conducting basic research on their halakhic methodology in general before even approaching their views on war, and that was a task that could not easily be accomplished within the scope of this study. An examination of R. Yosef's halakhic views on war alone could be an independent project in its own right. Nonetheless, I reiterate my hope that my choice of material will be justified by its richness and the insights gleaned from it.

It is important that I say something about the methodology of this study. I will be analyzing the issues and figures described here as an academic writing from the standpoint of the history of ideas. I must emphasize this point because much of the writing that has been done in the area of war in Halakhah has utilized the methodology of constructive ethics, which focuses on how ethics should applied. That is certainly the case with the rabbis who have engaged this issue. It is also the case with a good number of academics who have written on it. The goal in using this approach has been to discuss the subject of war in Halakhah from a philosophical and theological perspective in order to make judgments about how Israel should engage in war.[52] I have no such agenda. In analyzing the issue of war in Halakhah from the standpoint of the history of ideas, my aim is simply to understand what the five rabbis I will be examining have to say about this topic and to give insight into the way in which they formulated their views. My method is descriptive and analytical, not prescriptive and normative. I therefore bring no moral or political agenda to this study—at least not consciously. Whether I agree or disagree with the

52. As I point out in n. 9, the studies of Holtser and Firestone are academic in orientation, while the co-authored study of Rekhnits and Goldshtein takes the constructive approach. But there are some authors who have written on war and Halakhah whose methodology is difficult to classify because they make use of both methodologies. Complicating matters is that a number of individuals who write on war and Halakhah nowadays have both rabbinic ordination and academic doctoral degrees. Therefore, their work on this issue often reflects both perspectives.

rabbis I will be examining about when and how war should waged is immaterial to my concerns.

It is not that I have any objection to the constructive approach. In fact, quite the contrary. Engaging the subject of war in Halakhah with this methodology is critical if Jewish tradition is to serve as a vital source of guidance for Jews in our day and age. How the state of Israel deals with war is one of the most pressing moral questions that Jews have had to deal with in our time. Furthermore, an academic like myself would have little to write about on war in Halakhah were it not for thinkers who have dealt with this topic from the perspective of constructive ethics. After all, the rabbis explored in this study approach the topic precisely from this viewpoint, and their work furnishes me with material to scrutinize as an academic. Nonetheless, the difference between the two methodologies has to be made clear from the outset. As an academic, I stand "outside" the subject in way that those engaging in constructive ethics do not. I will therefore provide no instruction about when and how war should be waged by the state of Israel.

Using this approach, I hope to offer insights about war in Halakhah that do not emerge when it is examined from the standpoint of constructive ethics. Yet I would argue that those insights should be of interest to those who engage in the constructive approach. Normative judgments about war in Halakhah should be based on our best understanding of the views of the rabbis examined in this study, who have provided pioneering discussions of this topic, and an academic analysis of their thinking will add to that understanding.

I would like to conclude with some observations about the larger ramifications of this study. Exploring how the leading rabbis in the religious Zionist movement justified war in Halakhah from a moral standpoint will give us insight into important issues beyond the immediate subject matter. The body of Halakhah that has been produced on war since the creation of the state of Israel represents one of the most fascinating chapters in the history of Halakhah. The rabbis who composed this literature displayed remarkable boldness and ingenuity in attempting to formulate a comprehensive series of laws for war where none had existed. Halakhah tends to evolve slowly over time because its interpreters exercise great caution in formulating their rulings. Every halakhic decision must be grounded properly in precedent. After all, this is no ordinary law; it is a law that embodies God's will, and so it must be developed with great care. Significant change in Halakhah, therefore, may take centuries. Orthodox Jews in the modern period have tended to treat Halakhah in the same manner. Changes must be made slowly and cautiously. Yet here was an instance in which there was very little precedent on which to draw, and a group of Orthodox rabbis were able to build a significant corpus of halakhic literature on a subject in relatively short order. For this reason, the present study is not just about the treatment of war in Halakhah but about the halakhic process in general.

Perhaps more important, our study has implications for Middle East politics because it is focused on a community that is highly significant in the current political landscape of that region. The religious Zionist camp constitutes only 10 percent of Israel's population, but its influence on Israeli society has been far greater than its numbers would suggest. The settlement enterprise was largely spearheaded by this sector of Israeli society, and as everyone who follows current events knows, this enterprise has had an enormous impact on relations between Israel, on the one hand, and the Palestinians and Arab nations, on the other hand. Furthermore, Israelis in the religious Zionist camp are becoming increasingly influential in the Israeli army. Because of their high level of dedication to the state of Israel, they are often more eager to perform military service than their secular counterparts. Thus, by the 1990s, religious Zionists made up 20 percent of the soldiers in infantry brigades— twice the percentage of their numbers in the general population—and among combat lieutenants and captains, the ratio of religious to secular was two to one.[53] Probing the halakhic literature on war produced by the leading rabbis in religious Zionism will therefore help us understand an extremely important constituency in Israel's army and their views on its most important and consequential function, which is waging war. And given that so much of what has happened in the Middle East has been shaped by the successes of the Israeli army on the battlefield, these insights are of significance for the region as a whole.[54]

53. Cohen, "Quest," 38.
54. I might interject here that the question of whether Israeli soldiers who identify as religious Zionists feel more beholden to their rabbis or their army superiors is a complex one, and it is not an issue that we can delve into here. For a discussion of this matter, see Stuart A. Cohen, "Dilemmas of Military Service in Israel: The Religious Dimension," *War and Peace in the Jewish Tradition*, eds. Lawrence Schiffman and Joel B. Wolowelsky (New York: Yeshiva University Press, 2007), 313–40. Yet, it is safe to say that Israeli soldiers in the religious Zionist camp are, at the very least, influenced by what the leading rabbis in the religious Zionist community have to say about military matters, and thus, once again, it is imperative that we understand how these rabbis approach the topic of war.

CHAPTER 2

꧁

War in Jewish Law before Zionism

Before we turn to the five rabbis whose halakhic views on war we plan to examine, we must probe in greater depth how war is treated in Halakhah prior to Zionism in order to better understand the moral challenges these rabbis faced in engaging with the issue of war. Our review of this material will not be comprehensive. Although the volume of sources on war in early rabbinic and medieval Halakhah is much smaller than it is in other areas of Halakhah, there are still a fair number of them and some are quite complex; a full treatment of them would therefore require a lengthier exploration than we can embark on here. Nor is such a treatment necessary. A good many of the sources on war in Halakhah before Zionism are not relevant to issues we will be dealing with in this study. I therefore believe that I will serve my reader best by focusing my discussion only on halakhic material that is required for our concerns. Consequently, readers familiar with the sources on war in Halakah should not be surprised to find that some of the major talmudic texts on this topic will be dealt with here only in cursory fashion. For instance, I will not provide an in-depth analysis of the passages in the Babylonian and Jerusalem Talmuds in Tractate *Sotah* that deal with war, even though these passages constitute the most substantive treatments of this topic in early rabbinic literature. The thinkers in our study, when discussing the issues that concern us, certainly refer to these texts, but they do not deal with them in any detail, and therefore there is no need for us to do so either.[1]

---

1. A summary of sources on war in Halakhah prior to Zionism can also be found in Reuven Firestone's *Holy War in Judaism: The Fall and Rise of a Controversial Idea* (New York: Oxford University Press, 2012), part 2. Firestone provides a more thorough account of the treatment of war in early rabbinic sources than I do in this chapter. There are dozens of other treatments of war in Halakhah before Zionism, most

I will also limit my discussion to the halakhic sources that are cited most frequently in our study. I adopt this strategy because a full treatment of the halakhic sources discussed by our rabbis would require examining a myriad of disparate and fragmentary texts, many of which are utilized by only one or two rabbis in our study. It makes much more sense to take up such sources in the context of our treatments of the individual rabbis explored in the rest of this study rather than overburden my reader at this point with a discussion of these texts. In short, my discussion in this chapter will provide only the minimum background in Halakhah needed for what is to follow.

For this purpose, I have chosen as a framework for my discussion Maimonides' codification of the laws of war in the *Mishneh Torah*, which was mentioned in my introductory chapter.[2] Few medieval halakhic codes address this topic, seeing as it was no longer applicable in this period, and Maimonides is by far the halakhic authority of greatest stature to have done so. All modern halakhic authorities therefore regard Maimonides' codification of the laws of war as the foundational text for the treatment of this topic, and I will as well.

We will be aided in our analysis of Maimonides' halakhic rulings on war by his commentators, but we will focus primarily on those who lived before the advent of Zionism. There is no point in looking at how halakhic authorities have dealt with the laws of war in Maimonides since the advent of Zionism, because the rabbis we will analyze in this study are themselves commentators on Maimonides' laws of war, and their thinking was influential on other recent halakhic interpreters who have written on war. Therefore, if we were to look at treatments of Maimonides' halakhic views on war after the beginnings of Zioinism, we would end up having to delve prematurely into the opinions of the very halakhic thinkers we intend to examine in later chapters.

VARIETIES OF WAR AND LEGITIMATE AUTHORITY: THE MAIMONIDEAN FRAMEWORK

Maimonides addresses the laws of war in the *Mishneh Torah* in a section devoted to laws of kingship that functioned when Jews had their own state.

of them contained in journal articles and chapters in books, but Firestone's is one of the few that is historical in its orientation. Almost all other treatments of this subject are exercises in constructive ethics. Some academics have provided overviews of the laws of war in Halakhah that combine the historical and constructive approach. See, for example, Reuven Kimelman, "The Ethics of National Power: Government and War from the Sources of Judaism," *Authority, Power, and Leadership in the Jewish Polity*, ed. Daniel Elazar (Lanham, Md.: University Press of America, 1991), 247–94; Elliot N. Dorff, *To Do the Right and the Good: A Jewish Approach to Modern Social Ethics* (Philadelphia: Jewish Publication Society of America, 2002), 165–71.
  2. MT *Melakhim* 5–8.

The first paragraph of this section lays out a classification scheme for the types of wars that a king may wage:

> A king may initially wage only mandatory war (*milhemet mitsvah*). Which [war] is a mandatory war? It is a war against the seven [Canaanite] nations, a war against Amalek, and saving Israel from the clutches of the enemy that has attacked them ('*ezrat yisra'el mi-yad tsar she-ba 'aleihem*). Subsequently, the king may wage discretionary war (*milhemet ha-reshut*), which is war that he wages against the rest of the nations in order to widen the borders of Israel and to increase his greatness and prestige.[3]

Maimonides informs us that there are two major categories of war: mandatory and discretionary. Mandatory wars are of three types: those waged (1) to destroy the seven Canaanite nations who occupied the land of Israel before the Israelites conquered it in the time of Joshua, (2) to annihilate the Amalekite nation that attacked the Israelites just after the exodus from Egypt, and (3) to defend the nation from enemy attack, referred to here as wars for "saving Israel from the clutches of the enemy." Discretionary wars may be initiated by the king only when there is no mandatory war to be concerned about, and they include two types: those waged (1) to conquer territory outside the borders of the Jewish state, and (2) to increase the reputation of the king.[4]

Maimonides provides more detail about legitimate authority for waging war in the next paragraph:

> [For] mandatory war, he [i.e., the king] does not have to get the permission of a rabbinic court. Rather, he goes out [to war] of his own initiative at any time, and he forces the people to go out [to war as well]. However, [for] discretionary war, he takes the people out to it only with approval of a rabbinic court of seventy-one.[5]

Mandatory war is waged solely by the king, but discretionary war requires the king to seek the approval of a "rabbinic court of seventy-one," a reference to the Sanhedrin, the rabbinic Supreme Court that consisted of seventy-one rabbis.

3. MT *Melakhim* 5:1.
4. There is some ambiguity with regard to the latter type of war. When Maimonides says that discretionary war may be waged to "increase his greatness and prestige," the pronoun "his" may also refer to Israel the nation, which is mentioned earlier in the sentence. However, most commentators see the pronoun as referring to the king. It is also possible that the two types of discretionary war here are really one. That is, discretionary war may be waged to widen the borders of Israel *in order to* increase the prestige of the king. At least one of our rabbis will suggest this reading, but most commentators believe there are two types of war here.
5. MT *Melakhim* 5:2.

The distinction between mandatory and discretionary wars is talmudic in origin. The Mishnah, in Tractate *Sotah*, devotes an entire chapter to explicating Deuteronomy 20, one of the few sections of the Torah that provides us with laws for war. The Mishnah here focuses most of its attention on a number of verses in the biblical text describing a series of instructions that a specially designated priest is expected to dictate to the Israelite troops before they enter battle. These instructions include directions about a number of exemptions from military service. In particular, the priest must inform the soldiers that they need not go to battle if they have just planted a vineyard, built a house, or become engaged to be married. Also exempt are soldiers who are "fearful" or "soft-hearted" because their fears may affect the morale of the other troops.[6] At the end of the section of the Mishnah dealing with these rules, a dispute is recorded about when these military exemptions apply:

> To what does all the foregoing apply? To discretionary wars (*milhemet ha-reshut*), but in mandatory wars (*milhemet mitsvah*), all go forth [to war], even a bridegroom from his chamber, and a bride from her canopy. R. Judah says, to what does all the foregoing apply? To mandatory wars (*milhemet mitsvah*), but in obligatory wars (*milhemet hovah*), all go forth [to war], even a bridegroom from his chamber, and a bride from her canopy.[7]

The anonymous opinion in the Mishnah, which is always assumed to be the opinion of the majority of rabbis, claims that the exemptions apply only in discretionary wars (*milhemet ha-reshut*)[8] and not to mandatory wars (*milhemet mitsvah*). R. Judah claims they apply to mandatory wars (*milhemet mitsvah*), but not to obligatory wars (*milhemet hovah*).

We are given no information about the various types of war referred to in these opinions. We also have no information on the nature of the dispute between the two viewpoints. Compounding the difficulty is that some of the terminology used by the two opinions to distinguish between the types of wars seems awfully similar. It is not clear, for instance, what differentiates between a "mandatory" war (*milhemet mitsvah*) and an "obligatory" war (*milhemet hovah*). But what is important for our purposes is that Maimonides has clearly adopted the position of the rabbis who distinguish between discretionary wars (*milhemet ha-reshut*) in which the military exemptions apply, and

6. Deut. 20:5–9.
7. M *Sotah* 8:7. In translating this text, I benefited from the English translation of the Soncino edition of the Talmud.
8. Here and elsewhere in the Talmud, the phrase is *milhemet ha-reshut*, but in medieval and modern halakhic sources, the term *milhemet reshut* is often used, with the *ha-* missing before *reshut*. Readers, therefore, should not be surprised to see both variations used in this study. I tend to follow whatever convention was used by the author or text that I happen to be discussing.

mandatory wars (*milhemet mitsvah*) in which they do not.[9] Maimonides has also provided critical information about what types of war fall under these two rubrics.

Let us now look more closely at these wars. In the category of mandatory war, the first type of war Maimonides mentions is the series of wars the Israelites fought against the Canaanites, and why Maimonides includes these wars in this category is no mystery. In the Torah, God directly and repeatedly orders the Israelites, as they make their way to the land of Israel, to annihilate the Canaanite nations who reside in the land.[10] As wars explicitly mandated by God, one would presume that they are included in the category of war in which all able-bodied individuals must fight. And, in fact, the Gemara tells us that regarding this issue, there is no difference of opinion among the rabbis. All of them agree, including R. Judah, that in the wars against the Canaanites, everyone had to fight.[11] However, Maimonides states in a subsequent paragraph that the commandment to destroy the Canaanite nations is no longer in force because those nations have long ago disappeared.[12]

That the war to annihilate the Amalekites is mandatory, should also occasion no surprise. Here too, according to the biblical text, the commandment to wage war comes directly from God,[13] and thus one would once again presume that there are no exceptions for participating in this campaign. However, it is noteworthy that the Gemara makes no mention of this war in its deliberations on the Mishnah. In fact, nowhere in the Talmud is the war against the Amalekites referred to as mandatory war. It would seem, therefore, that Maimonides relies solely on the biblical text to include this war among those that are mandatory. Some commentators have noted that at no point does Maimonides inform us that the war against the Amalekites is defunct. Whether this omission is significant, however, is hard to say and has led to a good deal of speculation.

It is surprisingly difficult to find justification for Maimonides' inclusion of defensive wars among those that are mandatory. There is no law in the Torah that explicitly commands, or even allows, the Israelites to wage wars to defend themselves. Nor does one find reference to defensive wars in the Gemara that comments on the Mishnah in *Sotah*, though there is mention of preemptive war. One might argue that the rabbis did not have to provide justification for defensive war because they permit an individual to kill in self-defense.

---

9. R. Abraham de Boton (ca. 1560–ca. 1605) makes this observation in his commentary, *Lehem Mishneh*, on MT *Melakhim* 5:1.

10. See, for example, Deut. 7:1–2; 20:16–17.

11. BT *Sotah* 44b.

12. MT *Melakhim* 5:4. That the Canaanites no longer exist is attested to in early rabbinic sources. See M *Yadayim* 4:4; T *Kidushin* 5:6; BT *Berakhot* 28a.

13. Ex. 17:8–16; Deut. 25:17–19.

However, there are difficulties in Halakhah in extending that right to the nation as a whole, as I mentioned in chapter 1, and I will elaborate upon those difficulties later on in this discussion.

Some have found an authoritative source permitting defensive wars in the Jerusalem Talmud. In the Gemara on *Sotah* in the Jerusalem Talmud, we find a different series of opinions than those found in the Babylonian Talmud regarding the dispute between the rabbis and R. Judah in the Mishnah, and one of these opinions brings in the issue of defensive war. According to R. Hisda, R. Judah is of the opinion that defensive war is mandatory.[14] Maimonides' decision to identify defensive war as mandatory may have therefore been inspired by this viewpoint.

Some have also found a source for Maimonides' position on defensive war in a passage in the Babylonian Talmud, *'Eruvin* 45a:

> R. Judah stated in the name of Rav: If non-Jews besiege the cities of Israel, one does not go forth [to fight] against them with weapons and one does not desecrate the Sabbath for them. ... To what does the foregoing apply? When they [i.e., the non-Jews] have come [to fight] for financial gain. But if they have come to kill, one goes forth [to fight] against them with weapons and one desecrates the Sabbath for them. In the case of a city that is close to the border, even if they [i.e., the non-Jews] did not come to kill but only for [stealing] straw and stubble, one goes forth [to fight] against them with weapons and one desecrates the Sabbath for them.

Here we are told that when non-Jews wage war against a Jewish city with the intent of killing its inhabitants, all Jews are required to come to their defense, even on the Sabbath. If the enemy is intent only on stealing, this rule does not apply, except in cities located close to a border which, if overrun, would leave the rest of the nation vulnerable to further attacks. Maimonides codifies these rules in another section of the *Mishneh Torah* as well.[15]

The talmudic passage does not specifically mention mandatory war, nor does Maimonides when he codifies the rules that it contains, but a number of commentators hold that the wars being discussed in this talmudic text must be mandatory because they are initiated on the Sabbath and only a mandatory war may be commenced on that day. A discretionary war may be started no

---

14. JT *Sotah* 8:10. R. Judah, however, speaks of "obligatory war" (*milhemet hovah*), not "mandatory war" (*milhemet mitsvah*). There is some debate about the proper reading of the entire discussion in this text. See the commentary on this text of R. David Frankel (ca. 1704–1762), *Korban ha-'Eidah*, in standard editions of JT, which claims that the sources of the two opinions should be reversed. It is therefore the rabbis, not R. Judah, who believe that defensive war is mandatory and preemptive war, discretionary.

15. MT *Shabbat* 2:23.

later than three days prior to the Sabbath.[16] Therefore, it is possible that when Maimonides in *Hilkhot Melakhim* identifies defensive war as mandatory, he had in mind the talmudic text in *'Eruvin*, as well as his own ruling elsewhere in the *Mishneh Torah* that was based on that source. However, one should note that neither the talmudic source in *'Eruvin*, nor the one in the Jerusalem Talmud, cites a biblical passage as support for the notion that Jews may fight a defensive war. In both sources, the rabbis simply declare that such wars are allowed.

Let us now turn to discretionary wars. Maimonides' notion that this type of war can be waged to widen the borders of Israel is attested to in the Gemara that comments on the Mishnah in *Sotah*. The Gemara informs us that, in addition to the consensus of the rabbis that the wars fought by Joshua against the Canaanites were mandatory, there is also agreement among them that the wars that King David fought for "expansion" (*li-revahah*) were discretionary.[17] However, Maimonides' idea that discretionary wars may be conducted to increase the prestige of the king has no obvious source in rabbinic literature.

We find other types of discretionary war in early rabbinic literature that Maimonides does not mention. According to the Gemara in *Sotah*, the opinion of the majority of rabbis in the Mishnah is that preemptive war is also discretionary. In fact, according to the Gemara, it is this form of war that is at the crux of the disagreement between the rabbis and R. Judah. Whereas the rabbis believe that preemptive wars are discretionary, R. Judah believes they are mandatory.[18]

A difficulty here is that it is not clear that the rabbis and R. Judah are using the terms "mandatory" and "discretionary" with respect to preemptive war in the same way that they do when discussing other forms of war. According to Rashi's reading, which is adopted by most later commentators, when R. Judah says that preemptive war is "mandatory," he means that if someone is engaged in a halakhic obligation when the call to war is issued, he must desist from that obligation in order to join the battle. The war is therefore mandatory in the sense that it takes priority over other commandments. When the rabbis say that preemptive war is "discretionary," they mean that a person may finish whatever halakhic obligation he may be pursuing at the time before joining the battle. The war is therefore "discretionary" in the sense an individual may choose to fulfill the alternative halakhic obligation before going to war.

16. Though once a discretionary war has begun, it may continue on the Sabbath. That mandatory wars may begin on the Sabbath is mentioned by R. Abraham de Boton in his commentary, *Lehem Mishneh*, on MT *Shabbat* 2:25. Rashi also makes this point in his commentary on the Torah in his remarks on Deut. 20:19.

17. BT *Sotah* 44b.

18. BT *Sotah* 44b.

We find another, less ambiguous example of a form of war in early rabbinic literature that is deemed discretionary but is not mentioned by Maimonides: a war waged for economic gain. The Mishnah in Tractate *Sanhedrin* lays down the rule that a king must consult the Sanhedrin when waging discretionary war, a rule that, as we have already noted, Maimonides adopts,[19] and the Gemara attempts to find a source for this rule by citing an aggadah, or rabbinic legend, about King David. The passage opens with a description of David waking up in the middle of the night to study Torah until dawn. As the day begins, his advisers come to him to complain that his people have no "sustenance" (*parnasah*); that is, they are economically deprived. David is initially dismissive of his advisers' concerns, but when they press him further for action, he orders them to go to war, with the apparent goal of solving the economic crisis through plunder. The advisers, before waging war, consult with David's chief adviser, Ahitophel, the Sanhedrin, and the *urim ve-tumim*, the oracle on the breast-plate of the High Priest. The aggadah concludes with a series of biblical prooftexts demonstrating that each of these consultations took place.[20] Most important for the Gemara's concerns is that in the aggadah David specifically asks for the Sanhedrin to be consulted before going to war, and a biblical source is provided to show that this step was necessary before David's army went into battle. The Gemara therefore finds proof here that the king must get the approval of the Sanhedrin before initiating a discretionary war.[21] But what is important for our purposes at this point of our discussion is that this source suggests that discretionary war can be waged for economic reasons, and this motivation for conducting a war of this type is nowhere mentioned by Maimonides.

This source provides a good transition to an examination of Maimonides' views on legitimate authority in waging war. Maimonides' notion that the king may wage discretionary only after consulting the Sanhedrin is clearly based on the Mishnah in *Sanhedrin*, which tells us in two places that the king must make the decision to wage discretionary war with this rabbinic body.[22] The aggadic passage in the Gemara regarding David also mentions consultation with the *urim ve-tumim* as a prerequisite for waging discretionary war, but in Maimonides' laws of war in the *Mishneh Torah*, he makes no reference to this oracle. It would seem that, in general, Maimonides did not put much credence in this particular aggadah. He does not adopt its notion that discretionary war can be waged for economic reasons, nor that one must get approval from the *urim ve-tumim* before conducting a war of this kind.

However, some commentators have noticed that in his *Sefer ha-Mitsvot* Maimonides mentions consultation with the High Priest as a prerequisite for

19. M *Sanhedrin* 1:5, 2:4.
20. BT *Sanhedrin* 16a–b. The same aggadah also appears in BT *Berakhot* 3a.
21. BT *Sanhedrin* 16a–b.
22. M *Sanhedrin* 1:5, 2:4.

waging discretionary war, and it is generally assumed that he is referring to the *urim ve-tumim*.[23] Why his position here is different from that in the *Mishneh Torah*, is not clear. We may also note here that other medieval halakhic authorities rule that the *urim ve-tumim* were to be consulted before going to war of any kind, mandatory or discretionary. Rashi takes this position, as does Nahmanides.[24]

In the *Mishneh Torah*, Maimonides provides no reason as to why the Sanhedrin is consulted before waging discretionary war, but others have speculated about its role. R. Nissim Gerondi (1320–76)—better known by his acronym, Ran—and R. Menahem ha-Meiri (1249–ca. 1310) give perhaps the simplest explanation by focusing on political authority.[25] They claim that the king by himself did not have sufficient authority to force the nation into a war of this kind and that the approval of the Sanhedrin was therefore needed. Rashi, in his commentary on the Mishnah, tells us the Sanhedrin had to be consulted for an entirely different purpose; it was needed to pray for victory.[26] We have yet another opinion provided by R. Samuel Eidels (1555–1631)—better known by his acronym, Maharsha—who believes that the Sanhedrin was part of the decision to wage discretionary war because it had to provide halakhic guidance on the conduct of the war.[27]

Maimonides provides no reason why in the case of mandatory war, the king alone may take the nation into battle. However, one commentator makes the suggestion that this ruling can be inferred from the Mishnah's insistence that the Sanhedrin must be consulted for conducting discretionary war. The Mishnah's ruling here implies that in the one other major category of war, the Sanhedrin's help is not needed.[28]

NAHMANIDES: THE COMMANDMENT
TO CONQUER THE LAND OF ISRAEL

Although Maimonides' framework for laws of war in the *Mishneh Torah* becomes the basis for all subsequent discussions of the topic in later halakhic literature, not all halakhic authorities are satisfied with his views, and some of their differences with him are important for our study. Perhaps the most significant critique of Maimonides on laws of war is found in Nahmanides, who quarrels with

---

23. *Sefer ha-Mitsvot, shoresh*, 14.

24. Rashi, *Peirush 'al ha-Torah*, Num. 27:21; Nahmanides, "Addenda to Negative Commandments," *Sefer ha-Mitsvot*, addendum #17.

25. Ran on BT *Sanhedrin* 20b; and Meiri, *Beit ha-Behirah: Sanhedrin*, ed. Avraham Sofer (New York, 1962), on BT *Sanhedrin* 16a.

26. Rashi on BT *Sanhedrin* 3b, s. v. "*ve-nimlakhin*."

27. Maharsha, *Hidushey Halakahot ve-Aggadot*, on BT *Sanhedrin* 16a.

28. R. Joseph Karo (1488–1575), in his commentary, *Kesef Mishneh*, on MT *Melakhim* 5:2.

his predecessor's formulation regarding the prescription to wage mandatory war against the seven Canaanite nations. If one reads Maimonides' language carefully, this commandment is focused solely on annihilating the Canaanites, not on taking possession of the land of Israel per se. Moreover, as we have already noted, Maimonides believes that since the Canaanites no longer exist, the commandment to annihilate them is no longer in force. Nahmanides strenuously objects to these positions. In his commentary on Maimonides' *Sefer ha-Mitsvot*, a work devoted to a description of the 613 commandments, Nahmanides lists a number of commandments he believes Maimonides has mistakenly omitted, and one of them is the commandment to both conquer the land of Israel (*kibush ha-arets*) and settle it (*yishuv ha-arets*). Annihilating the Canaanites, for Nahmanides, was only a means to these ends. Moreover, the commandment to conquer and settle the land is eternally in force.

Given the importance of Nahmanides' views on this issue, they are worth citing in full:

The fourth commandment [that Maimonides omitted] is that we are commanded to inherit the land that God, may He be blessed and exalted, gave to
our forefathers—to Abraham, to Isaac, and to Jacob—and not leave it in the
possession of others among the nations, nor [to leave it] desolate. This is [the
meaning of] His statement to them, "And you shall take possession of the land
and settle in it, for I have assigned the land to you to possess. You shall appor-
tion the land among yourselves" (Num. 33:53). This notion regarding this commandment was repeated in other passages, as when He, may He be blessed, said,
"Go, take possession of the land that the Lord swore to your forefathers" (Deut.
1:8). He detailed this commandment to them in its entirety with respect to its
[i.e., the land's] borders and boundaries, as it says, "Start out and make your way
to the hill country of the Amorites and to all the neighbors in the Arabah, the hill
country, the Shephelah, the Negeb, the seacoast" etc. (Deut. 1:7), so that they
would not neglect any place within it. Evidence that this was a commandment,
was His statement regarding the matter of the spies, "Go up, take possession, as
the Lord, God of your fathers, has promised you. Fear not and be not dismayed"
(Deut. 1:21). He further said, "And when the Lord sent you on from Kadesh-
barnea, saying 'Go forth and take possession of the land I am giving you,'" and
when they did not want to go forth in accordance with this statement, it is written, "you flouted the command of the Lord your God; you did not put your trust
in Him and did not obey Him" (Deut. 9:23), indicating that it was a commandment, not a promise or assurance.[29] This is what the sages call mandatory war

---

29. Nahmanides is ruling out the possibility that when God says to the Israelites, "And you shall take possession of the land and settle in it" (Num. 33:53), it is merely a prediction of what will happen in the future. For Nahmanides, God's statement is an actual command that the Israelites must actively fulfill.

(*milhemet mitsvah*). Thus, they say in the Gemara, *Sotah*, "Rav Judah says, 'the war[s] of Joshua for conquest, everyone agrees, were obligatory; the war[s] of David for expansion, everyone agrees, were discretionary.'" [According to] the language of *Sifrey*, "'And take possession of it and settle in it' (Deut. 17:14): By virtue of taking possession of it, you shall settle it."[30]

Do not be confused and say that this commandment is the commandment of [waging] war against the seven nations that we were commanded to anni-hilate, as it says, "you shall surely annihilate them" (Deut. 20:17). That is not the case. For we were commanded to kill those nations when they made war against us, but if they wanted to make peace, we were to make peace with them, and leave them alone, in accordance with explicit stipulations. But the land, we were not to leave in their hands nor [in the hands of] other nations in any generation. Thus, if those [seven] nations had fled from us or went on their way—in accordance with their statement, "The Girgashites left and went on their way, and God gave them a good land like this one: Africa"[31]—we were [still] commanded to enter the land, conquer [its] territories, and settle our tribes in it. Likewise, if, after our destruction of the nations mentioned [above], they [i.e., the Israelites] had wanted subsequently to leave the land and to conquer for themselves the land of Shinar, or the land of Assyria, or any other place, they would not have been permitted to, for we have been commanded to conquer it [i.e., the land of Israel] and settle it.[32] Also, under-stand from their statement [i.e., that of the sages], "the war[s] of Joshua for conquest,"[33] that this commandment is in the [act of] conquest. Thus, they said in *Sifrey*,

"Every spot on which your foot treads, shall be yours etc.," (Deut. 11:22): [Moses] said to them, "Every place you shall conquer, except these places, shall be yours." Or was it [i.e., this statement] to permit them to conquer places out-side the land of Israel before conquering the land itself? [No], for Scripture says first, "You shall dispossess nations greater and more numerous than you" (Deut. 11:23), and afterwards, "Every spot on which your," etc.[34]

And they said "Should you ask, 'Why do the commandments not apply to Aram-Naharaim and Aram-Zobah which were conquered by David?,' the answer

---

30. *Sifrey Devarim* on Deut. 17:14.

31. *Devarim Rabbah*, 5:13–14. According to this midrash, Joshua offered the Canaanite nations the option of leaving the land of Israel in order to avoid war, and the only one that took him up on his offer was the Girgashites, who were given Africa as a reward.

32. With emphasis on "and settle it." That is, the commandment did not specify that they should merely conquer the land. They also had to then live in it.

33. Cited earlier in this passage from BT *Sotah* 44b.

34. *Sifrey Devarim* 51. I have been helped here by the translation of Reuven Hammer in *Sifre: A Tannaitic Commentary on the Book of Numbers* (New Haven, Conn.: Yale University Press, 1987).

is, David disobeyed the Torah. The Torah said, 'After you have conquered the land of Israel, you may conquer places outside the land,' but he did not do so." Hence, we have been commanded to conquer [the land] for all generations.[35]

I also say that the commandment about which the sages make emphatic statements—that is, [the commandment] to live in the land of Israel—so much so that they say that "anyone who leaves it and lives outside the land should be regarded by you as one who worships idols, as it says, 'For they have driven me out today, so that I cannot have a share in the Lord's possession, but am told, Go forth and worship other gods'" (I Sam. 29:19),[36] as well as other strongly emphatic statements that they make about it—all [these statements] are due to the positive commandment that we were commanded to inherit the land and settle in it. Consequently, it is a positive commandment obligating every individual, even in the period of the exile, as is explicit in several places in the Talmud.[37]

According to Nahmanides, the purpose of the wars against the Canaanites was not to annihilate those nations, as Maimonides tells us, but to take charge of the actual land and establish Jewish sovereignty in it. Moreover, the commandment to conquer the land of Israel is by no means defunct. It is eternal. Nahmanides also adds that included in this commandment is the imperative to live in the land of Israel. It is therefore a requirement incumbent upon every Jew to settle in the land of Israel even during the period of exile when it is ruled by non-Jewish nations.

A difficulty with Nahmanides' views here is that, as mentioned in chapter 1, a number of early rabbinic sources claim that the Jewish people pledged to God that they would not attempt to retake the land of Israel by force during the period of the exile but would wait patiently for the coming of the messiah. This difficulty is discussed by R. Isaac Leon ben Eliezer ibn Tsur, a sixteenth-century Spanish figure, whose commentary *Megilat Ester* appears in standard editions of Maimonides' *Sefer ha-Mitsvot*. R. Isaac adduces the early rabbinic sources about the three oaths to defend Maimonides' position against the attacks of Nahmanides.

While the sources about the three oaths will not be central to our study, they are cited by some of the rabbis we will explore, and we should therefore take a brief look at them. The inspiration for the notion of the three oaths is that in Song of Songs, the male lover cryptically "adjures" the "daughters of Israel" in three different places not to "wake or rouse love until it please."[38] The Hebrew term for "adjure" (*hishbiʻa*) here literally means "to exact an oath," and

35. *Sifrey Devarim* 51
36. BT *Ketubot* 110b.
37. Nahmanides, "Addenda to Positive Commandments," in Maimonides' *Sefer ha-Mitsvot*, addendum #4.
38. Song of Songs 2:7, 3:5, 8:4.

because the male lover is identified in rabbinic and medieval Jewish literature with God, a number of rabbis take the three passages as references to three oaths that God required the Jewish people and the nations of the world to take in order to define the terms of the relationship between the Jews and their non-Jewish overlords during the era of Jewish exile. The oaths would remain in effect until the messianic period, for, as the passage tells us, the male lover urges the daughters of Israel not to "wake" or "rouse" until the time that "it please." That is, the Jews and the nations of the world should adhere to the terms of these oaths until the messianic era when the Jews would once again have an intimate relationship with God. The key opinion in the talmudic passage about the oaths is that of R. Jose ben Hanina who spells out their content as follows:

> One, that Israel would not go up in a wall; another, that God made Israel swear that they would not rebel against the nations of the world; and another, that God made the nations of the world swear that they would not oppress Israel overly much.[39]

In the first oath, the cryptic phrase that Israel would not "go up in a wall" is understood by most commentators to refer to military conquest. Thus, with this oath, the Jewish people makes a promise not to make use of military might to re-establish sovereignty in their homeland before the coming of the messiah. According to the second oath, the Jewish people also promises not to cast off the yolk of subjugation to the nations of the world during the period of exile. The third oath is taken by the nations, and it consists of a promise not to oppress the Jewish people during the exile more than necessary. It is primarily the first oath that is of greatest relevance to our discussion. Here, military conquest to retake the land of Israel is ruled out until the arrival of the messiah. Yet, Nahmanides appears not to support this prescription. He states quite clearly that the commandment to conquer the land did not go into abeyance with the exile but, in fact, is in force for all time.

PREEMPTIVE WAR

One other difficulty with Maimonides' treatment of the laws of war in the *Mishneh Torah* that should be mentioned is that he says nothing about preemptive war. As we noted earlier in our discussion, this type of war was alluded to in the Gemara in *Sotah* in an attempt to make sense of the Mishnaic dispute between the majority opinion of the rabbis and that of R. Judah regarding

---

39. BT *Ketubot* 110b–111a. See also parallel passages in *Song of Songs Rabbah* 2:78:1, 2:18, 8:11.

the exemptions from military service. According to the Gemara, the rabbis view preemptive war as discretionary, while R. Judah sees it as mandatory.[40] However, it was unclear how the terms "mandatory" and "discretionary" were being used here, and Maimonides, in failing to make any reference to preemptive war, does not clarify matters. Subsequent halakhic interpreters would attempt fill in the gap and would provide a wide range of opinions on this issue, with some rabbis arguing that preemptive is indeed mandatory in the fullest sense of the term, and other arguing that it is discretionary. These rabbis would also be divided about what precise situations warrant the waging of preemptive war.[41]

ISRAEL AND THE WAGING OF WAR:
THE HALAKHIC OBSTACLES REVISITED

In my introductory chapter, I described the major difficulties halakhic authorities faced when the state of Israel was created and immediately thrust into war, and I would now like to take a closer look at these problems. As I explained in my introduction, in this study I am interested primarily in exploring the moral challenges that halakhic authorities in Israel had to confront when dealing with war, and therefore I will focus my discussion here only on issues of this kind.

Mandatory War, Discretionary War, and Legitimate Authority

The most basic challenge that the rabbis in the religious Zionist camp had to face was whether the halakhic categories of war laid out in early rabbinic literature and in Maimonides still applied. Could a modern Jewish state wage defensive wars? Could it wage discretionary wars that were more aggressive in nature? What about Nahmanides' view that there was an eternal commandment for Jews to conquer the land promised by God to Abraham? Could Jews conduct wars to fulfill this commandment?

As has been noted, these questions were in turn dependent on the issue of legitimate authority. If a king was needed to initiate a mandatory war, was the Jewish state then forbidden to wage a war of this kind, given that the institution of kingship had not existed for centuries and was not expected to be revived until messianic times? If a king was indeed needed to wage wars of this kind, Jews would not be permitted to conduct even a defensive

---

40. BT *Sotah* 44b.

41. This issue is thoroughly analyzed in J. David Bleich, "Preemptive War in Jewish Law," in *Contemporary Halakhic Problems* (New York: Ktav, 1989), 3:251–92.

war, and they certainly would not be allowed to wage war in accordance with Nahmanides' view that the command to conquer the land of Israel was still in effect. The halakhic obstacles to waging discretionary war were even greater because with this form of war, not only was a king needed, but also a Sanhedrin, and perhaps the *urim ve-tumim* as well, entities that had also not existed for centuries and, like kingship, were not expected to be reconstituted until the messianic era.

Conscription

The second major halakhic challenge that rabbinic authorities in the religious Zionist camp had to confront when it came to war was that even if these rabbis could somehow surmount the foregoing difficulties concerning legitimate authority, there were questions about whether Halakhah permitted such a modern Jewish state to assemble an army through conscription. I will concentrate my efforts on explicating the difficulty by focusing first on wars of self-defense, for it was here that the problem was most evident. If there were obstacles to drafting soldiers for defensive wars, the same problem would certainly arise for discretionary wars, which were more aggressive in nature, not to mention Nahmanides' notion of wars waged for the sake of conquest.

Let us begin by looking at how Halakhah views the issue of self-defense as it pertains to individuals. It is a sacrosanct principle in Halakhah that a person may kill another human being who threatens his life. If that person can neutralize the threat by merely wounding his attacker, he must do so. But if the only way he can dispense with the threat is by killing the assailant, he is permitted. This principle is based on a passage in the Torah which states that a person may kill a thief attempting to break into his home: "If a thief is caught breaking in, and is struck and killed, there is no bloodguilt in this case" (Ex. 22:1). The Mishnah in *Sanhedrin* explains this rule with a rather cryptic statement: "A [thief] who breaks in is judged in accordance with his outcome."[42] In the Gemara, Rava explains the statement as follows:

> It is assumed that a man does not restrain himself regarding his property. And this one [i.e., the thief] will [therefore] say, "If I go [to rob the house], he [i.e., the owner] will stand up against me, and will not allow me [to steal], and if he stands up against me, I will kill him," and the Torah says, "He who come to slay you, slay him first."[43]

42. M *Sanhedrin* 8:6.
43. BT *Sanhedrin* 72a.

What the Mishnah means, according to Rava, is that a thief who intends to steal from a home is likely to assume that if he encounters the owner of the home in the course of the robbery, the owner will prevent him from committing the crime because people naturally care about their property. We can therefore assume that, in this situation, the thief will come prepared to kill the owner. The owner thus has every right to kill the robber with impunity, for as the Torah teaches us, "he who comes to slay you, slay him first;" that is, one may kill in self-defense.[44] It is for this reason that the Mishnah says that the robber is "judged in accordance with his outcome." The thief, from a halakhic standpoint, has the legal status of a dead person from the minute he attempts to break into the owner's home because of the owner's right to kill him, and therefore the robber's death incurs no penalty for the owner. After all, one cannot kill someone who is already legally dead. Or to put it another way, one can kill such an individual, but it cannot be called murder in any legal sense.

One may wonder why Rava's explanation is so convoluted, but it would seem that, besides attempting to make sense of the Mishhah, he is struggling with a specific difficulty. One could argue that, in the case under consideration here, the owner of the home should simply let the thief rob him because the owner's property is of less worth than another person's life, even if that person happens to be a thief intending to take his belongings. Yet, the Torah clearly states that one may kill a thief who has broken into his home for that purpose. What, then, accounts for the Torah's position? Rava argues, in effect, that the owner has a right to kill in this instance, not in order to defend property, but in order to defend his own life, for we can assume that a thief who is willing to break into a person's home is also someone who will be intent on killing the owner if he encounters him during the robbery. The owner may therefore kill on the assumption he is defending himself from a lethal threat.

But what is most important for our purposes is that early on in the development of Halakhah, the rabbis rule that one is allowed to kill in self-defense. Moreover, it is a right that is never questioned in later halakhic literature.

Another halakhic principle connected to this one and equally important for our purposes is that an individual is permitted to kill not only in his own defense but also in defense of others. In fact, he is required to. If an innocent person is being pursued by an attacker who is intent on killing him, and a bystander has the opportunity to kill the attacker, the bystander must do so. This rule is known in halakhic literature as the law of the *rodef*, the "pursuer," and it is first dealt with in the Mishnah in the same chapter of *Sanhedrin* that takes up the case of the thief we just examined.[45] As with the latter case, the Mishnah states the general principle, but it is the Gemara that attempts to find a biblical source for

---

44. Though as a number of medieval and modern commentators point out, there is actually no place in the Torah where we are told that one may kill in self-defense.
45. M *Sanhedrin* 8:7.

it. The Gemara's first suggestion is that the law of the pursuer is based on the verse, "Do not stand idly by the blood of your fellow" (Lev. 19:16), which could be understood to include the imperative to rescue a fellow Israelite who is being pursued by someone intent on killing him.[46] However, the Gemara rejects this suggestion because a tannaitic source interprets that biblical verse as a general prescription to rescue a person whose life is at risk in any dangerous situation— such as one who is drowning, being mauled by animals, or being robbed—and the verse does not specifically permit a person to rescue another individual by killing his attacker. For this rule, the Gemara turns to another tannaitic source quoted in the name of R. Judah the Patriarch that comments on Deuteronomy 22:25–27, a passage that imposes the death penalty on a man who rapes a young woman engaged to be married. R. Judah focuses on a statement in the biblical passage that specifically compares the rape of the young woman to murder: "for this case is like that of a man attacking another and murdering him" (Deut. 22:26). R. Judah draws the following lesson from this comparison:

> Just as one may rescue an engaged young woman [from rape] by [taking] his life [i.e., that of the attacker], so too [in the case of] a murderer, one may rescue [the potential victim] by [taking] his life [i.e., that of the attacker].[47]

R. Judah tells us that what the biblical text is teaching us is that one must kill a person who is pursuing another to murder him just as one must kill a person who is pursuing an engaged young woman to sexually assault her. But the Gemara asks the obvious question: where does R. Judah learn that one should kill a would-be rapist pursuing his victim? The biblical text does not give such an instruction, at least not explicitly. This imperative, according to the Gemara, is drawn from another statement at the end of the same passage in Deuteronomy which informs us that "though the engaged young woman cried for help, there was no one to save her" (Deut. 2:27). The Gemara reasons from this addendum that "had there been someone to save her, [that person should have] rescued her by any means possible," which includes killing the attacker before he has a chance to commit the crime.[48]

The foregoing considerations should have made it easy for the rabbis in our study to justify conscription for wars of self-defense. Wars of this kind are, after all, instances in which one is both defending oneself and defending others from lethal attack, and in both cases, one may kill the assailant. In fact, in the latter instance, one is required to. However, matters are not so simple, as the rabbis in our study will point out. First, a soldier fighting in a defensive war is not necessarily defending himself. He may, in fact, be living at some

46. BT *Sanhedrin* 73a.
47. Ibid.
48. Ibid.

distance from the battlefront, and the threat posed by the enemy, therefore, may not be immediate for him. Moreover, surrender is always an option, especially if the attacking nation merely wants territory.

The case of the pursuer is perhaps more apt to characterize the position of a soldier fighting in a defensive war than that of simple self-defense, for even if one's own life is not immediately threatened, surely the attacking nation poses a threat to at least some of one's fellow countrymen, and one is therefore obligated, according to the law of the pursuer, to rescue them from harm. But here too, matters are not so simple, as we have already noted in chapter 1. According to Halakhah, one is not required to endanger oneself to rescue another from harm because the law of the pursuer is not applicable if rescuer has to risk his own life to save the victim.

Why the potential rescuer has no obligation to endanger himself here is due to a halakhic principle that one is not required to fulfill a divine commandment at the cost of one's life. The only exceptions to this rule are the prohibitions against idolatry, murder, and the most egregious of sexual violations, such as adultery and incest. One must sooner die than violate these commandments.[49] Yet, all other commandments may be transgressed if one's life is endangered by their fulfillment. The source for this principle is a Mishnah in *Yoma*, where we are told that one must violate the Sabbath to save a life that is endangered, even if there is some uncertainty about whether the danger is lethal: "One sets aside [the laws of the Sabbath] in [instances] of possible danger."[50] One must therefore transgress the Sabbath to rescue victims of a disaster, even if it is not certain that they are alive. Thus, if someone is buried in a landslide, one must conduct a rescue mission in violation of the Sabbath so long as there is even a possibility that the individual survived.[51] The Gemara entertains a number of opinions regarding the source of this rule, but the preferred one is that of Samuel, who bases it on Leviticus 18:5, which states, "You shall keep my decrees and laws, which a person will do and live by them, I am the Lord." The phrase "and live by them" is taken here as an imperative which requires us to "live" by the laws, not to die by them.[52] The same principle, therefore, applies in the case of the pursuer. Here too, one need not sacrifice one's life to fulfill the commandment of saving another person from his attacker.

Of course, the case of risking one's life to kill a pursuer is complicated by the fact that here, as opposed to the case of the Sabbath, two lives are stake, not just one: that of the pursued and that of the rescuer. However, Halakhah gives clear priority to the rescuer; he need not give up his life in such a situation. That point comes through with abundant clarity in a well-known talmudic

49. T *Shabbat* 16:14; BT *Sanhedrin* 74a.
50. M *Shabbat* 8:4.
51. M *Shabbat* 8:6.
52. BT *Shabbat* 85b.

source that takes up the question of two men traveling together, presumably at some distance from civilization, and one of them has a container with just enough water for one person to survive the journey. The question is whether the individual with the water is required to share it with his companion, in which case they will both die, or whether he may drink the entire quantity of water himself with the result that he will survive but his companion will not:

> Two people are on a journey, and one has a container of water. If both drink, they will die. If one of them drinks, he will reach civilization. Ben Petura taught: It is best that they both drink and die so that neither of them sees the death of his companion. Until R. Akiva came and taught, "so that your brother may live with you" (Lev. 25:36). Your life takes precedence over the life of your companion.[53]

The ruling of R. Akiva is the ruling generally accepted by later halakhic authorities, and it states that the person with the container of water has no obligation to share the water with his companion and may drink it all himself in order to save his own life. We therefore learn from here that when two lives are at stake, one's own and that of another, one has no obligation to give up one's own life to save another person from death. This principle can be applied to the case of the pursuer as well. Here, too, the bystander need not give up his life to save another person from his attacker.

These considerations would seem to rule out assembling an army through conscription. One may perhaps form an army in which soldiers serve on a voluntary basis, for while one is not obligated to save others from a pursuer at the cost of one's own life, some halakhic authorities permit an individual to do so voluntarily. One may therefore fight in a defensive war to defend one's countryman if one wishes to. However, it would seem that one cannot be forced to do so, which is precisely what conscription demands. Yet, the rabbis we will examine in our study knew full well that the state of Israel could not depend on the good will of its citizens to defend itself. Conscription was necessary for the state's survival.

But perhaps there is a way out of this conundrum. As some of our halakhic authorities in this study will point out, not all soldiers who fight in a war lose their lives. Therefore, a soldier who participates in a defensive war is not necessarily giving up his life for others but only putting it at risk. This distinction is significant because it is recognized in Halakhah. Medieval and early modern halakhic authorities tend to treat a scenario in which a person enters a situation of "possible danger" (*safek sakanah*) to save someone from "certain danger" (*vaday sakanah*), as different from one in which the rescuer himself is subject to "certain danger" and is likely to die in attempting to save another individual. The question is whether this fine distinction makes a difference as

---

53. BT *Bava Metis'a* 62a.

far as the halakhic outcome is concerned. A person does not have to subject himself to "certain danger" to rescue another in the same situation, but is he perhaps required to take on "possible danger" for that end? Some halakhic authorities say he is, and they do so on the basis of a passage in the Jerusalem Talmud that states the following:

> R. Immi was caught in a riot and captured.[54] R. Johanan said, "Let the dead person [i.e., R. Immi] be wrapped in his death shroud" [i.e., he will not survive his captivity]. R. Simeon ben Lakish said, "Either I will kill [those who hold R. Immi captive], or I will be killed." I will go and rescue him with force. He went and appeased them [i.e., those holding R. Immi], and they gave him [i.e., R. Immi] to him [i.e., R. Simeon ben Lakish].[55]

Here we are told that R. Simeon ben Lakish risked his life to save R. Immi, which indicates that perhaps one should subject oneself to possible danger to save someone in certain danger. This approach is endorsed by a number of later medieval authorities, including R. Joseph Karo, author of the *Shulhan Arukh*.[56] But the majority of latter-day halakhic authorities seem to incline away from this position. Most of them see no difference between merely risking one's life to save another person, and giving up one's life for that individual. In neither instance is the would-be rescuer required to act. He is permitted to put his own interests first.[57]

This brings us back to square one. It seems difficult, if not impossible, to justify conscription for the sake of a defensive war within the normal parameters of Halakhah. And, as we noted in the previous chapter, if that is the case with respect to defensive war, the difficulty would be even greater with discretionary wars, which are usually more aggressive in nature. The same goes for Nahmanides' notion of war for conquering the land of Israel, for here there is certainly no issue of self-defense. The rabbis in our study therefore had to ask how, within the strictures of Halakhah, the state of Israel could field an army that would allow the state to survive.

I pointed out in our introductory chapter that the rabbis in the religious Zionist camp were, of course, aware of the fact that in the Bible and rabbinic

---

54. Following Marcus Jastrow's dictionary for the phrase, *"ityatsid be-safsifa."*
55. JT *Terumot* 8:4.
56. See his commentary *Kesef Mishneh* on MT *Rotseah* 1:14, and his commentary *Beit Yosef* on *Tur, Hoshen Mishpat* 426. In agreement with this position is R. Joshua Falk (ca. 1555–1614), in his *Sefer Me'irat 'Einayim, Hoshen Mishpat* 426.
57. See R. David ben Solomon ibn Zimra (ca. 1479–1573), *Teshuvot Radbaz*, vol. 3, responsum 1,052; R. Joseph ben Meir Te'omim (1727–92), *Peri Megadim, Mishbetsot Zahav* 328:7; R. Yehi'el Mikhal Epshtein (1829–1908), *Arukh ha-Shulhan* on *Shulhan Arukh: Hoshen Mishpat* 426:4. A discussion of this issue can be found in Nahum Rakover, *Mesirut Nefesh: Hakravat ha-Yahid le-Hatsalat ha-Rabim* (Jerusalem: Moreshet ha-Mishpat le-Yisra'el, 2000), chapter 9. See also Bleich, "Preemptive War in Jewish Law," 275.

literature, conscription was permissible. But they could not approve of it for a modern Jewish state until they had an understanding of why it was allowed despite the fact that no individual could be forced to endanger his life for others. The source of the difficulty was that medieval Halakhah had developed laws governing individual behavior over a period of centuries without developing a corpus of laws for war, and in this case the laws regulating the conduct of the individual were difficult to maintain in war.

Civilian Casualties

The third major halakhic challenge that rabbis in the religious Zionist camp had to deal with in the moral sphere was civilian casualties. As noted in chapter 1, the problem is a universal one. Ethicists throughout the ages and in different cultures generally accept the fact that in war soldiers die. After all, war is not war without soldiers being killed. Soldiers in opposing armies may therefore target each other with impunity. But the same ethicists often argue that unarmed civilians should not be harmed, and if the demands of war make it impossible to avoid harming them, the harm should at least be minimized. In modern times, this issue has become especially important because the numbers of civilian casualties in wartime have risen dramatically, especially in the last century, due to the nature of modern warfare. Armies no longer battle each other, as they once did, in areas separate from population centers, and modern weaponry has become so powerful that an army cannot easily discriminate between enemy soldiers and civilians when pressing forward with a military campaign.

As we noted in our previous chapter, the rabbis in our study had to deal with the same issue from the standpoint of Halakhah, and here again Halakhah posed serious challenges. According to early rabbinic and medieval Halakhah, one may kill an assailant in self-defense, but not if it results in the death of innocent bystanders. One has to accept death at the hands of the assailant rather than harm someone who poses no threat. Thus, to use a modern example, if a person is being shot at by a gunman surrounded by innocent people, one may not return fire if there is any chance that he may kill one of the bystanders.

The basis for this principle is the following case that appears in several passages in the Gemara:

> Someone came to Rabbah and said to him: "The governor of my town said to me, 'Go kill so-and-so, and if [you do] not, I will kill you.'" [Rabbah] said: "Let him kill you, but you may not kill. Who is to say that your blood is redder? Perhaps that man's blood is redder."[58]

---

58. BT *Sanhedrin* 74a; *Yoma* 82b; *Pesahim* 25a.

Rabbah rules here that one may not obey a tyrant who orders him to kill some-one, even if the tyrant threatens him with death. One should sooner die than kill an innocent individual. Therefore, the prospect of losing one's life is no excuse for taking someone else's.

In some sense, this case is the reverse of the one examined earlier in which two men are on a journey, and only one has a sufficient quantity of water for a single person to survive. In that case, the question is whether one is required to sacrifice one's life for another. In the scenario now under consideration, the question is whether one may sacrifice the life of another for one's own. We can shed valuable light on the rulings the rabbis make in both instances by noting the unstated moral logic that underlies the two judgments. The general principle seems to be that a person who is in a position of safety has every right to remain in that position. He is therefore not required to take on any risk to relieve another individual who is in danger. Thus, a bystander who witnesses a pursuer intent on killing another person has the right to refrain from helping the one being pursued if the bystander has to risk his life to ren-der assistance. The bystander is permitted to maintain his position of safety. By the same token, if a tyrant threatens a person with death unless that per-son kills someone else who is innocent, the person may not do so to save his own life because in this situation, the person who is in immediate danger is the one to whom the tyrant is giving orders. The individual whom the tyrant wants killed is in a position of relative safety—at least, for the time being—and has every right to remain safe. The person to whom the tyrant is giving the order must therefore accept death rather than follow through with the king's demand.

But let us get back to war. If transferred to the battlefield, the ethic encap-sulated in Rabbah's ruling regarding an individual who is ordered to kill or be killed, would again make war virtually impossible to wage, even in self-defense. War always poses a danger to innocent civilians on the enemy side—more so nowadays than ever before—and yet it is quite clear from Rabbah's ruling, that one may not take the lives of innocent people to spare one's own. A Jewish army under attack from an enemy nation should therefore be barred from responding with military force, seeing as innocent lives are likely to be lost.

Here too, we must be reminded that the rabbis in the religious Zionist movement were well aware of the fact that the biblical and rabbinic sources sanctioned war despite this problem. However, these rabbis still had to explain why the Bible and early rabbis did not see it as an obstacle to the waging of war. And once again, the source of the problem was that Halakhah had devel-oped a comprehensive body of laws governing individual behavior without having to consider their ramifications for war. Thus, when the state of Israel was thrust into war, the rabbis were faced with instances of laws governing individual behavior that made war difficult, if not impossible, to wage.

Our goal in this chapter was to review the material on war in Halakhah before Zionism that is relevant to the issues discussed in our study.[59] For this purpose, we based our discussion on Maimonides' treatment of war in the *Mishneh Torah* because it provides the fundamental framework for all subsequent halakhic discussions of war, including those of the rabbis explored in our study. Maimonides' halakhic positions on war, however, are not the last word on the subject. We made note of some early rabbinic views on war that Maimonides did not adopt, as well as instances in which his successors either supplemented his views on war or disagreed with them, and these too will be important for our study.

According to Maimonides, there are two major categories of war: mandatory and discretionary. This division is based on the opinion of the rabbis in a Mishnah in *Sotah* which distinguishes between wars in which a number of military exemptions apply, and wars in which they do not. The latter wars are termed "mandatory," since all able-bodied adults must go into battle, while the former are designated "discretionary," because the exemptions apply here.

In Maimonides' view, mandatory wars include the wars against the Canaanites, the wars against the Amalekites, and wars waged in self-defense. The identification of the Canaanites wars as mandatory seems to have been taken from the Gemara in *Sotah*. The notion that the Amalekite wars are mandatory has no rabbinic source, but in the Bible these wars are directly commanded by God just as the Canaanite wars are, and therefore it is not hard to understand why Maimonides would see them as mandatory. It is not clear how Maimonides justified the inclusion of defensive wars in the category of mandatory wars, but two early rabbinic sources, one from the Babylonian Talmud and another from the Jerusalem Talmud, may have prompted him to do so.

The second major category of wars in Maimonides' scheme, those that are discretionary, include wars to expand the borders of the Jewish state or to increase the prestige of the king. The first type of war is explicitly identified as discretionary in the Gemara in *Sotah*, but not the second which appears to have been Maimonides' own innovation. Maimonides also appears to have passed over two other types of war identified as discretionary in talmudic sources: wars that are preemptive in nature, and wars waged for economic reasons.

59. In addition to this summary, I have also provided an appendix at the end of the chapter that reviews the same material in point form. I encourage readers who have little background in the treatment of war in Halakhah to refer back to this appendix while reading the coming chapters if they need a refresher on what medieval Halakhah has to say about war. All the rabbis in our study assume that their audience is familiar with this material, and so my hope is that the appendix will be of help to those who are not.

Besides the motives which determine whether a war is mandatory or dis-cretionary, the two categories of war are distinguished from each other by the issue of legitimate authority. According to Maimonides, only a king is required to initiate wars that are mandatory, while discretionary wars also require the approval of a Sanhedrin. However, in one source, Maimonides also appears to require that a king consult with the *urim ve-tumim* before waging discre-tionary war, and Rashi and Nahmanides take that position as well. Here too, Maimonides seems to have drawn from earlier rabbinic sources. The three authoritative entities he mentions that are needed to wage war—the king, the Sanhedrin, and the *urim ve-tumim*—are all dealt with in these sources.

We identified two features of Maimonides' scheme that would elicit much discussion among later halakhic interpreters. Nahmanides finds fault with Maimonides for identifying the first type of mandatory war with the command-ment to annihilate the Canaanites and for insisting that this commandment is no longer in effect. According to Nahmanides, God commanded the Israelites to conquer and settle the land of Israel, and the killing of the Canaanites was merely a means to those ends. Moreover, these commandments are still in force. However, commentators have wondered how Nahmanides could have claimed that these imperatives were still valid, seeing as there was an explicit talmudic source that seemed to rule out conquering the land of Israel by force prior to the messianic period. Another feature in Maimonides' scheme that would get the attention of later commentators was the absence of any treat-ment of preemptive war. These commentators would provide a wide range of opinions on this matter. They would debate whether preemptive war was mandatory or discretionary, as well as the precise circumstances under which a war of this kind could be waged.

We also explicated in greater detail than we did in our introductory chap-ter, the halakhic challenges in the moral sphere that religious Zionist rabbis had to confront when dealing with wars waged by the state of Israel. First, these rabbis had to decide which types of war could be conducted. Was the state permitted to wage only defensive wars, or could it wage aggressive wars as well, such as those that are discretionary? Could the state wage a war for the sole purpose of fulfilling the commandment to conquer the land of Israel as understood by Nahmanides? Closely tied to these questions was the issue of legitimate authority. Could war of any kind be waged in the absence of a Jewish king, a Sanhedrin, and the *urim ve-tumim*?

Other formidable halakhic obstacles in the moral realm had to do with the carnage of war. Could a modern Jewish state assemble an army through conscription, even for defensive purposes, if, according to Halakhah, one could not force an individual to endanger his life to save others from harm? Could a Jewish army, once assembled, wage war if Halakhah forbade the kill-ing of innocent individuals, even for the sake of self-defense, and war inevi-tably involves the loss of innocent civilian life? Even if biblical and rabbinic literature had permitted wars in the past despite these challenges, the rabbis could not assume that the same permission applied to a secular modern Jewish state established prior to the messianic era.

Before we move on to the next chapter, it should be noted that some of the halakhic challenges endemic to war had already been noted by a number of European halakhic authorities in the nineteenth century before the advent of Zionism. As noted in the previous chapter, these authorities took an interest in war due to the fact that, in this period, Jews were being emancipated across Europe and were invited to become citizens of their respective countries, and Jews were now required to perform military service. Jews were therefore participating in wars in larger numbers than at any time in the past many centuries.

The views of one major nineteenth-century halakhic authority on the moral problems inherent in war are worth mentioning here because they are quoted by a number of the thinkers examined in this study. I am referring to R. Naftali Tsevi Yehudah Berlin (1816–93), better known by his acronym, Netsiv. One passage in the Netsiv's writing, in particular, addresses the carnage of war. It appears in his commentary on the Torah in a gloss on Genesis 9:5–6. In these verses, God issues a number of commandments to Noah upon his exit from the ark, one of which addresses the prohibition of murder and its punishment:

> But for you own life-blood, I will require a reckoning: I will require it of every beast; of man, too, will I require a reckoning for human life, of every man for that of his fellow man. Whoever sheds the blood of man, by man shall his blood be shed; for in His image did God make man.

The Netsiv's comments on these verses are as follows:

> When is a person punished [for murder]? At a time when one is supposed to act with fellowship [toward others], which is not the case in a time of war and a time of hatred. In that instance, it is a time to kill, and there is no punishment for it at all, for that is the way the world was founded (*kakh nosad ha-'olam*). An Israelite king is even permitted to wage discretionary war, although a number of Israelites will be killed because of this.[60]

This passage contains a lot more information than its brevity would indicate. The Netsiv argues that though God imposes the death penalty for murder, the wording of the biblical text contains a loophole that allows human beings to indulge in killing in wartime. God says to Noah that a man must be put to

60. *Ha'amek Davar* on Gen. 9:5.

death when he takes the life of his "fellow" man. However, the Nestiv notes, when war is waged, it is time when there is no "fellowship" between men, and therefore in war, there is no punishment for killing; one is allowed to do so with impunity. The Netsiv also mentions that war is exceptional in another regard. In war, Jewish kings were permitted to endanger the lives of their subjects by sending them out to battle, even in discretionary wars, which, as we have noted, do not usually serve a defensive purpose. The Netsiv notes as well that the rules of war are different from those of ordinary life because "that is the way the world was founded," a statement implying that we must accept the carnage of war because war is a natural phenomenon.

Thus, in this passage the Netsiv addresses both the halakhic challenge of killing enemy civilians and that of conscription. The Netsiv's view is that war functions on a moral plane that is entirely distinct from that of everyday life, and therefore in Halakhah both activities are permitted. A Jewish king may send out soldiers to war to kill and be killed in a way that he could not in other situations.

The problem of conscription is taken up again by the Netsiv and expanded on in another remarkable passage in his commentary on the Torah. The Netsiv addresses the issue of conscription in a gloss on Deuteronomy 20:8, which spells out some of the exemptions from military service we referred to earlier that the Israelite soldiers are encouraged to take advantage of before going into battle. The biblical text reads as follows:

> The officials shall go on addressing the troops, and say, "Is there anyone afraid and disheartened? Let him go back to his home so that he not cause the courage of his comrades to flag like his."

The Nestiv makes the following comment on this prescription:

> But, [the verse] did not prohibit him—as its plain meaning indicates—from endangering himself [in war], for it is possible that a man who is depressed and bitter would like to die, but it is forbidden for him to commit suicide, and he sees it as a good thing to fall in war. There is no prohibition [against doing this] in war, just as the king is not forbidden from conducting discretionary war which results in endangering lives. For war is different [from everyday life]. There is no prohibition against a person going to war and endangering himself, but he must "not cause the courage of his comrades to flag."[61]

According to the Netsiv, the biblical text specifically prohibits a person who is fearful from going to war because his fear may damage the morale of his fellow

---

61. *Ha'amek Davar* on Deut. 20:8.

soldiers, but it does not prohibit a person who actually *wants* to die in war from doing so. Thus a person who is in a depressed state of mind and has a desire to end his own life may do so by going to war, even though suicide is normally forbidden in Halakhah. That is because there is no prohibition against risking one's life in war. The Nestiv also adds that this observation explains why a king may risk the lives of his troops by sending them into battle, even in a discretionary war. Again, the underlying principle here is that the laws of war are different from those of ordinary life.

Thus, in both passages, the Netsiv is able to deal with moral challenges of war by arguing that wartime Halakhah is different from everyday Halakhah. As we shall soon see, this way of thinking will have a significant impact on a number of the rabbis in this study. In fact, echoes of the Netsiv's viewpoint will be evident in the approach to war taken by the first halakhic authority we will examine in this study: R. Abraham Isaac Kook.

APPENDIX: SUMMARY OF LAWS OF WAR IN MEDIEVAL HALAKHAH

The classification below is based on Maimonides' *Mishneh Torah, Hilkhot Melakhim* 5, unless otherwise specified in parentheses:

A. Mandatory War
  1. Goals:
     a. conquest and annihilation of the Canaanites
     b. annihilation of the Amalekites
     c. defense
     d. conquest of the land of Israel (Nahmanides)
  2. Authority:
     direct divine command, or initiative of the king
B. Discretionary War
  1. Goals:
     a. expansion of the borders of Israel
     b. increase of the king's prestige
     c. economic benefit (Talmud)
  2. Authority:
     initiative of the king, approval of the Sanhedrin, and *urim ve-tumim* (Talmud)

CHAPTER 3

⚬∿⚬

R. Abraham Isaac Kook

The first thinker we will analyze is by far the best known. R. Abraham Isaac Kook (1865–1935) was born in Griva, which is now in modern-day Latvia. He received a traditional Jewish education in the famed Volozhin Yeshiva, where he was soon recognized for his prodigious intellectual talents. He then went on to serve as a rabbi in a number of Jewish communities in eastern Europe. During these years, R. Kook also became a supporter of Zionism, and in 1904 he emigrated to Palestine, where he assumed the position of Chief Rabbi of the city of Jaffa. It was not long before he was acknowledged as a leading figure in the nascent Jewish community in Palestine. He was also able to make inroads into the secular community of Jews in Palestine because of his positive outlook on secular Zionism, which was unusual for a rabbi of his religious background. In 1919, R. Kook became Chief Ashkenazi Rabbi of Palestine, and he held that post until his death at age seventy in 1935.[1]

R. Kook left behind a large body of writings in theology, poetry, and Halakhah. His theology became by far the best-known part of his corpus and his most lasting legacy. It represents a unique blend of homiletic teaching, aggadic interpretation, philosophy, and mysticism. It also reflects knowledge of the major currents in Western thought in R. Kook's time—again, unusual for a man of his background. We have already described the major tenets of R. Kook's theology. Central in R. Kook's thought was the view that God's being underlies the entire universe as a dynamic, pulsating presence which is

---

1. As noted in chapter 1 n.14. an excellent biography of R. Kook has recently been published by Yehudah Mirsky, *Rav Kook: Mystic in a Time of Revolution* (New Haven, Conn.: Yale University Press, 2014).

constantly moving the world toward greater perfection, a state of being that is identified with messianic redemption. Our task as human beings is to get in touch with God's dynamic presence in order to assist Him in bringing about the redemption. The Jewish people has a unique role to play in this process because of its special closeness to God. R. Kook also believed that the messianic redemption was moving toward its conclusion. The advent of Zionism was evidence of this belief. Zionism heralded the beginning of the return of Jews to their homeland, a critical event in the messianic process. Hence, R. Kook's positive outlook on secular Zionism. He believed that secular Zionism was unwittingly serving this goal.[2]

R. Kook died before the founding of the state of Israel, but after his lifetime his thinking exerted an enormous impact on Orthodox Israelis in the religious Zionist camp and still does. As mentioned earlier, R. Tsevi Yehudah Kook (1891–1982) shaped his father's thinking for a generation of followers in the newly founded Jewish state, inculcated in them the belief that the state of Israel was indeed the beginning of the messianic redemption, and inspired them to further the redemptive process by establishing Jewish settlements in territory conquered in the Six Day War in 1967. The goal here was to ensure that all the lands initially promised to Abraham would be in Jewish hands for the coming redemption.[3]

R. Kook—that is, the elder—also produced a substantial body of writings on Halakhah, and he brought to this discipline new and innovative perspectives that followed from his theology. He believed that if Jewish settlement in Palestine represented a critical development in the unfolding of the messianic process, Halakhah would have to undergo substantial change as well, both in content and method, in order to guide the Jewish people in this phase of its history. R. Kook referred to the new form that Halakhah would take as *torat erets yisra'el*, "the Torah of the land of Israel." It would be a Halakhah newly energized and revitalized by the experience of Jews being in control of their destiny in their homeland for the first time in almost two thousand years. This Halakhah would cultivate both the physical and spiritual dimensions of Jewish life in way that it had not been able to in the Diaspora because of the limitations of life in exile. The methodology of Halakhah would also have to adjust to the new reality. Halakhah would become far more dynamic and flexible than it had been in the Diaspora. It would also make use of a far greater range of Jewish sources than it had in medieval halakhic discourse. Rabbinic authorities would depend not just on strictly legal sources for halakhic decisions, but also on sources from rabbinic aggadah, Kabbalah, philosophy, and even sources outside Judaism. These, too, would inform the halakhic process.

---

2. I have already provided a partial list of studies from the vast corpus of academic literature that has been produced on R. Kook in chapter 1 n. 14
3. Above, pp. 8–10.

R. Kook also spoke of a renewal of the prophetic spirit that would affect halakhic decision-making as Jews became more settled in the land of Israel.[4]

How R. Kook's thinking here played out in his actual halakhic rulings has been the subject of some discussion. There seems to be consensus that a number of these rulings do indeed bear the earmarks of "the Torah of the land of Israel," both in method and content. But R. Kook is often not explicit about his halakhic methodology when rendering halakhic decisions, and therefore the extent to which his innovative theology of Halakhah affected these decisions is not always clear.[5]

R. Kook is frequently cited in the halakhic literature on war composed by religious Zionist rabbis, but in the academic world there has been relatively little analysis of R. Kook's halakhic views on war. This is not surprising because academics have devoted little attention to the topic of war in Halakhah in general. More importantly, we must recognize that while R. Kook has much to say about war, he provides relatively little information on the halakhic aspects of the topic, leaving academics with little to probe.

However, the little that R. Kook does say about war in Halakhah is very much worth examining because of its significant influence on later religious Zionist thinkers who deal with war. We will also find his few words on the subject rich in nuance and suggestive in their implications.[6]

***

4. Three studies have opened up our understanding of R. Kook as halakhic authority: R. Neryah Gutel, *Hadashim gam Yeshanim: Bi-Netivey Mishnato ha-Hilkhatit Hagutit shel ha-Rav Kuk* (Jerusalem: Magnes Press, 2005); Avinoam Rosenak, *Ha-Halakhah ha-Nevu'it: Ha-Filosofiyah shel ha-Halakhah be-Mishnat ha-R"'YH Kuk* (Jerusalem: Magnes Press, 2007); Hagi Ben-Artsi, *Ha-Hadash Yitkadesh: Ha-Rav Kuk ke-Posek Mehadesh* (Tel Aviv: Yedi'ot Ahronot and Sifrey Hemed, 2010). Ben-Artsi gives a particularly fine introduction to R. Kook's notion of "the Torah of the land of Israel" in part 1 of his book. All three authors analyze R. Kook's innovative halakhic methodology. R. Gutel is focused on R. Kook's inclusion of non-halakhic sources in his halakhic deliberations. Rosenak analyzes R. Kook's views on the role of the prophetic spirit in making halakhic rulings. Ben-Artsi, like R. Gutel, is interested in how non-halakhic sources played a role in Kook's halakhic methodology but focuses specifically on R. Kook's halakhic rulings in his early years in Palestine when he was Chief Rabbi of the Jaffa community.

5. See Rosenak, *Ha-Halakhah ha-Nevu'it*; Gutel, *Hadashim gam Yeshamin*; and Ben-Artsi, *Ha-Hadash Yitkadesh*.

6. As noted in chapter 1, it is not always easy to differentiate between academic and religious treatments of war in Halakhah because many of the religious Zionist rabbis writing on this subject have academic training, are affiliated with academic institutions, and are influenced by academic methodology. Treatments of R. Kook's halakhic views on war that are mostly academic in orientation are those of Nahum Rakover, *Mesirut Nefesh: Hakravat ha-Yahid le-Hatsalat ha-Rabim* (Jerusalem: Moreshet ha-Mishpat le-Yisra'el, 2000), 117–22; and Yitzchak Avi Roness, *"'Al Musariyutah shel ha-Milhamah be-Sifrut ha-Halakhah shel ha-Me'ah ha-'Esrim—Musar, Milhamah, ve-Le'umiyut,"* in *'Amadot: 'Am—Medinah—Torah*, vol. 1, ed. Moshe Rahimi (Elkanah / Rehovot, Israel: Mikhlelet Orot Yisra'el, 2010), 206–7. An analysis of the same subject that is mostly religious in orientation can be found in R. Yehudah Shaviv, *"Le-Mi Mishpat ha-Melukhah?"* in *Berurim be-Hilkhot ha-Re'iyah*, eds. R. Moshe Tsevi Neryah, R. Aryeh Shtern, and R. Neryah Gutel (Jerusalem: Beit ha-Rav, 1992), 147–54. Several

THE EXCHANGE WITH R. PINES: WAR AND RISKING
ONE'S LIFE FOR OTHERS

R. Kook's halakhic views on war are to be found mostly in a lengthy correspondence between him and R. Shlomo Zalman Pines (1874–1955) that took place
in the fall and winter of 1916–17. Both were in Switzerland at the time; R. Pines
was a prominent rabbi in Zurich, and R. Kook was residing temporarily in St.
Gallen.[7] The correspondence was not focused on war but on the question of when
it was appropriate, according to Halakhah, for a Jew to endanger his life to save
others from harm. The issue of war came into the discussion because war often
involves this very question, particularly wars waged in self-defense. In this type
of war, soldiers are sent into battle on the premise that they must risk their lives
to protect their fellow countrymen from harm. A full analysis of R. Kook's correspondence with R. Pines is, therefore, not necessary here. Our interest will be
in those sections of the exchange that deal with war. We will deal with other
matters in the correspondence, but only to the extent that they are necessary for
understanding the views of the two rabbis on war.

The correspondence between R. Kook and R. Pines was initiated by R. Kook
who turned to R. Pines for advice about assisting a hospital in Jerusalem that

other chapters in this volume also touch on R. Kook's views on war and are written from
a religious perspective. See references in n. 7 below. R. Kook's theological views on war
have received more attention from academics than have his halakhic perspectives on
this issue. See Aviezer Ravitzky, *Messianism, Zionism, and Jewish Religious Radicalism*,
86–124; Eli Holtser, *Herev Pipiyot be-Yadam: Aktivism Tseva'i be-Hagutah shel ha-Tsiyonut
ha-Datit* (Jerusalem: Keter, 2009), chapter 2; Avinoam Rosenak, "The Conquest of the
Land of Israel and Associated Moral Questions in the Teachings of Rabbi Kook and
His Disciples: Thoughts in Light of the Book, *Herev Pipiyot be-Yadam*," in *The Gift of
the Land and the Fate of the Canaanites in Jewish Thought*, eds. Katel Berthelot, Joseph
E. David, and Marc Hirshman (New York: Oxford University Press, 2014), 399–428;
idem, "*Musar, Milhamah, ve-Shalom be-Mishnat ha-Rav Kuk ve-Talmidav: Ha-Mifgash
bein Utopiyah le-Metsi'ut*," *Mayim mi-Dalyo* 25–26 (2014–15): 235–62.

7. R. Kook's letters to R. Pines are printed in a collection of R. Kook's responsa,
Mishpat Kohen (henceforth MK), responsa 143, 144, 145, and 148. Citations will be
from the 1966 edition printed in Jerusalem and published by Mosad ha-Rav Kuk.
R. Pines's letters to R. Kook have been printed and annotated by Rakover, *Mesirut
Nefesh*, Appendix II, 201–69. This correspondence has been analyzed in a number
of studies. Large portions of Rakover's book are devoted to that task. See especially,
chapters 9–12. Analyses of the correspondence can also be found in Gutel, *Hadashim
gam Yeshanim*, 134–47; and Ben-Artsi, *Ha-Hadash Yitkadesh*, 239–64. Explorations of
the correspondence from a more religious perspective can be found in several essays in
Neryah, Shtern, and Gutel, eds., *Berurim be-Hilkhot ha-Re'iyah*. Besides the chapter in
this volume by Shaviv, "*Le-Mi Mishpat ha-Melukhah?*", see also the chapters by R. Yig'al
Ari'el, "*Mesirut Nefesh 'avur ha-Kelal*," 73–89; R. Neryah Gutel, "*Samkhuyot Manhigey
Yisra'el*," 107–20; R. Menahem Fruman, "*Le-'Inyan Mesirut Nefesh 'avur ha-Kelal*," 121–
46; and R. Hayim Yisra'el Shteiner, "*Malkhut Hashmona'im le-'Or Tefisat Rabeinu be-
Mishpat Kohen Siman 144 ve-ha-Hashlakhah le-Yameinu*," 155–82.

was having financial difficulty and was in danger of closing.[8] In response, R. Pines suggested that R. Kook turn to a certain individual for help in raising money, and R. Kook apparently did.[9] In a subsequent letter, R. Pines commends R. Kook for his efforts in this matter, seeing as the lives of the patients in the hospital were at stake. As support for his praise of R. Kook's actions, R. Pines refers to Maimonides, who tells us that in situations in which a large group of people is in danger, a person must come to their aid even at the risk of his own life.[10]

In his response to R. Pines, R. Kook expresses great surprise at R. Pines's reference to Maimonides because he knows of no statement in the latter's writings or that of any other major halakhic authority, requiring an individual to risk his life to save others who are in danger, even if it is a large group of people. R. Kook does offer one qualification to this judgment. When the entire Jewish people is threatened with destruction, matters are different; Halakhah requires an individual to do anything necessary to save them, an imperative that includes the sacrifice of one's life. In subsequent discussion, it becomes clear that R. Kook is referring specifically to those relatively rare and dramatic situations in which the survival of the Jewish people depends on the actions of a single person, such as Queen Esther, the biblical figure who was called upon by Mordecai to use her influence with King Ahasuerus to save the Jews of the latter's kingdom from Haman's evil machinations.[11] According to R. Kook, such instances are exceptional, and one must come to the aid of the Jewish people regardless of whether one's own life is in danger.[12] However, in all other instances, one is not required to endanger one's life to rescue others from harm.

R. Kook's major point here is certainly backed up by numerous halakhic sources, as we have already noted in chapter 2. In fact, according to most halakhic authorities, an individual has no obligation to put his life at risk for others who are in danger.[13] Therefore, in a subsequent letter to R. Kook, R. Pines

8. The letter containing this request is printed in *Igrot ha-Re'iyah* (Jerusalem: Mosad ha-Rav Kuk, 1985), vol. 3, letter #743, pp. 6–7. The correspondence between R. Kook and R. Pines is quite complex and intricate and thus not easy to follow. I have therefore provided an outline of the exchange at the end of this chapter in which the letters of R. Kook and R. Pines are numbered and the main points summarized. In my notes, I will provide the letter number in my outline alongside the citations of the primary source so that my reader can more easily keep track of the discussion. Thus, the current letter is letter 1 in my outline.

9. As reported in R. Kook's letter in *Igrot ha-Re'iyah*, vol. 3, letter #742, pp. 5–6 (outline, letter 2).

10. Rakover, *Mesirut Nefesh*, Appendix II, 202–4 (outline, letter 3).

11. The example of Esther is mentioned in MK, responsum 142, p. 316, in the continuation of the passage just cited.

12. MK, responsum 142, pp. 305–6 (outline, letter 4).

13. Above, pp. 46–7.

is forced to revise his position. R. Pines now claims that while there is no *obligation* for a person to risk his life to save a large group of people, one is permitted to do so *voluntarily* as an act of piety.

R. Pines also goes on to express agreement with R. Kook's secondary point that when the entire Jewish people is threatened with destruction, the rules are different. A person who is in a unique position to avert the catastrophe is indeed obligated to do so even at the risk of his own life. R. Pines justifies this last point with his own argument that brings the issue of war into the debate:

> However, regarding the salvation of the community of Israel (*kelal yisra'el*), one can also find an argument for the obligation [of someone] placing his life in danger with the following reason: that one is obligated to go to out [and fight] in a mandatory war (*milhemet mitsvah*), one type of which is to the save [the people of] Israel from the clutches of an enemy that has attacked them, as Maimonides has written in *Hilkhot Melakhim* 5:1.[14]

Halakhah mandates that in a defensive war, all able-bodied adults must serve as soldiers and risk their lives in battle in order defend the Jewish nation, and it therefore stands to reason that even in non-war situations, an individual should risk his life to save the Jewish people when it is threatened with destruction.[15]

The discussion now focuses on the latter point. R. Kook responds to R. Pines's remarks in a letter that appears as responsum 143 in *Mishpat Kohen*, and in it he specifically objects to R. Pines's argument regarding war. R. Kook reiterates his agreement with R. Pines that an individual must indeed risk his life to save the entire Jewish people when he is in a unique position to do so. However, according to R. Kook, this imperative cannot be deduced from the laws of war as R. Pines has attempted:

> When it comes to saving the community of Israel (*kelal yisra'el*), I have already written above that in my humble opinion [one must risk one's life] because it is akin to an emergency measure (*hora'at sha'ah u-le-migdar milta*), but that it is something so straightforward that one does not need a rabbinic court [to rule] on it. But in my humble opinion, from [the laws of] mandatory war (*milhemet mitsvah*) we must not deduce anything [regarding individual behavior] because the concerns of the matter of war are separate from this matter of "you shall live by them" (Lev. 18:5). For discretionary war (*milhemet reshut*) is also permitted, and how is it that we find a dispensation to place many lives in danger for the sake of expansion [of territory] (*harhavah*)?[16] But war and the laws of

14. Rakover, *Mesirut Nefesh*, Appendix II, 213 (outline, letter 5).
15. Ibid., 207–11 (outline, letter 5).
16. As mentioned in chapter 2, discretionary wars can be waged for this purpose.

the collective are different [from those of the individual]. Perhaps it [i.e., the body of laws regarding war] was part of the laws of kingship that were undoubtedly many [in number] and given to the nation, as Maimonides has written in [Hilkhot] Melakhim 3:8 [where he says that] the king may not kill except with a sword, and that he does not have the authority to declare the money [of the executed individual] ownerless, and if he declared [it] ownerless, it is considered theft. ... All these [laws] and others like them are a small remnant left to us from the laws of kingship that are not in accordance with the strictures of the Torah concerning the laws of the individual. (In another place, I have explained that these too [i.e., the laws of kingship] have their source in the Torah, but the methods of biblical interpretation (darkey ha-derashah) in this [area of law] were given to every king in accordance with his broad wisdom. ...) Among them [i.e., the laws of kingship] are also laws of war, both mandatory war and discretionary war. But it is impossible to learn from this [i.e., the laws of war] about another area [i.e., the laws governing individual behavior]. Rather, the ongoing obligation to give up one's life for the community [of Israel] (ha-kelal) is because of an emergency measure (le-migdar milta ve-hora'at sha'ah).[17]

R. Kook begins here by providing an in-depth explanation of why an individual must risk his life to save the Jewish people from destruction when its survival is dependent on him and him alone. R. Kook understands this imperative as falling under the rubric of hora'at sha'ah and migdar milta. These phrases are closely related in talmudic discourse, and they refer to actions in violation of Halakhah that one is allowed to undertake in times of national crisis.[18] In halakhic sources, it is usually a prophet or rabbinic court who takes this kind of action. Thus, for example, the Talmud cites the case of Elijah who performed a sacrifice in his contest with the prophets of Baal on Mount Carmel in I Kings 18, even though Halakhah prohibits sacrifices outside the Temple precincts. According to this source, Elijah lived in a time of religious crisis when many Israelites had become idol-worshipers, and he therefore had to invoke the principle of hora'at sha'ah and violate the halakhic prohibition in order to demonstrate to the people of Israel that the God of Israel was the true God.[19] Similarly, R. Kook believes that when an individual is in a unique position to save the entire Jewish people from destruction but can do so only at

17. MK, responsum 143, pp. 315–16 (outline, letter 6).
18. Analysis of this principle can be found in s. v. "Hora'at Sha'ah," Entsiklopediyah Talmudit, eds. R. Me'ir Berlin and R. Shelomoh Yosef Zevin (Jerusalem: Yad ha-Rav Hertsog, 1947–), 8:513–27; Haim H. Cohn, "Extraordinary Remedies," The Principles of Jewish Law, ed. Menachem Elon (Jerusalem: Keter, 1974), 552.
19. BT Yevamot 90b; Maimonides, MT Mamrim 2:4. The phrases hora'at sha'ah and migdar milta are usually interchangeable, but the first phrase is the more common designation. For the sake of convenience, I therefore refer only to hora'at sha'ah in my discussion.

the risk of his own life, he too must act despite the danger involved because of the principle of *hora'at sha'ah*. Such a person is required to go beyond the strictures of Halakhah in that one is not usually mandated to endanger oneself to assist others who are in harm's way. R. Kook adds that an individual risking his life to save the entire Jewish people has no requirement to consult a rabbinic court before acting, as one normally would with *hora'at sha'ah*. His obligations in this instance are so obvious that no rabbinic guidance is needed.[20]

Yet, R. Kook disagrees vehemently with R. Pines's claim that one's obligation in this type of unique situation can be inferred from the laws of war. According to R. Kook, the laws of war belong to a realm of Halakhah that is completely separate from that which governs individuals outside of war. Laws of war are focused on communal welfare, and all laws connected to the latter issue are under the jurisdiction of a Jewish king. Proof that the laws of war are different from those of non-war situations is that in discretionary war, the king may require the nation to go into battle for the expansion of territory, a cause that would hardly merit the sacrifice of life under any other circumstance.

R. Kook goes on to speculate that the laws of war were part and parcel of a larger body of statutes in ancient Israel that were communal in nature. These laws were given to the king to administer and, like the laws of war, they

---

20. This ruling has received a fair amount of attention from academic and rabbinic commentators. Rakover notes that not all halakhic authorities agree with this position (Rakover, *Mesirut Nefesh*, 116–18, 144–45). Ari'el has focused on R. Kook's application of the concepts of *hora'at sha'ah* and *migdar milta* here and has argued that his use of these concepts in this instance is innovative in two respects (Ari'el, "*Mesirut Nefesh* 'avur ha-Kelal*," 77–79). For one, these principles are generally applied in halakhic literature to situations of spiritual crisis. The prophet and rabbinic court are allowed to violate halakhic norms when the people of Israel have strayed from their faith, as in the example of Elijah's sacrifice on Mount Carmel. R. Kook, by contrast, also applies *hora'at sha'ah* and *migdar milta* to situations of *physical* crisis. One can invoke these principles when the Jewish nation is being threatened with destruction. Second, *hora'at sha'ah* and *migdar milta* are generally implemented by a rabbinic court. However, in R. Kook's application, these principles are implemented by any Jew whose actions may save the Jewish people from destruction on the premise that a rabbinic court, without doubt, would approve of such actions. I will note one other innovation in R. Kook's thinking that, to my knowledge, has not been discussed by commentators. While the principles of *hora'at sha'ah* and *migdar milta* generally refer to outright violations of Halakhah, Kook applies these principles to actions that do not quite fit this description. In his correspondence with R. Pines, R. Kook argues that while an individual is not *required* to risk his life when someone else is in danger, he may do so voluntarily. Not all halakhic authorities agree with R. Kook on this issue, but he is quite adamant that a person is permitted to give up his life in a situation of this kind if he so chooses, especially if he can save many people (MK, responsum 143, p. 311; responsum 144, pp. 338–39; Rakover, *Mesirut Nefesh*, 89–92). Therefore, when R. Kook rules that an individual must risk his life for the sake of the Jewish people, he is not really requiring that person to do something in violation of Halakhah, but only to perform an action that, at least in R. Kook's thinking, would normally be considered voluntary.

were separate in kind from those that governed the individual.[21] He cites as an example a series of prescriptions in Maimonides' *Hilkhot Melakhim* that permit a king to kill any of his subjects who disobey his will, even regarding relatively trivial matters. Such an action would normally be considered outright murder in Halakhah, but the king is allowed to kill people in these circumstances because of the unusual nature of the laws that regulate his authority and conduct. The example here is apt to R. Kook's discussion because Maimonides' ruling helps explain why a king is allowed to send people out to war at the risk of their lives. R. Kook's point is that even in non-war situations, the king has the power of life and death over his subjects when it comes to matters far less important than obeying his command to go to war.[22] However, R. Kook goes on to explain that we retain only a small remnant of the king's laws. These laws have their source in the Torah, but the methods of interpretation for deducing them from the biblical text were given only to the kings, and those methods are now lost to us.

Yet, the main point is that, according to R. Kook, one cannot infer from the laws of war how a lone individual should behave in non-war situations, even in instances when the survival of the Jewish people is at stake. A Jewish soldier engaging in battle against a lethal enemy may be facing a situation similar, in some respects, to that of Queen Esther, who also was attempting to defeat a fearsome enemy; but in R. Kook's thinking, the similarities are only apparent. Situations of war and those outside war are governed by entirely different sectors of Halakhah.

The notion that the laws of war are in a separate category of Halakhah is not original to R. Kook. As we noted in our previous chapter, this issue cropped up in the writings R. Naftali Tsevi Yehudah Berlin (1816–93), or the Netsiv. The Netsiv addresses this issue in a gloss in his Torah commentary on Genesis 9:5–6 where God speaks to Noah and issues a prohibition against murder to Noah and his descendants. According to the Netsiv, the wording of the divine command in the biblical text allows human beings to kill in wartime. The Netsiv also mentions that it is this dispensation that permits Jewish kings to endanger the lives of his own people by waging war, even war that is discretionary.[23]

We might also mention a similar position taken by R. Joseph Babad (1800–1874), who is usually referred to by the title of his major halakhic work, *Minhat Hinukh*. The *Minhat Hinukh* addresses a similar concern with respect to the wars of the Israelites against the Canaanites. The *Minhat Hinkuh* notes that while an individual is not normally required to risk his life for the sake

21. MT *Melakhim* 5:1.
22. This interpretation is noted briefly by R. Ya'akov Ari'el, *Be-Oholah shel Torah*, vol. 4 (Kefar Darom, Israel: Makhon ha-Torah ve-ha-Arets, 2003), 162.
23. *Ha'amek Davar* on Gen. 9:5. Above pp. 53–4.

of others, that right was overridden by the divine command to annihilate the Canaanites.[24]

However, R. Kook appears to echo the thoughts of the Netsiv more closely than those of the *Minhat Hinukh*. R. Kook seems to follow in the Netsiv's footsteps by addressing the issue of war in relation to the rest of Halakhah in a way that the *Minhat Hinukh* does not and by using the permissibility of discretionary war as evidence that the laws of war are fundamentally different from those governing everyday life.

Yet, R. Kook differs from the Netsiv on one important point. The Netsiv addresses the issue of war as it pertains to all human beings, not just Jews. His notion that in war there is no punishment for killing is a principle given to Noah, a pre-Sinaitic figure who is forefather to the entire human race, and thus it is a principle for all humanity. There is also the innuendo in the Netsiv's briefs comments that this principle is based on natural law. The Netsiv tells us that killing in wartime is allowed because "that is the way the world was founded." R. Kook, by contrast, is focused entirely on the imperatives of Halakhah. The distinction he draws between norms that govern everyday life and those that govern war is therefore a concern for Jews alone. Implied here as well is that the imperatives regulating war emanate from the divine will, not from natural law. In short, we may characterize the Netsiv's approach to war as naturalistic-universalistic in orientation, while that of R. Kook is halakhic-particularistic.

We should note that R. Pines's point of view is also not without precedent in prior halakhic literature, though the precedent here is somewhat more obscure than it is for R. Kook. R. David Frankel (ca. 1704–62), in his commentary, *Shiyarey Korban* on the Jerusalem Talmud takes a position on conscription that anticipates that of R. Pines. R. Frankel's views on this matter appear in his remarks on the Gemara that discusses the Mishnah in *Sotah* spelling out the military exemptions for Israelite soldiers. We pointed out in chapter 2 that in this section of the Gemara, R. Judah classifies defensive war as mandatory and that Maimonides, who takes the same position in his *Mishneh Torah*, may have been inspired by R. Judah's viewpoint. R. Frankel comments on this theory by focusing on the views of a previous halakhic authority who supports it: R. Hayim Benveniste (1603–73), author of *Keneset ha-Gedolah*:

> The rabbi, author of *Keneset ha-Gedolah*, wrote in the section on *Orah Hayim*, in his novella on Maimonides, chapter five of *Hilkhot Melakhim*, that because Maimonides wrote, "Which [war] is a mandatory war? It is a war against the seven [Canaanite] nations ... and saving Israel from the clutches of the enemy that has attacked them," we can infer that [Maimonides] agrees with R. Judah.

24. *Minhat Hinukh* (Jerusalem: Jerusalem Institute, 1998), chapter 425.

For this reason, [the author of *Keneset ha-Gedolah*] gave a tendentious interpretation of [the parallel passage in] the Babylonian Talmud. His words are surprising. Is there anyone who says that "saving Israel from the clutches of the enemy" is not a commandment? For even in the case of an individual who is being pursued [by an attacker], there is a positive and negative commandment to rescue him, as it says, "Do not stand idly by the blood of your fellow" (Lev. 19:16), and "you shall return it to him" (Deut. 22:2), the latter referring to the loss of a person's life [which must be "returned" to the person].[25]

R. Frankel does not understand why R. Benveniste resorts to R. Judah's opinion in the Jerusalem Talmud as a source for Maimonides' view that defensive wars are mandatory. The imperative for all Jews to participate in such wars is clear from the biblical commandment that every individual is required to rescue another from harm. Implied in R. Frankel's comments is that there is no distinction between wartime Halakhah and everyday Halakhah when it comes to saving the lives of fellow Jews, just as R. Pines argues.

But let us get back to the debate between R. Kook and R. Pines. Each of them has now staked out a position that will be defended throughout the rest of their exchange. They agree that in the sector of Halakhah that governs non-war situations, an individual Jew is obligated to do whatever is necessary to save the Jewish people from destruction, even to the point of risking his life. However, R. Pines believes that this obligation can be deduced from the laws of war—specifically defensive war—while R. Kook denies that claim and argues that wartime Halakhah is a completely separate area of Halakhah governed by unique communal laws administered by the king.

The next round in the debate begins with R. Pines challenging R. Kook's position by looking more carefully at the issue of discretionary war:

> All of his statements [i.e., R. Kook's], forgive me, are not acceptable to me at all. For this "expansion of territory" (*harhavah*) in discretionary war has already been explained there by Maimonides, may his memory be blessed; it is a war "for expanding the border of Israel and for increasing his [i.e., the king's] greatness and reputation."[26] And how could one say for a goal as exalted as this that here too there is no [halakhic] dispensation (*heter*) for all generations for one to place his life in danger?"[27]

R. Kook had claimed that the laws of discretionary war provide proof that the laws of war in general are in a special category because the reasons for

---

25. BT *Sanhedrin* 73a; *Shiyarey Korban, Sotah* 8:10, in standard editions of JT, s. v. "*milhemet ha-reshut*."
26. MT *Melakhim* 5:1.
27. Rakover, *Mesirut Nefesh*, Appendix II, 233–34 (outline, letter 7).

waging this type of war, such as the expansion of territory, would not normally require an individual to place his life in danger. R. Pines dismisses this argument. Indeed, discretionary war can be initiated for "expanding the border of Israel and for increasing his [i.e., the king's] greatness and reputation," as Maimonides tells us. R. Pines takes Maimonides to mean that the king may expand the borders of the nation *for the sake of* making his name great. That is, what are usually taken as two causes for discretionary war—territorial expansion and increasing the king's prestige—are regarded by R. Pines as one. The king conquers in order to strengthen his reputation.[28] And as far as R. Pines is concerned, making the king's name great is, from a halakhic standpoint, a perfectly sound reason for an individual to put his life at risk. Therefore, for R. Pines, the imperative to place oneself in danger in a discretionary war is fully justified according to the normal strictures of Halakhah that are directed at the individual in his everyday life, and thus one can make sense of the laws of discretionary war without placing them in a special category of Halakhah as R. Kook has done. To support his argument, R. Pines cites a midrash, adduced by him earlier in his discussion with R. Kook,[29] that teaches us that suicide, though normally forbidden in Jewish law, is permitted in instances in which "the dignity of Israel and the needs of the nation" are at stake. The imperative for an individual to sacrifice his life in discretionary war for similar reasons should therefore be understood as an everyday halakhic norm as well.[30]

R. Pines provides another rebuttal to R. Kook's notion that war is governed by unique laws by bringing in the issue of defensive war, which is more at the heart of the debate between the two:

> Moreover, the assumption that this [i.e., the body of laws governing war] belong to laws of kingship, I do not recognize. For the laws of kingship are statutes that deal with the rights [and obligations][31] of the king, and the laws of mandatory war are not concerned with this matter, for it [i.e., mandatory war] is not for

28. R. Pines's precise wording therefore refers to the "goal" of discretionary war in Maimonides in the singular. Others have also read Maimonides in this manner. See, for instance, R. Yehudah Amital, *"Milhamot Yisra'el 'al pi ha-Rambam," Tehumin* 8 (1987): 454–61.

29. *Bereishit Rabbah* 34:12; Rakover, *Mesirut Nefesh*, Appendix II, 222–24 (outline, letter 7).

30. Rakover, *Mesirut Nefesh*, Appendix II, 233–34 (outline, letter 7). Note that there is some disparity between the case of permission to commit suicide and that of self-sacrifice in discretionary war. Whereas the first is presented by R. Pines as optional (*heter*), the second is required. However, this does not affect R. Pines's main point, which is that R. Kook is incorrect in claiming that the causes of discretionary war are inexplicable in terms of the halakhic norms that govern individual behavior.

31. Rakover, *Mesirut Nefesh*, 235n162, explains that he brackets these words because the manuscript was pierced at this point, and he could only guess what the precise words were.

the sake of the king; rather the king is for its sake, as Maimonides expresses in his fine language ... at the end of chapter 4 in *Hilkhot Melakhim* with this language: "that we do not appoint a king to begin with except to implement justice and wage wars. ..."[32] In the days of the Hasmoneans when there was no king in Israel, was there not an obligation on everyone to go out to war against the soldiers of Syria when they came to the land of Israel to do battle?

In sum, in my humble opinion, one can learn the obligation of rescuing the community of Israel at the risk of one's life from the obligation to go out [and fight in] a mandatory war.[33]

R. Pines concedes to R. Kook that there were indeed special laws pertaining to kingship; however, he believes, contra R. Kook, that the laws of war were not among them. The laws of kingship were concerned only with the privileges of the king, while the laws of war served the needs of the people and were therefore part of everyday Halakhah. Proof for this assertion is the citation from Maimonides' *Hilkhot Melakhim*, which R. Pines takes to mean that it is the people who appoint the king to implement justice and wage war. That is, the king is given the duty to administer such matters as justice and war on behalf of his subjects, and therefore these duties are not regulated by special laws given solely to the king. R. Pines illustrates his point by referring this time to the laws of mandatory war rather than discretionary war, and as the discussion proceeds it becomes clear that he is specifically speaking of mandatory wars of self-defense.[34] These wars do not even require a king, as is evident from the example of the Hasmonean wars which took place when no king governed Israel. It goes without saying, R. Pines argues, that in those wars, every Jew was obligated to fight and defend the nation. Thus, defensive war is the same as discretionary war in being governed by laws that make perfect sense within the strictures of everyday Halakhah. They do not belong to the special body of laws for the king which had an entirely different purpose.

R. Pines's original position is thus confirmed as he states in the last line in the passage above. The imperative for all Jews to fight in a defensive war teaches us that even in non-war situations an individual must risk his life if he is uniquely positioned to rescue the entire Jewish people from destruction. Neither the laws of defensive war—nor those of discretionary war, for that matter—belong in a separate category of Halakhah, and they are not the sole prerogative of the king, as R. Kook claims. They therefore can be used

---

32. MT *Melakhim* 4:10.

33. Rakover, *Mesirut Nefesh*, Appendix II, 235 (outline, letter 7).

34. As explained in my introductory chapter, the category of mandatory war also includes the wars fought by the Israelites against the Canaanites and the Amalekites. R. Pines is not concerned with these wars here.

to deduce laws for how an individual should act in situations that do not involve war.[35]

R. Kook responds to R. Pines with yet another attempt to establish the notion that the laws of war are in a special category of Halakhah that is the prerogative of the king. In a letter that appears as responsum 144 in *Mishpat Kohen,* he says the following:

> With regard to what I wrote, that the issues of war are part of the laws of king-ship, R. Pines objects and says that the laws of kingship only concern those things that have to do with the honor of the king. This is not the case. Rather, every general matter that touches on [the concerns of] the nation, and every amelioration [of society] (*tikkun*) consequent upon [implementing] an emer-gency measure (*hora'at sha'ah*) to protect [the nation] against evil-doers—all [of these things] are included in the laws of kingship. For the king has the author-ity to implement them [i.e., emergency measures] as he pleases, even when it has nothing to do with his well-being and honor, as it is written in [*Hilkhot*] *Melakhim* 3:10: "Anyone who commits murder without there being sufficient proof [for conviction] etc., the king has the authority to put them to death and to ameliorate the world in accordance with the need of the hour (*ke-fi she-ha-sha'ah tserikhah*) etc. and to break the hand of the wicked people of the world." Thus, the powers of laws of kingship reach well beyond the realm of the honor and the rights of the king. ... Therefore, there is nothing new [in saying] that this [i.e., ameliorating the world] would be the great need of the hour (*tsorkeh ha-sha'ah ha-gadol*) of war—in particular, discretionary war, which is waged with the advice of a court of seventy-one.[36] There are [thus] two reasons for it [i.e., discretionary war]: [because it is] an emergency measure (*migdar milta le-hora'at sha'ah*)—which is dependent on the opinion and approval of the court—for the spiritual and physical well-being of the nation that are always connected to each other, and because of the authority of the laws of kingship. But it is not proper to learn from this [i.e., the laws of war] about anything else.[37]

R. Kook rejects R. Pines's view that the laws of kingship were concerned only with the rights of the king and therefore did not include the laws of war, which were focused on the needs of his people. The people's needs were, in fact, cen-tral to the king's duties. He was obligated to do whatever was necessary to protect the nation and improve its well-being.

R. Kook's point here is that the laws of war must certainly be included among the special duties of the king because those duties are focused on safe-guarding and enhancing the welfare of his people, and war served those very

---

35. Rakover, *Mesirut Nefesh*, Appendix II, 235 (outline, letter 7).
36. Referring to the Sanhedrin.
37. MK, responsum 144, p. 335 (outline, letter 8).

purposes. R. Pines is therefore wrong in assuming that the king's duties concern only his personal privileges. R. Kook does not explicitly address the issue of defensive war that is at the center of the debate between him and R. Pines, but he does not really have to. He seems to assume that the obligation to wage defensive war falls squarely on the shoulders of the king as part of his charge to protect the nation. Yet R. Kook does devote attention to discretionary war, which is not surprising given that its connection to the duties of the king are somewhat more opaque. R. Kook explains that permission for a king to wage discretionary war was also a manifestation of his special duties. This type of war was meant to improve the material or spiritual well-being of the nation. Here R. Kook seems to be referring to situations of national crisis. R. Kook explains that the king was allowed to initiate these wars because of the principle of *hora'at sha'ah* that was invoked by the king in consultation with the Sanhedrin, and, as we have already noted, this principle refers to actions taken in times of national emergency.[38]

Thus, while R. Pines had attempted to remove the laws of war from the prerogative of the king and place them in the sphere of everyday obligations for all Jews, R. Kook has returned them to the king's sphere. For this reason, R. Kook concludes the passage just cited by saying that the laws of war cannot be used as a source of guidance for "anything else"—that is, individual conduct in everyday life.

A bit further on in his exchange with R. Pines, R. Kook also provides an answer to R. Pines's challenge regarding the Hasmonean wars. R. Pines had argued that these wars were proof that the laws of kingship did not include laws of war because during this period the Jews had no king, but the Hasmoneans waged war anyway. R. Kook offers a number of answers to this challenge, two of which we will recount. First, the Hasmonean wars were waged in a "time of persecution" (*she'at ha-shemad*) against a people that was bent on destroying the Jewish religion, and in such dire circumstances it goes without saying that there was no need for a king to lead the Jewish people into war.[39] A second answer to R. Pines's challenge is that R. Kook takes the position that when the Jews have no king, the responsibilities of this office devolve upon the individual or governmental body leading the Jewish community at the time. Such an individual or governmental body would have the de facto status of a king:

38. Rakover, *Mesirut Nefesh*, 120n15, claims that R. Kook does not respond to R. Pines's argument regarding discretionary war, and that is because the latter's argument is not a "rebuttal" (*kushya*) of R. Kook's position but merely a "rejection of evidence" (*dehiyat re'ayah*) that R. Kook had adduced as support for his view. In my reading, R. Kook does indeed respond to R. Pines's argument regarding discretionary war as explained here.
39. MK, responsum 144, p. 336 (outline, letter 8).

In a period in which there is no king, because the laws of kingship concern the general condition of the nation, these rights of [administering] the laws return to the jurisdiction of the nation as a collective. ... When it comes to the laws of kingship which concern leadership of the collective, there is no doubt that ordained judges and leaders of any kind (*nesi'im kelaliyim*) stand in the place of the king.[40]

The Hasmoneans served in that role, and therefore an argument can be made that they were permitted to authorize a war just as a king would.[41] As we shall see throughout our study, this position will have wide influence. Almost every figure in our study will use R. Kook's insight to justify the notion that an Israeli government may wage war in place of the king.

R. Kook's position here has been the subject of much discussion. Commentators have noted that there is no real precedent for this position in medieval halakhic sources. Jewish communities in the medieval period were generally allowed by their non-Jewish overlords to install their own governments and run their own internal affairs, and some rabbinic authorities justified the authority of these governments by claiming that, in the period of the exile, each Jewish community had the authority of a Jewish monarch in biblical times and could therefore choose its own representatives. Some rabbis even allowed community leaders to make amendments to Jewish civil law just as in former days a Jewish king could.[42] However, these sources are rather vague on this point and are not nearly as explicit as R. Kook is in investing a Jewish government chosen by the people with all the powers of the monarchy. Moreover, R. Kook does not mention any halakhic precedents for his view. Instead, he seems to formulate it on the basis of theological considerations. In

---

40. Ibid., p. 337 (outline, letter 8).

41. Ibid., pp. 337–38 (outline, letter 8). This issue is discussed in Yig'al Ari'el essay in *Berurim*.

42. Menachem Elon, introduction to *The Principles of Jewish Law*, ed. Menachem Elon (Jerusalem: Keter, 1974), 31; idem, "Public Authority and Administrative Law," in Elon, *Principles of Jewish Law*, 645; idem, "Power and Authority: Halachic Stance of the Traditional Community and Its Contemporary Implications," in *Kinship and Consent: The Jewish Political Tradition and Its Contemporary Uses*, ed. Daniel J. Elazar (Lanham, Md.: University Press of America, 1983), 188–91; Michael Walzer, Menachem Lorberbaum, and Noam J. Zohar, eds., *The Jewish Political Tradition*, vol. 1 (New Haven, Conn.: Yale University, 2000), 379–439. According to another approach, some halakhic authorities recognized the community as having the status of a rabbinic court. Communal amendments were therefore justified because the community as a whole effectively had rabbinic authority. Another important precedent for conferring authority on communal leaders in matters of Halakhah is found in talmudic sources which recognize that "the townspeople" (*beney ha-'ir*) could impose legislation on themselves regarding monetary matters. See Elon, "Public Authority and Administrative Law," 645; Elon, "Power and Authority," 188–91; Walzer, Lorberbaum, and Zohar, *Jewish Political Tradition*, 378–439.

R. Kook's thinking, the Jewish people as a collective has a unique status among the nations of the world because it is the locus of God's spirit and revelation on earth, and it would therefore follow that its choice of government would be invested with the maximum political authority envisioned in Halakhah. In short, it would seem that we have here an excellent example of "the Torah of the land of Israel" as R. Kook conceived it. R. Kook formulates a halakhic position based on theological insights. While he does not say so explicitly, it would seem that his thinking here is guided in part by a desire to accommodate the new reality created by the Zionist movement in Palestine. R. Kook is, in effect, giving his approval to the elected Jewish political bodies that govern the Jewish community in Palestine, even though they were secular in nature.[43]

We can now summarize the positions of R. Pines and R. Kook that emerge from their debate. According to R. Pines, when a Jew finds himself in a rare position to save the Jewish people in a time of crisis, as Queen Esther did, he—or she in this case—must do so even at the risk of his—or her—own life. This imperative applies to non-war situations, but it can be deduced from the laws that govern war, specifically defensive war. Just as an individual Jew must be prepared to endanger his life by serving in the king's army to defend the Jewish nation in times of war, so, too, must he endanger his life for similar purposes in other circumstances. R. Pines concedes R. Kook's claim that the king has special laws that apply only to him, but these laws are concerned only with his rights and privileges, not the needs of the people. The laws of the king therefore have nothing to do with the laws of war, as R. Kook claims, and are therefore irrelevant to their discussion. The laws of war can be explained perfectly well within the strictures of everyday Halakhah that govern the actions of the individual and can therefore be used to determine the obligations of the individual in non-war situations, as well.

R. Kook agrees with R. Pines on the basic premise that in non-war situations a Jew has an obligation to risk his life when he is in a unique position to save the Jewish people, but in R. Kook's thinking the laws of war do not provide a source for this obligation. Those laws are governed by a special category of imperatives given to the king that require him to serve the needs of his people. Defensive war fulfills this purpose because it is meant to protect the nation from a hostile enemy. So does discretionary war, which the king may initiate as a matter of *hora'at sha'ah* when the nation faces some sort of material or spiritual crisis.

We can sharpen our understanding of R. Kook's approach by noting that what he is saying, in effect, is that the bar for being obligated to risk one's life in non-war situations is much higher than it is in war. In non-war situations, the individual is required to risk his life for the sake of the Jewish people, but

43. Gutel, *"Samkhuyot Manhigey Yisra'el"*; idem, *Hadashim gam Yeshanim*, 144–47; Ben-Artsi, *Ha-Hadash Yitkadesh*, 81–86.

only when the entire people is facing demise. Yet, in war, a Jew must participate in war, defensive or discretionary, when the threat facing the Jewish people is not necessarily an existential one. After all, defensive war is not always
waged against an adversary seeking the destruction of the Jewish people, and
discretionary war certainly is not. Therefore, the soldier serving in the king's
army is more readily required to face danger for the sake of the Jewish people
than the lone individual in non-war situations.

One difficulty with R. Kook's thinking is his emphasis on the complete disjunction between laws of war and those governing non-war situations. One
cannot insist on such a distinction without running the risk of detaching
the laws of war entirely from the rest of Halakhah. Yet, one could argue that
R. Kook still maintains a bridge between the two realms, at least implicitly. He
would concede that both the lone individual risking his life to save the Jewish
people in non-war situations and the soldier serving in an army at the order of
the king are working for the same purpose: the welfare of the Jewish people.

R. KOOK ON DISCRETIONARY WAR: FURTHER REFLECTIONS

An issue that deserves further analysis is R. Kook's treatment of discretionary
war. In his initial statement about war in responsum 143, R. Kook appears to
accept Maimonides's understanding of discretionary war, according to which
a king is permitted to wage war of this type for two reasons: to expand the
borders of Israel and to increase the king's greatness and prestige. As we have
seen in responsum 143, R. Kook alludes to the first of these reasons.[44] Yet
later on in the correspondence, in responsum 144, R. Kook informs us that
discretionary war is waged in instances of *hora'at sha'ah* in order to improve
the physical and spiritual well-being of the nation. It is not clear how this
latter understanding of discretionary war squares with that of Maimonides.
According to Maimonides, discretionary wars are offensive military campaigns for the conquest of land and the enhancement of the king's name.
R. Kook's second description of discretionary war suggests that such wars are
more defensive in nature in that the king wages them because he is forced to
respond to a national crisis.

The inconsistency may be due to some ambivalence on R. Kook's part
regarding discretionary war. In a study of attitudes to militarism in religious Zionism, Eli Holtser demonstrates that R. Kook's theological views on
war were quite negative. R. Kook was committed to building a Jewish state
through peaceful action and did not believe that Jews should employ violence

---

44. Rakover, *Mesirut Nefesh*, Appendix II, 207–11 (outline, letter 5).

for that purpose. R. Kook's views on this issue were part of a larger theology in which he saw the return of the Jewish people to its homeland as the beginning of the final stage of messianic redemption that had been unfolding throughout history. An important component of this stage of the messianic process was that the Jews would model a nonviolent ethic to the gentile nations, an ethic that the nations would adopt as their own, thereby fulfilling the expectation that the messianic period would mark the end of warfare among human beings. In the background to this theology were the horrors of the First World War. R. Kook believed that this war, with its unprecedented carnage, was an important factor in the messianic redemption because it was meant to teach the gentile nations once and for all about the corruption of their ways and that their only hope was to follow the example of the Jewish people, whose values were divine in origin and peaceful to the core. Divine providence had timed the growth of Zionism perfectly to convey this lesson because it would focus the attention of the gentile nations on the Jewish people and the critical lessons about peace that these nations needed to learn, precisely at the point in history when the world had witnessed the worst violence it had ever known. Thus, the return of the Jews to their homeland was not only the beginning of their own redemption but the redemption of the non-Jewish world as well.[45]

R. Kook's negative views on violence and war also colored the way he viewed the biblical period. Most telling is the following passage that appears in R. Kook's letters:

> With regard to the matters of wars, it was completely impossible at a time when all the neighboring nations were truly wolves of the steppe,[46] that only Israel would not engage in war. Otherwise, they [i.e., the nations] would have gathered and annihilated them [i.e., the Israelites], God forbid. In fact, conversely, it was also an extreme necessity [for the Israelites] to bring fear upon the unruly [nations] also through cruel conduct, only with an expectation to bring humanity to that which it was supposed to be, though not [with the purpose of] hastening the time [of redemption].[47]

R. Kook begins here by explaining that the wars of Israel in the biblical period were defensive in nature because the Israelites lived in an environment in which the nations were so violent and aggressive that they had no choice but to engage in war. R. Kook also notes that at times the Israelites themselves had to act with cruelty toward other nations, but they did so only for the purpose of perfecting humanity, not to hasten the redemption.

45. Holtser, *Herev Pipiyot be-Yadam*, chapter 2.
46. A reference to Zeph. 3:3.
47. *Igrot ha-Re'iyah*, 1:100; Holtser, *Herev Pipiyot be-Yadam*, 73.

One can see how R. Kook struggles here with the moral challenges presented by the wars of the Israelites in the Bible and that he is attempting to give an interpretation of these wars that avoids any suggestion that they were motivated by pure aggression. Moreover, R. Kook's insistence that such wars were meant to perfect humanity but not bring about the redemption may have been inspired by his concern about the potential for renewed violence initiated by Jews in his own period. He seems to be cautioning his fellow religious Zionists that the coming redemption cannot be achieved through war.

The same tendency to soften the aggressiveness of violence on the part of the Israelites in the biblical period is evident in another passage in R. Kook's writings that focuses specifically on the Canaanite conquest. R. Kook claims that the wars fought against the Canaanites were a punishment for the sin of the golden calf. Had the Israelites not sinned, R. Kook tells us, the Canaanites would have surrendered peacefully out of recognition and fear of the God of Israel.[48]

With all this in mind, it is understandable that R. Kook would have an ambivalent attitude toward Maimonides' interpretation of discretionary war. R. Kook could not ignore Maimonides' views on this type of war because Maimonides' entire discussion of war in *Hilkhot Melakhim*, in which these views appear, was the most authoritative and systematic treatment of the laws of war in the history of Halakhah. However, as we have noted, discretionary wars as described by Maimonides are offensive campaigns for the purpose of expanding territory and increasing the prestige of the king, and they therefore do not fit well with R. Kook's view that Jews were meant to be a beacon of peace for the world. Thus, it should occasion no surprise that R. Kook would initially mention Maimonides' views on discretionary war but then, in a later passage, give his own spin on the matter that was at odds with Maimonides' perspective. When R. Kook refers to discretionary war as a form of war waged in times of national crisis in order to improve the physical and spiritual condition of the Jewish people, he is clearly giving this form of war a meaning that is more acceptable to his larger theology of the eschaton. Discretionary war, according to this reading, is more defensive than offensive in nature in that it is meant to help the Jewish people in times of physical and spiritual crises. Of course, we could have benefited from more details from R. Kook about what types of crises he was referring to and how discretionary war was meant to improve the physical and spiritual condition of the Jewish people in such situations. Nonetheless, the general direction of his thinking here is clear, as are its underlying motivations.

There is one other passage in R. Kook's collection of responsa that deals with discretionary war and that also seems to reflect his ambivalence toward this type of war. In a responsum composed in 1918, R. Kook

48. R. Abraham Isaac Kook, *Orot* (Jerusalem: Mosad ha-Rav Kuk, 1982), 14; Holtser, *Herev Pipiyot be-Yadam*, 73.

addresses a question posed to him by a R. Menasheh Grasberg about a ruling in Maimonides' *Hilkhot Melakhim* regarding the biblical prohibition against Jews settling in the land of Egypt.[49] According to Maimonides, this prohibition does not affect any portion of Egypt that is captured in war by an Israelite king.[50] R. Grasberg has two questions regarding this latter ruling. First, he asks R. Kook whether the land in Egypt captured by a Jewish king would have the status of the land of Israel "in all matters." The concern here is with the status of the biblical commandments that apply only to the inhabitants of the land of Israel. Second, R. Grasberg asks whether Maimonides' ruling also applies to an Israelite "judge" who captures land in Egypt. R. Grasberg is referring here to political leaders in ancient Israel who were not formally given the title of king but who nonetheless united the people of Israel for the purposes of waging war.

These two questions were obviously of a strictly academic nature, seeing as neither of them had any practical significance at the time they were posed. However, in response to R. Grasberg's second question, R. Kook provides an answer that gives us some insight into his views on discretionary war. To the question of whether Maimonides's ruling would apply to land in Egypt captured by a judge, R. Kook responds in the negative:

> We have learned from what we have concluded that there is no place for the question of whether this law applies to a judge. For as long as there is no king, it is not possible to capture the land of Egypt in war because without a king there is no place for discretionary war; it is possible [to wage discretionary war in such a situation] only with a prophet. One can also say that this [permission to wage discretionary war] applies if one [i.e., the judge] goes out [to war] with the consensus of all of Israel seeing as the reason that one needs a king [for discretionary war] is specifically for the matter of coercing [the Israelites to fight]. ... Nonetheless, this [conclusion] is not certain, for one can say that as long as the conditions [for waging discretionary war] are not sufficient to force [the people to fight], it is, in this instance, akin to mere murder, and that it is forbidden to wage a discretionary war. Still, this much is certain: that there is a distinction between a king and a judge, for it is possible to say that a king may capture the land of Egypt with [the approval] of a rabbinic court and [may] force the people [to fight] regarding this, but a judge is certainly forbidden [to do so] when it is not in accordance with the will of the people. ... But in my humble opinion, it makes sense to forbid [a judge from waging discretionary war] as long as the elements of the rabbinic court and the king or the prophet are not in place.[51]

49. MK, responsum 145, pp. 348–51; Maimonides, MT *Melakhim* 5:7; Ex. 14:13; Deut. 17:16; 28:68.
50. MT *Melakhim* 5:8.
51. MK, responsum 145, p. 350.

R. Kook forbids a Jewish judge from waging war on Egypt because this war would be discretionary, and this type of war can be waged only with the authority of a prophet or with the authority of a king in consultation with a Sanhedrin. R. Kook entertains the possibility that a judge may wage a discretionary war in place of a king if he has the firm consensus of the people, because the reason that one needs a king to initiate war here is that only he has the right to force the people to fight against their will. But in the final statement in the passage, R. Kook backtracks from this suggestion and concludes that without a prophet, or the combination of a king and Sanhedrin, a discretionary war should not be waged.

A number of commentators have been perplexed by one element of R. Kook's position here. As we have already noted, R. Kook believes that while the institution of kingship no longer exists for Jews, any individual or governmental body appointed by a Jewish community to run its political affairs has the de facto status of a king. This ruling is one of R. Kook's best known.[52] Why then does R. Kook rule in responsum 145 just quoted that a judge may never substitute for a king when it comes to waging discretionary war? The judge, of course, could not act alone and would require the consensus of a Sanhedrin to initiate such a war. But if that condition were in place, why does R. Kook take the position that a judge would still be prohibited from waging a war of this kind?

A number of solutions have been proposed, but to my mind the one that comes closest to the truth is that of R. Yehudah Shaviv, who claims that Jewish tradition has great reservations about war in general and that R. Kook is merely echoing those reservations by placing restrictions on discretionary war.[53] I would put the matter another way. The Jewish tradition is not the issue here. In fact, its viewpoint on war is ambiguous; some of its sources speak out against war, while others are quite bellicose. Rather, it is R. Kook himself who had reservations about war, as is evident from his other writings. It is therefore not surprising that he would place tight restrictions on who could wage discretionary war. His message to us is that this form of warfare is to be used only under a series of narrowly defined conditions that no longer exist.

If my reading here is correct, it would indicate that R. Kook had more than one strategy for dealing with the moral challenge of discretionary war. In his debate with R. Pines, he deals with that challenge by reinterpreting the purpose of discretionary war—it was an emergency measure taken only in times of national crisis. Far from being an offensive war, it was defensive in

---

52. MK, responsum 144, pp. 337–38. Above, pp. 70–1.
53. Shaviv, *"Le-Mi Mishpat ha-Melukhah?"*, 154. Other solutions are proposed by R. Menashe Shmerlovski, *"Milhemet Mitsvah ve-Milhemet Reshut,"* *Sefer Har'el*, ed. R. Eli'ezer Hayim Shenvald (Hispin, Israel: Ha-Golan, 1999), 62–64.

some sense. In his responsum to R. Grasberg, R. Kook handles the moral challenge of discretionary war by restricting its use via the issue of authority. This
type of war could be fought only in ancient Israel and only when a king and
Sanhedrin were in place.

Yet, despite our efforts at clarifying R. Kook's views on discretionary war,
we would have benefited from more explanation on his part about when this
type of war can be waged. More precisely, in his exchange with R. Pines, R.
Kook informs us that discretionary war can be initiated when the physical or
spiritual well-being of the nation is threatened, but he does not specify what
situations he is referring to. We might speculate that when R. Kook refers to
war being waged for the sake of the physical well-being of the Jewish people,
he might be alluding to some of the reasons for waging discretionary war
discussed in early and medieval rabbinic Halakhah—such as the preemption
of attack by an enemy or poor economic conditions. However, it is not clear
what he is referring to when he alludes to discretionary war being fought for
spiritual reasons. Now, R. Kook does say that the spiritual well-being and the
physical well-being of the Jewish nation are inextricably tied up with each
another. His apparent point is that the spiritual condition of the Jewish
nation is dependent on its material welfare. Thus, perhaps the physical causes
of waging discretionary war discussed in earlier halakhic literature ipso facto
serve the spiritual mission of the Jewish people, as well. Yet all of this is quite
speculative in the absence of greater elaboration by R. Kook himself.

R. Kook has opened our discussion of war in Halakhah with the claim that the
Jewish people may engage in war because war is governed by a special class of
halakhic imperatives that are administered by the king and the purpose of which
is to protect or enhance the well-being of his subjects. The king may therefore
make use of war to defend the nation from outside attack. He may also use it to
confront crises of lesser urgency that affect the material or spiritual well-being
of the nation, a form of war known in rabbinic sources as discretionary war.

The special imperatives of the king allow him to draft soldiers and send them
into combat, even though Halakhah does not normally allow anyone to be forced
to endanger his life, even to save others from a lethal threat. Undergirding the
king's permission to act in this manner is the notion that the king has the power
of life and death over his subjects, which includes his right to send them into
combat. In separating the norms of war from those that govern the individual
in everyday life, R. Kook appears to have followed in the footsteps of the *Minhat
Hinukh* and the Netsiv, who take similar positions in their brief remarks on matters of war, though R. Kook's views on this issue seem closer to those of the Netsiv.

What inspires R. Kook to deal with these matters is a debate with R. Pines
on the question of whether a lone individual in a unique position to save the
Jewish people from destruction, such as Queen Esther, is required to risk
his or her life for that purpose. R. Kook and R. Pines agree that a person in

a situation of this kind must act despite the dangers involved, but R. Pines insists that this obligation can be deduced from the requirement for all Jews to fight in a defensive war, whereas R. Kook claims that this obligation has nothing to do with war because war is governed by a realm of Halakhah that is entirely separate from that which governs the individual in everyday life. It is in the course of conducting this debate that R. Kook shares with us his insights about war.

Therefore, for R. Kook, Halakhah is always concerned with the welfare of the Jewish people in both everyday life and wartime; it is just that the individual acting alone has a higher bar for taking action to safeguard that welfare than the king does when going to war. While an individual in a non-war situation is required to endanger his life only when the Jewish people faces utter destruction, the king may order a soldier to risk his life in situations that are far less threatening. In fact, he may even do so to wage discretionary war in which there is no hostile enemy to speak of.

What also emerged in our analysis was R. Kook's ambivalence toward war, which had already been documented in his theological writings. This ambivalence came through in his treatment of discretionary war. At first, R. Kook follows Maimonides' lead, depicting this type of war as offensive in character in permitting the king to conquer territory and expand his kingdom. However, he also portrays it as a type of war with a defensive purpose of sorts in that it is meant to be waged in situations of material or spiritual crisis. We explained the tension between these two depictions by surmising that R. Kook felt bound by Maimonides' authoritative but bellicose understanding of discretionary war, yet at the same time wanted to portray this form of war as serving a defensive function that was more in line with the pacifist tendencies that underlay his theology.

All in all, R. Kook's insights into the laws of war are somewhat sketchy, but this is perhaps to be expected. The debate with R. Pines that produced R. Kook's reflections on war was not focused on the subject. It centered on the more general question of when an individual is required to endanger his life for the sake of others. The issue of war was only tangential to this question, and the amount of space devoted to it in the correspondence was quite limited. It is perhaps for this reason that R. Kook did not work out his views on the laws of war in more detail.

We must also appreciate that R. Kook engaged in his correspondence with R. Pines well before the creation of the state of Israel, and while their correspondence was composed at a time when Zionism had existed for twenty years, it was still a relatively young movement. Questions surrounding war and how a sovereign Jewish state would conduct it were therefore of little immediate practical relevance to either thinker.

However, the general questions raised by R. Kook and R. Pines regarding wartime Halakhah and its relationship to everyday Halakhah would be taken up by later halakhic authorities. Moreover, R. Kook's specific views on war would have a direct influence on those authorities soon after his lifetime. The first was R. Isaac Halevi Herzog, the first Chief Rabbi of Israel, who would witness the establishment of a Jewish state and watch it immediately become engulfed in war. R. Herzog is the subject of our next chapter.

APPENDIX: OUTLINE OF THE DEBATE ON WAR BETWEEN R. KOOK AND R. PINES

Letter 1: R. Kook
- asks R. Pines for advice about closing of a hospital

Letter 2: R. Kook
- thanks R. Pines for guiding him to a donor to keep the hospital open

Letter 3: R. Pines
- commends R. Kook for his efforts
- cites Maimonides that a person is obligated to save a large group of people even at the risk of his own life

Letter 4: R. Kook
- refutes R. Pines with two reasons:
  A. no such statement in Maimonides,
  B. but a person *does* have an obligation to risk his life to save the entire Jewish people

Letter 5: R. Pines
- corrects statement in Letter 3:
  A. a person is not *obligated* to risk his life to save a large group of people, but he can do so *voluntarily*
  B. agreement with R. Kook's statement (Letter 4B) that a person has an obligation to risk his life to save the entire Jewish people
  C. proof for B is the requirement for individuals to fight in defensive wars

Letter 6: R. Kook
- refutes Letter 5C
- war provides no proof that an individual must risk his life to save the Jewish people
  A. the individual has this obligation in non-war situations because of *hora'at sha'ah* that applies *only* to the individual
  B. laws of war are different because they were governed by special laws of the king
- proof is discretionary war which is for expansion of territory, a cause that would not normally require risking lives

Letter 7: R. Pines
- refutes Letter 6: imperative of individual to risk his life to save the Jewish people *can* be learned from laws of war

- refutes Letter 6B: laws of kings are only concerned with the king's rights and privileges, not needs of the people, and therefore laws of war do *not* belong to special laws of kings and can be explained within bounds of Halakhah governing the individual
- specifics of argument:
  A. laws of discretionary war
    - expansion of territory and increasing prestige of king is a good reason for war without invoking special laws of king
    - proof is that suicide is allowed for such purposes
  B. laws of defensive war:
    - defense is a good reason for war without invoking special laws of king
    - evidence is Hasmonean wars which were fought even without a king

Letter 8: R. Kook

- refutes Letter 7: imperative of the individual to risk his life to save the Jewish people *cannot* be learned from laws of war
- special laws of king *do* serve the needs of the people—and these include laws of war
- this is the case, not just with defensive war, but also with discretionary war
- discretionary war serves the needs of the people because it is *hora'at sha'ah* for the well-being of the nation
- Maccabean wars were allowed without the king—because others could serve in his place

CHAPTER 4

༺ঙ৹

R. Isaac Halevi Herzog

Rabbi Isaac Halevi Herzog (1888–1959) was perhaps the first major rabbinic figure in religious Zionism to apply the laws of war in Halakhah to an actual war waged by the state of Israel. He wrote a handful of important responsa on this issue in 1948, as Israel's War of Independence was just getting underway. These responsa bear the imprint of R. Kook's influence, but they also contain a good deal of original thinking on R. Herzog's part as well.

R. Herzog was born in Poland and emigrated at age ten to Leeds, England, when his father became Chief Rabbi of the Jewish community there. He received his rabbinic education through private lessons with his father. At age sixteen, he began pursuing secular studies and quickly earned a high school equivalency degree. He then went on to receive a bachelor of arts degree and master's degree from the University of London, a master's from the Sorbonne, and a doctorate from the University of London. His doctoral thesis was on *tekhelet*, the blue dye mentioned in the Bible that is used for the ritual fringes (*tsitsit*) on prayer shawls, and his work on the subject made him well-known in the Jewish world on account of his claim that he had rediscovered the source of the dye, the knowledge of which had been lost for centuries.

R. Herzog's professional rabbinic career began in 1916 when he became Chief Rabbi of Belfast. He went on to become Chief Rabbi of Dublin, in 1919, and then Chief Rabbi of Ireland, in 1922. In 1936, he accepted the position of Ashkenazi Chief Rabbi of the Jewish community in Palestine, replacing R. Kook, who had died a year earlier, and he continued in that position after the founding of the state of Israel in 1947 until his death in 1959. Throughout his professional life, R. Herzog was a leading spokesman of religious Zionism, and he produced a large corpus of writings that helped shape the movement.[1]

R. Herzog did not produce theological writings, but from scattered references to theological matters in his works, one can construct the outline of a theology that undergirds his worldview. R. Herzog did not see Zionism in the same dramatic eschatological terms one finds in R. Kook's thinking. Zionism did not represent the beginning of the messianic redemption, nor were secular Zionists being impelled by the divine spirit for messianic purposes. However, R. Herzog certainly viewed Zionism as an important development in Jewish history. A Jewish state would serve the immediate goal of helping the Jewish people rebuild after the Holocaust, and in the longer term, it would give Jews a land in which they could improve their material conditions because they could live in it freely and without persecution.

And yet, the messianic element was not entirely absent from R. Herzog's views on Zionism. R. Herzog supported a naturalistic messianism, and he therefore saw Jewish history as steadily progressing toward the messianic redemption, even though he believed that the final stages of the messianic period would come about through miracles. That meant that Jews had to take initiative at all times to prepare the way for the messiah. Zionism presented one such opportunity because it drew Jews to the land of their redemption and allowed them to improve their material conditions. Therefore, in R. Herzog's thinking, if Zionism was not a critical step in the messianic process, it still had messianic import, though one that was more muted than that which we see in R. Kook's theology.[2]

Most of R. Herzog's writings were devoted to halakhic issues involving the political affairs of the Jewish state. He appreciated the fact that the application of Halakhah to the renewal of Jewish political sovereignty was a novel challenge, but he had full confidence in the capacity of Halakhah to deal with it. R. Herzog's view was that Halakhah had always been dynamic, flexible, and adaptive to changing times, and it was therefore very much up to the task in this instance as well.[3]

---

1. R. Herzog's biography has been treated in the following studies: Shmu'el Avidor, *Yahid be-Doro: Megilat Hayav shel ha-Ga'on Rabi Yitshak Aizik ha-Levi Hertsog, Rosh Rabaney Yisra'el* (Jerusalem: Keter Publishing House, 1980); Sha'ul Meizlish, *Rabanut bi-Se'arat ha-Yamim: Hayav u-Mishnato shel ha-Rav Aizik ha-Levi Hertsog, ha-Rav ha-Rashi le-Yisra'el* (Tel Aviv: Merhav, 1991).

2. Yitzchak Avi Roness, "*Medinat Yisra'el be-Mishnato ha-Hilkhatit shel ha-Rav Hertsog*" (MA thesis, Touro College, Jerusalem, 2005), chapter 2. An important essay by R. Herzog for exploring his theological views on Zionism can be found in *Peskaim u-Khetavim be-Diney Orah Hayim*, ed. Shlomo Shapira (henceforth *PKOH*) (Jerusalem: Mosad ha-Rav Kuk, 1989), vol. 2, chapter 116.

3. Yitzcahk Avi Roness, "*Milhamot Yisra'el—Halakhah ve-Idi'ologiyah be-Mishnat ha-RY' Hertsog*," *Masu'ah le-Yitshak*, eds. R. Shelomit Eli'ash, R. Itamar Varhaftig, and R. Uri Dasberg (Jerusalem: Yad ha-Rav Hertsog, 1989), vol. 1, pp. 469–71.

War was one political issue that R. Herzog had to grapple with, and, as noted, he produced a number of responsa on this topic in the initial stages of Israel's War of Independence. These works were written in the winter and the early spring of 1948, in the period between the passing of UN Resolution 181, on November 29, 1947, that approved the partition of Palestine into Arab and Jewish states, and the conclusion of the British Mandate on May 14, 1948. In this period, the fighting had already broken out between Jewish and Palestinian forces in what was shaping up to be an extended war. R. Herzog also addressed the topic of war in passages in writings composed in other contexts, and these, too, are helpful for understanding his views on war.

Relatively little has been written on R. Herzog's treatment of war, but pioneering studies have been done by Yitzchak Roness and Neryah Gutel to define some of his key positions on the issue, and my remarks in this chapter are very much indebted to their work.[4] Yet, a difficulty with these studies is that they have not paid close enough attention to the dating and chronology of R. Herzog's writings on war, a deficiency that, in turn, has hampered efforts to understand how his views on war evolved. Therefore, one of the contributions of this chapter will be an attempt to address these issues by establishing the order in which R. Herzog's writings on war were composed and tracing how his ideas developed in them.

THE TWO RESPONSA TO THE EZRA MOVEMENT

One of the most important communications that R. Herzog composed on war is a responsum he issued on April 5, 1948, to address a series of questions posed by Tuvia Bir, a representative of the Ezra youth movement in Palestine. The questions—seven in all—focused on halakhic issues involving military operations against the Arabs. The first six questions were about Sabbath law. Bir was concerned about several activities that commanders were asking Jewish soldiers to perform on the Sabbath that were in violation of Halakhah. He wanted to know whether, in R. Herzog's opinion, halakhically observant Jews were permitted to volunteer for such activities, despite the violations. The seventh and final question was whether, in the conflict with the Arabs, Halakhah allowed for conscription. Could Jews be required to serve in the newly formed Jewish army? The alternative, it would seem, was an all-volunteer army. This last question, of course, is most central to our study.[5]

---

4. Roness, *"Milhamot Yisra'el,"* in *Masu'ah le-Yitshak*, vol. 1, pp. 451–73; R. Neryah Gutel, *"Hagdaratan ha-Hilkhatit shel Milhamot Yisra'el be-Mishnat ha-Rav Hertsog,"* *Masu'ah le-Yitshak*, vol. 2, pp. 311–22.

5. PKOH, vol. 1, chapter 48.

In his responsum, R. Herzog answers each of these questions in turn and, in the course of doing so, spells out some of his major positions on war in Halakhah. This responsum has therefore received much attention from scholars interested in R. Herzog's views on this subject, and deservedly so. However, there is another responsum that R. Herzog composed to the Ezra organization that has received much less attention. It appears to be an alternative version of the responsum just described,[6] and most importantly, it also seems to be the earlier of the two communications. The latter piece of information is easy to miss because no date is given at the beginning of the alternative version. However, in an addendum to the text, R. Herzog informs us that it was composed on February 17, 1948, a few weeks before the better known one was written.[7]

It is not at all clear what the precise relationship between the two versions is. While there is a good deal of overlap between them, there are important differences as well. A number of the questions asked in the earlier responsum do not appear in the later one, and vice versa. The same goes for R. Herzog's responses to those questions. He takes up issues in the first that are not dealt with in the second, and vice versa.

Nonetheless, we must begin our analysis of R. Herzog by looking at the earlier, lesser known version of the responsum. Not only is it first of the two versions, it also seems to be the first responsum that R. Herzog wrote on anything having to do with war. It also provides a great deal of information about his views on that topic.

The First Responsum

We start with a section of this responsum that deals with Sabbath law. The first question that is raised regarding this issue is whether Jewish soldiers may violate the Sabbath by volunteering to participate in military operations being conducted for defensive purposes. R. Herzog responds to this question as follows:

> This question is one that I find almost incomprehensible. In the present situation, if we did not volunteer for defensive operations, then, God forbid, the danger of annihilation would be expected for all of us. We are certainly obligated [to volunteer], because what alternative do we have? To surrender to the

6. PKOH, vol. 1, chapter 52.
7. Ibid., p. 245. The addendum is dated to "the third day of 'to raise the eternal light' 5708," which was the third day of the week preceding the Sabbath on which the Torah portion of *Tetsaveh* was read that year. "To raise the eternal light" is a phrase taken from the first verse of that Torah portion.

enemy? If, God forbid, we were to surrender to [them] and be captured by them, it is clear that in the end they would destroy us, God forbid, because the enemy would make the assessment that there would certainly be [Jewish] fighters underground, and [this] underground [force] would surface from time to time, and they [i.e., the enemy] would thus have an excuse to destroy those who were liable to surface, and there is no danger greater than this. And this is according to a simple assessment without addressing the desecration of [the divine] name that would be caused by this [destruction] in the eyes of the world. We [i.e., the Jewish people] would also be forfeit, because there would be no refuge for [the people of] Israel in the event of persecutions, may God help us, that are likely to arise outside the land [of Israel]. We have already learned from experience to what extent one can rely upon the humanity of the gentiles, even the cultured ones, and all the more so [is this true regarding] the humanity of the race waging war on us, and we have had enough. And besides this, this [situation] touches on the survival of Judaism among the hundreds of thousands of Jews in the world after the terrible Holocaust, when the entire hope of [the people of] Israel is tied to the revival of [the people of] Israel in its holy land, for when the masses of [the people of] Israel will give up hope completely, the entire religion will collapse, and no more [need be said] for those who are insightful.[8]

R. Herzog expresses consternation that such a question even needs to be asked. One may indeed volunteer for defensive military operations on the Sabbath, and for a number of reasons. First and foremost, under the present circumstances, there is simply no alternative. The Arab forces are bent on destroying the Jewish community in Palestine, and even if the Jewish community were to surrender to the Arabs, it would not be spared; confrontations between Jews and Arabs would likely continue, and the Arabs would use them as a pretext to destroy the Jewish community anyway. Underlying R. Herzog's ruling is the assumption that Sabbath law is always overridden to save lives, and given that the danger to life here is immediate and affects all Jews in Palestine, there is no question that in these circumstances, Sabbath law may be disregarded.

Two other reasons are provided for this ruling. R. Herzog argues that the victory of Jewish forces is critical not only for saving the Jewish community in Palestine but for the survival of Jews throughout the world. In light of the Holocaust, it is abundantly clear that Jews need an independent state as a place of refuge to which they can flee when persecution strikes again. Furthermore, R. Herzog claims that the Jews must defeat the Arabs for the survival of Judaism as a religion. If the Jewish forces in Palestine are defeated, the faith that Jews have in their religion, already compromised by

8. Ibid., p. 230.

the Holocaust, would only be further weakened. These considerations also provide warrant for violating the Sabbath in order to participate in defensive military operations.[9]

Yet R. Herzog seems to have adopted R. Kook's position that everyday Halakhah and wartime Halakhah are different from each other, and the arguments he has offered thus far are apparently only in accordance with everyday Halakhah on the presumption that the conflict with the Arabs is not necessarily a war in the formal halakhic sense. This presumption becomes clear in the next paragraph, where R. Herzog goes on to argue that, according to his opinion, the conflict with the Arabs is, in fact, a halakhically sanctioned mandatory war, and it therefore brings into effect a whole new set of halakhic regulations not yet discussed and unique to wartime:

> [I]n my view, this is a mandatory war, for because the United Nations has decided to return to us, at the very least, a portion of the land of Israel to establish an independent government, this is a war for the conquest of the land (*kibush ha-arets*), and for Nahmanides ... this is an obligatory commandment. ... And indeed to wage mandatory war one does not need a court of seventy-one [i.e., a Sanhedrin], which we do not have nowadays. It [i.e., the authority to wage war] is one of the powers of the king—of course, after consulting with military commanders. And even though we do not have a king [nowadays], the majority of the community together with its institutions, the rabbinate etc., have the legal status of a king. ... There is no doubt that this is a mandatory war to conquer the land [of Israel], besides the reason of "saving Israel from the clutches of the enemy" (*'ezrat yisra'el mi-yad tsar*). And all the more so is it "saving Israel from the clutches of the enemy," because [in this instance] there is no alternative [but war]. But, of course, the military headquarters [of the Jewish forces] is equivalent to the minister of defense. Also, the obligation to volunteer does not apply except to those whom it [i.e., the military headquarters] calls upon to serve. But to volunteer is permitted even for those who have not yet been called on to be drafted. It is more than permitted; it is also a divine commandment. That is my opinion.[10]

R. Herzog informs us here that the fight against the Arabs is indeed a mandatory war, for two reasons. First, it is a fulfillment of the commandment to conquer the land of Israel—*kibush ha-arets*—in accordance with Nahmanides' view. Second, it is a defensive war in accordance with Maimonides' notion that Jews are required to "save Israel from the clutches of the enemy"—*'ezrat*

---

9. See Roness, "*Medinat Yisra'el*," 60–66, for a discussion of the impact of the Holocaust on R. Herzog's thinking regarding Zionism and the establishment of the state of Israel.

10. PKOH, vol. 1, pp. 230–31.

yisra'el mi-yad tsar.[11] R. Herzog also addresses the concern that in Halakhah a mandatory war may be waged only by a Jewish king, an institution that has long been in abeyance. He circumvents this problem by claiming that in the absence of a king, the Jewish community together with its governing institutions, including the chief rabbinate, can function in his place. Here, R. Herzog seems to be alluding to R. Kook's position on this matter, though R. Kook is not specifically mentioned. As for the original question about violating Sabbath law for defensive military operations, the equation of the conflict with a mandatory war makes the matter even easier to handle than was the case in everyday Halakhah. The Sabbath is no obstacle to the prosecution of a mandatory war. One is even allowed to initiate a mandatory war on the Sabbath.

R. Herzog thus issues the same ruling for wartime Halakhah that he did for everyday Halakhah: a soldier may volunteer for defensive operations on the Sabbath. The two sectors of Halakhah bring us to the same conclusion.

Further information about R. Herzog's views on the conflict with the Arabs can be found in the next section of his responsum in which he takes up the question of whether Jews may participate in military operations on the Sabbath if the operations are offensive in nature. Here, the questioner seems to have in mind primarily operations conducted for the sake of deterrence. This type of military operation presents a bit more of a challenge with respect to Sabbath law than defensive operations because the threat to life that made the latter type of operation permissible on the Sabbath was immediate, while that is not necessarily the case here. Deterrence implies the preemption of a future danger, not one that is at hand.

Here, too, R. Herzog deals with the matter from the standpoint of both everyday Halakhah and wartime Halakhah. But first he digresses on why the rabbinic tradition about the three oaths do not present an obstacle for Jews to fight for their land. First, the oath forbidding Jews to reclaim their land by rebelling against the nations of the world is not in effect in the current situation. Britain is in charge of Palestine only temporarily according to the mandate arrangement, and the United Nations has voted that Jews should have their own independent state. Therefore, the Jews are not rebelling against anyone; they are fighting for possession of what is already theirs. Second, R. Herzog casts doubt on whether the oaths are, in fact, binding halakhic imperatives,

11. R. Herzog also appears to acknowledge that the standard for waging defensive war is much lower than the present situation with the Arabs dictates when he notes that "all the more so is it 'saving Israel from the clutches of the enemy' because [in this instance] there is no alternative [but war]." R. Herzog implies here that a defensive war may be conducted in any situation in which an enemy initiates a war, even if they do not intend total destruction; yet, in the present situation in which the enemy has this intention, defensive war is all the more justified.

and he adduces evidence that they are not. For instance, Maimonides, in his *Mishneh Torah*, does not codify the oaths into law. Third, R. Herzog claims that even if the oaths are regarded as law, they would no longer be in effect because one of the oaths consists of a pledge by the nations of the world not to oppress the Jewish people excessively, but that is precisely what they have done, as was evident in the Holocaust. Because the nations have broken their oath, the oath of the Jewish people to refrain from rebelling against them is no longer in effect as well.[12]

R. Herzog then moves on to address the main question about whether one may violate Sabbath law to participate in an offensive military operation with a deterrent purpose. In his treatment of the previous question about Sabbath violations, R. Herzog began with everyday Halakhah, but here he begins with Halakhah in wartime:

> To conclude, my opinion is that this war against the Arabs, who are seeking to deny our right [to our land], and, in an indirect manner, against Britain which has abused its office, is a mandatory war in four respects: 1) with respect to rescuing [the people of] Israel, for if we allow the Arabs to do as they intend, we will end up being forfeit, and we have had enough 2) with regard to the commandment of conquering the land of Israel when we have been given the possibility of doing so 3) so that [the people of] Israel do not get to the point of despondence and Reform [Judaism] and assimilation increase, and we have had enough 4) after the recent bitter experience with respect to the most cultured nation, it is necessary that we have a place of refuge for every trouble that comes. And because [the situation] is so, this struggle of ours [against the Arabs] has the legal status of an actual mandatory war, and in a mandatory war, the rule is that [we] lay siege to the cities of gentiles on the Sabbath from the outset (Jerusalem Talmud, *Shabbat* 1:8). This is the procedure of every war, even a defensive war: to attack for the sake of defense.[13]

In this passage, R. Herzog again establishes the fact that the conflict with the Arabs is a mandatory war, but here he gives a more comprehensive list of reasons for this position than he did in his answer to the previous question. There are four such reasons. The struggle with the Arabs is a mandatory war because (1) it fulfills the commandment to conquer the land of Israel (*kibush ha-arets*); (2) it fulfills the commandment to defend the Jewish nation from attack (*'ezrat yisra'el mi-yad tsar*); (3) in wake of the Holocaust, Jews throughout the world must have a permanent place of refuge when persecutions arise; and (4) a defeat would threaten the spiritual well-being of the Jewish people, which the Holocaust has already weakened.

12. PKOH, vol. 1, chapter 52, pp. 231–32.
13. Ibid, p. 233.

The first two are familiar to us from R. Herzog's response to the previous question about purely defensive military operations conducted on the Sabbath. The last two reasons are also familiar to us from his discussion of the previous question, though in that context they were used to justify Sabbath violations from the standpoint of everyday Halakhah, while here they have been co-opted for the purposes of justifying such violations from the perspective of Halakhah in wartime.

With the notion again established that conflict with the Arabs is a mandatory war, R. Herzog concludes the passage just cited with the ruling that Jews may violate the Sabbath to participate in offensive military operations that serve the purpose of deterrence. The justification of this judgment is based on a source in the Jerusalem Talmud that allows Jews to initiate a siege on the Sabbath in cases of mandatory war. R. Herzog also adds that military operations for the sake of deterrence are a normal part of the strategy used in the prosecution of any war, even those waged in self-defense, and thus, if Halakhah permits the violation of the Sabbath for the sake of mandatory war, that dispensation must extend to these operations as well.

R. Herzog then goes on to justify his position from the standpoint of everyday Halakhah:

> [E]ven according to the narrow standpoint of saving lives [of individuals], the great sage, the *Noda' bi-Yehudah*[14] admits (first edition, part 14, pericope 210) that one can perform an autopsy in order to determine the cause of the illness [that caused the person's death], when there is only a possibility to heal a [living] sick person similar to this one [who died], and the sick person is in our presence.[15] In the present situation, and as long as it continues, every Jewish settlement that is situated close to those places that are in danger from the non-Jews, has the legal status of someone in danger or in possible danger who is in our presence, and because the experts in that matter[16] are of the opinion that the [military] operation will result in protecting them, it [i.e., the military operation] is permissible [on the Sabbath]. And in the case of a sick person who is in danger, one may desecrate the Sabbath even if the treatment may not work because there is a possibility that it will work. See [*Shulhan Arukh*] *Orah Hayim* 328.[17]

Even if the conflict with the Arabs is not regarded as a war in the formal halakhic sense, violations of the Sabbath to conduct offensive military operations with deterrent value would still be justified because in everyday Halakhah one

---

14. A work containing the collected responsa of R. Ezekiel Landau (1713–93).
15. Lit., "who is before us."
16. The reference here is to the military experts guiding the Jewish war effort.
17. PKOH, vol. 1, chapter 52, p. 233.

is permitted to transgress halakhic norms to save lives, even if the danger is not certain or immediately present. Thus, one may perform an autopsy, which is normally forbidden, if there is any chance that the knowledge gained from it will help save the lives of others. One may also violate the Sabbath to save others from danger, even in instances in which it is not certain that the danger constitutes a threat to life. Thus, an offensive military operation for deterrent purposes may be performed on the Sabbath as well because here, too, there is a possibility that it will save lives by preempting a future attack.

Much closer to our concerns than the issues we have discussed thus far is R. Herzog's response to yet another question that he entertains a little later on in his responsum addressing the risk to life that all soldiers face when going into battle. Should Jews who participate in military operations against the Arabs be at all concerned about the halakhic imperative not to place themselves needlessly in danger? R. Herzog begins his answer by engaging the problem from the standpoint of everyday Halakhah:

> This question is almost incomprehensible to me because the [military] operations are to rescue the lives [of the people] of Israel. For it is as clear as the sun at noon that were it not for "the [military] operations,"[18] the enemies would destroy us unless we were to completely surrender, and thus in the end ... we would not only lose our right to the land of Israel—until the coming of the messiah—but there would be no place of refuge for [the people of] Israel, and that is the case even if we do not rule that this conflict has the legal status of a mandatory war. Moreover, complete surrender is not an option for it is clear that Jews would remain in the underground [to continue fighting], and these enemies that are not at all cultured, will find an excuse to kill the Jews whenever they are able to, to rape our daughters, and to steal our goods. ... Therefore, it astonishes me how the question would come to mind as to whether it is permitted [to risk one's life to fight]. It is not only permitted, we are required to.[19]

R. Herzog's answer here is similar to the one he gave to the question about volunteering on the Sabbath for defensive military operations. He expresses surprise that such a question even needs to be asked. If Jews do not fight the Arabs, the Jewish community in Palestine will be destroyed, and surrender is no option because the Arabs will find pretexts to annihilate the Jewish community regardless. The point here seems to be that the risk to one's life in taking up arms against the Arabs could not be any less than the risk of *not* doing so, given the violent intentions of the enemy. Therefore, one should

---

18. These words are in quotation marks because R. Herzog is citing the wording of his questioner.

19. PKOH, vol. 1, chapter 52, pp. 235–36.

not worry about placing oneself in needless danger in the current circumstances because here the danger is anything but needless; every Jew is, in
fact, fighting for his own survival. R. Herzog also adds here that Jews must
face the dangers of participating in the battle against the Arabs because if
the Jews are defeated, again there will be no place of refuge for Jews elsewhere in the world who have to flee persecution. In light of all these considerations, R. Herzog concludes with the ruling that, even according to everyday
Halakhah, Jews may not only place themselves in danger to fight the Arabs,
they are required to do so.

Most significant for our purposes is that with this last statement, R. Herzog
has opened the halakhic door to conscription. The fight against the Arabs cannot be considered a voluntary matter; it is requirement—and it is a short step
from here to the approval of forced enlistment. We will soon see that in the
later version of R. Herzog's responsum, he will make this reasoning explicit.

Yet what R. Herzog has said up to this point about self-endangerment is
only according to everyday Halakhah. R. Herzog goes on to reiterate that,
according to his opinion, the conflict with the Arabs is a war in the formal
halakhic sense, and in that case there is no question that Jews may participate
in military operations without concern for violating the prohibition against
needlessly endangering one's life. In fact, once again, they are required to do
so. As support for this position, R. Herzog bypasses the obvious point that
in Halakhah there is universal agreement that a mandatory war obligates all
Jews to fight, and instead he cites the views of the Netsiv, most likely because
the Netsiv provides reflection, absent in earlier halakhic sources, about why
wartime Halakhah is different from that of the everyday. As we saw earlier
in our study, the Netsiv believes that actions normally forbidden in everyday
Halakah are permitted in wartime because war is a natural phenomenon—it
is "how the world was founded." Thus, a king may send soldiers into battle at
the risk of their lives, even though under any other circumstances, one may
not force an individual to subject himself to danger. The Netsiv notes that this
rule applies even in instances of discretionary war in which the motivation for
war may have nothing to do with self-defense.[20]

In the responsum under examination, R. Herzog also takes up another
major ethical issue central to our study, which has to do with killing of enemy
civilians. We do not have the original question that prompted R. Herzog to
address this problem, but he seems to have been asked whether it is permissible to kill Arab civilians on the Sabbath in revenge for the killing of Jewish
civilians. His questioner appears to have believed that retaliatory measures of
this sort were, in fact, justified because they would eventually save Jewish lives
by instilling fear among the Arabs that their actions would not go unpunished.

20. Ibid., p. 236.

The only question was whether the Sabbath presented a halakhic obstacle to taking such action.

The question is rather specific, but in the course of answering it, R. Herzog confronts the broader ethical issues it raises. R. Herzog responds by first noting that the Sabbath is really not a factor here. The question is whether one can kill Arab civilians for the purpose described on *any* day of the week. In R. Herzog's opinion, that is not an easy question to answer. In everyday Halakhah, the killing of innocent non-Jews is most certainly forbidden, but in war, Jews are not culpable for doing so in the course of battling an enemy army, because no war can be won without killing civilians who happen to be in the line of fire. The scenario presented by the questioner, therefore, presents a dilemma. On the one hand, the type of killing being asked about here may be forbidden because the Arab civilians being targeted are not necessarily anywhere near the line of fire; they have been chosen to be killed at random. On the other hand, such killing may be permitted because it could deter the Arab forces, which themselves have shown a willingness to kill Jews at random, from repeating their murderous actions, and it may therefore save Jewish lives.[21]

After looking at the question from a number of angles, R. Herzog eventually concludes as follows:

> If it [i.e., killing of enemy civilians] does not serve the needs of the war, it is forbidden even on weekdays, and if it does serve the needs of the war and is therefore permitted on weekdays, it is also permitted on the Sabbath. Nonetheless, I would not dare to make a decision about this [issue] even regarding weekdays, not to mention regarding the Sabbath, when it comes to innocent people among the enemy. A lot depends on an examination of the issue with respect to the influence [it would have] on the progress of the war. Sometimes, there is reason to be concerned that a particular non-Jew who appears to be innocent may go and give information about the location of a Jewish army division and bring disaster on it. But to take him prisoner and to hold him in a secure place is not possible, and [if] the army division takes him along, we should be even more concerned when he is freed, and enough [said] for those who are insightful. This matter has to be examined thoroughly, but this is not the place for in-depth discussion.[22]

R. Herzog reiterates that the issue of violating Sabbath law is beside the point. The important question is whether the random killing of innocent non-Jews in wartime for the sake of deterrence is permitted at any time. R. Herzog

---

21. Ibid., pp. 233–34.
22. Ibid., p. 235.

seems to rule out killing for this purpose. However, he is reluctant to issue a blanket condemnation of killing unarmed civilians because in some instances, this type of action may be necessary. If an army unit encounters a civilian who may divulge its location to the enemy army thereby endangering the unit, killing the civilian here may be imperative.[23]

R. Herzog's first responsum on war has yielded a wealth of information, and it behooves us to take stock of what we have discovered in this work. R. Herzog appears to adopt R. Kook's approach in creating a sharp division between wartime Halakhah and everyday Halakhah, but he is called upon to apply this model to concrete reality in a way that R. Kook was not.

R. Herzog considers the conflict with the Arabs a mandatory war in the formal halakhic sense, and he provides no fewer than four reasons to justify this judgment. The first two rely on traditional halakhic categories. The conflict with the Arabs is a fulfillment of the imperative to "save Israel from the clutches of the enemy," 'ezrat yisra'el mi-yad tsar, championed by Maimonides, as well as the commandment of "conquering the land of Israel," kibush ha-arets, endorsed by Nahmanides. The third and fourth reasons, however, have to do with R. Herzog's own perceptions about the unique historical circumstances of the Jewish people in the period in which he lived. In wake of the Holocaust, it is clear to him that Jews around the world need a state of their own as a place of refuge from persecution, and they therefore must fight the Arabs. They must also fight because defeat at the hands of the Arabs would imperil the spiritual well-being of the Jewish people worldwide seeing as many Jews would likely lose their faith as a result.

By classifying the conflict with the Arabs as a mandatory war, R. Herzog is then able to justify a series of activities by Jewish military forces that would normally be forbidden in Halakhah, including violations of the Sabbath and requiring Jews to endanger their lives in order to save others from harm. Thus, one may violate the Sabbath to participate voluntarily in both defensive and offensive military operations because halakhic sources explicitly allow Sabbath law to be disregarded for activities that have to be performed for prosecuting a mandatory war. Requiring Jews to risk their lives for others by serving in the army is also permissible because halakhic sources tell us that in mandatory war all Jews have an obligation to fight despite the danger involved, a point which the Netsiv explains in accordance with his view that war is a natural phenomenon. R. Herzog also takes up the question of whether wartime Halakhah permits the killing of innocent Arab civilians at random to deter the Arab forces from doing the same, but he offers no clear answer.

23. See also Ibid., pp. 236–37, where R. Herzog expresses similar thoughts about the danger posed by seemingly innocent civilian Arabs. Yet, here again, R. Herzog resists issuing a ruling that all Arab civilians should be considered dangerous and that Jews therefore have license to kill them.

Yet what is perhaps most interesting about R. Herzog's responsum is that he also strives to justify his positions within the strictures of everyday Halakhah. In fact, he tends to deal with this aspect of Halakhah first, before considering wartime Halakhah and its unique prescriptions. On the issue of Sabbath violations, this task is fairly easy because Halakhah allows for the transgression of Sabbath law for saving lives, even in non-war situations, and this point therefore becomes the basis for allowing Sabbath violations for both defensive and offensive military operations, seeing as they are intended to protect Jews from harm. R. Herzog also makes his case on the basis of what he believes are the unique circumstances of the Jewish people in his time. The consequences of a Jewish defeat would be so dire both for the Jewish community in Palestine and the Jewish people as a whole, that even according to everyday Halakhah, activities that are normally forbidden are permitted if they can aid the Jews in achieving victory over the Arabs.

Somewhat more challenging for everyday Halakhah is the prohibition against requiring Jews to risk their lives for others, a prohibition that poses serious problems for conscription, but here, too, R. Herzog manages to get around the problem. Certainly, in everyday Halakhah, Jews cannot be forced endanger themselves for the sake of others, but in the current conflict with the Arabs, every Jew is, in fact, fighting for his own life because the Arabs are clearly intent on destroying the Jewish community in Palestine. Therefore, the issue here is not really the defense of others but the defense of oneself, which requires no special halakhic dispensation. And here again, the wider concerns are an issue as well. If the Jewish forces are defeated, the survival of the Jewish people and the Jewish religion will be threatened, and therefore, once again, Jews have no choice but to risk their lives to participate in the struggle against the Arabs. Thus, even according to everyday Halakhah, conscription is permitted in the current circumstances.

In many of his subsequent responsa, R. Herzog continues to justify his positions regarding the conflict with Arabs from the standpoint of both everyday Halakhah and wartime Halakhah, and a question that has been asked by commentators is why R. Herzog saw the need to adopt this twofold approach. It is not only redundant, but it is clear in all his responsa that R. Herzog preferred to view the hostilities between Jews and Arabs as falling under the category of mandatory war. Why, then, did he insist on consistently finding support for his rulings from the standpoint of everyday Halakhah as well?

Yitzchak Roness and Kalman Neuman both suggest that R. Herzog took this approach because he knew that applying the halakhic categories of war to the events of 1948 might not be accepted by those in some of the more traditional sectors of the Orthodox community that would insist that the realm of Halakhah involving political matters, including war, could not be revived until messianic times, when the Davidic kingship is to be reconstituted. We also have to keep in mind that the entire Zionist enterprise was viewed with deep skepticism or outright hostility by the most traditional elements of the Orthodox community in Palestine. R. Herzog therefore made a point of addressing this audience by defending his positions in accordance with halakhic categories that were outside the parameters of war.[24]

Neuman adds several more explanations for R. Herzog's twofold approach to war. According to Neuman, one has to keep in mind that R. Herzog was writing his responsa on war early in 1948, when it still was not clear that the violence between Arabs and Jews was indeed a full-scale war. After all, there had been violence between the two communities for well over a decade, though it tended to be episodic in nature. Moreover, the British were in charge throughout this period, including the early months of 1948 when R. Herzog was writing the responsa being examined here, and they tended to clamp down on violence between the communities. R. Herzog's twofold approach to the events of 1948 may therefore have been due to this ambiguity. He himself believed that the violence between Jews and Arabs was, in fact, in the category of war from a halakhic standpoint, but he had to address the situation from the standpoint of everyday Halakhah for those who may not have been convinced that the situation, as yet, could be characterized in this manner.[25]

Neuman also notes that another factor influencing R. Herzog's thinking is that it was not clear to some Jewish factions that a war between Jews and Arabs was necessary. Some Jews argued that war could be avoided if they did not declare independence. Those holding this viewpoint included the left-wing secular organization *Ihud* and the ultra-Orthodox group *Neturey Karta*. Thus, R. Herzog may have seen the need to address those who held this viewpoint by arguing for his position from the standpoint of everyday Halakhah, in addition to wartime Halakhah.[26]

The Second Responsum

Let us now turn to the later version of R. Herzog's responsum to the Ezra movement. We have already noted some of its major features: The responsum is dated to early April of 1948, and it was therefore written just a few weeks after the earlier one was composed. The responsum consists of answers to seven questions regarding war, of which six address Sabbath law, and the

---

24. Roness, "*Milhamot Yisra'el*," 455; Kalman Neuman, "The Law of Obligatory War and Israeli Reality," in *War and Peace in Jewish Tradition: From the Biblical World to the Present*, eds. Yigal Levin and Amnon Shapira (London: Routledge, 2012), 189.

25. Neuman, "Law of Obligatory War," in Levin and Shapira, *War and Peace in Jewish Tradition*, 189.

26. Ibid. This last explanation strikes me as a bit more tendentious than the others. It's not clear that R. Herzog would have much concern with the view of *Ihud* or *Neturey Karta*.

seventh takes up the issue of conscription. The later version shares many similarities with the earlier one but differs from it in a number of respects as well.
It is not clear, however, what the relationship is between the two responsa.

I would like to focus primarily on how the second responsum deals with the
final question regarding conscription because this topic is the most central to
our study. Moreover, what the second responsum has to say about the first
six questions involving Sabbath law does not differ significantly from what is
found in the first responsum, and it therefore does not give us much to examine here.[27] The issue of conscription is another story. On this topic, R. Herzog
presents new perspectives not found in the earlier text.

In the later responsum, R. Herzog once again explores the issue of conscription in accordance with his twofold framework. With respect to everyday
Halakhah, R. Herzog rules, as he did in the first version of the responsum, that
Jews are required to participate in the armed struggle against the Arabs, even
at the risk of their lives. Yet the justification for this position differs from that
of the earlier text. R. Herzog now casts doubt on the ruling that in everyday
Halakhah an individual is not required to risk his life to save another person
who is in danger:

> [E]ven if we judge this [matter] only from the narrow viewpoint of rescuing [the
> people of] Israel with respect to [the commandment of] saving the lives of many
> [people], the ruling would be that with regard to this commandment of saving
> the lives of the entire [Jewish] community, we force [a person to perform the
> commandment]. ... There is a debate between halakhic authorities ... whether
> the Halakhah is according to the Jerusalem Talmud (*Terumot*, end of chapter 8)
> [which says] that a person must subject themselves to possible danger in order
> to rescue someone from certain death. According to those who say that one is
> required [to do so], here [in the conflict with the Arabs] there is definitely the
> certain danger [of death] for hundreds of thousands of [the people of] Israel, for
> if we do not stand up to our enemies, they will destroy us.[28]

R. Herzog now argues that under certain circumstances, an individual must
endanger himself for others, even according to everyday Halakhah. He supports his ruling by citing a passage in the Jerusalem Talmud that we saw earlier in our study which implies that a Jew is required to subject himself to a
"possible" life-threatening situation (*safek sakanah*) in order to rescue a fellow
Jew from a situation in which the threat to life is "certain" (*vaday sakanah*).[29]
R. Herzog's presumption seems to be that by serving in an army and going

27. PKOH, vol. 1, chapter 48, pp. 212–14.
28. Ibid., p. 217.
29. JT *Terumot* 8:4. Above, p. 48.

into battle, one is subjecting oneself to a "possible" risk to life in order to save fellow Jewish civilians from a risk to life that is "certain." The difference, it would seem, is that soldiers in combat have weapons with which to defend themselves from the enemy, while civilians do not, and therefore the latter are more at risk than the former.[30]

R. Herzog notes, however, that the view of the Jerusalem Talmud is supported by only a minority of later halakhic authorities, and he therefore strengthens his position by arguing that in the conflict with the Arabs, there is another reason why Jews must serve in the military, with all the risk that this commitment entails:

> However, there are those who disagree, and the opinion of the Netsiv ... is that this is an optional act of kindness to subject oneself to possible danger as described above, but is not [required] by the actual law, and therefore it would appear that one does not force [a person to do so]. But in [the book] *Mishpat Kohen* of my predecessor, the great sage [R. Kook] ... ruled that to rescue the community of Israel (*kelal yisra'el*), one must subject oneself to possible danger, and even certain danger, even if one can escape [harm]. And because the community [in Palestine] is thought of as "the congregation of Israel" (*kahal yisra'el*), it should be said that we force [the person to act], even if there is no ruling here of [the situation being] mandatory war, given that we have no king nowadays. However, this [ruling] is nonetheless something that is dependent on the inference that in this matter as well, the community [in Palestine] is considered the community of Israel (*kelal yisra'el*), or the majority of [the people of] Israel. Indeed, one can say that the destruction of the community [in Palestine], God forbid, is liable to cause the destruction of the community of Israel (*kelal yisra'el*), or the majority of [the people of] Israel. But there is, as yet, no clear decision regarding this [matter], and therefore I hesitate to make a decision in favor or against [this idea], and it still requires much examination.[31]

R. Herzog makes use here of an idea that originates with R. Kook and that we encountered in our previous chapter. According to R. Kook, an individual Jew in everyday life is not normally obligated to risk his life to rescue fellow Jews from danger, but if the entire Jewish people is threatened with destruction, and one is in a unique position to save them, there is no question that one must take action even if it is certain that he will die. R. Herzog adopts this view and combines it with the notion, found in a number of rabbinic sources as well as R. Kook's writings, that the Jewish community in the land of Israel

---

30. One could, of course, quarrel with this assessment. Depending on the circumstances, soldiers may be in far greater danger than unarmed civilians. Nonetheless, R. Herzog assumes the alternative perspective.

31. PKOH, vol. 1, chapter 48, p. 217.

is considered equivalent to the Jewish people as a whole. R. Herzog mentions this idea in a number of places in his writings, and it has halakhic implications. In the present context, it means that a Jew must sacrifice his life to save the Jewish community in the land of Israel if it is threatened with destruction, just as he would were the entirety of world Jewry similarly at risk.[32]

R. Herzog adds that in the present circumstances the Jewish community in the land of Israel is equivalent to the Jewish people as a whole in a concrete sense, for if the Jewish community in Israel is destroyed, it could very well mean the end of the Jewish people elsewhere as well. Here R. Herzog is clearly alluding to views laid out in his earlier responsum according to which the future well-being of the Jewish people, both physically and spiritually, is dependent on the survival of the Jewish community in Palestine. All Jews must therefore join in the fight against the Arabs to save that community, not just because of a technical halakhic equivalence between Jewish community in the land of Israel and the Jewish people in general, but also because the survival of the latter is dependent on the former in a very concrete way. R. Herzog concludes by voicing some reservations about whether his reasoning here is correct, though he does not inform us what precisely troubles him.

R. Herzog's approach here is quite different from the one we saw in the earlier responsum. There, R. Herzog argued that conscription could be justified according to everyday Halakhah because in the current crisis Jews were not just concerned about risking their lives to save others; all Jews in Palestine were in danger, and therefore the issue was really one of self-defense for each and every person. Moreover, military defeat would bring with it dire consequences for the physical and spiritual well-being of the Jewish community worldwide. In the later responsum, the argumentation is more subtle and complex both in its reasoning and its use of halakhic sources. Here, R. Herzog casts doubt on the very assumptions on which the original question is based. Is it really the case that there is a prohibition to begin with against forcing an individual to risk his life to save others? R. Herzog argues that the source in the Jerusalem Talmud indicates otherwise. He acknowledges that this source may not be authoritative because it is supported only by a minority of later

---

32. Roness, "*Milhamot Yisra'el*," 464–68, analyzes R. Herzog's notion that the Jewish community living in Israel has the halakhic status of the Jewish people in its entirety. Roness argues that this idea is based on R. Herzog's reading of Maimonides' views on sanctification of the new moon and rabbinic ordination, but he also points out that R. Herzog seems to have also been influenced by modern nationalism which was predicated on the notion of deep ties between a people and its homeland. Roness also notes that R. Kook suggests an equivalence between the Jewish community in the land of Israel and the Jewish people as a whole (*Mishpat Kohen* 143, p. 308). However, R. Herzog takes the idea further than R. Kook by suggesting that, in light of this idea, a Jew must sacrifice his life in order to save the Jewish community in the land of Israel from destruction.

halakhic authorities, but an argument can still be made for forcing Jews to risk their lives for others because of R. Kook's ruling that a Jew must risk his life to save the Jewish people from destruction when he is in a unique position to do so. In the present historical circumstances, all Jews in Palestine are in such a position. All Jews must be willing to fight the Arabs at the cost of their lives, because the future of the Jewish people is at stake. Thus, if the general principle of the Jerusalem Talmud is not quite strong enough to warrant action, the historical circumstances of the Jewish people and R. Kook's ruling tip the balance in its favor.

Yet, as we have already seen in the earlier responsum, R. Herzog was convinced that the struggle with the Arabs was, in fact, a mandatory war, and in mandatory war all Jews are required to fight, and therefore conscription was certainly permitted. He takes the same position in the later responsum as well. R. Herzog also confronts once again the question of how a mandatory war can be waged in the absence of a king, and he solves this difficulty in much the same way that he did in the earlier responsum. When there is no king, the government of the Jewish community has the authority of a monarch. However, this time R. Herzog cites R. Kook to make his argument, which he did not do in his earlier discussion.[33]

R. Herzog says very little in the later responsum about the category of mandatory war to which the conflict with the Arabs belongs. In the earlier responsum, he cited four reasons for equating the conflict with mandatory war and provided explanations for each of them. Two were drawn from halakhic sources—'ezrat yisra'el mi-yad tsar and kibush ha-arets—and another two were suggested based on R. Herzog's perceptions about the unique historical circumstances in which the conflict was taking place. However, in the later version of the responsum, the phrase 'ezrat yisra'el mi-yad tsar is not mentioned, nor is there any clear reference of any other sort to the notion that the war against the Arabs is defensive in nature.[34] The imperative of kibush ha-arets is treated in the section dealing with conscription but primarily in order to show that Rashi's view is in agreement with that of Nahmanides regarding the notion that the commandment to conquer the land is still in force in the period of the exile.[35]

33. PKOH, vol. 1, chapter 48, pp. 215–17. R. Herzog first identifies the conflict with the Arabs as mandatory earlier in his discussion when dealing with the issue of Sabbath law. See ibid., p. 212.

34. In PKOH, vol. 1, chapter 48, pp. 212 (bottom)–213 (top), R. Herzog does refer to the "defense of Israel" (haganah 'al yisra'el) to characterize the military functions Jews are permitted to perform on the Sabbath in their conflict with the Arabs. However, this reference is in the context of a discussion about everyday Halakhah, not wartime Halakhah.

35. Ibid., p. 216.

Also included in R. Herzog's treatment of conscription in wartime Halakhah in the later responsum are a number of points not found in the earlier responsum. He discusses the halakhic provision of exemptions from army service in discretionary war that are granted to those who are unable to handle the rigors of battle due to fear.[36] R. Herzog cites halakhic sources stating that those exempted still had to perform other functions to support the war effort, such as providing food and water for their fellow Jews on the battlefield.[37] His point seems to be that participating in the struggle against the Arabs need not be confined to participating directly in combat. Other forms of service are also possible. Now, it may seem odd that R. Herzog is using a rule about discretionary war to comment on the conflict with the Arabs, which he has classified as mandatory in nature. Yet, R. Herzog seems to be making a pragmatic point. He is implicitly acknowledging that not all Jews will have the courage to go into battle against the Arabs, even though they are halakhically obligated to do so in the current conflict, but he says that these people should nonetheless be encouraged to participate in the war effort in some other manner. We may also surmise that his remarks here were directed to the ultra-Orthodox community, which, besides their halakhic reservations about entering combat, were not at all physically fit or trained for such activity. R. Herzog was signaling to them here that they could serve the war effort by other means.

Another issue R. Herzog deals with in the later responsum that is not discussed in the earlier one is the proper attitude that soldiers should have when going to war. R. Herzog cites a lengthy statement by Maimonides in his *Mishneh Torah* that in all wars a Jewish soldier must fight solely for *kidush ha-shem*, "sanctification of the divine name."[38] He explains Maimonides' view by claiming that Jews accomplish this purpose by going to war, because Jewish victories on the battlefield will convince non-Jews that the Jewish God is the one true God, and this, in turn, will bring humanity closer to the messianic period.[39]

R. Herzog also argues against any complacency on this matter predicated on the premise that much of the world has already been won over to monotheism by the successes of Christianity and Islam. Christians are not real monotheists, and even though Muslims are, they believe in Muhammad, and monotheism cannot flourish without acknowledgment of its true source in the Torah or without acquiescence to the belief in the validity of the Oral Torah that was imparted to Moses alongside the written one. Nonreligious Jews also come in for criticism here as being similarly distant from true belief and therefore in need of remediation as well.[40]

---

36. Ibid., p. 215; Deut. 20:8; M *Sotah* 8; BT *Sotah* 44b; MT *Melakhim* 7:4–14.
37. BT *Sotah* 43a; MT *Melakhim* 7:9.
38. MT *Melakhim* 7:15.
39. PKOH, vol. 1, chapter 48, pp. 215–16.
40. Ibid., p. 216.

R. Herzog finishes his thoughts on this issue by expressing certainty that the establishment of a Jewish state in its ancient homeland represents the final stages of the Jewish exile, which will be followed by the messianic redemption. Thus, anyone who helps to bring the redemption closer is also working to bring true religious belief to the nations of the world, as well as to wayward Jews. R. Herzog's message here is quite clear. Jews who participate in the struggle against the Arabs are fulfilling a messianic function on a number of levels. They are bringing about the revival of Jewish sovereignty in the Jewish homeland as predicted in prophetic teachings. They are also helping to convince non-Jews adhering to other religions, as well as Jews who have lost their religious faith, that Judaism is, in fact, the true religion.[41]

We should not be surprised by the messianic element in R. Herzog's thinking here. As I pointed out in the introduction to this chapter, even though R. Herzog did not go as far as R. Kook in identifying Zionism as serving a critical role in the unfolding of the messianic redemption, he still saw it as serving the function of preparing the way for the messiah by giving Jews a place of refuge and by bringing them back to their homeland. Apparently, war has a role to play here as well.

What is most perplexing is that much of R. Herzog's discussion of conscription in the later responsum is tangential to the original question that was asked of him regarding this issue. The question was simply whether conscription is allowed, and yet little of what he says seems addressed to this problem. This is particularly evident when he takes up the issue from the standpoint of wartime Halakhah. As we have seen, he spends a good deal of effort explaining that Rashi is in agreement with Nahmanides' view that the conquest of the land is in force in the period of the exile; that Jews can be of service to the war effort through nonmilitary activities; that when soldiers are in combat in any war, mandatory or discretionary, they are fighting for victory in order to convince the world of the truth of Judaism and to bring the messianic redemption closer; and that the current conflict has to be won for this very reason. Yet, issues discussed in the earlier responsum that are far more central to R. Herzog's thinking on conscription have been passed over here, such as why the conflict with the Arabs is a mandatory war in the first place. The key notion of *'ezrat yisra'el mi-yad tsar*, so central in the earlier version of the responsum, receives no attention. The notion of *kibush ha-arets* is dealt with, but only for the sake explaining Rashi's agreement with Nahmanides on this matter. An explication of Nahmanides' own views is never given.

What these observations may indicate is that R. Herzog composed the later version of the responsum for readers who had read the earlier version, and his intent was to provide glosses and supplementary commentary on the

41. Ibid.

positions he had already explicated in the previous version. This would explain why in the later responsum many of his remarks about conscription in wartime Halakhah are tangential to the main issue. R. Herzog was merely filling in information that he had not imparted in the earlier text. Yet, this hypothesis does not explain other features of the second responsum, such as why, in this responsum, R. Herzog appears to discuss some halakhic matters as if he is starting from scratch. Nor does it explain why each of the two texts deals with halakhic questions not found in the other.

THE EXCHANGE WITH R. MESHULAM ROTH

We can learn more about R. Herzog's halakhic views on war by examining an exchange he had about his positions on this topic with R. Meshulam Roth (1875–1962), a prominent rabbi of Ukranian origin who had managed to find his way to Palestine in 1944 while the Holocaust was unfolding. R. Herzog frequently consulted fellow rabbis about his halakhic decisions, especially when they concerned major issues, such as those we have been examining. Thus, R. Herzog informs us at the end of the earlier version of the responsum to the Ezra organization, that R. Tsevi Pesah Frank (1873–1960) had been asked to review its contents, and it had met with the latter's approval.[42] R. Herzog sent the second version of the responsum to R. Roth, but this time the reaction was different. R. Roth was quite critical of R. Herzog's views and wrote up a communication to that effect on April 7, 1948, just two days after R. Herzog's responsum was issued.[43]

R. Roth voices criticisms of R. Herzog's views on both Sabbath law and conscription, but since our focus has been primarily on the latter issue, we will concentrate on what R. Roth has to say about this particular matter. R. Roth rejects R. Hezog's position that conscription can be justified within the parameters of everyday Halakhah. He argues that, according to the majority view in halakhic sources, a Jew is not obligated to risk his life in order to rescue others from danger. R. Roth makes no mention of the contrary minority opinion based on the passage in the Jerusalem Talmud that R. Herzog had used as support for his viewpoint. More important, R. Roth entirely ignores R. Herzog's argument that all Jews must be willing to take up arms against the Arabs with all the risks involved because of R. Kook's notion that a Jew must sacrifice his life to save the Jewish people from destruction. Apparently, R. Roth was not at all convinced by this argument.[44]

42. PKOH, vol. 1, chapter 52, p. 245.
43. R. Meshulam Roth, *Kol Mevaser* (Jerusalem: Mosad ha-Rav Kuk, 1955), vol. 1, chapter 47, pp. 124–25.
44. Ibid., p. 125. For the sake of clarity, my presentation of R. Roth's views is not according his own order of presentation.

R. Roth also expresses doubt that the conflict with the Arabs can be classi-fied as a mandatory war.[45] R. Roth is particularly troubled by R. Herzog's pre-sumption that the conflict is a war of this type because of Nahmanides' view that the commandment to conquer the land of Israel is still in force. R. Roth seems to be under the impression, though he never says so explicitly, that the reason the Jewish forces are fighting is to capture land designated by the United Nations for the Palestinian state, and this he believes is a mistake. The implementation of the partition agreement endorsed by the UN is the best arrangement that Jews can hope for in settling the dispute with the Arabs, and thus any land captured in territory meant for the Palestinians, or in the environs of Jerusalem that had been deemed an international area, will have to be returned eventually in order to implement the partition. According to R. Roth, this type of scenario is not what Nahmanides had in mind when he spoke of the commandment to conquer the land of Israel. For Nahmanides, conquest meant taking full control of territory in the land of Israel the same way that Joshua did in biblical times. R. Roth is not necessarily denying the validity of Nahmanides' position; he is just making the point that it does not apply in the present circumstances, seeing as Jews appear to be bent on fight-ing to gain control of land beyond that which was given to them by the UN resolution, land that would therefore have to be returned.[46]

R. Roth has no objection to Jews volunteering for army duty. He also believes that Jews may be forced to aid those who have taken up arms against the Arabs by providing them food or by doing guard duty, as R. Herzog had suggested. However, forcing Jews to serve as full-fledged soldiers and to engage in combat is out of the question.

R. Herzog composed a rejoinder to R. Roth dated April 12, 1948.[47] He responds to R. Roth's criticisms regarding the issue of conscription in everyday Halakhah as one might expect: by reiterating the points that R. Roth chose to ignore. R. Herzog repeats his view that conscription is permitted in this sphere of Halakhah on the basis of R. Kook's notion that a Jew is obligated to sacri-fice his life to save the Jewish people from destruction, an imperative that, in R. Herzog's opinion, is very much applicable in the current circumstances. R. Herzog also reminds R. Roth of the minority view in the Jerusalem Talmud, which is that regardless of whether or not one is speaking about war, a Jew is required to expose himself to "possible" danger in order to save a fellow Jew from "certain" danger. Again, R. Herzog appears to be arguing that while the position of the Jerusalem Talmud is a minority one, it can be relied upon in this instance if considered in conjunction with R. Kook's viewpoint and its relevance in the present historical circumstances. Moreover, the uncertainty

45. Ibid.
46. Ibid., p. 124.
47. PKOH, vol. 1, chapter 49, pp. 219–22.

that R. Herzog had expressed about this reasoning in the previous responsum has now disappeared. He now seems quite sure of his position.[48]

R. Herzog reacts to R. Roth's criticisms of his view that the current conflict is a mandatory war by revising his positions—though he seems reluctant to admit that his thinking has changed:

> My primary support [for identifying the conflict with mandatory war] is that it is in the category of "saving Israel from the clutches of the enemy" ('ezrat yisra'el mi-yad tsar) which is explained in Maimonides ..., and I depended on [the opinion] of Nahmanides ... only as an addendum.[49]

R. Herzog responds to R. Roth's critique of using Nahmanides' views to understand the conflict with the Arabs by contending that R. Roth has misunderstood him. The central reason that the conflict with the Arabs is a mandatory war, R. Herzog argues, is that it has all the features of a defensive war in accordance with Maimonides' notion of 'ezrat yisra'el mi-yad tsar. R. Herzog insists that this position is the one that he had held all along, and that his discussion of Nahmanides' views was nothing more than an "addendum" to this main point. Yet, a look back at both of R. Herzog's responsa to the Ezra organization will show that this is not really the case. In the first version of the responsum, he gives Nahmanides' viewpoint equal billing with that of Maimonides, and in the second version, he comments primarily on the viewpoint of Nahmanides. Therefore, Nahmanides' view seems to have been far more important to R. Herzog than he is willing to admit here.

Be that as it may, R. Herzog has to explain to R. Roth why, in their war against the Arabs, Jews must fight for territory beyond the borders designated for them by the UN partition plan, an issue that R. Roth had raised in his critique of R. Herzog's views:

> However, regarding [the battle for] Jerusalem, this is rescuing [the people of] Israel from the danger of death and famine alike, for they [i.e, the Arabs] are not allowing [anyone] to bring any food to Jerusalem, and [therefore] we should rule that those who are defending the holy city are fulfilling [the commandment] of conquering the land. And even though this region will not be ours entirely, nonetheless we will have great strength there because we are the majority. The goal of the enemy, as is known to me with great clarity, is to force the remaining [population of Jews] to flee Jerusalem after they do much killing, God forbid. ... I say that this [defense of Jerusalem] is in the category of conquest [of the land]—that is, to preserve the [Jewish] community. ... And with regard to the

48. Ibid., pp. 219–21.
49. Ibid., p. 222.

Arab villages in the Arab region: Even if the goal here is not total conquest but rather weakening the power of the enemy, this [action] in itself is in the category of conquering Jerusalem in that we will nonetheless be able to hold on to the portion [of land] that in the end belongs to us, thank God. And for this [goal], we must rely on experts who thoroughly understand [how to fight] the war.[50]

R. Herzog focuses his retort mostly on why Jews must continue to fight for Jerusalem, even though it is supposed to become an international capital. R. Herzog contends that the military campaign here is necessary, first, because the Jewish sectors of Jerusalem, at present, are under siege from Arab forces and their inhabitants are in danger of dying at the hands of the enemy or from starvation, and they therefore need to be rescued. That is, the fight for Jerusalem is very much part of the imperative of *'ezrat yisra'el mi-yad tsar*. R. Herzog also adds that the fight for Jerusalem is necessary, for even if Jerusalem is ultimately given up to international control, the preservation of the Jewish communities in the city is still included in the fulfillment of the commandment to conquer the land in accordance with Nahmanides' views. R. Herzog indicates here that this commandment can be performed not just by military means but by Jewish settlement. That is, "conquest" is to be equated with property ownership, not necessarily political sovereignty. Indeed, a number of interpreters have claimed that when Nahmanides spoke about conquering the land, he meant the former rather than latter. R. Herzog, however, seems to feel that both types of conquest fulfill the precept.

Why, then, should Jews continue to fight for territory other than Jerusalem that is outside the designated boundary of the Jewish state? R. Herzog handles this question by claiming that capturing this territory weakens the enemy so that Jews can hold on to the parts of Jerusalem that belong to them. It is not entirely clear what R. Herzog means here, but he seems to be suggesting that by fighting for Arab territory, Jews will diminish the strength of the Arabs forces as a whole, so that the latter will be incapable of driving the Jews out of Jerusalem.

R. Herzog's exchange with R. Roth is an excellent illustration of the challenges that R. Herzog faced in convincing some of his Orthodox compatriots of the gravity of the situation in Palestine. As we saw earlier, R. Herzog seemed to be aware of this challenge, and that is why he expended so much effort attempting to prove that Jews must join the armed struggle against the Arabs, despite the halakhic obstacles involved. Moreover, as Roness and Neuman have argued, R. Herzog attempted to establish his views within the parameters not just of wartime Halakhah but everyday Halakhah as well because he had to answer the doubts of his fellow Orthodox Jews who questioned

50. Ibid.

whether the conflict with the Arabs could be classified as a war in the formal halakhic sense and whether there was therefore an obligation to fight. R. Roth resists R. Herzog's thinking on all these issues. He not only rejects the notion that the conflict is a halakhically sanctioned war, he has serious doubts about whether Jews are required to participate in the fight against the Arabs within the strictures of everyday Halakhah, as well.

R. Roth's skepticism may have come as a surprise to R. Herzog. It is possible that R. Herzog consulted R. Roth because the latter had escaped eastern Europe in 1944, during the Holocaust, and he may have assumed that R. Roth would be sympathetic to his views on the conflict with the Arabs, seeing as they were based, at least in part, on judgments about the dire situation of both the Jewish community in Palestine and the Jewish people in the world as a whole. However, R. Roth would have none of it. The conflict could not be justified as a halakhic war, nor as a struggle serious enough to require Jews to fight from the standpoint of everyday Halakhah.

R. Herzog composed a number of other responsa having to do with the subject of war, but on the issues central to our study, they mostly reiterate the views that he presented in the responsa we have just examined.[51] We are therefore ready to sum up what we have learned from this material.

R. Herzog is the first thinker in our study to apply Halakhah to an actual war, and he does so in a fairly consistent fashion. He provides four reasons that the conflict with the Arabs is a mandatory war. Two are drawn from traditional halakhic sources. The conflict is a mandatory war because it is a war of self-defense in accordance with Maimonides' notion of 'ezrat yisra'el mi-yad tsar and because it fulfills the commandment to conquer the land of Israel in accordance with Nahmanides' position on kibush ha-arets. We witness some development in R. Herzog's thinking regarding these first two reasons. In his rejoinder to R. Roth's criticisms of his views, R. Herzog plays down the

---

51. See, for instance, PKOH 1:45, pp. 195–96, in which R. Herzog addresses a question posed by a R. Werner in Tiberias. We do not have the original query, but from R. Herzog's reply, it would seem that R. Werner inquired of R. Herzog about whether it was permitted to violate Halakhah by building a fence on the Sabbath around the Jewish neighborhood of Kiryat Shmu'el because of fear that it would be attacked by Arab forces. The exact date of the responsum is not given, but Neuman argues that the historical evidence indicates that this responsum must have been written before April of 1948. See Neuman, "Law of Obligatory War," in Levin and Shapira, eds. War and Peace in Jewish Tradition, 187, and sources cited p. 196n16. That would place this responsum between the earlier and later versions of the responsum composed to the Ezra organization. Another noteworthy essay is "'Al Hakamat ha-Medinah Kodem Bi'at ha-Mashiah," PKOH 2, Appendix 1, pp. 121–33. This essay is undated and was published after R. Herzog's lifetime, and it contains a rich discussion of most of the issues dealt with in this chapter. However, while the essay contains some information not dealt with in the responsa we have analyzed, it does not add anything substantive to the points most central to our concerns.

association of the conflict with the Arabs with Nahmanides' notion of *kibush ha-arets* compared to previous writings, while also playing up Maimonides' conception of *'ezrat yisra'el mi-yad tsar*. He also broadens his understanding of *kibush ha-arets* to include private property ownership in addition to military conquest.

Two other reasons are provided by R. Herzog for viewing the conflict with the Arabs as mandatory war that are based on his perceptions of the historical circumstances of the Jewish people. It has become clear in wake of the Holocaust that Jews must have an independent state as a place of refuge. Moreover, the faith of Jews throughout the world, having already been compromised by the Holocaust, would further be weakened were the Jews to be defeated.

These reasons for identifying the conflict with the Arabs as a mandatory war are innovative and bold. Here, R. Herzog is no longer drawing from traditional halakhic categories on war to justify his thinking; he is basing it on his own personal observations about the specific needs of the Jewish people in his time. Moreover, R. Herzog was surely aware that according to Halakhah, Jews may not wage a defensive war until an enemy has actually attacked—or, in the case of preemptive war, is about to attack—but he was willing to rule here that war is warranted for threats that have not yet materialized because of the potential danger they posed to the well-being of the Jewish people as a whole. In effect, R. Herzog is speaking here in the spirit of *hora'at sha'ah* but without using that terminology. In his judgment, the Jewish people are in such dire condition, both physically and spiritually, that emergency action is required.

The identification of the conflict with the Arabs with mandatory war allows R. Herzog to approve of military activities that are normally forbidden in non-war situations. The premise here is that wartime Halakhah is different from everyday Halakhah in permitting Jews to commit transgressions essential for waging war. Thus, R. Herzog allows Jews to participate in defensive and offensive military operations in violation of Sabbath law. He also permits conscription, even though one is not normally allowed to force an individual to endanger his life for others. R. Herzog also permits the killing of enemy civilians on the assumption that no war can be fought successfully otherwise. However, he is unable to come up with a definitive position on whether Arab civilians may be killed at random to deter the enemy from doing the same to Jewish civilians.

The absence of a Jewish king does not trouble R. Herzog because he believes that the Jewish people as a whole can assume the authority of a king. And even though the Jewish community fighting the war against the Arabs represents only a fraction of the Jewish people, R. Herzog believes that from a halakhic standpoint, the Jewish community in the land of Israel is equivalent to the Jewish nation in its entirety.

But most intriguing is R. Herzog's attempt to justify many of the same halakhic positions from the standpoint of everyday Halakhah. He seems to have been motivated to do so out of a desire to address his fellow Orthodox Jews, some of whom may have been skeptical that the conflict with the Arabs was indeed a war in the formal halakhic sense. R. Herzog was also undoubtedly mindful of the fact that the ultra-Orthodox community was opposed to the Zionist enterprise to begin with. R. Roth's negative reaction to R. Herzog's views is evidence of the challenges R. Herzog faced in convincing some of his Orthodox compatriots of his positions.

R. Herzog had little difficulty demonstrating that according to everyday Halakhah, Sabbath law could be violated in the conflict with the Arabs because Sabbath transgressions are always permitted when there is immediate danger to life. Conscription posed more of a challenge for everyday Halakhah, and here R. Herzog's views went through some development. In his earlier responsum to the Ezra organization, he argues that conscription can be justified within everyday Halakah because the Arabs are determined to annihilate the Jewish community, and thus all Jews are fighting in self-defense, which is perfectly permissible in everyday Halakhah. Moreover, because the physical security and spiritual well-being of Jews elsewhere is at stake, Jews once again have no choice but to take up arms. However, in the later version of the same responsum, R. Herzog provides a more complex halakhic argument for conscription in everyday Halakhah by questioning the assumption that Jews are not required to risk their lives to save others. A passage in the Jerusalem Talmud rules to the contrary. R. Herzog admits that this ruling is not accepted by the majority of later halakhic authorities, but he feels that it must be considered in light of another ruling by R. Kook dictating that a Jew must always be ready to risk his life to save the Jewish people from destruction whether or not the situation is one of war. According to R. Herzog, R. Kook's principle most certainly applies to the conflict with the Arabs because of what he feels is at stake with respect to the well-being of the Jewish community not just in Palestine but elsewhere.

These observations bring up R. Herzog's relationship with R. Kook on matters of war. R. Kook appears to have played an important role in R. Herzog's thinking on this subject. R. Herzog explicitly draws two key points from his predecessor: the one just mentioned regarding the obligation incumbent on every Jew to save the Jewish people from destruction, and, most important, the notion that in the absence of a king, the Jewish people as a whole has the authority to wage war. It is also likely that R. Herzog is indebted to R. Kook for the two-level framework that he uses to examine war in Halakhah. Like R. Kook, R. Herzog believes that there is a sharp division between everyday Halakhah and wartime Halakhah. It is also possible that R. Herzog's two-level approach was influenced by the Netsiv, who suggests a similar division between everyday Halakhah and wartime Halakhah. We saw that in his first responsum to the Ezra organization, R. Herzog, in fact, quotes the Nestiv on this point.

It is noteworthy that R. Herzog does not invoke R. Kook's notion that the laws of war are part of a larger body of special laws that were the prerogative of the king—*mishpat ha-melekh*—and concerned with communal welfare. R. Herzog treats the body of laws dealing with war as an independent area of Halakhah in its own right. While it is always perilous to make inferences from what an author does *not* say, here I believe R. Herzog's silence is significant. R. Kook's theory of *mishpat ha-melekh* would not have appealed to R. Herzog, for obvious reasons. According to R. Kook, this sector of Halakhah is in large part lost to us. The theory is therefore inimical to R. Herzog's view that Halakhah contained everything needed to guide Jews in their quest to re-establish Jewish sovereignty in their ancient homeland.

R. Herzog also goes beyond R. Kook in a number of important ways. Confronted with the reality of a Jewish state and the threat to its existence posed by its Arab enemies, R. Herzog was required to think about war in ways that R. Kook was not, seeing as he died before the state of Israel came into existence. Much of R. Herzog's challenge was to figure out whether the conflict with the Arabs qualified as a war in the formal halakhic sense and, if so, what kind of war it was, and as we have seen, he affirms that it was a mandatory war and provides no fewer than four reasons for that assessment.

R. Herzog also goes beyond R. Kook in arguing that the struggle with the Arabs is a mandatory war because it fulfills the commandment to conquer the land of Israel. R. Herzog's position here is inimical to R. Kook's way of thinking. The notion that Jews should wage war to conquer the land is one that R. Kook would not have considered, even if he had lived in R. Herzog's time. R. Kook did not believe the Jewish state should be founded through war or violence. To the contrary, the state had to be a beacon of peace in a world in danger of being destroyed by war and violence. Therefore R. Kook would not have approved of R. Herzog's position here.

This last point leads us to one of the most important differences between R. Herzog and R. Kook, which is that R. Herzog's overall view of war is far more positive than that of his predecessor. This difference is in part due to the different historical contexts in which they lived. R. Herzog wholeheartedly supported the Jewish community in Palestine waging war, in part because he felt he had no choice. War was necessary because of the immediate threat to the Jewish community in Palestine as well as the potential threats to Jews around the world. R. Kook never had to face this kind of situation. However, R. Herzog also seems to have had a more positive view of war quite apart from the historical context. His notion that conflict with the Arabs is a fulfillment of the commandment to conquer the land is proof of that. Here war is not about self-defense but takes on an offensive character for the purpose of fulfilling messianic goals that transcend the immediate situation.

I conclude with some thoughts about the place of R. Herzog's halakhic views on war in the history of religious Zionism. With the outbreak of the 1948 war, other religious Zionist rabbis were grappling with halakhic questions involving military matters similar to those that preoccupied R. Herzog. Perhaps the most prominent of these figures was R. Kook's son, R. Tsevi Yedudah Kook (1891–1982). The younger Kook published a pamphlet, on June 6, 1948, at the beginning of Israel's War of Independence, entitled *Regarding the Commandment of the Land* (*Le-Mitsvat ha-Arets*) in order to argue that yeshiva students were required to serve in the Israeli army. The pamphlet was written to counter a view that was being publicized at the time in R. Tsevi Yehudah Kook's circles claiming that his father did not approve of yeshiva students serving in the army. The proponents of this position cited as proof a letter the elder R. Kook had composed during the First World War, when he lived in England, in which he had adamantly opposed the drafting of yeshiva students into the British army. R. Tsevi Yehduah Kook angrily rejected this position with the argument that the situation in England was completely different from that in Palestine, and that his father's views therefore could not be used to draw any conclusions about whether yeshiva students should take up arms in the conflict with the Arabs. R. Tsevi Yehudah Kook composed the pamphlet to spell out his positions on why yeshiva students were indeed required to fight.[52]

One of the essays in R. Tsevi Yehudah Kook's pamphlet was devoted to the halakhic aspects of the issue, and what is striking about it is that he uses many of the same arguments that R. Herzog did to make the case for conscription.[53] In the first section of the essay, R. Tsevi Yehudah Kook explores reasons for joining the Israeli army that are concerned with what he terms "temporal life" (*hayey sha'ah*), and the arguments he presents here are very similar to those that R. Herzog offered regarding conscription within the parameters of everyday Halakhah. R. Tsevi Yehudah Kook tells us that Jews are required to serve because of the imperative to save the lives of other Jews who are in danger. The Jerusalem Talmud is cited as support for the notion that a Jew must subject himself to possible danger in order to save a fellow Jew who is in certain danger, though R. Tsevi Yehudah Kook shows little concern about the fact that this is a minority opinion. R. Tsevi Yehudah Kook also argues that, according to his father, a Jew must even subject himself to certain danger

52. The five essays are reprinted in *Li-Netivot Yisra'el* (Beit El, Israel: Mei-Avney ha-Makom, 2003), vol. 1, chapters 15, 21–24. The historical background to the composition of this pamphlet is recounted in R. Neryah Gutel, "'*Hufshah Li-Veney Yeshivateinu' o Mitsvat Giyus: 'Al Igeret hR'YH Kuk ve-Pulmus Parshanutah*," in *'Amadot: 'Am—Medinah—Torah*, vol. 1 ed. Moshe Rahimi (Elkanah / Rehovot, Israel: Mikhelet Orot Yisra'el, 2010), vol. 1, pp. 25–40, especially pp. 31–36; R. Shlomo Aviner, "*Korot Rabeinu 'al Giyus Talmidey Yeshivot*," *'Iturey Yerushalayim* 85 (Elul, 5773 [2013]): 3–12.

53. "*Le-Mitsvat ha-Arets*," *Li-Netivot Yisra'el*, vol. 1, chapter 23, pp. 168–83.

when the Jewish people is threatened with destruction. All these arguments, as we have seen, are critical to R. Herzog's approach to conscription when it comes to everyday Halakhah.[54]

In the second section of the essay, R. Tsevi Yehudah Kook provides reasons for army service having to do with what he terms "eternal life" (*hayey 'olam*), and here the arguments assume that the conflict with the Arabs is a war in the formal halakhic sense. Once again, we find remarkable similarities to the views of R. Herzog. R. Tsevi Yehudah Kook is convinced that the conflict with the Arabs fulfills the commandment of conquering the land in accordance with Nahmanides' opinion, and he spends a good deal of energy making this point. However, he also mentions that the conflict is about the commandment to "save Israel from the clutches of the enemy," in accordance with Maimonides' views.[55] Toward the end of the essay, R. Tsevi Yehudah Kook also invokes the notion of sanctification of the divine name (*kidush hashem*) as a motivation for fighting the Arabs. These arguments are very similar to those used by R. Herzog to argue for conscription within the context of wartime Halakhah.[56]

R. Tsevi Yehudah Kook is generally credited with having pushed religious Zionism in a militaristic direction. His influence had an enormous effect, not just on religious Zionism, but also on Israeli politics in general, especially after the Six Day War. Moreover, as Eli Holtser has shown, the turn in R. Tsevi Yehudah Kook's thought toward a more militaristic Zionism began much earlier than many scholars assume.[57] In fact, his thinking began to take on a militaristic hue not after the Six Day war, but with the publication in 1948 of the very pamphlet just described.[58] However, what emerges from our analysis in this chapter is that the halakhic aspects of the transformation in R. Tsevi Yehudah Kook's thinking may owe something to R. Herzog. Both of R. Herzog's responsa to the Ezra movement in which he lays out his positions on conscription predate the essay of R. Tsevi Yehudah Kook on that subject, the first one by a full three months. We cannot be sure that R. Tsevi Yehudah Kook borrowed his ideas from R. Herzog. In his essay, R. Tsevi Yehudah Kook does not refer to his contemporary. However, there is remarkable similarity between R. Tsevi Yehudah Kook's views and those of R. Herzog. Moreover, it is likely that R. Tsevi Yehudah Kook was familiar with R. Herzog's views, seeing as R. Herzog was the Chief Ashkenazi Rabbi of the Jewish community

54. "*Le-Mitsvat ha-Arets*," 168–71.
55. "*Le-Mitsvat ha-Arets*," 171–80.
56. "*Le-Mitsvat ha-Arets*," 180–83.
57. Eli Holtser, *Herev Pipiyot be-Yadam: Activizm Tseva'i be-Hagutah shel ha-Tsiyonut ha-Datit* (Jerusalem: Hartman Institute, 2009), chapter 6.
58. Holster, *Herev Pipiyot be-Yadam*, 207–8.

in Israel, and his views would have been widely publicized in religious Zionist circles. Therefore, it is certainly possible that R. Tsevi Yehudah Kook did indeed adopt R. Herzog's views. If that is case, R. Herzog should be seen as having played a critical role in the development of R. Tsevi Yehudah Kook's militaristic Zionism, an ideology that would have such a significant impact in subsequent years.

CHAPTER 5

⌒⋎⌒

R. Eliezer Yehudah Waldenberg

R. Eliezer Yehudah Waldenberg (1915–2006) was an eminent halakhic authority, best known for his monumental work *Tsits Eli'ezer*, a collection of responsa consisting of twenty-two volumes.[1] He was born in Jerusalem and lived there his entire life. He served in a number of rabbinic positions, the most prestigious of which was judge on the Rabbinic Supreme Court of Jerusalem, from 1981 to 1985. He was perhaps best known for his expertise in medical Halakhah. He was the rabbi of the Shaare Zedek hospital in Jerusalem, a position that provided him the opportunity to formulate many of his halakhic decisions on medical matters. In 1976, he was awarded the Israel Prize for rabbinic literature.

With respect to the subject of war in Halakhah, R. Waldenberg is perhaps best characterized as a figure of moderate importance. On the one hand, he produced a pioneering work on this subject as part of a three-volume set on Halakhah and politics, *Hilkhot Medinah*.[2] Written in the 1950s, this work was one of the first attempts by a major halakhic authority living in the newly established state of Israel to deal with the reality and consequences of the Jewish return to political power. Moreover, R. Waldenberg authored several responsa on war that appear in *Tsits Eli'ezer*. On the other hand, R. Waldenberg's treatment of war in *Hilkhot Medinah* is of little practical importance because of its utopian character. Much of the discussion in this work is on such issues as the structure of the army in biblical times and the laws for maintaining holiness within the army camp, topics that would be of little relevance to a modern and secular Israeli army. By contrast, not much attention is paid in this

---

1. *Tsits Eli'ezer* (Jerusalem, 1945–1994).
2. *Sefer Hilkhot Medinah* (Jerusalem, 1951).

work to such timely issues as combat ethics. As for R. Waldenberg's responsa on war, some of them deal with practical issues, but the number of responsa focused on war occupy only a tiny fraction of his *Tsits Eli'ezer*. Against this background, it is not surprising that though R. Waldenberg's views on war are cited in modern halakhic and academic discussions of the topic, it is not with as much frequency as those of other halakhic authorities.[3]

Yet regardless of R. Waldenberg's influence on rabbinic authorities who grapple with war, his views on the questions central to this study are very much worthy of our attention. R. Waldenberg deals with the halakhic challenges of war in the moral sphere in a number of places in his writings. He is particularly concerned with the issue of conscription, a topic that for him serves as the focal point for the moral difficulties that war raises. Moreover, his treatment of the topic provides new perspectives on conscription that we have not yet seen in our study.

HILKHOT MEDINAH II, 4:3

R. Waldenberg first raises the difficulty of making halakhic sense of conscription in the second volume of *Hilkhot Medinah*, in a chapter devoted to discretionary war. R. Waldenberg asks specifically why a Jewish king is allowed to endanger the lives of his subjects in this type of war.[4] He does not elaborate on the motivation for this question, but he appears to be bothered by the fact that unlike mandatory wars, discretionary wars are not commanded directly by God, nor are they fought necessarily for defensive purposes. Why, then, may a king risk the lives of his soldiers for this kind of war?

R. Waldenberg responds by arguing that discretionary wars are permitted despite the risks to Jewish soldiers who fight in them because war in general functions by its own set of halakhic norms that are different from those that

---

3. The legacy of R. Waldenberg's treatment of war in Halakhah is discussed by Yosef Ahituv, *"Min ha-Sefer el ha-Sayif: 'Al Demuto ha-Hazuyah shel ha-Tsava ha-Yisra'eli 'al pi ha-Torah ba-Shanim ba-Rishonot le-Kum ha-Medinah,"* in *Sheney 'Evrey ha-Gesher: Dat u-Medinah be-Reshit Darkah shel Yisra'el*, eds. Mordekhai Bar-On and Tsevi Tsameret (Jerusalem: Yad Yitshak ben Tsevi, 2002), 425–31. The following are examples of recent studies on war in Halakhah in which R. Waldenberg's views are cited and analyzed: Michael J. Broyde, "Just Wars, Just Battles and Just Conduct in Jewish Law: Jewish Law is Not a Suicide Pact!" in *War and Peace in the Jewish Tradition*, eds. Lawrence Schiffman and Joel B. Wolowelsky (New York: Yeshiva University Press, 2007), 2–3; Yitzchak Avi Roness, *"'Al Musariyutah shel ha-Milhamah be-Sifrut ha-Halakhah be-Me'ah ha-'Esrim,"* in *Sefer 'Amadot: 'Am—Medinah—Torah*, vol. 1, ed. Moshe Rahimi (Elkanah / Rehovot, Israel: Mikhlelet Orot Yisra'el, 2010), 202–4.

4. *Hilkhot Medinah*, vol. 2 (henceforth HM 2), 4:3, p. 119. This chapter is reproduced in a later responsum in *Tsits Eli'ezer* (henceforth TsE) (Jerusalem, 1994), 20:43, pp. 103–13.

govern everyday life.[5] The reason war has this special status is that it is a natural and universal phenomenon for human beings, and all nations are therefore
allowed to engage in this activity. The presumption here seems to be that if
war is natural and universal, it must have God's approval despite the loss of
life it incurs. As his discussion proceeds, it becomes clear that R. Waldenberg's
inspiration for this position ultimately comes from the Netsiv, whose views
on this matter we have already encountered on several occasions in our study.
According to the Netsiv, war is permissible because "that is the way the world
was founded," a statement suggesting that war is both natural and universal.[6]

In addition, R. Waldenberg argues that R. Kook's views on war are exactly
the same as those of the Netsiv. R. Kook also believes that wartime Halakhah
is different from everyday Halakhah, that Halakhah creates norms unique to
war because it is a natural and universal phenomenon, and that conscription
is permitted for this reason. This interpretation of R. Kook is at odds with the
one we presented earlier in this study. We argued that while R. Kook appears
to have followed the Netsiv on the general notion that wartime Halakhah is
different from everyday Halakhah, R. Kook does not adopt the Netsiv's view
that war is allowed in Halakhah because it is natural and universal. Rather,
war is permitted because of halakhic decree. It is therefore sanctioned because
of divine norms, not natural law, and those norms are directed only to Jews,
not to all of humanity. We encapsulated the differences between the two
approaches by characterizing the Netsiv's view as naturalistic-universalistic
and that of R. Kook as halakhic-particularistic.[7]

But let us see how R. Waldenberg arrived at his interpretation of R. Kook.
R. Waldenberg believes that R. Kook supports a naturalistic view of war based
on a statement the latter makes in his exchange with R. Pines. We have already
examined a portion of this exchange in chapter 3, but R. Waldenberg's interest

---

5. My analysis does not follow the precise sequence of the arguments presented
by R. Waldenberg. I have reordered them in order to provide a clear exposition of
his views.

6. Some commentators reject this reading and claim that the the Netsiv's intent
is only that war is a universal convention among human beings for the purpose of
settling conflicts. That is, "the world" that "was founded" such that war has become
ubiquitous, is the world of human convention, not the world of nature. This appears
to be the manner in which R. Sha'ul Yisraeli understood the Netsiv's position in his
essay on Kibiyeh which will be discussed in the next chapter. Yitshak Kofman also
rejects the notion that the the Netsiv saw war as natural. See his article, *"Et Milhamah
ve-'Et Shalom 'al pi ha-Netsiv," Merhavim* 6 (1997): 285–97. This matter is also discussed
by Ahituv, *"Min ha-Sefer el ha-Sayif,"* 344–45, and Roness, *"'Al Musariyutah,"* 201–2.
However, I believe that the reading of the the Netsiv according to which war is an
expression of human nature is the better one because it reads less into the text than
the alternative interpretation. Attempts to deny that the Netsiv viewed war as natural
betray an apologetic intent. It also appears that R. Waldenberg adopted the reading of
the Netsiv that I support.

7. Above, pp. 64–65.

is in a section of the discussion that we have not yet looked at. In this section, R. Pines takes the position that in mandatory war one is allowed to violate all halakhic prohibitions, even the most serious ones, in order to ensure victory, and he cites as proof the biblical example of Yael.[8] According to rabbinic tradition, Yael agreed to engage in sexual relations with the Canaanite general Sisera so that she could kill him and save the Israelites from the Canaanite army Sisera had just led into battle against them.[9] According to rabbinic law, engaging in illicit sexual relations is forbidden even on pain of death, and yet Yael is lauded by the rabbis for her actions on behalf of the Jewish people. R. Pines concludes, therefore, that the need to achieve victory in mandatory war allows for the transgression of any and all prohibitions.[10]

R. Kook firmly rejects R. Pines's opinion:

> Where have we found a dispensation for [committing sins involving] illicit sexual relationships with respect to mandatory war? Even [with] other prohibitions, we find no dispensation—except for those matters that they [i.e., the rabbis] allowed in the [army] camp, [reported] in [Mishnah] 'Eruvin 17, and all the [dispensations] for [eating] forbidden foods and the like, when they [i.e., the soldiers] cannot find permitted [food], [all this being] in accordance with Maimonides' [ruling] in [Hilkhot] Melakhim 8:1. And in this [matter], there is no difference between mandatory war and discretionary [war]. And aside from [the dispensations for] these prohibitions, there are no [other] dispensations, even in mandatory war. Moreover, one cannot by any means infer anything from [the fact] that in it [i.e., war] *we expose ourselves to the dangers of killing and being killed in accordance with the nature of the world.* For that is the very commandment [of war]. ... [From] the explanation for the matter of the dispensation of sending [soldiers to be exposed] to the dangers of wars—whether it [i.e., this dispensation] is something unique in being part of the laws of kings, or [unique] in some other fashion—one does not, by any means, make a ruling from it regarding other prohibitions [in war].[11]

R. Kook rebuts R. Pines's interpretation of Yael's actions by arguing that war does not give us wholesale license to violate the commandments, and certainly not a commandment as serious as the prohibition against adultery.[12] Indeed, R. Kook admits, there are some commandments that the rabbis allowed Jewish soldiers to violate while fighting a war, such as certain prohibitions

---

8. Judges 4:17–24.

9. BT *Yevamot* 103a, *Nazir* 23b, *Horayyot* 10b.

10. Rakover, *Mesirut Nefesh*, 224. See also 142–43 for Rakover's explication of this passage.

11. HM 2, p. 120; R. Kook, MK, responsum 144, pp. 326–27 (my emphasis).

12. In subsequent discussion, R. Kook claims that Yael's behavior was nonetheless justified because she was acting according to the principle of *hora'at sha'ah*.

involving the consumption of forbidden foods. However, these are exceptions, and beyond them there are no dispensations. R. Kook also preempts any argument that in war all commandments can be violated because war allows us to override the prohibition to murder. Permission to kill in war in no way entails permission to transgress other halakhic norms, for the very essence of the commandment to wage war requires the taking of life, and thus no commandment is really being "overridden" when in war we are permitted to kill.[13]

What does all this have to do with R. Waldenberg's views on war? First of all, in the passage just quoted R. Kook provides precedent for R. Waldenberg's contention that war is governed by unique halakhic norms in allowing a king to send soldiers into combat despite the dangers involved—though R. Kook emphasizes that one must not use this dispensation to justify other violations when fighting a war. However, in R. Waldenberg's subsequent discussion, it becomes clear that just as important for him is R. Kook's reference in this passage to war as an activity in which "we expose ourselves to the dangers of killing and being killed in accordance with the nature of the world," a statement which I have highlighted with emphasis in the citation above because it can easily be missed. The last part of the statement that refers to the killing of war being "in accordance with the nature of the world" is taken by R. Waldenberg to allude to the position of the Netsiv, for whom war is justified because "that is the way the world was founded." R. Waldenberg subsequently summarizes R. Kook's views and informs us that R. Kook "alluded with this—[that is,] with the essential notion that war is different [from ordinary activities]—to the words of the Netsiv."[14] R. Waldenberg believes that like the Netsiv, R. Kook holds the view that a king may endanger the lives of his soldiers in war because war is a natural and universal phenomenon and it thus has divine approval.

In the course of his discussion, R. Waldenberg also cites verbatim another passage from R. Kook's exchange with R. Pines that elaborates on the special halakhic norms that govern war. This passage is one that we have already seen in our earlier discussion of R. Kook:

> [T]he concerns of the issue of wars are separate from this matter of "you shall live by them" (Lev. 18:5). For discretionary war (*milhemet reshut*) is also permitted, and how is it that we find a dispensation to place many lives in danger for the sake of expansion [of territory] (*harhavah*)?[15] But war and the laws of the collective are different [from those of the individual]. Perhaps it [i.e., the body

13. According to a portion of the passage omitted here, the same point can be illustrated with the administering of the death penalty which again should not be viewed as overriding the commandment to preserve life, for here too the very essence of the commandment to implement the death penalty requires the taking of life.

14. HM 2, p. 120.

15. MT *Melakhim* 5:1.

of laws regarding war] was part of the laws of kingship that were undoubtedly many [in number] and given to the nation. ... Among them [i.e., the laws of kingship] are also laws of war, both mandatory war and discretionary war.[16] But it is impossible to learn from this [i.e., the laws of war] about another area [i.e., the laws governing individual behavior].[17]

R. Kook informs us that a solider is required to endanger his life in war, even though in normal situations the passage in Leviticus, "and you shall live by them," ordinarily absolves one of the obligation to risk one's life in order to fulfill a commandment. The reason that war is exceptional is that it is governed by a sector of Halakhah that is communal in focus, and these laws are completely separate from the norms that govern individuals in everyday life. Proof for the exceptional nature of war is that a king is permitted to wage a discretionary war for the expansion of territory, a cause that does normally justify the loss of life. Yet we must keep in mind that R. Waldenberg reads this passage in light of his view that, in R. Kook's thinking, war is permitted despite the loss of life it causes because it is a natural and universal phenomenon.

The connection that R. Waldenberg makes between the views of the Netsiv and those of R. Kook regarding war as a natural and universal phenomenon is elaborated on in a passage that appears later on in R. Waldenberg's responsum:

> Moreover, from the words of the explanations of *Ha'amek Davar* and *Mishpat Kohen* emerges and sprouts the seed of a distinction that the matter of exposing oneself [in war] to "the dangers of killing and being killed in accordance with the nature of the world" is different [from other matters], and that one [may] say [about war] that "that is the way the world was founded." We have found something like this [notion] also in the book *Shem Aryeh* 14:27 [the author of which] writes by way of explanation that [with regard to] even those things that are a source of danger, when it concerns a matter that is [in accordance with] the custom of the world and is by way of necessity, one should not be wary etc. And similarly, it is permissible to [engage] in every matter that is necessary for [our normal activity in] the world, such as going to war which is [a situation of] certain danger—even a discretionary war.[18]

16. The last two sentences appear only in the original text of R. Kook. I have included them here because they make the passage more understandable, and R. Waldenberg appears to have assumed that his reader would be familiar with the full text.

17. HM 2, p. 120; MK, responsum 143, pp. 315–66. Above, p. 66. R. Waldenberg's text of R. Kook has minor differences with the published version. I have translated from the latter.

18. HM 2, p. 121. This passage is, in fact, one long and complex sentence that is difficult to translate. I have therefore broken the sentence up in order to make it readable in the English.

In this passage, R. Waldenberg assumes again that R. Kook and the Netsiv both view war as a natural activity. A clear equation is made between R. Kook's statement that war is "in accordance with the nature of the world" with the Netsiv's view that war is permitted because "that is the way the world was founded."

Moreover, R. Waldenberg informs us here that the viewpoint of the Netsiv and R. Kook is in turn explained by the position of R. Aryeh Leib Lifshits (1808–88), a halakhic authority to whom R. Waldenberg refers by the title of his major halakhic work, *Shem Aryeh*. The *Shem Aryeh* briefly alludes to the issue of war in a responsum dealing with the general question of how one assesses whether an action is dangerous enough to one's life to render it forbidden from a halakhic standpoint. Halakhah does not permit an individual to risk his life unnecessarily, but given that there are dangers in many of the ordinary activities we engage in on a day-to-day basis, what criteria does one use to determine when an activity carries with it sufficient risk to be deemed impermissible? For instance, does a merchant embarking on a voyage by sea to conduct business, place himself in a position of sufficient danger that he should be forbidden from traveling in this manner? The *Shem Aryeh* concludes that actions that bring with them some degree of danger are not forbidden if they are performed in accordance with the "customs of the world" (*minhago shel 'olam*) or are done "by way of necessity" (*derekh hekhreah*) in that they are required for everyday life. Therefore, the merchant is by no means forbidden from traveling by sea, seeing as this action is the normal way merchants do business, and it is necessary for his livelihood. Most interesting—and relevant for R. Waldenberg's purposes—is that the *Shem Aryeh* includes the waging of war among "normal" activities that carry an acceptable level of risk. Here, too, according to the *Shem Aryeh*, war is in accordance with the ways of the world and is required by necessity, and it is for this reason that Halakhah allows the waging of war despite the danger it presents to its participants.[19]

At no point does the *Shem Aryeh* mention the Netsiv's views on war. However, R. Waldenberg sees the remarks of the *Shem Aryeh* as an explication of the latter's position. The Netsiv tells us that war is justified despite the dangers to human life because "that is the way the world was founded," and, according to R. Waldenberg, the *Shem Aryeh*'s statement that war is in accordance with "customs of the world" is meant as a reference to the Netsiv's viewpoint. Therefore, the *Shem Aryeh*'s reflections on war are an attempt, in R. Waldenberg's thinking, to make sense of the Netsiv's elliptical remarks on that subject.

---

19. *She'elot u-Teshuvot Shem Aryeh*, (Vilnius: Rom Family, 1874), 2:27 pp. 37b–39b. See also TsE, 15:37, pp. 95–96, where the *Shem Aryeh*'s views are applied by R. Waldenberg to a case of experimental medical treatment.

The key points that emerge from R. Waldenberg's discussion of war in *Hilkhot Medinah* is that despite the loss of life it causes, war is permitted on the basis of the notion that it is natural and universal, and therefore the halakhic directives that regulate it are different from those that govern day-to-day life. R. Waldenberg views both the Netsiv and R. Kook as authoritative sources for this approach, citing the *Shem Aryeh* as added support. Therefore, R. Waldenberg has an answer to his original question. The reason that a Jewish king may force his soldiers to fight in a discretionary war despite the dangers involved, is that war is governed by a special set of laws.

TSITS ELI'EZER 12:57, 13:100

The issue of conscription is again taken up by R. Waldenberg in a later discussion contained in a responsum in volume 12 of *Tsits Eli'ezer*, which was published in 1976.[20] In the very next volume of the same work, published two years later, R. Waldenberg presents a revised version of the responsum that was inspired by deeper reflection on the issues it discusses.[21] The positions in the second responsum do not differ in substance from those of the first, but they are significantly expanded and supplemented by more supporting material. We will therefore focus our analysis on this second responsum.

The question that prompted the initial responsum is not about conscription. It is about whether a soldier is required, or even allowed, to save the life of a fellow soldier who is lying wounded in the field of combat. However, in dealing with this query, R. Waldenberg addresses the question of conscription as well.[22]

In his attempt to unpack the question, R. Waldenberg informs us that a soldier lying wounded in the field of battle would have, at the very least, the halakhic status of someone who is in a situation of "possible danger" (*safek sakanah*), seeing as he may die of his wounds or be killed by the enemy. Alternatively, depending on the circumstances, he may even be in a situation of "certain danger" (*vaday sakanah*). Moreover, according to R. Waldenberg, the presumption is that a person who attempts to rescue such an individual would have to place *himself* in a situation of possible danger. Therefore, the essential question in halakhic terms is whether a soldier in the heat of a battle

---

20. TsE, 12:57, pp. 157–59.

21. TsE 13:100, pp. 203–7.

22. TsE, 12:57, p. 157; 13:100, p. 203. Broyde (p. 2) describes these two responsa as dealing with the case of soldiers being held captive by the enemy, and the question is whether other soldiers are obligated to risk their lives in order to rescue them. That is not the scenario being discussed here—though there are certainly some similarities between the case of captive soldiers and that of soldiers wounded in the field of combat, the scenario that R. Waldenberg, in fact, discusses.

may enter a situation of possible danger to rescue a wounded comrade who is either in a situation of possible or certain danger.[23]

R. Waldenberg begins his response with the observation that in non-war situations, one is not required to endanger oneself to save the life of another individual. As support for his position, R. Waldenberg cites R. David ben Solomon ibn Zimra (1479–1573), better known by his acronym, Radbaz, who remarks that one who attempts such a rescue is a "pious fool" (*hasid shoteh*), a statement suggesting that such an action is not absolutely prohibited, but is strongly discouraged.[24] R. Waldenberg also rules that if the individual requiring rescue is only in a situation of possible danger, one is not even *permitted* to endanger oneself to save him, presumably because the wounded individual may, in fact, survive without any help, and risking one's life to rescue someone in this situation would therefore place one needlessly in danger.[25]

However, R. Waldenberg goes on to argue that war is different from other situations, and therefore in war these rules do not apply. Proof for this conclusion begins with an analysis of the more general question of why a king is permitted to wage war at all, seeing as he is endangering the lives of his soldiers by taking them into combat. According to R. Waldenberg, the permissibility of war is implied in *Tosafot*'s interpretation of a talmudic passage in *Shevu'ot* 35b, according to which a king may sacrifice the lives of up to a sixth of his army when waging a discretionary war. R. Waldenberg proceeds to explain why Halakhah allows for such mayhem. One explanation is that of the Netsiv, whom R. Waldenberg had cited in his earlier discussion in *Hilkhot Medinah*. War is a natural phenomenon, and therefore we must accept it and its consequences, which include risking the lives of soldiers whom the king sends into combat. R. Waldenberg also cites R. Kook, as he did in his earlier discussion in *Hilkhot Medinah*. Yet here R. Waldenberg departs from his earlier discussion by presenting R. Kook's views as an *alternative* to those of the Netsiv:

> What emerges from the words of these eminent sages is that we have before us two definitions and explanations for the unique laws of war, and they are: A. because in this way and on this foundation the world has been established B. because the laws of the collective and the guidance of the nation are different [from those governing individuals]—that is to say, that this [category of laws] is for the improvement and security of the people and the nation.[26]

In this passage, R. Waldenberg sees the Netsiv and R. Kook as defending two different positions. R. Waldenberg's views of the Netsiv are unchanged

23. TsE, 13:100, p. 203.
24. *Teshuvot Radbaz* (New York: Otsar ha-Sefarim, 1966), 3:1, p. 52.
25. TsE, 13:100, pp. 203–4.
26. TsE, 13:100, p. 204.

from his earlier presentation. As before, the Netsiv is depicted as upholding the view that war is permitted because it is a natural and universal phenomenon. However, R. Waldenberg's description of R. Kook's view is now quite different. R. Kook is no longer presented as supporting the position that war is permitted because it is natural and universal, but because of special halakhic norms that are communal in focus and apply, it would seem, to Jews alone. Most tellingly, nowhere in this discussion do we see any mention of the passage in R. Kook cited by R. Waldenberg in the earlier treatment in *Hilkhot Medinah* in which R. Kook alludes to the notion that war is "in accordance with the nature of the world." In his responsum, R. Waldenberg has therefore brought R. Kook's thinking on war into line with the way he was presented in our own discussion of him earlier in this study. R. Kook's approach to war is halakhic-particularistic versus that of the Netsiv which is naturalistic-universalistic.

R. Waldenberg also cites two authorities, each of whom, he claims, supports one of the two theories. The first is R. Moses Schreiber (1762–1839) better known by his book *Hatam Sofer*, who, in a responsum in this work, speaks of wars waged by a Jewish king as being justified because they are for "the good and welfare of the Jewish nation," a position that echoes that of R. Kook.[27] The second is the *Shem Aryeh*, whom we encountered earlier. He supports the viewpoint of the Netsiv because he sees war as a natural activity. Thus, the dichotomy between the Netsiv and R. Kook is not confined to these two thinkers. They represent different approaches to war found among other halakhic authorities.

At this point, R. Waldenberg is ready to respond to the original question about whether a soldier is required to risk his life in order to rescue a fellow soldier who is wounded in combat:

> Given that we have learned from what has been stated that war is different [from everyday situations], it is reasonable to say that just as one must not learn from an [activity being] permitted in war that it would be permitted in another situation [i.e., in everyday life], so too one must not learn from an [activity being] forbidden in another situation [i.e., in everyday life] that it would be permitted in war. That is to say, that just as the principle of "and you shall live by them" (Lev. 18:5) does not apply in war, it is also reasonable to say that the principle of "and your kinsman shall live with you," [Lev. 25:36]—which they [i.e., the rabbis] interpret, to mean "your life takes priority over his" (BT *Bava Metsi'a* 62a)— does not apply in war. Rather, all men [fighting] in war are together obligated to give their lives, each and every one, for the rescue of their fellow [soldiers]. This

27. R. Moses Schreiber, *She'elot u-Teshuvot Hatam Sofer* (Bratislava, 1912), 5:44, pp. 20a–21a.

point is also one of the principles of laws governing the collective and is in the category of [actions meant for] leading the nation and advancing its welfare.[28]

R. Waldenberg concludes that a soldier is required to make every effort to rescue a comrade wounded in combat despite the dangers involved. Normally, one has no obligation to risk one's life to save another person who is in danger. That principle is based on the well-known talmudic passage discussed earlier in this study that focused on a situation in which two people are in the desert and one has with him a jug that contains enough water only for one person to survive the journey. Should the person carrying the jug share the water and both die? Or should the person with the jug drink the water himself for his own survival and allow his companion to die? The decisive ruling is that of R. Akiva, who supports the latter option.[29] However, according to R. Waldenberg, this principle does not apply in war. R. Waldenberg refers to the view of R. Kook that the laws governing the nation differ from those governing individuals in everyday life because the former are concerned with the well-being of the entire collective. R. Waldenberg therefore concludes that just as a soldier is required to risk his life for the nation when going to war, so too, is he required to risk his life to save a companion who is wounded in the course of battle.

R. Waldenberg supports his position by looking at other halakhic rulings by rabbinic authorities in situations that involve danger to life. Normally, in such situations we are required to issue rulings that preserve life. Thus, for instance, according to the halakhic principle of *safek nefashot le-hakel*, we must be lenient in judging ambiguous situations involving the death penalty.[30] If a defendant has been implicated in a crime that is punished by the death penalty, but it is uncertain whether that person is, in fact, guilty, we err on the side of lenience, and we do not put that person to death. However, R. Waldenberg goes on to argue that in some situations, the imperative to preserve life is not heeded. For example, if a person is in a situation in which the mandate for martyrdom is for some reason unclear, that person is nonetheless required to give up his life for the sanctification of the divine name (*kidush ha-shem*). In this instance, therefore, a halakhic ruling that could result in the loss of life errs on the side of stringency rather than lenience. This ruling can be explained by the fact that the Torah does not insist on safeguarding the life of a Jew when martyrdom is required, as it does in other situations, and therefore even in a situation in which the mandate for martyrdom is unclear, one must take the stricter approach. Another case that illustrates the same point involves the

28. TsE, 13:100, p. 205.
29. Above, pp. 46–47.
30. BT *Bava Batra* 50b.

prohibition against adultery, which is one of three commandments that one must fulfill even if it means giving up one's life *(yehareg ve-al ya'avor)*. If a man is confronted with a situation in which he is forced to have sexual relations with a woman or be killed, and it is unclear whether the woman is married or not, the man must still accept death rather than risk transgressing the prohibition against adultery. Here, too, a halakhic ruling involving the potential loss of life comes down on the side of stringency, and that is because in cases involving the violation of a cardinal prohibition, such as adultery, the Torah, again, does not insist on preserving Jewish life as it does in other instances, and, thus, even in situations of ambiguity, a person must sacrifice his life.[31] Most significantly, the same logic in R. Waldenberg's thinking applies to a case in which a soldier lies wounded in the field of combat. His fellow soldiers are required to rescue him despite the possible dangers involved, even though in non-war situations that would not be the case, because in war, all soldiers must risk their lives to begin with. Here again, we err on the side of the more stringent ruling that may result in loss of life.[32]

Yet let us not lose sight of our focus, which is the issue of conscription. As we have seen, a good portion of R. Waldenberg's responsum is devoted to this issue because he must first explain why a Jewish king is permitted to wage war in the first place, seeing as he endangers his soldiers—before he deals with the question of whether a soldier must risk his life to save a wounded comrade. R. Waldenberg provides two justifications for why the king has this permission: one that relies on the halakhic-particularistic approach to war of R. Kook, and the second that depends on the naturalistic-universalistic approach of the Netsiv. Moreover, in seeing a dichotomy here between the views of his two predecessors, he has taken a position different from that in *Hilkhot Medinah*, where he saw harmony between them.

What prompted R. Waldenberg to change his mind on the relationship between the Netsiv and R. Kook? The simplest explanation is that in his later discussion, R. Waldenberg came to the conclusion that his earlier attempt to harmonize the two had been mistaken. He may have come to the realization—to my mind, correct—that in R. Kook's thinking, war was permitted solely because it was governed by special communal laws to be implemented by the king for the welfare of the Jewish people, not because R. Kook saw war as a natural phenomenon. Therefore, in this revised reading, R. Kook did not support the naturalistic approach of the Netsiv. What we have here are, in fact, two separate approaches.

---

31. The sources of these rulings are the *Terumat ha-Deshen* (New York, 1958), p. 30b, of R. Israel ben Petahiah Isserlein (1390–1460); and the commentary of the *Shakh*, R. Shabbetai ben Me'ir ha-Kohen (1621–62), on the *Shulhan 'Arukh*, 157:101.
32. TsE, 13:100, p. 205.

However, I suspect there is also a deeper issue here. As mentioned in my introductory remarks to this chapter, one of the limitations of *Hilkhot Medinah* is its utopian character. It deals with war in a highly idealized form, as depicted in ancient times. However, in his responsa in *Tsits Eli'ezer*, R. Waldenberg had to deal with war as an actual reality. Confronted with practical questions, such as whether a soldier may rescue a wounded comrade, he had no choice but to approach war in this manner. The different contexts may help explain the different approaches to war. As long as R. Waldenberg was dealing with war as an idealized phenomenon, he could speak of the notion that war was permitted because it was natural and universal, and he could therefore depict the Netsiv and R. Kook as supporting this approach. But dealing with war as a living reality in which Jewish soldiers were risking their lives and dying may have caused R. Waldenberg to revise his thinking. The notion that war was natural and universal implied that Jewish soldiers were sacrificing their lives for no particular reason; war was simply part of the natural order. R. Waldenberg therefore re-examined his sources and presented R. Kook's halakhic-particularistic perspective as an alternative to the naturalistic-universalistic approach of the Netsiv. This reading of R. Kook's position had the advantage of presenting the wars that the state of Israel had to fight in a more positive light because war was an institution designed to serve the needs of the Jewish people and bolster its welfare. This perspective furnished a far better justification for the sacrifices that Israeli soldiers were making than did describing war as a phenomenon that we accept just because that is the way the world is.

R. Waldenberg does not provide us with a great deal of information about the issues central to our study, but what he does say about them is significant. R. Waldenberg is similar to R. Herzog in adopting R. Kook's notion that wartime Halakhah is fundamentally different from everyday Halakhah. However, R. Waldenberg introduces a new perspective on war in Halakhah by placing the viewpoint of the Netsiv on equal footing with that of R. Kook. The Netsiv believed, just as R. Kook did, that wartime Halakhah is distinct from everyday Halakhah, but whereas R. Kook held that wartime norms are governed by special directives within Halakhah meant to guide Jewish behavior, the Netsiv was of the opinion that these norms are anchored in natural law and applicable to all human beings. R. Waldenberg therefore concludes that we have two perspectives here on the origins of wartime Halakhah. Moreover, R. Waldenberg believes that the two viewpoints represent larger schools of thought in Halakhah regarding war, each of which is supported by other halakhic authorities.

Yet it seems to have taken R. Waldenberg some time to appreciate the difference between R. Kook and the Netsiv. At first, R. Waldenberg argued that R. Kook adopted the Nestiv's view that war was a natural phenomenon on the basis of wording in a single passage in R. Kook's writings. But R. Waldenberg eventually came to the realization that the perspectives of these two thinkers were, in fact, quite different from each other.

R. Waldenberg is certainly not the first figure in our study to cite the Netsiv's view on war. We saw that R. Herzog did so as well. But R. Herzog mentions the Netsiv only in passing and relies primarily on R. Kook in formulating his views on war, while R. Waldenberg treats the Netsiv as a figure equal in importance to R. Kook.

All of these considerations, however, were background for R. Waldenberg's treatment of conscription. What justified the fact that a Jewish king or his equivalent could order his soldiers into battle at the risk of their lives? The question was especially pressing for discretionary wars that were not directly commanded by God and served no obvious defensive purpose. R. Waldenberg relies on both the Netsiv and R. Kook to answer this question. Both these predecessors argued that wartime Halakhah was fundamentally separate from everyday Halakhah, even though they gave different reasons for their positions, and the unique nature of the laws governing war allowed the king or his equivalent to send his soldiers to war, even one that was discretionary.

I would like to conclude with the observation that R. Waldenberg unwittingly introduces yet another perspective on the relationship between wartime Halakhah and everyday Halakhah. R. Waldenberg demonstrates that the Netsiv's naturalistic-universalistic perspective on war is not a lone view by citing the *Shem Aryeh*. According to the *Shem Aryeh*, soldiers are allowed to risk their lives in war because they are taking on risks that are considered a normal part of everyday life. Just as a businessman is allowed to embark on potentially life-threatening voyages because that activity is considered part of his normal routine, so too may a soldier go to war and risk his life in war because war is a normal human activity as well. The *Shem Aryeh*'s views on war therefore support those of the Netsiv in that the *Shem Aryeh* conceives of war as a natural phenomenon.

But what R. Waldenberg does not seem to have noticed is that in one critical respect the *Shem Aryeh*'s views are actually inimical to those of the Netsiv, because the *Shem Aryeh* effectively erases the distinction between wartime Halakhah and everyday Halakhah. If, according to the *Shem Aryeh*, a soldier may risk his life in war because going to war is considered a normal everyday activity, the boundary between everyday Halakhah and wartime Halakhah, in essence, disappears. And not only do the *Shem Aryeh*'s views implicitly undermine the Netsiv's perspective; they also undermine that of R. Waldenberg himself, who also assumes in all of the discussions of war examined here that wartime Halakhah is fundamentally different from everyday Halakhah.

We should not exaggerate the importance of these observations. After all, the *Shem Aryeh*'s views are somewhat tangential to R. Waldenberg's thinking on war, and R. Waldenberg seems not to have been aware of their implications. However, the *Shem Aryeh*'s ruminations and R. Waldenberg's adoption of them have opened the possibility that the norms of war are not always to be distinguished from those of everyday Halakhah.

We saw that R. Herzog had attempted to go in a similar direction to that of the *Shem Aryeh* on the issue of conscription. In the second responsum to the Ezra organization, he entertained the possibility that conscription could be justified within the parameters of everyday Halakhah by citing the Jerusalem Talmud, according to which an individual is indeed required to endanger his life to save a fellow human being from harm even in non-war situations. However, we also saw that R. Herzog was reluctant to push this reasoning because it went against the viewpoint of the more authoritative Babylonian Talmud. He was able to justify conscription according to everyday Halakhah only because of the unique circumstances of the 1948 war and because of R. Kook's insight that an individual must sacrifice his life when the entire Jewish people is in danger and he is in a unique position to help.

What emerges from these observations is that up to this point in our study, the figures we have examined mostly concur that the norms of war are distinct from those governing ordinary life. But the thinking of R. Herzog and the *Shem Aryeh* on the issue of conscription suggests that the barrier between the two spheres may be permeable on some issues. As we shall see in the coming chapters, R. Sha'ul Yisraeli would eventually develop this approach much further than either R. Herzog or the *Shem Aryeh* did. However, R. Yisraeli would take this approach only after composing his well-known essay on Kibiyeh, which is the subject of our next chapter.

CHAPTER 6

✧

R. Sha'ul Yisraeli

The Essay on Kibiyeh

I f R. Kook is the best-known figure we have examined in this study, Rabbi
Sha'ul Yisraeli (1910–95) may be the most influential when it comes to the
specific subject of war in Halakhah. R. Yisraeli was born in Belarus and emigrated to Palestine in 1934. He had a long and distinguished career as a halakhic authority for the religious Zionist community in Palestine and then in
the state of Israel after its founding. Among his many leadership positions, he
served as communal rabbi for the Kefar ha-Ro'eh moshav from 1938 to 1966
and was head of the Mercaz ha-Rav Yeshiva from 1982 until his death. He
received the Israel Prize for Torah Literature in 1992.[1]

R. Yisraeli's halakhic writings were dedicated to applying R. Kook's notion
of "the Torah of the land of Israel" to political affairs in the Jewish state that
R. Kook never lived to see. Like R. Kook, R. Yisraeli believed that the establishment of a Jewish state in its ancient homeland was a critical step in the
unfolding of the messianic period, and he held that Halakhah had within it
the capacity to deal with this new reality. R. Yisraeli, therefore, devoted a good
portion of his life to providing halakhic guidance on political issues, and he

---

1. Biographical information on R. Yisraeli can be found in Yisra'el Sharir, *"Ish Emet
ve-'Anavah—Pirkey Hayim,"* in *Ga'on ba-Torah u-ve-Midot: Perakim le-Darko ve-li-Demuto
shel Maran ha-Ga'on Sha'ul Yisra'eli zts"l,* ed. Yisra'el Sharir (Jerusalem: Erez, 1999),
11–97; Ari'av Yost, *"Pesikat ha-Halakhah shel ha-Rav Sha'ul Yisra'eli, Nokhah Etgar ha-
Ribonut ha-Yehudit be-Me'ah ha-'Esrim* (MA thesis, Tel Aviv University, 2010), 20–33;
Yitzchak Avi Roness, *"Mishnato ha-Hilkhatit shel ha-Rav Sha'ul Yisra'eli"* (PhD diss., Bar-
Ilan University, 2012), 3–5.

became the leading spokesman of this enterprise for the religious Zionist community.[2]

Part of this enterprise included a number of essays on the theme of war. By far the best-known piece that R. Yisraeli composed on this topic was "The Kibiyeh Incident in Light of Halakhah," published in 1954.[3] It was a lengthy essay that grappled with an Israeli military raid conducted a year earlier on the Jordanian village of Kibiyeh, which was close to the Israeli border. The raid was meant to retaliate for previous attacks by Arab terrorists who had come from the area of Kibiyeh, crossed into Israel, and killed a number of Israeli civilians. The Kibiyeh operation resulted in the deaths of dozens of Arab civilians, including women and children. In his essay, R. Yisraeli attempted to determine whether such a raid was permissible according to Halakhah, but in the course of dealing with this question, he also spelled out positions on how Halakhah dealt with war in general.

At the time of its publication, the Kibiyeh essay was a more complex and sophisticated treatment of war in Halakhah than anything that had been produced by a halakhic authority since the advent of Zionism, and its influence in the religious Zionist camp has been enormous. However, R. Yisraeli continually revised his views on war throughout his career, and he produced a string of subsequent essays that touched on matters of war and took positions quite different from, or even at odds with, those in the Kibiyeh essay. The later essays have received far less attention from halakhic authorities and academics, even though they, too, are remarkable for their complexity and sophistication.

The current chapter is devoted to the essay on Kibiyeh, and our next chapter, to the later essays. The Kibiyeh essay deserves a lengthy discussion of its own not only because of its importance and complexity but also because it has been frequently misunderstood. One of our major tasks here, therefore, will simply be to clarify its positions. The essay on Kibiyeh also deserves in-depth treatment because it has become somewhat controversial among R. Yisraeli's interpreters. The views expressed in this essay are regarded by a number of

2. R. Yisraeli's writings have received surprisingly little attention from academic scholars. However, Yost's master's thesis and Roness's doctoral dissertation, cited in note 1, are hopefully harbingers of expanding interest in this important figure. On R. Yisraeli's political views, two shorter studies are noteworthy: Gerald J. Blidstein, "*Torat ha-Medinah be-Mishnat ha-Rav Sha'ul Yisra'eli*," in *Sheney 'Evrey ha-Gesher*, eds. Mordekhai Bar On and Tsevi Tsameret (Jerusalem: Yad Yitshak ben Tsevi, 2002), 350–63; Hayim Burganski, "*Kehilah ve-Mamlakhah: Yahasam ha-Hilkhati shel ha-Rav Y"A Hertsog ve-ha-Rav Sha'ul Yisra'eli li-Medinat Yisra'el*," in *Dat u-Medinah be-Hagut ha-Yahadut be-Me'ah ha-'Esrim*, ed. Aviezer Ravitzky (Jerusalem: Ha-Makhon ha-Yisra'eli le-Demokratyah, 2005), 267–94.

3. "*Takrit Kibiyeh le-Or ha-Halakhah*," *Ha-Torah ve-ha-Medinah* 5–6 (1953–54): 71–113. The essay was later republished in a slightly expanded version under the title "*Pe'ulot Tseva'iyot le-Haganat ha-Medinah*," in *'Amud ha-Yemini* (Tel Aviv: Moreshet, 1966), 168–205.

these interpreters as militant and extreme. This assessment is understandable; however, I will attempt to demonstrate that with a careful analysis it can be shown that R. Yisraeli's positions in the Kibiyeh essay are less extreme and more nuanced than interpreters have claimed.[4]

CLARIFYING THE CONTENTS OF THE ESSAY

We begin our analysis of the essay by looking more closely at the historical events that inspired it. After the conclusion of Israel's War of Independence in the 1948 war, armed Arab groups from Jordanian towns bordering Israel began infiltrating into Israel and terrorizing its citizens. In one such raid, on the village of Yehud in 1953, a woman and her two young children were killed. In response to the incident, the government of Israel sent an elite army unit to attack the village of Kibiyeh, just across the Jordanian border, in reprisal for the Arab violence against Jewish villages. Kibiyeh was chosen as a target because the Israelis believed that the perpetrators of the violence in Yehud had come from there. In the Kibiyeh raid, sixty-nine Arabs were killed, including women and children. Condemnation of the raid from the international community was swift and harsh. Opinion in Israel was mostly supportive of the operation, though a vocal minority opposed it.[5]

In a long footnote at the beginning of his essay, R. Yisraeli presents his own version of the Kibiyeh raid and the events leading up to it.[6] The description is accurate except that he claims that the raid was conducted by Jews from the village of Yehud, when, as just noted, an elite army unit was in fact responsible. R. Yisraeli's understanding of events seems to have been influenced by initial government reports that identified the raiding party as consisting of Jewish vigilantes from the Israeli border-towns who were operating independently of the army.[7]

R. Yisraeli's description of the raid in his essay provides insight into his understanding of its motives. According to him, there were two. The first was

---

4. This chapter draws on material from an earlier article of mine, "War, Revenge, and Jewish Ethics: Rabbi Shaul Yisraeli's Essay on Kibiyeh Revisited," *AJS Review* 36, no. 1 (2012): 141–63. However, many of the positions in this article have been revised here.

5. Benny Morris, *Milhamot ha-Gevul shel Yisra'el: 1949–1956* (Tel Aviv: 'Am 'Oved, 1996); Ehud Luz, *Wrestling with an Angel: Power, Morality, and Jewish Identity*, trans. Michael Swirsky (New Haven, Conn.: Yale University Press, 2003), 207–12.

6. *"Pe'ulot Tseva'iyot,"* in *'Amud ha-Yemini*, p. 168 (section 1:1). Page numbers are from the 1992 edition of *'Amud ha-Yemini* published by Erets Hemdah. I have also added references in parentheses to sections and subsections of the essay to accommodate those who have other editions of the text with different pagination.

7. Luz, *Wrestling with an Angel,* 208.

that Jews in the Israeli border-towns could not "sit any longer with folded arms until, God forbid, there were more victims" of Arab terrorism. Here R. Yisraeli suggests that the motive was deterrence against future violence. Yet, in the same paragraph, R. Yisraeli also identifies the raid as "an operation of retaliation (*pe'ulat tagmul*) that emanated from the build-up of outrage of the residents of the village [of Yehud] and the community in the land [of Israel] in general."[8] Here R. Yisraeli indicates that the raid was for the purpose of revenge. As we shall see, R. Yisraeli discusses both possibilities from the standpoint of Halakhah, but the second possibility occupies most of his attention.

R. Yisraeli finishes the footnote by telling us that "it is incumbent on us to determine our most appropriate reaction according to the Torah" to the Kibiyeh operation, and in the opening paragraph of his essay, he spells out the halakhic dilemma that the operation raises:

> The activities of the murderous gangs [of terrorists] were done with the agreement, encouragement, and perhaps at the direction of the entire population [of Kibiyeh]. However, it is quite possible that the members of the gangs would have committed the acts of murder if they had not been sent or encouraged by others. What then is the ruling regarding the population? Does one hold it responsible for the actions of the gangs as if they did them [i.e., the violent actions] all together, or not?[9]

It is important to understand what R. Yisraeli's precise concern is. He seems to presume here and throughout the essay that the terrorists who had been attacking Jewish villages were not necessarily residents of Kibiyeh, nor were the terrorists present in the village when the raid on it occurred. Rather, the terrorists had received support and encouragement from the residents of Kibiyeh and other towns along the Jordanian border. The purpose of the raid, therefore, was not to kill the terrorists themselves but to target the civilian population that had supported them. This understanding is stated explicitly by R. Yisraeli in a later passage in the essay, when he says that in an operation like the one conducted in Kibiyeh, the military action was "not intended in its essence to harm the [terrorist] gangs themselves, but others, with the intention of frightening them and scaring them."[10] R. Yisraeli alludes here only to the deterrent value of such an operation; but, as we have seen, he also saw the operation as retaliation. Yet the important point is that he describes the operation here as being directed solely at the civilian population. The question,

8. "*Pe'ulot Tseva'iyot*,"168 (section 1:1).
9. Ibid.
10. Ibid., 190 (section 5:3).

then, is whether Halakhah would endorse this type of operation. Can Jews launch a military raid to kill Arab civilians who have supported terrorists and encouraged them to murder Jews, or is such an operation forbidden because the civilians did not perpetrate the violence themselves?

The rest of R. Yisraeli's essay is devoted to responding to this question, and it offers five different answers, each based on a different halakhic model. It is the last answer that R. Yisraeli adopts as the correct one, but important information is imparted in his discussion of the other answers—particularly the third and fourth—and we must therefore summarize these as well.[11]

In his first answer, R. Yisraeli entertains the possibility that a military operation such as that executed in Kibiyeh is justified because when Arab civilians support terrorists who murder Jews, they become, in effect, accessories to murder and therefore deserve to be punished as such. R. Yisraeli argues that the merit of this position depends on how Halakhah views instances in which a person convinces another individual to commit a sin on his behalf. Who is held responsible for the crime? The person who sends the agent to commit the transgression or the agent himself? Normally, in Halakhah it is only the person who performs the sinful action who is culpable, and therefore it is the agent who is deserving of punishment. Yet, R. Yisraeli notes that although this rule applies to Jews, it is not clear that it applies to non-Jews as well. If it does, then Arab civilians who encourage terrorists to kill Jews would not be held liable for the actions of the terrorists. However, if the rule does not apply to non-Jews, the Arab civilians could be held accountable and would be legitimate targets in a military operation meant to punish them. After much deliberation, R. Yisraeli ultimately rules that, according to Halakhah, non-Jews are no different from Jews when it comes to agency in committing sinful acts, and thus Arab civilians who encourage terrorists to perpetrate acts of violence cannot be held responsible for what the terrorists do as a result.[12]

The second possibility entertained by R. Yisraeli focuses on the notion that a military operation such as the one in Kibiyeh is justified because the Arab civilians were aware that the terrorists responsible for murdering Jews were

---

11. Good summaries of R. Yisraeli's essay on Kibiyeh can be found in R. Neryah Gutel, *"Lehimah be-Shetah Ravey Ukhlosiyah Ezrahit," Ha-Milhamah ba-Teror*, ed. Ya'ir Halevi (Kiryat Arba: Makhon Le-Rabaney Yishuvim, 2006), 64–66, 76–79, 87–98; Aryeh Edrei, "Law, Interpretation, and Ideology: The Renewal of the Jewish Laws of War in the State of Israel," *Cardozo Law Review* 28, no. 1 (2006): 211–17; idem, *"Mi-Kibiyeh 'ad Beirut: Tehiyatam shel Diney ha-Milhamah ha-Hilkhatiyim bi-Medinat Yisra'el,"* in *Yosef Da'at: Mehkarim be-Historiyah Yehudit Modernit Mugashim le-Prof' Yosef Salmon*, ed. Yossi Goldshtein (Be'er Sheva: Ben Gurion University, 2010), 111–18; Roness, *"Mishnato ha-Hilkhatit,"* 87–91; idem, "Halakhah, Ideology, and Interpretation: Rabbi Shaul Yisraeli on the Status of Defensive War," *Jewish Law Association Studies* 20 (2010): 186–90.

12. *"Pe'ulot Tseva'iyot,"* 168–73 (section 1).

living in their midst and they did not bring them to justice. This hypothesis is premised on a ruling by Maimonides stipulating that non-Jews must establish courts of law and a penal system to enforce the Noachide code, including the prohibition of murder, and that failure to do so is grounds for punishment.[13] Yet, in R. Yisraeli's thinking, this solution also fails because Arab civilians cannot be held accountable for the behavior of the terrorists if there is any suspicion that the civilians are fearful of them and are therefore reluctant to bring them to justice. Although he does not say so explicitly, R. Yisraeli seems to think that in the case of Kibiyeh, this suspicion was warranted.[14]

R. Yisraeli's third answer requires more attention than the first two because, even though it, too, is rejected by him, it provides information that will be important in his later deliberations. Here R. Yisraeli takes up the possibility that Arab civilians who support the terrorists are in the halakhic category of "pursuers" (*rodfim*). As we have already learned in chapter 2, in Halakhah a "pursuer" (*rodef*) is someone who is in the process of attempting to murder another individual, and in such an instance, a third party is permitted to kill the pursuer to save the life of the one being pursued.[15] Might we therefore consider Arab civilians as pursuers if they support terrorists who take Jewish lives, and if so, are Jews then not allowed to kill the civilians to prevent further violence? To clarify, the issue here is not the punishment of Arab civilians for their harmful actions in the past, as was the case with the first two halakhic models that R. Yisraeli entertained, but rather the preemption of such actions in the future.

R. Yisraeli concludes that Arab civilians who support terrorists can indeed be considered pursuers and that Jews may therefore kill these civilians. The Arab population "encourages the activity of the [terrorist] gangs in many ways, and this certainly aids in the strengthening and expansion of their activities in the future."[16] Thus, the Arab civilians who support the terrorists are no different from the terrorists themselves when it comes to assessing the danger they pose to Jews, and in accordance with the law of the pursuer, Jews may therefore kill the civilians who provide such support in order to preempt further violence.

At this point, it would seem that a solution has been found to R. Yisraeli's initial query. The Kibiyeh raid should be permitted. However, R. Yisraeli raises a critical difficulty:

> All of this [i.e., the pursuer hypothesis] is being said with respect to the adult sector of the population, the majority of which is equivalent to the total

---

13. MT *Melakhim* 9:14.
14. "*Pe'ulot Tseva'iyot*," 174–81 (section 2).
15. Above, pp. 44–45.
16. "*Pe'ulot Tseva'iyot*," 184 (section 3:5).

[population] (*rubo ke-khulo*) in encouraging the murderous operations [of the terrorists], as far as we know—which is not the case with respect to the children who are not in this category. It is forbidden to harm them deliberately and intentionally.[17]

The adult population can indeed be targeted as pursuers because the vast majority of them assisted the terrorists. However, what about the innocent people in Kibiyeh who did not support the terrorists—in particular, the children who by definition are presumed innocent? May Jews therefore proceed with a raid such as the one conducted in Kibiyeh knowing that innocents will be killed accidentally? At the beginning of the next section, R. Yisraeli describes the problem in greater detail:

[T]he question arises that in the [Arab civilian] population are also those who are innocent of sin, such as children and the like, but the operation [i.e., the one in Kibiyeh], when it is conducted, cannot differentiate [between the innocent and the guilty], and there are necessarily innocent victims. Is the operation permitted in general, or shall we say that because there is no way of avoiding the harming of innocent ones, it is forbidden to conduct this operation in general?[18]

R. Yisraeli conducts a detailed discussion of the matter and ultimately concludes that children cannot be held accountable for the sins of their elders, and, therefore, if there is any chance that a military operation against the adults of a village, such as Kibiyeh, will likely result in harm to children, it is forbidden. R. Yisraeli does not draw an explicit conclusion regarding Kibiyeh, but it is clear that this stipulation would effectively rule out the type of operation conducted there in which children were indeed killed.[19]

There is a significant inconsistency here that should be noted. R. Yisraeli seems to acknowledge that there were also adults in Kibiyeh who were innocent in that they did not aid the terrorists, but he expresses no concern for the possibility that they, too, may have been killed in the raid. In the first of the two passages just cited, he says that the pursuer hypothesis applies to "the adult sector of the population, the majority of which is equivalent to the total [population] (*rubo ke-khulo*) in encouraging the murderous operations [of the terrorists], as far as we know." Here R. Yisrareli informs us that the portion of the adult population in Kibiyeh that assisted the terrorists was "the majority," but according to the principle of *rubo ke-khulo*—which literally means "the majority is equivalent to the whole"—those adults who

17. Ibid.
18. Ibid., 184 (section 4:1).
19. Ibid., 181–89 (sections 3–4).

did not assist the terrorists would be considered part of the majority as far as guilt is concerned.[20] The question then is why R. Yisraeli objects to the killing of innocent children but not innocent adults. The latter group should not have been held accountable for the sins of the guilty any more than the children were.

R. Yisraeli provides no answer here, but perhaps in this thinking innocent children are different from innocent adults because children are not only innocent of wrongdoing, they are also easily identifiable by their very appearance, and therefore those who conduct the type of raid carried out in Kibiyeh have an obligation to avoid killing them. The same obligation would not exist for the innocent adults because they would *not* be easily distinguished from those who were guilty. R. Yisraeli, therefore, concludes that the raid in Kibiyeh was halakhically sanctioned, but that children should not have been attacked deliberately. However, there are problems with this solution. Halakhah forbids killing innocent individuals when trying to stop a pursuer, and therefore the fact that the majority of the adults in Kibiyeh were deemed to be pursuers would not justify killing the adults who were innocent if they could not be distinguished from the guilty ones.

Yet despite this difficulty, what is important to note here is that R. Yisraeli's third halakhic model for dealing with the Kibiyeh raid helps define the direction of the rest of his discussion. He has found a way to justify the bloodshed of the Kibiyeh raid with respect to the adult civilian population because they pose a threat to Jews no less than the terrorists themselves. However, this justification fails because it may result in the accidental killing of children who are innocent and whose lives cannot be risked for the purpose of the operation. With the final two models, R. Yisraeli will entertain halakhic approaches that will attempt to surmount this difficulty.

The Kibiyeh Raid as Discretionary War

These last two approaches take matters in a new direction. Up to this point, R. Yisraeli's halakhic models have been constructed from laws that regulate day-to-day interactions between individuals—that is, everyday Halakhah. He now considers the possibility that a military operation such as the one in Kibiyeh, should, in fact, be thought of as a battle within a formally declared war. If that is the case, then the killing of innocent civilians would present no halakhic problem:

20. In the second of the two quotations just cited, R. Yisraeli again seems to acknowledge that there could have been innocent adults in Kibiyeh when he states that "in the [Arab civilian] population are also those who are innocent of sin, such as children *and the like*" (my emphasis). But here he does not imply that they are guilty by being associated with the guilty majority.

We have also not found with respect to war an obligation to distinguish between people [in the enemy population].[21] And even though after the conquest of a city of the enemy, it is forbidden to kill women and children ... still, it is clear that this ruling is stated with respect [to the situation] after they [i.e., the Jews] have captured them and they are under our control. But in the course of war, when we besiege a city and the like, there is no obligation, nor is there even a possibility, to be meticulous in this matter.[22]

R. Yisraeli tells us that there is no halakhic obligation to be careful when it comes to the killing of innocent people in war, including children, nor is it even possible to avoid such casualties even if one wanted to.[23]

But we have to determine what kind of war are we talking about here. R. Yisraeli begins with the possibility that military action of the type taken in Kibiyeh is in the category of preemptive war, the purpose of which is to instill fear in an enemy nation so as to deter it from initiating a war of its own. According to R. Yisraeli, this type of war is precisely the kind that Maimonides refers to when he says that one of the reasons for engaging in discretionary war is to "increase the prestige of the king."[24] R. Yisraeli follows the interpretation of R. Abraham Hiya de Botton (ca. 1560–1605)—author of the *Lehem Mishneh*, a commentary on Maimonides's *Mishneh Torah*—in assuming that what Maimonides is alluding to here is a war meant to instill fear in the enemy so that they do not consider waging war any time in the future.[25] In the case of a military operation such as the one conducted in Kibiyeh, the goal was similar. Its goal was "not to harm the [terrorist] gangs themselves," seeing as they were no longer present, but "[to harm] others [i.e., the civilians] with the aim of scaring them and frightening them," presumably to deter them from supporting the terrorists in the future.[26]

The problem here is that according to most halakhic sources, this type of war is discretionary war, and it requires the approval of a Sanhedrin that no longer exists. However, R. Yisraeli argues that the Sanhedrin serves only a marginal role in the waging of discretionary war, and therefore its absence does not preclude the possibility of waging this type of war in our time. R. Yisraeli supports a statement made by Rashi in his commentary on the Talmud that the role of the Sanhedrin in the prosecution of discretionary war is to pray for victory.[27] R. Yisraeli theorizes, on the basis of Rashi's gloss, that at first the inclusion of the prayers of the Sanhedrin in the initiation of discretionary war

21. Lit., "between blood and blood."
22. *"Pe'ulot Tseva'iyot,"* 189 (section 1).
23. Ibid.
24. MT *Melakhim* 5:1.
25. This commentary is found in standard editions of MT.
26. *"Pe'ulot Tseva'iyot,"* 190 (section 5:3).
27. BT *Berakhot* 3b, s.v. *"ve-nimlakhin ba-sanhedrin."*

was nothing more than a custom, and it was therefore optional. However, that custom eventually became law, and once that occurred, all kings were required to seek the prayers of the Sanhedrin before they could wage war. Yet that custom was binding only on the king. If the Israelites wanted to wage discretionary war voluntarily, there was no requirement to involve the Sanhedrin.[28] The reason these considerations are relevant to military operations like the one in Kibiyeh is that R. Yisraeli believed—mistakenly, as it turned out—that the Kibiyeh operation had been executed by volunteers from the Israeli towns who had been affected by Arab terrorism from across the border, and there was thus no need to consult a Sanhedrin to approve such an operation.[29]

But R. Yisraeli raises an even bigger problem with discretionary war as a model for the Kibiyeh operation. He is deeply troubled by the fact that discretionary war as depicted in rabbinic sources has an aggressive dimension to it. While preemptive war presumes that there is an enemy that has to be deterred, that is not the case in other instances of discretionary war. R. Yisraeli notes, for example, that discretionary war can also be waged for economic gain. According to one talmudic passage, mentioned in an earlier chapter, King David wages discretionary war because his advisers tell him that the people require material sustenance and he must therefore go to war in order to take care of his people's needs.[30] R. Yisraeli expresses consternation that David was allowed to spill blood for such a reason: "What kind of argument is this that would permit the blood [to be spilled] of those created in the image [of God]?" Moreover, one is certainly not allowed to steal from a non-Jew, and yet, is that not what Jews are doing by waging discretionary war against gentile nations for the sake of economic gain?[31] R. Yisraeli makes no mention of the third reason for waging discretionary war mentioned in the Talmud and codified by Maimonides, which is the expansion of territory,[32] but one can assume that it would elicit a similar negative reaction on his part.

The challenge here inspires R. Yisraeli to take a new direction in his understanding of discretionary war, and he now presents a theory of this category of war that is highly original and the defense of which takes up a good many pages. According to R. Yisraeli, discretionary war, in fact, includes all wars waged by the nations of the world in accordance with international law and custom.[33]

---

28. *"Pe'ulot Tseva'iyot,"* 190–91 (section 5:6).

29. An interesting question that R. Yisraeli does not ask is whether this logic would allow the state of Israel to wage discretionary war without the permission of a Sanhedrin in our day and age, if the decision was in accordance with the will of the majority of the Israeli public. Would R. Yisraeli believe that such support amounts to waging this type of war voluntarily?

30. Above, p. 36.

31. *"Pe'ulot Tseva'iyot,"* p. 191 (section 5:8).

32. BT *Berakhot* 3b; MT *Hilkhot Melakhim* 5:1. Above, p. 35.

33. *"Pe'ulot Tseva'iyot,"* 189–202 (section 5:1–24).

Hence, this type of war is not permitted for Jews alone. In addition, the determination in Halakhah as to which discretionary wars are permissible for the nations to wage may change over time because that determination is entirely relative in being dependent on non-Jewish law and custom. Thus, at one point, R. Yisraeli mentions the views of groups in the international community in his own time who believe that war should be abolished, and he states quite explicitly that if these views were to be accepted by the majority of nations in the world, Jews would be required to desist from waging war as well.[34]

Unbeknownst to R. Yisraeli was the fact that the international community had, in effect, taken that position. In 1945, the United Nations Charter outlawed war as an instrument of national policy. Only wars waged in response to aggression by another nation were sanctioned.[35] Yet the fact that R. Yisraeli was not aware of this development is not our concern here. R. Yisraeli believed that war was permitted in international law for purposes other than defense, and even if that belief was erroneous, that was the premise on which he based his deliberations regarding discretionary war.

According to R. Yisraeli, the proof that Halakhah approves of discretionary war as defined by him is a ruling supported by a number of halakhic authorities and based on a passage in the Talmud explaining that when a king—Jew or non-Jew—conquers territory in war, he acquires legitimate ownership of it. R. Yisraeli could have said more about what this source proves, but it appears to demonstrate to him that the talmudic rabbis were conferring legitimacy, first, on wars waged by Jewish and non-Jewish kings alike, and, secondly, on wars waged in conformity to the customs of the period in which those rabbis lived.[36]

34. Ibid., 195 (section 5:15). However, it should be noted that at the beginning of his essay, when describing events leading up to the Kibiyeh raid, R. Yisraeli decries the condemnation of the operation by the international community claiming that their views are hypocritical because no similar condemnations were uttered when Jews were killed by Arab terrorists (ibid., p. 168). Apparently, R. Yisraeli feels that there is a significant gap between what international law says and the way in which it is applied by international community.

35. United Nations Charter, art. 4.2; Yoram Dinstein, *War, Aggression, and Self-Defence*, 4th ed. (New York: Cambridge University Press, 2005), 87–94; Gary D. Solis, *The Law of Armed Conflict: International Humanitarian Law in War* (New York: Cambridge University Press, 2010), 77. The Kellogg-Briand Pact of 1928, which preceded the UN Charter and was signed by sixty-three states, renounced war as an instrument of national policy, and therefore implied the notion that wars were permitted only for self-defense. However, the latter idea was stated unequivocally for the first time only in the UN Charter.

36. "Pe'ulot Tseva'iyot," pp. 191–92 (section 5:9–10). The talmudic source is BT *Gittin* 38a, and it is endorsed by such authorities as Maimonides in MT 'Avadim 9:4 and R. David ben Solomon ibn Zimra, *Teshuvot Radbaz* (New York: Otsar ha-Sefarim, 1966) 3:533.

R. Yisraeli never explains to us how, in light of this theory, one should view the forms of discretionary war described in early rabbinic and medieval halakhic sources, such as preemptive wars, or wars waged for more aggressive purposes, such as those waged for economic gain or the expansion of territory. Yet, here too one can presume that he would view such wars as having been permitted by Halakhah because they were regarded as legitimate according to the customs of the time in which these sources were composed.

R. Yisraeli goes on to argue that the laws and customs of nations are the key determinant for the legality of wars because of the halakhic principle of *dina de-malkhuta dina*, "the law of the kingdom is the law." Normally, this principle is used in Halakhah to define the responsibilities that a Jew has as a resident of a non-Jewish polity. The notion that "the law of the kingdom is the law" dictates that a Jew is required to obey the law of the land, even if it clashes with halakhic norms. This rule applies primarily to monetary and civil matters, not to ritual observances which are seen by Halakhah as immune to non-Jewish interference.[37] While this halakhic principle was originally meant to regulate the relationship between Jewish citizens and their government *within* nations, R. Yisraeli extends it to conduct *between* nations, Jewish and non-Jewish. In the latter application, "the law of the kingdom is the law" dictates that all states must obey international law and custom in the same way that an individual Jew must obey the law of the land in which he lives. This principle also governs the waging of war.[38]

One element in R. Yisraeli's discussion that creates some confusion is that he refers to international "law" and "custom" interchangeably as his standard for determining when discretionary war is permissible, but these are not necessarily the same.[39] When he speaks of "law," he seem to be referring to an actual body of law agreed on by all nations. Yet when he speaks of "custom," he seems to be referring to what the nations actually do. The gap between the two can be substantial when it comes to war. International law may dictate one set of norms for war, but what nations are accustomed to doing in war may be entirely different. Often, nations are far more brutal in war than international law allows. Commentators on R. Yisraeli have generally argued that he upheld the latter understanding of international norms.[40] It is what nations do that

37. A thorough discussion of the history of the principle of *dina de-malkhuta dina* can be found in Shmu'el Shiloh, *Dina de-Malkhuta Dina* (Jerusalem: Jerusalem Academic Press, 1974).

38. *"Pe'ulot Tseva'iyot,"* 191–92 (section 5:9), 194–95 (section 5:14–15).

39. When speaking of law, R. Yisraeli uses the noun *hok* and related terms, such as the adjective *huki*. When referring to custom, he uses nouns and verbs based on the root *nahag*, as well as nouns and verbs based on the *hif'il* of *sakam*, such as *haskamah*, *heskemi*. An example of a passage in which the terms "law" and "custom" are used interchangeably, can be found in *"Pe'ulot Tseva'iyot,"* 194–95 (section 5:15).

40. See, for instance, Gerald J. Blidstein, "The Treatment of Hostile Civilian Populations: The Contemporary Halakhic Discussion in Israel," *Israel Studies* 1, no. 2 (1996): 34; R. Neryah Gutel, *"Lehimah be-Shetah Ravey Ukhlosiyah Ezrahit,"* 94–95.

matters to R. Yisraeli, not what international law dictates. These commentators have a point, given his references to international "custom." However, at times, R. Yisraeli clearly refers to international "law," not custom, as his standard. In the course of his discussion, R. Yisraeli also alludes to specific examples of norms regulating war that are, without doubt, references to international law, such as the laws that determine what a proper declaration of war is and what types of weapons may be used in fighting a war.[41] Moreover, it is hard to imagine that R. Yisraeli would base his views about what is permissible in war solely on what the nations of the world actually do in war, because in that case he would have no objection to the atrocities committed in the two world wars, including the Holocaust, and this hardly could have been R. Yisraeli's intent.

One possibility is that when R. Yisraeli referred to international law and custom, he may have been referring to the distinction between laws established by multilateral treaties and those that are based on customary law, a distinction well-known in the field of international law. Laws based on treaties are binding on nations that are signatories to those treaties, while customary law refers to the body of unwritten rules that are viewed in international law as binding on all nations as the accepted norms by which they must behave, regardless of whether or not the nations have explicitly acknowledged them as such.[42]

However, there is no evidence that R. Yisraeli was aware of such a distinction. I therefore think it more likely that R. Yisraeli deliberately refers to both law and custom because he was aware that international law is a modern invention, and that prior to the modern period, the world had nothing more than custom to go by in regulating conduct between nations in the international sphere. Since the norms governing discretionary war change in accordance with the time period, he speaks of both "law" and "custom," because the first term was appropriate for the modern period in which he lived, and the latter term was appropriate for the period in which the sources of early rabbinic and medieval Halakhah were composed. This explanation, however, is admittedly speculative.

But let us get back to R. Yisraeli's discussion. Despite what he has said thus far, R. Yisraeli still expresses doubts about whether his insights regarding discretionary war provide enough justification for the killing that takes place when discretionary war is waged. The problem is that *dina de-malkhuta dina* does not normally apply to state laws that involve the taking of life, such as the administration of the death penalty. How then can it be used to justify killing in war? R. Yisraeli confronts this challenge with yet another innovative

---

41. "*Pe'ulot Tseva'iyot,*" 195 (section 5:15).
42. Solis, *Law of Armed Conflict,* 11–15.

move. He argues that nations have the right to wage war with the loss of life it entails because of metaphysical considerations. He cites a source claiming that the souls of non-Jews are inherently different from those of Jews because non-Jewish souls originate in the physical world, whereas Jewish souls have their origin in God.[43] Non-Jews therefore have possession over their souls in a way that Jews do not and can therefore waive their right to life if they so choose.[44] The waging of war is a situation in which they do precisely that. Thus, in this instance, the loss of life is no obstacle to applying the principle of *dina de-malkhuta dina.*[45]

This reasoning, however, seems to apply only when both nations willingly go to war for whatever cause they choose. What if one of nations has no interest in war and is being forced into combat by the aggression of the other nation? Here, the citizens of the nation that is not interested in war have in no way consented to waive their right to life. R. Yisraeli, however, does not confront this question.

It may seem strange that R. Yisraeli has resorted to a theological argument here, but it would appear that he is using the methodology of the "Torah of the land of Israel" as formulated by R. Kook. According to this methodology, one does not rely solely on halakhic texts to adjudicate on matters of Halakhah. One may draw from sources that are non-halakahic, such as aggadah, philosophy, theology, and Kabbalah.

R. Yisraeli concludes his discussion of discretionary war with the following statement:

> What emerges from this discussion is that even in our day, a military operation by [the people of] Israel under the rubric of discretionary war is [halakhically] possible. And in war there is no need to be meticulous and differentiate between righteous and wicked because the nature of war does not make it possible to be meticulous. Moreover, war [conducted] in this way is permitted as long as this conduct [in war] is accepted among the nations. Therefore, with regard to the matter under discussion (concerning Kibiyeh and similar situations), one must

43. R. Yisraeli specifically cites *Tanya*, composed by R. Shne'ur Zalman of Liadi (1745–1812), as a source for this idea. However, the notion that non-Jewish souls are different from Jewish souls permeates Kabbalistic thought and has its roots in the *Kuzari* of Judah Halevi (1075–1141).

44. R. Yisraeli cites the *Minhat Hinukh* as support for his position. The *Minhat Hinukh* rules that suicide is not a transgression for non-Jews as it is for Jews, a ruling that R. Yisraeli sees as an endorsement of his theory that non-Jews are in charge of their souls, while Jews are not. See *Minhat Hinukh* (Jerusalem: Jerusalem Institute, 1998), 187.

45. "Pe'ulot Tseva'iyot," 195–202 (sections 5:14–23). The implication here is that non-Jews may initiate wars against each other but not against Jews, due to the latter's special status. R. Yisraeli, however, does not explicitly draw this conclusion.

examine if a [military] response of this kind is supported and accepted among the nations, because [if it is accepted] one would have to view it as [something agreed upon by] a consensus on behalf of all those [nations] involved in the matter [of war], and there would be nothing about it involving the [prohibition against] the shedding of blood.[46]

This conclusion is rather anticlimactic. R. Yisraeli has spent a great deal of energy delineating his innovative position on discretionary war, but up to this point, he has said very little about how his position is relevant to the central concern of the essay—namely, whether military operations such as the one in Kibiyeh are permitted according to Halakhah. It is here that he finally broaches this question, only to tell us that the matter requires further investigation! He informs us that in order to determine whether the Kibiyeh raid was acceptable as a form of discretionary war, one would have to examine whether operations like it are permitted according to international law, and it is on this point that the discussion of discretionary war ends. No further discussion is forthcoming about whether the Kibiyeh raid did or did not conform to international law, and thus we have no determination about whether or not it qualifies as discretionary war.

But it is perhaps not surprising that R. Yisraeli would leave us hanging here. It may be that he did not feel sufficiently knowledgeable in international law to judge whether the Kibiyeh raid conformed to it. In the course of his discussion, R. Yisraeli demonstrates awareness of certain elements of international law on warfare. As we have noted, he refers to proper procedures for declaring war and to rules regarding which weapons may be used. However, his opinions are short on detail.

R. Yisraeli's preference not to discuss whether the Kibiyeh raid conformed to the standards of international law may also be due to the fact that equating the raid with discretionary war was not his preferred solution. R. Yisraeli does not explicitly reject the model of discretionary war for understanding the Kibiyeh raid, but ultimately, he finds it less satisfying than the last solution he proposes, and it is to that solution that we now turn.

The Kibiyeh Raid as Mandatory War

In the final section of his essay, R. Yisraeli concludes that a military operation like the one conducted in Kibiyeh is best understood as falling under the halakhic category of mandatory war. The Arabs initiated a war against the Jewish state upon its establishment in 1948, and the sporadic violence of terrorists

46. *"Pe'ulot Tseva'iyot,"* 202 (section 5:24).

crossing into Israel to kill its citizens since then has to be viewed as an extension of that war. The Kibiyeh raid, therefore, has to be seen as a military operation in the context of this war as well. What this means is that the raid was not preemptive in nature, as suggested in R. Yisraeli's discussion of discretionary war, but was in response to a war already in progress that had been initiated by an enemy nation. In Maimonides's terminology, such a war is described as *'ezrat yisra'el mi-yad tsar*—"saving Israel from the clutches of the enemy."[47]

It is important to be clear about what R. Yisraeli is saying here. Discretionary war, according to R. Yisraeli, encompasses all wars waged by nations against each other according to international law and custom, but this category of war does not include wars in which a Jewish state is confronted by an enemy nation that has initiated hostilities and crossed its borders. In this latter instance, a new category of war comes into effect that is mandatory in nature, and it is governed by a set of strictures different from those that govern discretionary war. Presumably, if a non-Jewish nation wages war in response to an enemy attack, in R. Yisraeli's thinking it would still be considered discretionary war, and the norms of the international community would apply. Only Jews have a special category of mandatory war to deal with this type of situation.

In the next section of his discussion, R. Yisraeli discusses one rule unique to mandatory war that he finds most troubling. It dictates that in mandatory wars all Jews are obligated to fight. Thus if wars waged in response to enemy attack are mandatory in nature, all Jews are required to fight here as well. But how is this possible? In Halakhah, one cannot force an individual to endanger himself to defend the lives of others, but in a war of this type, that is apparently what Jews are being asked to do.[48] In short, R. Yisraeli is asking, in effect, how conscription can be justified.

R. Yisraeli answers, surprisingly, that the cause of defense provides no such license. When Jews go to war in response to an attack by an enemy, it is not, in fact, for the purpose of defending their fellow Jews; it is for the purpose of wreaking revenge (*nekamah*) on the enemy. It is only for this reason that the war is considered mandatory and that a Jewish government can conscript its subjects. R. Yisraeli tells us that the source for this idea is the biblical account of the war against the Midianites in the book of Numbers. This war was commanded by God explicitly for the sake of revenge,[49] and it was also mandatory because all Israelites were required to fight.[50] According to R. Yisraeli, the war with the Midianites serves as a model for all future wars that are waged in

47. "*Pe'ulot Tseva'iyot*," 202–3 (section 5:25); MT *Melakhim* 5:1.
48. "*Pe'ulot Tseva'iyot*," 204 (section 5:29).
49. Num. 25:16–18; 31:1–18.
50. Num. 31:2.

response to enemy attack. These wars are also wars of revenge, and in them all Jews must also go into battle, as they did against the Midianites.[51]

We should clarify that in the biblical account, the Midianites never actually attacked the Israelites; we are told that they tempted the Israelites into idol-worship and that God sought revenge because of this action.[52] Nonetheless, R. Yisraeli treats the Midianite war as a response to violence on the basis of a midrashic source that he cites later in his discussion stating that the luring of the Israelites into practicing idolatry was an attack every bit as harmful to them as a physical assault—in fact, more so. While killing someone robs them of their life in this world, tempting them into idolatry robs them of their life both in this world and in the world to come.[53] The purpose of the Midianite war was therefore to avenge this "attack." Thus, this war serves as a paradigm for any war that is waged in response to enemy attack, which is normally of the physical variety.[54]

R. Yisraeli also claims that his views on wars of revenge are precisely those of Maimonides. According to Maimonides, the category of mandatory war includes wars for the purpose of 'ezrat yisra'el mi yad tsar.[55] This phrase, which we have rendered as "saving Israel from the clutches of an enemy," is usually understood by halakhic authorities as a reference to defensive wars. Yet, in a creative reading, R. Yisraeli gives the phrase a different meaning in line with his understanding of this type of war by linking the word tsar, or "enemy," with the term tsorer, or "assailant," that the Bible uses to describe the Midianites (Num. 25:18). Therefore, in R. Yisraeli's opinion, when Maimonides refers to 'ezrat yisra'el mi-yad tsar, he had in mind wars of revenge of the kind fought against the Midianites.[56]

But the important point here is that R. Yisraeli is now able to solve the problem of compelling soldiers to endanger themselves by fighting in wars waged in response to enemy attack. In the biblical account of the Midianite war, the entire Israelite nation was mobilized in this type of war, and thus we learn from here that in subsequent wars of this sort, everyone must fight as well, regardless of the dangers. Once again, these wars are not for the purpose of defense but of revenge, and it is the need to seek revenge that foists a special obligation on all Jews to participate in the war effort.

What R. Yisraeli is saying here is that there really is no such thing as a Jewish war of self-defense! At no point in his discussion of mandatory war does R. Yisraeli refer to "defense" (haganah) or terms related to it. He refers only to

---

51. "Pe'ulot Tseva'iyot," 204 (section 5:30).
52. Num. 25:16–8.
53. Ba-Midbar Rabbah 21:4; Tanhuma, Pinhas 3.
54. "Pe'ulot Tseva'iyot," 204 (section 5:31).
55. MT Melakhim 5:1.
56. "Pe'ulot Tseva'iyot," 204 (section 5:30).

wars in which the nation "has already come" (*kevar ba'u*)—that is, has already initiated hostilities. Thus, when an enemy initiates a war against a Jewish state, a mandatory war comes into effect, the purpose of which is revenge and nothing more.[57]

In the next section of his discussion, R. Yisraeli raises a question that brings us back to the central concern of his essay. Whom is one permitted to kill in a war of revenge? R. Yisraeli answers as follows:

> [O]ne applies to it [i.e., wars of revenge] all the laws of war, and [thus] there is no obligation to be meticulous in conducting the operation so that no one is hurt except those who participated, for this is the way of war in that the righteous die with the wicked.[58]

R. Yisraeli tells us that on this issue, mandatory wars are no different from all other wars, and he therefore reiterates what he said earlier about discretionary wars, with practically the same wording: in war, one does not have to be careful to differentiate between the "righteous" and the "wicked" because that is "the way of war." In other words, in war one may kill innocent people along with the guilty participants because there is no halakhic obligation to refrain from doing so, nor is it even possible to avoid such casualties if one wanted to.

R. Yisraeli goes on to express discomfort with the fact that in the Midianite war, Moses specifically instructs the Israelites to kill the Midianite children after the war was won.[59] According to R. Yisraeli, "[T]his seems amazing; what sin did they commit?"[60] He points out that halakhic sources are generally opposed to punishing children for the sins of their parents;[61] it is only God who can mete out punishment of this kind.[62] What is clearly troubling R. Yisraeli here is that if the Midianite war is the paradigm for future wars waged in response to enemy attack, then Israelis should be permitted to kill children in military operations, such as the one conducted in Kibiyeh, and to do so quite deliberately.

---

57. Roness, "*Mishnato ha-Hilkhatit*," 90–91, claims that, according to R. Yisraeli, Jews can also wage a defensive war under the rubric of discretionary war, but in such a war soldiers could not be conscripted and would have to fight voluntarily. Indeed, R. Yisraeli seems to take such a position in "*Pe'ulot Tseva'iyot*," 203–4 (section 5:26–28). However, I disagree with Roness's reading here. While the notion that Jews can fight a defensive war voluntarily is certainly entertained by R. Yisraeli in the section cited, this interpretation appears to be superseded by his discussion of wars of revenge in the very next section of the essay.

58. "*Pe'ulot Tseva'iyot*," 204 (section 5:31).

59. Num. 31:13–18.

60. "*Pe'ulot Tseva'iyot*," 204 (section 5:31).

61. Based on Deut. 24:16.

62. Ex. 24:5. We should point out here that R. Yisraeli is not concerned about innocent Midianite adults because his presumption seems to be that there were none. They were all guilty of tempting the Israelites into idol-worship and were therefore deserving of death.

R. Yisraeli's response to this problem begins with the observation that there are, in fact, some instances in which Jewish law sanctions the punishment of children because of the misdeeds of their parents. For example, in the Bible, when an entire Israelite city has engaged in idol-worship ('ir ha-nidahat), the city is destroyed and all of its residents are put to death—men, women, and children.[63] The Midianites who tempted the Israelites into idol-worship are punished in a similar way. Yet R. Yisraeli rules that this type of punishment should not be implemented in subsequent wars of revenge because, as noted earlier, tempting Jews into idol-worship is a far more serious crime than the physical violence perpetrated in most other wars. Thus, in wars of revenge waged in response to an ordinary physical attack, Jews should not deliberately target children. However, given that in war an army cannot engage in combat without risking the lives of children, Jews should not be held responsible if children are killed accidentally. What all this means, R. Yisraeli tells us, is that when it comes to the problem of killing innocent people, wars of revenge are really no different from all other wars in which the innocent die alongside the guilty. In halakhic sources, "special laws for wars of revenge were not mentioned."[64]

R. Yisraeli sums up his position in the concluding statement of the essay:

> What emerges from all this is that there is room for [military] operations of retaliation and revenge against those who assail Israel (tsorerey yisra'el), and an operation of this kind is in the category of mandatory war. And whatever disaster and harm is inflicted on the [enemy] perpetrators [of violence], their associates, and their children, it is their very own responsibility, and they will bear their sin. And there is no obligation to avoid [military] operations of retaliation because of the concern that the innocent will be harmed, for it is not we who are the cause [of this harm], but they themselves [i.e., the enemy]; we are guiltless.
>
> However, regarding the intention to harm children from the outset, this is something we have not found [in the Jewish tradition] except with the sin of idol-worship. Therefore, one should take care not to harm them.[65]

Here again, R. Yisraeli tells us that all wars that Jews fight in response to enemy attack are wars of revenge, and in such wars one need not be careful in sparing the lives of the innocent. R. Yisraeli also adds that if anyone is responsible for the death of the innocent in wars of this kind, it is the enemy that initiated hostilities in the first place, not the Jews. Still, special care should always be taken to avoid killing children deliberately because they are by nature innocent and cannot be held responsible for the sins of their parents.

---

63. Deut. 13:13–19; Maimonides, MT 'Akum 4:6.
64. "Pe'ulot Tseva'iyot," 204 (section 5:31).
65. Ibid., 205 (section 5:32).

HOW RADICAL AN ESSAY?

As I noted at the beginning of this chapter, a number of R. Yisraeli's interpreters believe that his final position in the Kibiyeh essay is extreme. In a
recent article, Yitzchak Roness captures this sentiment by claiming that
R. Yisraeli's position reflects a "radically militant worldview."[66] However, the
views expressed by these commentators are short on detail in explaining precisely what makes R. Yisraeli's views so extreme.

Some commentators are troubled by the fact that R. Yisraeli's viewpoint
does not seem to have a precedent in halakhic literature. Medieval Halakhah
contains no reference to a formal category of war waged for the purpose of
revenge. R. Neryah Gutel, despite his respect and reverence for R. Yisraeli's
authority, makes this point.[67] Roness is even more forthright in his criticism
of the Kibiyeh essay regarding this issue. According to him, "nowhere in the
halakhic literature do we find this biblical account transformed into a normative precedent for such wars in the future."[68] Thus, in Roness's opinion,
R. Yisraeli's position is tendentious from the standpoint of halakhic methodology.[69] Roness goes on to conclude that R. Yisraeli's radical views, combined
with the lack of halakhic precedent to support them, are proof that the Kibiyeh
essay was inspired more by ideology than by sober halakhic judgment.[70]

66. Roness, "Halakhah, Ideology, and Interpretation," 189; idem, "*Mishnato ha-
Hilkhatit*," 90; R. Yitzchak Blau, "Biblical Narratives and the Status of Enemy Civilians
in Wartime," *Tradition* 39, no. 4 (2006): 21–25; Aryeh Edrei, "Law, Interpretation, and
Ideology," 215n71. See also Luz's judgment that R. Yisraeli's theory of wars of revenge
"found a way of 'declaring pure something inherently impure'" (*Wrestling with an Angel*,
211). Blidstein is also disturbed by what he perceives to be the militancy of R. Yisraeli's
views, but Blidstein inexplicably renders this judgment by focusing only on halakhic
models that R. Yisraeli ultimately rejects, not on the concept of wars of revenge. Thus,
in his article "The Treatment of Hostile Civilian Populations," pp. 31, 33–34, Blidstein
addresses R. Yisraeli's views on the *rodef* and discretionary war. In his article, "The
State and the Legitimate Use of Coercion in Modern Halakhic Thought," *Studies in
Contemporary Jewry* 18 (2002): 13–14, he deals only with R. Yisraeli's views on discretionary war. Yet, R. Yisraeli finds both the *rodef* model and that of discretionary war to
be inadequate for understanding the Kibiyeh raid from a halakhic standpoint.
    67. Gutel, "*Lehimah be-Shetah Ravey Ukhlosiyah Ezrahit*," 94–95.
    68. Roness, "Halakhah, Ideology, and Interpretation,"192.
    69. Ibid., 192–93.
    70. Ibid., 192–95. Others voice objection to R. Yisraeli's views on wars of revenge
but without labeling him as an extremist. See, for instance, R. Menashe Shmerlovski,
"*Milhemet Mitsvah ve-Mmilhemet Reshut*," *Sefer Har'el*, ed. R. Eli'ezer Hayim Shenvald
(Hispin, Israel: Ha-Golan, 1999), 81–83. One could broaden this criticism beyond the
realm of Halakhah. A common assumption among Jewish scholars and thinkers is that
Judaism in general does not encourage revenge. Thus, it has been pointed out by more
than one commentator that in the Bible it is usually God who takes revenge, and that
human beings are discouraged from doing so. R. Yisraeli's position, therefore, seems
to be out of sync with the Jewish tradition as a whole. For a discussion of the issue of

Are R. Yisraeli's views as extreme as commentators have claimed? I do not believe so. To get an accurate understanding of R. Yisraeli's views, we must first recap the key points of his essay. First, it is important for us to keep in mind that the essay is focused on a very specific situation, one in which the adult population of an Arab town has aided and encouraged terrorists to kill Jews and has perhaps even helped to plan the violence. R. Yisraeli's sole concern is the halakhic status of this population. May they be attacked because of their complicity with the terrorists or not? R. Yisraeli is not interested in the terrorists themselves. In the case of Kibiyeh, the terrorists did not reside in the town and were presumed to have been absent at the time of the Israeli raid.

By the time R. Yisraeli gives us his final position in the Kibiyeh essay, he had concluded earlier in his discussion that in Kibiyeh the adult population had the halakhic status of pursuers (rodfim) and could therefore be killed. This point is important for understanding R. Yisraeli's final position because it establishes that the residents of Kibiyeh were culpable for assisting in the killing of Jews, and they were fair targets because of that complicity. For R. Yisraeli, these people were therefore anything but civilians who were "innocent."[71]

The difficulty with the pursuer hypothesis was that one cannot kill a pursuer if innocent people will be harmed as well. Therefore, the raid in Kibiyeh could not be permitted on the basis of this paradigm, seeing as the raid was likely to involve the death of children who were innocent of all wrongdoing. Yet, with his final position, R. Yisraeli circumvents this obstacle. If the operation in Kibiyeh was, in fact, part of a mandatory war of revenge, the adults of Kibiyeh could certainly be killed because they would be considered combatants in a war against the Jewish state for the same reason they were considered pursuers: they participated in that war by aiding and abetting those who carried out violence against Jews. But even more important, there was no need to worry about children being killed because in all wars there is no obligation to be "meticulous" in differentiating between "righteous" and "wicked," as R. Yisraeli puts it. It is accepted practice in war that in attacking those who are involved in the hostilities, innocent people may die as well. Thus, in the Kibiyeh raid, Israelis were justified in killing the "wicked" adults, even though the "righteous" children would be killed as well. That consequence was unavoidable.

revenge in the Hebrew Bible, see the thorough study of H. G. L. Peels, *The Vengeance of God* (Leiden: E. J. Brill, 1995), especially, 274–76.

71. It should be acknowledged that in equating the Kibiyeh raid with a war of revenge, R. Yisraeli has shifted his paradigm from a forward-looking ethic to a backward-looking one. That is, with the pursuer hypothesis, the object was to deter future violence, while the final hypothesis involving wars of revenge is focused on punishing violence in the past. Still, R. Yisrael's discussion of the pursuer hypothesis clearly establishes that the adult residents of Kibiyeh were participants in the violence against Jews and were culpable for their actions, and that judgment carries over into R. Yisraeli's discussion of his final position.

R. Yisraeli emphasizes, however, that in an operation such as the one in Kibiyeh, children may not be killed deliberately. Their deaths were excusable only if they occurred accidentally in the course of attacking the adults. R. Yisraeli tells us that this exception is due to the fact that wars of revenge in response to enemy attack are not of the same severity as the war waged by the Israelites against the Midianites who had tempted them into idolatry. Only in that instance could children be targeted.

In effect, R. Yisraeli's fifth and final response solves the one major problem that derailed the "pursuer" hypothesis earlier in his essay. With the pursuer hypothesis, R. Yisraeli demonstrated that the adult population of Kibiyeh were considered accomplices to the terrorists and could be attacked, but according to that paradigm, a military raid against the town was nonetheless forbidden because of the possibility that children would be harmed as well. R. Yisraeli's final response, which is based on the notion that the raid was part of a larger war of revenge, overcomes this obstacle. According to this model, the raid could proceed despite the danger posed to children because in war the innocent perish along with the guilty, and therefore, as long as the children were not intentionally targeted, the raid was within the bounds of Halakhah.

What comes out of this review of the major points of the Kibiyeh essay is that R. Yisraeli's is not as extreme or militant as his critics claim. One gets the impression from R. Yisraeli's critics that when he supported wars of revenge against Arabs, he meant that Jews were permitted to do to Arabs exactly what had been done to them. Jews could kill innocent Arabs in indiscriminate fashion in retaliation for the indiscriminate killing of innocent Jews. But that is not what R. Yisraeli argued. R. Yisraeli endorsed the killing of only those whom he deemed responsible for the violence against Jews, and, according to his halakhic ruling, this included the adults of Kibiyeh who had aided the terrorists, not just the terrorists themselves. Those who were innocent—in particular, the children—should not have been targeted, even though the Arab terrorists showed no compunction about killing Jewish children.

We can bring home this point by asking how R. Yisraeli would have reacted if Israelis had responded to the Arab terrorism emanating from the Jordanian border towns by attacking a Jordanian village elsewhere in the country that had no connection to the terrorists. I suspect that R. Yisraeli would have disapproved of such an action. Not only would the children of such a village have been innocent of all wrongdoing, the adults would have been innocent as well. A military operation such as the one in Kibiyeh was permitted only because it was meant to punish the adult population that bore responsibility for attacks against innocent Jews by aiding those who perpetrated the violence. Put in the language of current international law and just war theory, R. Yisraeli considered the adults of Kibiyeh as "combatants" because of their involvement in the violence against Jews, but that designation would not have applied to adults living in other Arab villages who had nothing to do with terrorism.

Our observations raise the question of whether the term *nekamah*, or "revenge," was really the right one for the type of military action that R. Yisraeli supported. A good deal has been written about the concept of revenge by Western thinkers in recent years, much of it spawned from a discussion by Robert Nozick, in his well-known work *Philosophical Explanations*, in which he argues for a distinction between revenge and retribution. Nozick claims that there are three differences between the two terms: (1) Retribution is in response to a wrong, whereas revenge may be perpetrated for any injury, harm, or slight whatsoever, even if no wrong was committed. (2) The amount of retribution is proportional to the harm done, whereas revenge can exceed that proportionality. (3) Retribution need not be personal, whereas revenge generally is ("I am doing this because of what you did to my father").[72]

R. Yisraeli's understanding of wars of revenge fails to meet Nozick's standards for true revenge. According to R. Yisraeli, one does not initiate a war of revenge in response to any harm or slight. Such wars are a response to a full-scale attack by an enemy. Moreover, wars of revenge in R. Yisraeli's thinking do not exceed the proportionality of the harm done, as we have just shown. Only those responsible for conspiring with terrorists are punished for their crimes. One may also argue that in R. Yisraeli's thinking, wars of revenge, in fact, fall short of proportionality. While the terrorists killed children intentionally, Jews are forbidden to do so. And finally, wars of revenge in R. Yisraeli's thinking need not be personal, though one might argue that in the Kibiyeh raid, this element may have been present to some degree.

A much more appropriate term for the type of war R. Yisraeli is describing may be Nozick's notion of retribution, or just the term "punishment." In common parlance, the latter word is really what R. Yisraeli is referring to in his discussion of wars of revenge. Arab civilian populations that actively support terrorists who kill Jews should be punished for their role in the perpetration of such violence.[73]

More could be said about the matter of revenge and its meaning. As we have noted, Nozick's distinction has inspired much discussion. However, for our purposes, there is no need to delve further into the issue. What we learn from Nozick is that, at the very least, there are serious doubts about whether the term "revenge" as used by R. Yisraeli was appropriate for what he was

---

72. See Robert Nozick, *Philosophical Explanations* (Cambridge, Mass.: Harvard University Press, 1981), 366–74.

73. One should not be perplexed by the fact that at the beginning of his essay, R. Yisraeli had rejected the possibility that the operation in Kibiyeh was for the purpose of punishment. It would seem that R. Yisraeli rejected the punishment paradigm in the first two models because these models were based on everyday Halakhah governing the lives of individuals. However, he seems to have presumed that situations of war were different and that in these situations punishment was appropriate for civilian populations who support terrorists.

trying convey. We also learn that the critics who take R. Yisraeli to task for supporting a radical and militant viewpoint are off the mark. His endorsement of wars of revenge should not conjure up images of Israeli soldiers gunning down innocent Arab civilians in retaliation for Arab terrorism. What he was really speaking about was a war meant to punish those guilty of conspiring with terrorists, who were, in effect, combatants in a war against Israel.

That R. Yisraeli's notion of wars of revenge is not as militant as critics claim is also evident from the fact that his approach toward civilians in such wars is no different from that which he supports for all other wars. He says this quite explicitly; wars of revenge have no unique laws when it comes to the treatment of civilians.[74] In such wars, one can kill the innocent alongside the guilty, but the innocent should not be deliberately targeted. According to R. Yisraeli, that is the same ethic that governs discretionary wars, which, in R. Yisraeli's definition, include all wars waged in conformity with international law and custom. In R. Yisraeli's thinking, what therefore separates wars of revenge from other wars seems to be the intent in waging such wars, not the conduct of Jewish soldiers toward civilians once war has been initiated.

Casting further doubt on the judgment that R. Yisraeli is a radical is that it is not clear that he, in fact, endorsed the military operation that was actually conducted in Kibiyeh! All commentators on R. Yisraeli's essay on Kibiyeh assume that his final position was meant to give approval to the operation retroactively. This assumption is not necessarily warranted. What has not been noticed in the Kibiyeh essay is that at no point in R. Yisraeli's discussion of his final position does he examine what, in fact, happened in the raid. All he tells us is that an attack against the village was warranted. Moreover, in the concluding statement of the essay cited earlier in which he sums up his views, Kibiyeh is not even mentioned. Let us look again at this statement in its entirety:

> What emerges from all this is that there is room for [military] operations of retaliation and revenge against those who assail Israel, and an operation of this kind is in the category of mandatory war. And whatever disaster and harm is inflicted on the [enemy] perpetrators [of violence], their associates, and their children, it is their very own responsibility, and they will bear their sin. And there is no obligation to avoid [military] operations of retaliation because of the concern that the innocent will be harmed, for it is not we who are the causes [of this harm], but they themselves [i.e., the enemy]. We are guiltless.
>
> However, regarding the intention to harm children from the outset, this is something we have not found [in the Jewish tradition] except with the sin of idol-worship. Therefore, one should take care not to hurt them.[75]

---

74. Above, pp. 146–47.
75. *"Pe'ulot Tseva'iyot,"* 205 (section 5:32).

The terms here are prescriptive rather than descriptive. R. Yisraeli seems interested in setting forth general principles on how Jews should deal with the Arab terrorist threat in the future, not in commenting on events that have already occurred.

Roness provides insights that can help explain R. Yisraeli's approach here. Roness argues that R. Yisraeli often formulated his halakhic views regarding the state of Israel in theoretical terms because he knew that the political establishment was not ready to be guided by halakhic norms. R. Yisraeli takes this approach even in cases that deal with actual events. R. Yisraeli saw value in making halakhic rulings of this sort in order to prepare for the time when the Jewish state would be governed by Halakhah.[76] It would seem that it is precisely this approach that R. Yisraeli takes in his essay on the Kibiyeh raid. That is why his language in the essay is prescriptive rather than descriptive.

Other factors may have also caused R. Yisraeli to speak in theoretical terms in his essay on Kibiyeh. He may not have said more about the raid itself because he felt he was in no position to do so. Given that he did not actually witness the raid, he may have believed that he could not determine whether the actions of the Jews who conducted it conformed to his ruling. Thus, for example, he could make no informed judgment about whether those who participated in the raid had killed children intentionally. The thrust of his essay was therefore to use the Kibiyeh raid as a springboard for discussion about operations of this sort so as to provide guidance in the future, not to pronounce judgment on what had already happened.

Yet, it is also possible that R. Yisraeli avoided discussion of the Kibiyeh raid because he had mixed feelings about what happened there. Children were indeed killed in Kibiyeh, and it is therefore possible that in his mind the military operation had gone too far. This may explain why he voices special concern about the killing of children and why he concludes his essay by emphasizing that concern. Thus, his essay may have been as much an attempt to place restrictions on Jewish military action as it was an attempt to determine what was permitted.[77]

76. Roness, "*Mishnato ha-Hilkhatit*," 300.

77. Roness criticizes me for making this suggestion in my earlier article on R. Yisraeli's essay on Kibiyeh. See Roness, "*Mishnato ha-Hilkhatit*," 300n1047. As we have just noted, Roness claims that R. Yisraeli tended to speak about halakhic issues involving the state of Israel in theoretical rather than concrete terms, and he therefore believes it highly unlikely that R. Yisraeli would have had concerns about the carnage in Kibiyeh as I suggest. While I have no quarrel with Roness's argument about the theoretical thrust of R. Yisraeli's writings on the state of Israel, I see no reason to insist that his writings be viewed only in this manner. It is quite possible that while focusing on theoretical issues, R. Yisraeli was also affected—even subliminally—by the concrete events he was addressing. That possibility is even greater with respect to the Kibiyeh operation, seeing as it was such a highly charged issue.

These observations may help account for a curious detail that has been noted by commentators on R. Yisraeli's essay on Kibiyeh but has never been explained. The original title of the essay on Kibiyeh was "The Kibiyeh Incident in Light of Halakhah." However, the title was changed twice in later printings to exclude references to Kibiyeh. Thus, in the expanded version of the original essay in *'Amud ha-Yemini*, the title became "Military Operations in Defense of the State." In a reprint of the earlier shorter version, the title was, "Retaliatory Attacks in Light of Halakhah."[78] We can make sense of these changes by noting that the new titles better reflect the purpose of the essay according to our reading.[79] In the essay, R. Yisraeli is not as much concerned with the matter of Kibiyeh per se as he is with the general question that the Kibiyeh affair raised: can Jews conduct a military operation to kill Arab civilians if they support terrorists who kill Jews? Again, the essay is prescriptive rather descriptive. The change of title, therefore, appears to have been quite deliberate in excluding references to Kibiyeh.

But R. Yisraeli's critics may still insist he was an extremist because none of the attempts that we have made thus far to inject nuance into the Kibiyeh essay gets around the fact that he advocated the killing of unarmed civilians. Indeed, those civilians were complicit in aiding and abetting terrorism against Jews, but one could argue that there is a world of difference between terrorists, on the one hand, and civilians who provide food, shelter, and encouragement to terrorists, on the other hand. Those in the first group deserve to be killed, while those in the second category, despite their immoral behavior, do not.

In fact, international law clearly takes that position. According to international law, an army is not culpable for civilian casualties in war so long as two conditions are met: the civilians who are killed are not deliberately targeted, and the number of civilian deaths in a given military operation is in conformity with the principle of proportionality, which dictates that the number of casualties not be excessive in relation to the military advantage gained by the operation.[80] Civilians can be targeted if they aid the war effort because in

---

78. This reprint is contained in *Be-Tsomet ha-Torah ve-ha-Medinah* (Alon Shevut, Israel: Tsomet, 1991), 253–89. These details have been gleaned from Kalman Neuman, "The Law of Obligatory War and Israeli Reality," in *War and Peace in the Jewish Tradition: From the Biblical World to the Present*, eds. Yigal Levin and Amnon Shapira (London: Routledge, 2012), 197n29.

79. See n. 3 above for the Hebrew titles of these essays.

80. The principle of distinction, which requires that civilians not be targeted is contained in Additional Protocol I, arts. 48, 51.1, 51.2. See Solis, *Law of Armed Conflict*, 232–34, 251–58; Yoram Dinstein, *The Conduct of Hostilities under the International Law of Armed Conflict*, 2nd ed. (New York: Cambridge University Press, 2010), 8, 89, 121, 123–24. The principle of proportionality is found in Additional Protocol I, arts. 51.5(b), 57.2(b). See Solis, *Law of Armed Conflict*, 272–85; Dinstein, *Conduct*, 128–34.

that case they become combatants, but this rule applies only if their actions have a direct connection to military actions that cause harm to the enemy, and the civilians are caught in the actual performance of those actions. Civilians who provide shelter and encouragement to military personnel, even if they are classified as terrorists, do not fall into this category. International law also expressly forbids attacking civilians for the purposes of retaliation.[81]

Therefore, international law in its present form would clearly oppose R. Yisraeli's view that the civilians in Kibiyeh could be targeted on account of their support for the terrorists who were launching attacks on Israeli villages. The civilians were in no way participating directly in those operations by the standards of international law, and they were therefore to be treated as noncombatants.[82]

However, it is important to recognize that most of the prescriptions in international law summarized here were issued after R. Yisraeli composed his essay on Kibiyeh. On the question of civilian casualties, R. Yisraeli formulated his views before international law had given precise guidance on this matter. The targeting of civilians in war was indeed outlawed by international customary law, but this prohibition had not yet been put explicitly into writing in the form of a multilateral treaty. There was also little guidance on who was to be classified as a civilian. Some progress had been made on these questions with the signing of the Geneva Conventions in 1949 which gave protection to civilians in wartime, but that protection was accorded only to certain groups of people. Only with the promulgation of Additional Protocol I of 1977, which supplemented the Geneva Conventions, did the international community afford civilians full protection in the form of a multilateral treaty. Subsequently, efforts were also made to define precisely which individuals

81. Additional Protocol I, art. 51.3, with further clarification in a report by the International Commission of the Red Cross in 2009. See Solis, *Law of Armed Conflict*, 202–6, 252–53, 539, 543–44; Dinstein, *Conduct*, 146–52. However, the state of Israel has a broader definition than most states of what constitutes direct participation in hostilities. According to Israel, civilians that help recruit for terror groups or develop and operate funding activities for those involved in terrorism, are legitimate targets. See Solis, *Law of Armed Conflict*, 543–44.

82. Michael Walzer, the most authoritative spokesman for just war theory in recent years, discusses the Kibiyeh raid in his classic work, *Just and Unjust Wars: A Moral Argument with Historical Illustrations* (New York: Basic Books, 1977). He concludes that the raid was criminal (pp. 217–18). This judgment follows from Walzer's general position on attacking civilians, which is close to that of international law. He argues that armies are permitted to target civilians if they aid the enemy war effort in a direct material manner (p. 146). The paradigmatic example is that of civilians who work in munitions or bomb factories. However, Walzer does not believe that such civilians should be directly targeted. What is targeted is the factory, not the civilians working there, and the destruction of the facility should take place at a time that the minimum loss of civilian life would be expected.

should be classified as civilians and therefore immune from attack, and it eventually included anyone not directly involved in violent activities, as noted above. Yet, these developments happened well after R. Yisraeli composed his essay.

Therefore, in its time, R. Yisraeli's views on civilian casualties were not as extreme as they would be today. That did not stop the international community from condemning the Kibiyeh raid. Public opinion was clearly moving in the direction of giving civilians comprehensive protections, even if international law had not yet fully concretized that sentiment. Nonetheless, R. Yisraeli's views, evaluated within the context of international legal opinion in his own period, would have seemed less militant than they do in our own time.

R. Yisraeli's essay on Kibiyeh is thus more difficult to evaluate from a moral standpoint than commentators have appreciated, both because of the nuances of its arguments which are easy to miss, as well as the historical context in which it was written. Yet we cannot let R. Yisraeli off the hook entirely. There are still elements of his final position in the essay on Kibiyeh that may be deemed objectionable. First of all, in his use of the notion of revenge, R. Yisraeli can be faulted for invoking an incendiary concept that could easily be misunderstood—even if, as we have shown, he did not mean to use this concept in the same way that others have. Moreover, as Roness has pointed out, R. Yisraeli's choice of this concept seems to have been quite deliberate. R. Yisraeli had at his disposal other authoritative arguments that he could have easily called on to justify wars in response to enemy attack and had nothing to do with revenge.[83] Therefore, it is likely that R. Yisraeli's invocation of the notion of revenge was motivated in part by anger against Arabs and their support for terrorism, not just sober halakhic judgment.

We must also note that R. Yisraeli never grapples in a satisfactory manner with the possibility that innocent adults may have been killed in Kibiyeh along with the guilty. He acknowledges that possibility; when he entertains the "pursuer" hypothesis, he alludes to the notion that a minority of adults in Kibiyeh may not have aided the terrorists. However, he implies that these adults could be targeted because they were subsumed under the majority of the adult population that participated in that activity. And that approach seems to carry over into his final hypothesis when he equates the Kibiyeh raid with a battle in a war of revenge. Here too, the problem of killing innocent people is focused only on the children of Kibiyeh, not on any of the adults. Yet, it is hard to understand, according to either hypothesis, why the killing of innocent children is any more problematic from a halakhic standpoint than the killing of innocent adults.

83. Roness, "*Mishnato ha-Hilkhatit*," 91–93; idem, "Halakhah, Ideology, and Interpretation," 192–93.

I would like to examine briefly one more element in R. Yisraeli's essay that has aroused a good deal of criticism with respect to his ethics. As we have seen, R. Yisraeli bases his justification of discretionary war on the notion that the principle of *dina de-malkhuta dina* applies to international laws governing the relationships between nations. Since the gentile nations permit war, Jews can wage war as well. Yet, in order to justify the killing that takes place in war, R. Yisraeli makes use of a metaphysical argument predicated on the notion that there is a fundamental distinction between the souls of Jews and non-Jews. While Jews have souls that belong to God, non-Jews have full owner-ship over their souls, and therefore the non-Jewish nations as a group have a right to permit wars in which their lives may be taken.

A number of commentators have been disturbed by this argument for obvi-ous reasons: it seems to assume that non-Jewish life is cheaper than Jewish life.[84] Yet, a closer examination of R. Yisraeli's essay will reveal yet again that the issues are more complex than they seem. First of all, let us not ignore the irony that while R. Yisraeli appears to denigrate non-Jews here, he does so while arguing that the rules of war for Jews are determined by non-Jews in accordance with the principle of *dina de-malkhuta dina*. While non-Jews are inferior in a metaphysical sense, it is they who decide how Jews should con-duct themselves when it comes to the practice of war in the real world.[85]

Second, R. Yisraeli is not entirely lacking in compassion for non-Jewish life. As we have seen, R. Yisraeli at no point endorses the wanton killing of non-Jews. He expresses concern throughout his deliberations for innocent non-Jewish civilians who die in war. Most poignant are his views on the killing of non-Jewish children. This issue seems to have particularly disturbed him.

His method of dealing with the problem of killing children in war is also noteworthy. As we saw, R. Yisraeli addresses the killing of children when dis-cussing the Midianite war in which children were deliberately put to death. Why, R. Yisraeli asks, were they killed if there is a prohibition in Jewish law against holding children responsible for the sins of their parents? R. Yisraeli answers that children were killed in the Midianite war only because the Midianites had "attacked" the Israelites by tempting them into idol-worship, an assault far worse than a physical war. That is why there is also a biblical mandate to kill children when destroying an Israelite city that has adopted idolatry. The Midianite war therefore does not provide precedent to act in

---

84. See especially Yosef Ahituv, *"Milhamot Yisra'el u-Kedushat ha-Hayim,"* in *Kedushat ha-Hayim ve-Heruf ha-Nefesh,* eds. Aviezer Ravitzky and Isaiah Gafni (Jerusalem: Merkaz Zalman Shazar, 2003), 267–71; Blau, "Biblical Narratives," 24–25.

85. One could argue, however, that R. Yisraeli's position here is still ethically prob-lematic. When it comes to the ethics of warfare, he is willing to follow gentile practice, but when it comes to their humanity, he suddenly becomes a chauvinist! I would like to thank an anonymous reviewer of my earlier article on R. Yisraeli for this insight.

a similar manner in defensive wars when the enemy has attacked in a more conventional manner. What is striking about this line of reasoning is that R. Yisraeli treats the matter of killing non-Jewish children with halakhic principles and injunctions that normally apply to Jews! In their biblical and rabbinic contexts, the prohibition against holding children responsible for the sins of their parents, as well as the case of the idolatrous Israelite city, are focused on Jews. Therefore, in this instance, the distinction between Jews and non-Jews seems to be ignored.

THE QUESTION OF HALAKHIC PRECEDENT

What about the charge of Roness and Gutel that R. Yisraeli's concept of wars of revenge is invalid because it has no precedent in halakhic literature? Here, too, I believe that R. Yisraeli's critics have been too quick to render harsh judgment. There is evidence that R. Yisraeli formulated his views on wars of revenge with the help of a number of rabbinic sources. The first one we have already discussed. It is a midrashic passage that appears in *Ba-Midbar Rabbah* and *Tanhuma* and is critical for understanding R. Yisraeli's views on the Midianite war. The full passage reads as follows:

> "Assail the Midianites" (Num. 25:17): Why? "For they assailed you" (Num. 25:18). From this the Sages have derived the maxim: If a man comes to kill you, kill him first. R. Simeon says: How do we know that one who causes a man to sin is even worse than one who kills him? Because one who kills him, does so only with respect to this world but leaves him a share in the world to come. One who causes him to sin, however, kills him in this world and in the next.[86]

As we have already seen, R. Yisraeli adopts R. Simeon's implied claim that in tempting the Israelites into idolatry, the Midianites were perpetrating violence against them that was worse than murder because someone who tempts another person into idolatry affects the latter's fate not just in this life but in the afterlife as well. It was for this reason, according to R. Yisraeli, that the wholesale slaughter of the Midianites was justified.

Yet, other aspects of the passage may have had an influence on R. Yisraeli as well. The passage not only justifies the killing of the Midianites, it also deduces from the Midianite episode the general principle that one may kill in self-defense in any situation in which one's life is threatened. Moreover, the biblical source upon which the midrash relies is concerned with war, and

---

86. According to the version in *Ba-Midbar Rabbah* 21:4. A similar passage appears in *Tanhuma, Pinhas* 3.

therefore the midrash implies that what the Midianite story teaches us is that killing in self-defense is permitted not just for individuals but for the Jewish nation as a whole. R. Yisraeli therefore appears to have drawn from this midrash the notion that the Midianite war was paradigmatic for all future instances in which the Jewish people had to defend itself from enemy attack.

One may wonder why R. Yisraeli does not explicitly mention this midrashic source when he initially formulates his concept of wars of revenge. It may be that he was aware of the fact that the lesson he was drawing from it was somewhat different from what the original source intended. After all, R. Yisraeli departs from the midrash by rejecting the notion that the Midianite war was paradigmatic for wars of self-defense. For him, there are no such wars; wars that respond to an enemy attack are wars of revenge. Thus, the Midianite war is paradigmatic only for wars of the latter type.[87]

An explicit precedent for R. Yisraeli's views on wars of revenge is found in a passage in the writings of R. Judah ben Betsal'el Loew (1520–1609), better known by his acronym, Maharal, a famous sixteenth-century figure. The Maharal addresses the topic of war in comments on Genesis 34 that reports the story of the rape of Dinah, Jacob's daughter, by Shechem son of Hamor. The Maharal is troubled, as many commentators are, by the violent rampage of Simeon and Levi, Dinah's brothers, who slaughter the entire male population of Shechem in response to the sexual assault, even though only one person committed the crime. The Maharal justifies their actions as follows:

It would appear that [the killing of the men of Shechem] is not at all a problem. For matters are different when two nations [are involved in battle], such as the Children of Israel and the Canaanites, which are two nations. ... Therefore, they [i.e., the Children of Israel] were permitted to wage war with the same legal justification of a nation that comes to wage war against another nation, which the Torah permits. And even though the Torah says, "When you approach a town to attack it, you shall offer it terms of peace" (Deut. 20:10), that is only when they [i.e., the enemy nation] have not done anything to Israel. But if they have done something to Israel, such as in this case in which they [i.e., Shechemites] attacked them in committing an abominable act against them, even though only one of them did [it]—because he was one of the people [of Shechem], [and] they [i.e., the Shechemites] initiated the attack on them [i.e., the Children of Israel],

---

87. In making this move, R. Yisraeli is merely reinstating the theme of revenge that is found in the biblical text and that the midrash seems to have attempted to avoid. When God commands Moses to wage war, He tells him, "Avenge the Israelite people on the Midianites" (Num. 31:2), and shortly afterward, Moses gathers an army and implores it to "wreak the Lord's vengeance on Midian" (Num. 31:4). By bringing in the issue of revenge, R. Yisraeli is therefore going back to the meaning of the original biblical text upon which the midrashic reading is based.

they [i.e., the Children of Israel] are permitted to take revenge on them [i.e., the Shechemites]. This is the case with all wars, such as "Assail the Midianites" etc. (Num. 25:17). Even though there were many [Midianites] who did not do [anything], this makes no difference. Because they [i.e., the innocent Midianites] belonged to that nation that perpetrated evil against them [i.e., the Israelites], they are permitted to wage war against them [i.e., the Midianites]. This is the case with all wars.[88]

The Maharal's argument here is that Simeon and Levi acted correctly in attacking the Shechemites because the Children of Israel and the Shechemites were, from a halakhic standpoint, two nations at war. The war that the Children of Israel initiated was a war of "revenge" in response to the assault by the Shechemites. The fact that only one person perpetrated the assault on Dinah is of no consequence. The nation to which that person belonged could be held responsible for his actions because that is the case with all wars. Nations may be held responsible for the crimes of the few. The war against the Midianites sets the precedent here. One can presume that not all Midianites were guilty of leading the Israelites astray. Nonetheless, the nation as a whole was held responsible, and therefore the Israelites were ordered to take revenge on them.

Most of the ingredients of R. Yisraeli's views on wars of revenge are contained in this passage. If a nation assaults the Jewish people, the Jews may wage a war of revenge in response, and in a war of this type, one need not be concerned about taking innocent life, because in war, those who are innocent are considered part of the collective. Moreover, the war against the Midianites provides the paradigm for this kind of war. R. Yisraeli does not cite the Maharal in formulating his views on wars of revenge, but the similarities between the Maharal's views and those of R. Yisraeli are quite striking. And given the Maharal's stature, there is a likelihood that R. Yisraeli was familiar with the passage of the Maharal under discussion here. It is possible, therefore, that the Maharal influenced R. Yisraeli's thinking on wars of revenge.

R. Yisrael's critics may not be satisfied with the rabbinic sources cited here in support of his notion of wars of revenge because they are drawn from aggadic and exegetical texts, not texts that are strictly halakhic. The fact remains that there is no formal category of wars of revenge in medieval Halakhah. Yet we have to be careful in our judgment of what R. Yisraeli considered halakhic literature. We saw an instance, earlier in our discussion, in which R. Yisraeli relied on non-halakhic sources for halakhic purposes. He cited sources from Kabbalistic theology to explain why discretionary war is permitted despite the carnage it causes. We also surmised that in citing this type of source, R. Yisraeli was applying R. Kook's methodology of the "Torah of the land of

88. *Gur Aryeh* (Tel Aviv: Pardes, 1956) on Genesis 34:13.

Israel" according to which non-halakhic sources were legitimate resources for halakhic decision-making. We therefore have to keep an open mind about which texts are considered proper halakhic precedent in R. Yisraeli's rulings. He may very well have regarded the passage in the midrash aggadah about the Midianite episode, as well as the source of the Maharal regarding the Shechem story, as perfectly legitimate precedents for halakhic deliberation. In relying on these sources, R. Yisraeli was once again applying the methodology of the "Torah of the land of Israel."

The focus of R. Yisraeli's essay on Kibiyeh is whether Halakhah approves of a military operation of the kind conducted in Kibiyeh, an operation that was directed at an Arab civilian population on account of its support for terrorism against Jews. Was it permissible to kill these civilians in retaliation for their role in the violence?

R. Yisraeli proposes five halakhic models for answering this question. The first three approach the question via norms from everyday Halakhah, but he rejects all three. With the fourth and fifth models, R. Yisraeli takes a new direction by attempting to deal with the question with the help of norms from wartime Halakhah. The fourth model entertains the possibility that the type of raid conducted in the Kibiyeh operation falls into the category of discretionary war, but this model does not yield a conclusive answer to R. Yisraeli's question. It is the fifth and final model that R. Yisraeli favors. According to this paradigm, a military raid such as the one conducted in Kibiyeh is permitted because it is to be viewed as a battle in an ongoing war that was initiated by the Arab side upon the establishment of the state of Israel. In Halakhah, all wars waged in response to enemy attack are mandatory wars, and their purpose is to wreak revenge on the nation that has done them harm. The authoritative source for this type of war is the biblical account of the Midianite war. Most important for R. Yisraeli's purposes is that in wars of revenge one may kill the innocent with the guilty, as one is permitted to in all wars. Thus, in the military operation conducted in Kibiyeh, it was permissible to target adult civilians because they were combatants in being complicit in terrorist operations against Jews, and permission to do so was granted even if innocent children were killed, as long as there had been no intention to target them deliberately. Once again, in war, one must accept the fact that the innocent will die alongside the guilty.

Critics have been disturbed by R. Yisraeli's position. Yet, we have shown that his position is more nuanced and complex than the critics have assumed. His rhetoric is more incendiary than his actual views. First of all, R. Yisraeli did not endorse indiscriminate violence against Arab civilians as retaliation for violence of this sort perpetrated against Jews. Only those complicit in the violence against Jews could be attacked. Second, when it came to the actual waging of wars of revenge, the rules were no different from all other wars. The innocent can be killed alongside the guilty because war does not allow one to easily differentiate between them, not because we should have no interest in sparing the innocent. Third, while R. Yisraeli believed that killing the innocent is permitted in wars of revenge, he also believed that it should not be intentional. Thus, children should never be targeted, seeing as they should always be viewed as innocent bystanders. Finally, R. Yisraeli's critics have overlooked the fact that at no point in his essay does he clearly endorse what actually happened in Kibiyeh. His essay is prescriptive rather than descriptive in its emphasis. It attempts to set halakhic policy for how Jews should conduct military operations against civilian populations in the future, rather than endorse the carnage that took place in the Kibiyeh raid.

In light of these observations, the term "revenge" may have been the wrong one for R. Yisraeli to use. The terms "retribution" or "punishment" may have been more appropriate. R. Yisraeli seems to have chosen to speak about revenge more for its rhetorical effect than for its substantive meaning with respect to war ethics. Like most Israelis, he was enraged by the terrorist violence against Jews, and the notion of revenge allowed him to vent to his feelings on this issue. But, once again, his actual positions on how to treat civilian populations in war were more nuanced than this language suggests.

We also have to keep in mind that R. Yisraeli's views would not have appeared as radical when assessed according to the standards of international law in his time. When R. Yisraeli composed his essay, the protections of civilians from the ravages of war were not yet fully developed. It was only later on that those protections were put in place.

Still, R. Yisraeli's views are open to criticism. His invocation of the concept of revenge could be viewed as irresponsible. Even if that notion is more complex than his readers have appreciated, its subtleties can be easily lost on his readers and interpreters, and that is a consequence he might have foreseen.

Moreover, R. Yisraeli does not clarify why he was so concerned about the innocent children who died in Kibiyeh while showing little interest in the deaths of innocent adults. He seems to acknowledge in places that some of the adult casualties in Kibiyeh may have been innocent of wrongdoing. But he never takes up that issue, except to imply that such individuals were to be considered part of the guilty majority, a position that hardly justifies their killing from a halakhic standpoint.

Let us now turn to examining what is most important for our concerns: where does R. Yisraeli's essay on Kibiyeh leave us with respect to the major questions about war that are at the center of our study? Because R. Yisraeli's two most important paradigms for dealing with the Kibiyeh raid are focused on war, he has a great deal to say about these questions.

We will begin with the issue of which types of war are permitted in our time. R. Yisraeli believes that Jews may engage in wars to respond to an enemy attack, but he takes the original position that these wars are not for the purpose of self-defense; rather they are meant to take revenge on the enemy.

R. Yisraeli also has innovative views regarding discretionary war. He is the only figure in our study thus far who permits discretionary wars to be waged in our time. He also takes the unprecedented position that discretionary wars refer to all wars sanctioned by international law and custom in accordance with the principle of *dina de-malkhuta dina*, "the law of the kingdom is the law."

The difficulty with discretionary war is that, according to R. Yisraeli, Jews may not wage this type of war without a king and Sanhedrin. The only reason he entertains the possibility that the military operation in Kibiyeh was permitted as a discretionary war is that he presumes that the operation was conducted by a group of volunteers from the village of Yehud, a presumption that, as it turned out, was mistaken. The same restriction regarding legitimate authority does not seem to affect non-Jewish nations, perhaps because they have no Sanhedrin to begin with. Therefore, R. Yisraeli presumes they can still wage discretionary war in the present era.

It is not clear what all this means for the state of Israel. It would seem that in R. Yisraeli's thinking all the nations of the world are allowed to wage discretionary war—except Israel. For Israel, discretionary war would be permitted only if its army were composed entirely of volunteers. One may speculate that R. Yisraeli would also permit the Israeli government to wage discretionary war with a conscripted army on the premise that the government in Israel is democratically elected, and it thus represents the will of the people. Therefore, when the Israeli government sends its troops to war, the action, in effect, emanates from the will of the people as well—or at least, its majority. However, these ruminations are purely speculative.

R. Yisraeli also has good deal to say about more specific issues pertaining to war. When it comes to conscription, R. Yisraeli argues that in wars that respond to enemy attack—what R. Yisraeli calls wars of revenge—all Jews are required to fight. He bases his position on the biblical account of the Midianite war in which all Israelites were obligated to go into battle. We learn from this source that the imperative to wreak revenge on an enemy overrides the prohibition against forcing someone to endanger his life.

With respect to discretionary war, R. Yisraeli does not discuss the problem of conscription in any detail. However, as we have just noted, he does indicate that in the absence of a king and Sanhedrin, Jews may wage discretionary war only if the army is composed of volunteers. Thus, it would seem that the Israeli government would not be allowed to conscript soldiers for a war of this type. But once again, it is not clear whether in R. Yisraeli's thinking, the democratic character of the Israeli government would have an impact on this matter.

As for the problem of casualties among enemy civilians, R. Yisraeli believes that killing the innocent is in the very nature of war, and it therefore cannot be avoided. However, R. Yisraeli indicates that in war one should not take innocent life any more than is necessary. In the case of Kibiyeh, R. Yisraeli therefore rules that the children of the village should not have been killed intentionally. It is also likely that he would extend the same principle to adult civilians in other situations. The adult population of Kibiyeh were regarded as combatants because of their participation in the violence against Jews, and they therefore deserved to be killed. But presumably adults in other Arab villages who had no role in the violence would not have been regarded by R. Yisraeli as legitimate targets of attack.

The problem of killing the innocent in a discretionary war occupied less of R. Yisraeli's attention than an even more basic challenge: how does one justify killing of any sort in this kind of war, even that of enemy soldiers? If Halakhah envisions waging discretionary war for such reasons as economic gain or expanding territory, Halakhah, it would seem, approves of wanton killing. R. Yisraeli surmounts this difficulty by a combination of halakhic and theological considerations. He argues that the permissibility of discretionary wars is determined by international law and custom, and if the latter dictate that wars can be initiated for purely aggressive purposes, then one can kill for motives that would not normally be halakhically acceptable. This position, however, is ultimately based on theological considerations. Non-Jews are masters of their souls in a way that Jews are not, and they can therefore forfeit their right to life in discretionary war if they so choose.

We might interject here that this explanation is not without problems. It seems to work when nations engaged in a war are spoiling for a fight and fully willing to use war as a means to settle their differences. But if a nation is not interested in war and is merely being victimized by the aggression of another, it is hard to see how its citizens have "chosen" to give up their right to life.

In some places, R. Yisraeli speaks as if the dichotomy between the "innocent" and the "guilty" is relevant to discretionary war, as it was for wars of revenge. He tells us that when conducting military operations in a discretionary war, an army need not differentiate between the innocent and the guilty. But notably absent in R. Yisraeli's ruminations on discretionary war is any suggestion that one should spare the innocent when possible, as he tells us in his discussion of wars of revenge. All in all, R. Yisraeli's views on civilian casualties in discretionary war do not seem to be fully worked out.[89]

89. Moreover, one could argue that R. Yisraeli should have differentiated between the various types of discretionary war with respect to this issue. In discretionary war of the preemptive variety, for instance, one could perhaps differentiate between the guilty and innocent because the guilty would be the soldiers preparing for attack, while the innocent would be civilians uninvolved in such activity. The distinction between innocent and guilty, however, would have less meaning, or perhaps none at all, if war were to be waged for economic gain or expansion of territory. Here, everyone would presumably be in the category of the innocent. Yet, R. Yisraeli does not broach these questions.

R. Yisraeli's overall approach to the laws of war is similar to that of R. Kook, R. Herzog, and R. Waldenberg. Like them, he believes that the laws of war are different in kind from those that pertain to everyday life. However, he has introduced a whole new series of concepts in delineating the precise manner in which the two bodies of law differ, both with respect to the questions of conscription and loss of life among enemy civilians.

One may have expected that R. Yisraeli would follow R. Kook in believing that the reason wartime Halakhah supersedes everyday Halakhah is that communal interests are at stake here and they need to be protected.[90] In other instances involving such interests, R. Yisraeli came up with innovative halakhic positions on matters pertaining to the state in order to ensure that Halakhah was responsive to the needs of the public. Thus, for instance, R. Yisraeli was extremely lenient when it came to the question of halakhically observant policemen violating Sabbath law in order to fulfill their duties. Public welfare was the paramount consideration here, and therefore R. Yisraeli was willing to compromise on Sabbath law in order to ensure that the needs of the public be addressed.[91] It would therefore make sense for R. Yisraeli to adopt the view that the laws of war were designed to protect the communal welfare as well.

However, in his essay on Kibiyeh, R. Yisraeli sends mixed signals about whether the laws of war were meant to serve this function. Certainly, discretionary war is depicted by R. Yisraeli in the Kibiyeh essay as addressing communal needs since it is waged for such purposes as economic gain and settling disputes between nations, purposes that benefit the collective. However, when it comes to mandatory wars waged in response to enemy attack, R. Yisraeli informs us that the motivating principle is revenge—or, perhaps more accurately, punishment. Here justice is served as mandated by God, but not necessarily the needs of the community of Israel. In fact, R. Yisraeli rules out the notion that communal needs are at stake here by denying that wars waged in response to enemy attack are defensive in nature. In such wars one does not fight to protect fellow Jews but instead to punish the enemy.[92]

---

90. Above, pp. 63–64.

91. This matter is discussed extensively by Yost, *"Pesikat ha-Halakhah shel ha-Rav Sha'ul Yisra'eli*, especially chapters 3 and 4. See also Yost, "Me'afyeney ha-Pesikah ha-Tsiburt be-Mishnato ha-Hilkhatit shel ha-Rav Sha'ul Yisra'eli: Haf'alat ha-Mishtarah be-Shabbat ke-Mivhan," *Diney Yisra'el* 28 (2011): 145–85.

92. In later essays, R. Yisraeli explicitly rejects R. Kook's view that the king had special communal laws that included those regulating war. See "Pe'ulot Tseva'iyot," 104–5; and *Havat Binyanim*, ed. R. Neryah Gutel (Kefar Darom, Israel: Makhon ha-Torah ve-ha-Arets), vol. 1, pp. 94–95 (pagination according to the text as it appears in www.hebrewbooks.org). However, it is unclear whether this viewpoint is relevant here seeing as it appears in an essay written over twenty years after the Kibiyeh essay.

Yet, the essay on Kibiyeh will not be R. Yisraeli's last word on war. After its publication, R. Yisraeli authored a series of subsequent essays over a span of thirty years that continued to dwell on halakhic matters pertaining to wars initiated by an enemy nation. We shall see in our next chapter that in these writings, the positions R. Yisraeli set forth in his essay on Kibiyeh regarding wars of this type will be substantially revised, and the new positions will be no less innovative than those we have encountered thus far.

CHAPTER 7

༫ঌ

R. Sha'ul Yisraeli

The Later Writings

The task of analyzing R. Yisraeli's writings on war after the Kibiyeh essay is no less daunting than analyzing the Kibiyeh essay itself. None of the later essays is nearly as lengthy as the essay on Kibiyeh, but most of them are still quite complex. Moreover, even when they discuss the same issues, none of the later essays takes positions precisely identical to those found in the Kibiyeh essay, nor are they always consistent with each other. R. Yisraeli had a penchant for continually revising his ideas from one essay to the next without acknowledging or explaining his revisions, and this feature of his work is on full display in his later writings on war.

The challenge of examining R. Yisraeli's views in the later essays will be made easier by the fact that I have chosen to focus exclusively on how he treats mandatory wars waged in response to enemy attack. The treatment of discretionary war in these writings will have to wait for another occasion. There are two reasons for my preference for exploring R. Yisraeli's views on wars of the first type. First, it is the form of war that R. Yisraeli discusses most in his later writings. He does engage the subject of discretionary war in some of the later works, but not nearly as frequently or extensively as he does mandatory war. Second, my study has concentrated primarily on how halakhic authorities have dealt with war as a concrete reality for the state of Israel, and mandatory wars waged in response to an attack by an enemy nation are clearly the type of war most relevant to this concern. From the time of its founding, Israel has been under the constant threat of war from hostile Arab neighbors, and it is undoubtedly for this reason that R. Yisraeli is most preoccupied with war of this character in his later writings. Of course, in the essay on Kibiyeh, R. Yisraeli permits Jews to wage discretionary war in our day and age, as well, which would suggest that this form of war is also relevant in our time. However, R. Yisraeli does not take a clear position on the circumstances under which this type of war may be conducted, and in his later writings, he does not bring any more clarity to the matter. Thus, once again, given that this study is focused primarily on how war is dealt with by halakhic authorities as an actual reality, it is best to concentrate on R. Yisraeli's views on wars waged in response to enemy attack.[1]

Yet, despite the narrowed focus in this chapter, the material we will be looking at is still quite challenging. Even on the specific topic we will be examining, R. Yisraeli presents a bewildering variety of views across a series of essays, and it will take some effort to untangle them.

PRELIMINARY REFLECTIONS

Because of the complexity of the material to be analyzed here, let us begin our discussion by anticipating the direction it will take. First, we should note that while in the essay on Kibiyeh, R. Yisraeli was concerned with both the challenge raised by conscription and that of enemy civilian casualties, in the later essays R. Yisraeli's concern is only with the first issue. Second, and more important, most of R. Yisraeli's later writings on war take a position on conscription that represents a sharp departure from the one we saw in the Kibiyeh essay. In that essay, R. Yisraeli held the view that conscription for wars initiated by an enemy nation could not be justified on the basis of an imperative for Jews to rescue their fellow Jews from danger, because no Jew could be required to endanger his life for that purpose. R. Yisraeli therefore made the case for conscription on the basis of an imperative that was unique to wars initiated by an enemy and was drawn from the Midianite episode in the Bible: the requirement to wreak revenge on the attacking nation. This imperative overrode the prohibition against forcing people to risk their lives for the sake of saving others. In his later writings, R. Yisraeli does something of an about-face on this issue. The preponderant approach he takes in these works is that in everyday situations, Jews are indeed required to risk their lives to save other Jews from a lethal threat, and they must therefore do so in war as well.

R. Yisraeli has taken a position here that we have not yet seen in our study. R. Kook, R. Herzog, and R. Waldenberg all assume a distinction between wartime Halakhah and everyday Halakhah, as does R. Yisraeli himself in the essay

---

1. The selection of material in this chapter, as well as the structure of my discussion therein, owe a great deal to Yitzchak Roness's treatment of R. Yisraeli's writings on war in his *"Mishnato ha-Hilkhatit,"* 85–110, 305–11. My analysis here has also benefitted from a number of Roness's insights. However, I approach R. Yisraeli's writings from an angle that is different from Roness's in a number of respects, and I also depart from him on a number of specific points.

on Kibiyeh.[2] In his later writings, however, R. Yisraeli completely erases that distinction, at least with respect to the issue of conscription.

R. Yisraeli bases this approach to conscription on reasoning that bears some resemblance to that which we saw in R. Herzog. According to R. Yisraeli, the imperative to risk one's life to save others from harm applies in situations in which those being rescued are in a position of "certain danger" (*vaday sakanah*) and the rescuer faces only a "possible danger" (*safek sakanah*). This situation is precisely the one that all soldiers face when they fight in wars waged in response to enemy attack. They, too, are placing themselves in "possible danger" in order to rescue fellow Jews who are in "certain danger." As with R. Herzog, the presumption seems to be that in war, civilians who do not serve in the army are more vulnerable to the enemy than soldiers who are armed.[3] Thus, conscription can be justified on the basis of everyday Halakhah and requires no special dispensation for situations of war. R. Yisraeli, like R. Herzog, also makes use of the Jerusalem Talmud to support his thinking here, though, as we shall see, he will attempt to find a basis for this approach in other sources as well.

However, despite some overlap with R. Herzog, R. Yisraeli's thinking is categorically different from that of his predecessor. R. Herzog did not believe that he had a sufficient case for justifying conscription for defensive wars within the parameters of everyday Halakhah, only for the 1948 war because of its unique circumstances. R. Yisraeli, by contrast, provides an argument for conscription that is not only based on everyday Halakhah but applies in principle to any and all defensive wars.

Not all of R. Yisraeli's later writings take the new approach. As we shall see, in one essay he returns to the notion that the imperative to risk one's life in wars initiated by an enemy has nothing to do with everyday halakhic norms, and he will again invoke the Midianite episode as the source for his position— though this time with an interpretation somewhat different from that found in the Kibiyeh essay. However, the approach that clearly dominates his later writings is the one just described, an approach that justifies conscription on the belief that in everyday Halakhah, Jews are required to save others from danger even at the risk of their own lives and that the same obligation therefore applies in war.[4]

2. Though as we have noted, R. Waldenberg unwittingly opens the door to the possibility that there is no distinction between the two realms in his citation of the *Shem Aryeh* on the issue of conscription.

3. As we pointed out in our chapter on R. Herzog, one might question this assumption on the premise that in wartime soldiers are often in greater danger than civilians. See above, p. 98n30.

4. Tables 7.1 and 7.2, at the end of this chapter summarize R. Yisraeli's views on war in all of the essays examined in this chapter as well as those in the Kibiyeh essay that were explored in the last chapter. Readers may want to consult these tables periodically while reading this chapter because of the complexities of R. Yisraeli's positions as they evolve in his writings after Kibiyeh.

The intriguing question is why R. Yisraeli's views on this matter went through such a dramatic change. However, before we tackle that question, we must first establish that such a change indeed took place, and it is to this task we now turn.

ERETS HEMDAH I: THE NEW PARADIGM FOR CONSCRIPTION

The first essay in R. Yisraeli's later writings to take up the issue of war initiated by an enemy nation was composed in 1957, just four years after the essay on Kibiyeh was published, and it appeared in a collection entitled, *Erets Hemdah*, a two-volume work.[5] R. Yisraeli's discussion here is initially focused on the question of whether a Jew may leave the land of Israel when a war of this kind is in progress so as to avoid danger. However, the discussion quickly becomes centered on the issue of conscription because that is really the key question here. If, in situations of war initiated by an enemy nation, all Jews must serve in the army to fend off the threat, then clearly no Jew would be allowed to leave the state of Israel after such a war has begun to find safe refuge elsewhere. But if in such situations, Jews do not have to serve in the army, then the door is open to the possibility that an individual may leave the country for a more secure haven.[6]

R. Yisraeli entertains a number of answers to his query, but in the last section of the essay he concludes that a Jew is not allowed to leave the land of Israel when a war has been initiated by an enemy because in this type of war, every Jew is, in fact, required to join the army and fight the adversary. As Maimonides tells us, wars meant to "save Israel from the clutches of an enemy" (*'ezrat yisra'el mi-yad tsar*) are mandatory, and all Jews must participate in the effort to defeat the enemy. Yet, what is most significant here is that R. Yisraeli claims that this ruling is based on the principle that Jews are required, even in non-war situations, to subject themselves to "possible danger" in order to save fellow Jews who are in "certain danger." In R. Yisraeli's thinking, war waged in response to enemy attack is merely an instance in which this requirement applies to all Jews because of the nature of the situation. As noted, the presumption seems to be that soldiers and civilians alike are endangered by the

---

5. *"Berihah min ha-Arets bi-She'at Sakanah," Erets Hemdah be-Hilkhot Erets Yisra'el* (Jerusalem: Mosad ha-Rav Kuk, 1989), 49–52. There is some uncertainty as to when the material in this collection was composed. However, Roness believes there is evidence that this particular essay was written not long before its publication. See Roness, *"Mishnato ha-Hilkhatit,"* 97n363, 104–5n384.

6. *Berihah min ha-Arets*, 49.

enemy onslaught, but that soldiers are in a somewhat less dangerous situation during war because they are armed.[7]

R. Yisraeli also claims that his reasoning is rooted in both Talmuds. Most innovative is his claim that the Babylonian Talmud endorses his thinking. The Jerusalem Talmud is easily co-opted into R. Yisraeli's viewpoint. As was noted in earlier chapters, a discussion in the Jerusalem Talmud cites an opinion that war a waged in response to enemy attack is a mandatory war in which all Jews must fight.[8] Moreover, the notion that a Jew is required to subject himself to possible danger in order to rescue a fellow Jew in certain danger is implied in another passage in the Jerusalem Talmud.[9] Thus, both elements of R. Yisraeli's position are found here: the idea that all Jews must fight in wars initiated by an enemy, and the notion that in everyday situations an individual Jew is required to subject himself to possible danger to save another Jew from certain danger.[10]

The Babylonian Talmud, however, is less amenable to R. Yisraeli's viewpoint. We find no statement here that wars waged in response to enemy attack are mandatory, nor do we have any passage suggesting that in ordinary circumstances a Jew must place himself in any kind of danger in order to rescue another Jew whose life is at risk. Moreover, in later halakhic sources, the silence of the Babylonian Talmud on this matter is taken as a deliberate statement that in non-war situations a Jew may not be forced to endanger himself to save others from danger.[11]

Yet, R. Yisraeli finds a source in the Babylonian Talmud that appears to be in alignment with the approach of the Jerusalem Talmud. He cites a Mishnah, 'Eruvin 4:3, that takes up a case in which a group of Jews has to travel outside the parameters of their city on the Sabbath with weapons in hand to rescue fellow Jews who have been attacked by non-Jews. The Mishnah rules that the rescuers are allowed not only to carry their weapons into battle, but also to return home with their weapons after defending their fellow Jews, even though Sabbath law would not normally allow them to do so. The reason for this ruling is a matter of debate among halakhic authorities. R. Yisraeli, on the basis of remarks made by Maimonides, surmises that the rescuers must be allowed to return home with their weapons because otherwise they would be forced to remain where they were with their weapons until the end of the Sabbath, and they would therefore be reluctant to perform similar missions

---

7. Ibid., 51–52.

8. Above, p. 34.

9. Above, pp. 47–48.

10. R. Yisraeli also cites R. David Frankel's *Shiyarey Korban*, a commentary on the Jerusalem Talmud, that, as we have seen in an earlier chapter, grounds this opinion in everyday Halakhah. See above, pp. 65–66.

11. Above, pp. 47–48, 122.

in the future on account of the inconvenience involved.[12] Most important, R. Yisraeli infers from this reading of the Mishnah that Jews are required to risk their lives to defend other Jews who have been attacked, even when no war has been declared. After all, there is no suggestion in the Mishnah that the situation being dealt with here is one of war in the formal halakhic sense, and yet Jews are still expected to endanger themselves to fight on behalf of their fellow Jews. Moreover, the rescuers are expected to come to the assistance of Jews not just on this one occasion but on all future occasions as well:

> Those who go out to rescue [their fellow Jews] are certainly endangering themselves ... though the individuals going out are without doubt in possible danger. ... And this [requirement of] going out [to rescue others] is certainly not under the category of mandatory war because it is not the result of an announcement by a Sanhedrin or any other authoritative body for this purpose, rather they go out on their own in order to rescue. ... And from this amendment (*takanah*) that they should not refrain from rescuing [their fellow Jews] on another occasion, we learn that it is not only permitted to endanger oneself to rescue others, but there is a commandment to this effect. ... And because there is no definition of mandatory war [applicable] in this case, we learn that there is a commandment to place oneself in the category of possible danger in order to save those in Israel who have been placed in certain danger.[13]

It would seem, therefore, that the Babylonian Talmud is no different from the Jerusalem Talmud in requiring Jews in non-war situations to risk their lives to save other Jews from danger. The Mishnah, is, after all, the common text upon which both Talmuds are based. It also stands to reason, according to R. Yisraeli, that the same imperative would apply in situations of war as well; here, too, Jews would have to defend their fellow Jews at the risk of their own lives. Thus, R. Yisraeli concludes that the Babylonian Talmud supports his viewpoint on conscription no less than the Jerusalem Talmud.[14]

In the essay in *Erets Hemdah*, we therefore have the first instance of the dramatic shift that we described in general outline earlier. Here R. Yisraeli is claiming that there is halakhic consensus on the principle that all Jews must fight in wars responding to an enemy attack because every Jew must be willing to face possible danger in order to rescue fellow Jews who are in certain danger. The latter principle is by no mean unique to war. It applies to individual Jews in everyday life, and in wars initiated by an enemy, it merely becomes incumbent on all Jews because of the nature of the situation.

---

12. MT *Shabbat* 2:23.
13. "*Berihah min ha-Arets*," 51.
14. Ibid., 51–52. I am indebted here to Yost's discussion of R. Yisraeli's reasoning. See Yost, "*Pesikat ha-Halakhah shel ha-Rav Sha'ul Yisra'eli*," 48–49.

'AMUD HA-YEMINI: RASHI'S POSITION
ON DISCRETIONARY WAR

The next essay in which R. Yisraeli takes up the issue of wars waged in response to enemy attack appears to represent yet another shift in viewpoint, but we will see that this is not the case. The essay appeared in *'Amud ha-Yemini* that was published in 1966, and it was devoted primarily to the subject of discretionary war.[15] It was prompted by R. Yisraeli's effort to explain a gloss of Rashi on a passage in the Babylonian Talmud, in which Rashi states that the Sanhedrin has to be consulted when a king initiates a discretionary war so that it may pray for victory.[16]

After a lengthy discussion, R. Yisraeli concludes that we can make sense of Rashi's suggestion about the role of Sanhedrin in discretionary war by showing that Rashi's understanding of the distinction between mandatory and discretionary war is radically different from that of Maimonides. Rashi informs us in a comment on the first chapter of Mishnah *Sanhedrin* that the only wars that are in the category of mandatory war are the wars waged by Joshua against the Canaanites to conquer the land of Israel.[17] According to R. Yisraeli, Rashi adopts this position because he believed that those wars were distinctive in being the only wars in which the commandment to go to war was directed at individual Jews. All other wars, according to R. Yisraeli's understanding of Rashi, are discretionary because the commandment to fight is incumbent only on the collective. Such wars are termed "discretionary" because an individual who happens to be occupied with fulfilling one of the divine commandments when a war of this kind has been declared, need not desist from fulfilling that commandment in order to join the fight. Since the war is incumbent on the Jewish people as a whole, others can initiate the military campaign until that person is finished with his halakhic obligation and can participate in the war. These wars are therefore "discretionary" because an individual is not immediately required to participate in the fighting, seeing as it will depend on whether or not he is engaged in the performance of another commandment when the call to arms is issued. This reasoning does not apply in the wars waged by Joshua to conquer the land of Israel, for here the imperative to go war was incumbent on each and every person, and therefore even someone occupied with another commandment had to immediately abandon his efforts to fulfill the commandment in order to fight.

---

15. *"Milhemet Reshut u-Gedareha,"* *'Amud ha-Yemini*, 153–60.

16. BT *Berakhot* 3b, s.v. *"ve-nimlakhin ba-sanhedrin;"* above, p. 137.

17. M *Sanhedrin* 1:1, s.v. *"be-milhemet reshut."* Rashi, in fact, refers to "obligatory war" (*milhemet hovah*), not "mandatory war" (*milhemet mitsvah*), but R. Yisraeli seems to regard the two designations as synonymous.

According to R. Yisraeli, Rashi still views the wars he terms "discretionary" as having a mandatory dimension because waging these wars does fulfill a divine commandment. It is just that the requirement to participate in wars of this kind may be overridden, at least initially, by a competing halakhic obligation, and therefore these wars may also be termed "discretionary."[18]

Against this background, R. Yisraeli attempts to explain the role that the Sanhedrin plays in discretionary war in Rashi's thinking. According to R. Yisraeli's reading, Rashi believes that the approval of the Sanhedrin could not have been a necessary condition for waging discretionary wars because, as already noted, waging these wars still fulfills a commandment despite their being termed "discretionary," and therefore the Sanhedrin could not have possibly been allowed to interfere with their execution. Rashi must have therefore reasoned that the role of the Sanhedrin here was ancillary to the war itself, and he thus concludes that the Sanhedrin's role was to offer prayers for victory. It was appropriate for the Sanhedrin to perform this function for discretionary wars in particular because these wars are incumbent on the Jewish people as a collective, and the role of the Sanhedrin in general was to serve the needs of the nation as a whole. The same reasoning does not apply to the mandatory war waged by Joshua because there the obligation to fight was incumbent upon each Jew as an individual, and therefore the Sanhedrin was not needed here at all.[19]

What is most important for our purposes is what R. Yisraeli has to say about Rashi's views regarding wars waged in response to enemy attack. R. Yisraeli does not discuss these wars here in any depth, but he does group such wars under the category of discretionary war. That may seem odd, but because in Rashi's scheme, all wars except the ones waged by Joshua are termed "discretionary", a war waged in response to enemy attack would be discretionary as well. That is, it, too, is a war incumbent on the collective, not on the individual, and therefore competing halakhic obligations initially take precedence when the war has been waged. Most significant for us is that in discussing wars waged in response to enemy attack, R. Yisraeli refers to them as wars initiated for the purpose of "defense" (*haganah*). He also notes that the biblical source for this type of war is the Midianite war in the book of Numbers.[20]

What are we to make of this essay? R. Yisraeli's views here are confusing. They bear some resemblance to those he took in the previous essay in *Erets Hemdah* because there, too, he seems to have abandoned the idea proposed in the Kibiyeh essay that wars initiated by an enemy are waged for the sake of revenge, and he now claims that they are, in fact, wars of defense. But he

---

18. "*Milhemet Reshut u-Gedareha*," 157–59 (sections 7–9).
19. Ibid., 159–60 (section 10).
20. Ibid., 158 (section 7).

seems to have gone back to the Kibiyeh essay in identifying the Midianite episode as the source for these wars, an idea that does not appear in the essay in *Erets Hemdah*. He also identifies these wars as discretionary, while in the Kibiyeh essay and the essay in *Erets Hemdah* they were only mandatory.

However, I believe we can cut through the confusion here by recognizing that in his essay on Rashi, R. Yisraeli is attempting to explain a position that is ultimately not his own. Up to this point in his writings on war, he assumes that Maimonides' views on mandatory and discretionary war are authoritative, and my sense is that he has not abandoned that assumption. What he is trying to do in the essay on Rashi is to explicate a position that he thinks is worthy of attention but is not one that he himself adopts. In short, R. Yisraeli, in probing Rashi's views here, is engaging in a purely academic exercise in order to understand those views, and nothing more.

The difficulty is that at no point in this essay does he say this explicitly, and there are passages in the essay in which he seems to attempt to harmonize Maimonides' views with those of Rashi. Still, it would seem that he views the two positions as quite distinct and that his personal loyalties remain with Maimonides. Evidence for this reading is that when R. Yisraeli brings Maimonides into his discussion of Rashi's views of defensive wars, he makes no mention of the critical passage in the *Mishneh Torah* in which Maimonides speaks about defensive wars as wars waged for the sake of "saving Israel from the clutches of an enemy," *'ezrat yisra'el mi-yad tsar*. R. Yisraeli, it would seem, has no interest here in bringing Rashi's views into line with Maimonides' central halakhic statement on wars of this type. One would have imagined that he would try to do so if he believed that Rashi's views were authoritative. R. Yisraeli does cite Maimonides' *Sefer ha-Mitsvot* in two places in the essay while presenting his final theory about Rashi's viewpoint, but only to show harmony between Rashi and Maimonides on specific issues that are critical to Rashi's thinking, not to demonstrate that the two authorities had the same views on how they approached war in general.[21]

TORAH SHE-BE-'AL PEH 10: RASHI AND MAIMONIDES ON WAR

This reading of R. Yisraeli's essay on Rashi receives support from a subsequent essay that R. Yisraeli published two years later, in the journal *Torah she-be-'al Peh*, that discusses the differences between mandatory war and discretionary war. Here again, R. Yisraeli shares reflections on the Rashi's views regarding

---

21. The two points that Rashi and Maimonides share in common is that there is a distinction between commandments directed to the individual and the collective, and that the commandment to destroy Amalek was directed at the collective. See *"Milhemet Reshut u-Gedareha,"* pp. 157–58 (section 7).

wars initiated by an enemy, but he does it this time in explicit comparison with those of Maimonides.[22] R. Yisraeli reiterates the view in his earlier essay on Rashi that such wars are termed "discretionary" by Rashi because the obligation to participate in them is directed at the Jewish nation as a whole, not the individual, and therefore the individual has a right to finish fulfilling a competing halakhic obligation before going into battle in such wars. However, R. Yisraeli adds a new insight here with the claim that Rashi bases his viewpoint on the Babylonian Talmud, as opposed to the Jerusalem Talmud. Rashi, according to R. Yisraeli, holds the view that the Babylonian Talmud does not require an individual to risk his life to save others from danger and that it is for this reason that the requirement to participate in wars waged in response to enemy attack has to be directed only at the collective. Only the nation as a whole can be required to enter a situation of danger, not the individual per se. R. Yisraeli goes on to argue that Maimonides' viewpoint in the *Mishneh Torah* is entirely different from that of Rashi. Maimonides sees wars waged in response to enemy attack as mandatory wars, and therefore the obligation to participate in such wars is incumbent on each and every individual. The reason Maimonides takes this position, according to R. Yisraeli, is that Maimonides follows the Jerusalem Talmud, according to which an individual *is* required to risk his life to save others from danger, and that Maimonides therefore draws the conclusion that this principle applies in war as well.[23]

What is important to recognize here is that R. Yisraeli's reading of Maimonides' position in the article in *Torah she-be-'al Peh* is almost identical to the one R. Yisraeli argued for earlier in *Erets Hemdah*, the first essay we examined in this chapter: wars waged in response to enemy attack are mandatory because even in non-war situations every Jew is required to endanger his life to rescue other Jews whose lives are threatened. There are differences between the two essays. Thus, for instance, in the essay in *Erets Hemdah* R. Yisraeli argued that this position was supported by both Talmuds but without invoking Maimonides; whereas in the current essay, he argues that this position is supported only by the Jerusalem Talmud and that it is endorsed by Maimonides as well. However, the differences between the essays are relatively minor.

---

22. "*Milhemet Mitsvah ve-Milhemet Reshut*," *Torah she-be-'al Peh* 10 (1968): 46–50.

23. Ibid., 49–50. R. Yisraeli admits that in his *Peirsuh 'al ha-Mishnah*, Maimonides' viewpoint is the same as Rashi's with respect to the definition of mandatory and discretionary war (ibid., 50). However, it is clear that in R. Yisraeli's thinking, this work of Maimonides was not meant to impart Maimonides' halakhic decision on this matter and that this latter function was reserved for the *Mishneh Torah* which clearly departs from Rashi. After R. Yisraeli states that Maimonides in his *Peirush 'al ha-Mishnah* follows Rashi, R. Yisraeli introduces Maimonides' views in the *Mishneh Torah* with the clause, "but with respect to the halakhic ruling (*akhen le-halakhah*)," and this ruling, according R. Yisraeli, reflects Maimonides' differences with Rashi.

Most important, there is little doubt that Maimonides' position as depicted in the essay in *Torah she-be-'al Peh* is the one that R. Yisraeli himself supports, not Rashi's. This is evident not just from the fact that it matches R. Yisraeli's own view as described in *Erets Hemdah*, but also from looking at the overall trajectory of R. Yisraeli's writings on war after the Kibiyeh essay. While R. Yisraeli expends effort to explain Rashi's position in some of these works, his interest in Rashi's viewpoint is confined to only two of seven essays written on war after the essay on Kibiyeh. Moreover, it would be difficult to imagine R. Yisraeli giving serious support to Rashi's views on war given that Rashi had so little to say about this issue and that in the history of Halakhah, Rashi's influence on laws of war is negligible compared to that of Maimonides. It is, therefore, Maimonides' view that R. Yisraeli undoubtedly considers authoritative.

Thus far, the position that R. Yisraeli takes after his essay on Kibiyeh regarding wars waged in response to enemy attack seems fairly consistent. He follows Maimonides' view that these wars are mandatory and that all Jews must therefore fight in them. He also believes that this view is rooted in the halakhic imperative that even in non-war situations a Jew must risk his life to rescue other Jews whose lives are endangered. Rashi presents a different position on these issues, but R. Yisraeli does not accept his view. The only major point of uncertainty for R. Yisraeli is whether Maimonides' position is supported by both Talmuds. In the *Erets Hemdah* essay, he argues that it is, but in the article in *Torah she-be-'al Peh*, he maintains that Maimonides' position is supported only by the Jerusalem Talmud.

The next essay R. Yisraeli composed that deals with wars initiated by an enemy appeared in 1977 in the journal *Shevilin*, and it seems, in large part, to return to the views that R. Yisraeli argued for in the Kibiyeh essay.[24] However, I would like to skip this essay for the time being and take it up at the end our discussion because it represents something of an exception in the writings on war that R. Yisraeli composed after the Kibiyeh essay. R. Yisraeli published two more essays on war after the one in *Shevilin*, and the positions of these works align with those that we have seen thus far in R. Yisraeli's post-Kibiyeh writings. We will therefore deal with these essays first before returning to the one in *Shevilin*.

TEHUMIN 2: A THEOLOGICAL APPROACH TO CONSCRIPTION

In an article published in 1981 in the journal *Tehumin*, R. Yisraeli again deals with war waged in response to enemy attack but, this time, as a tangent to

---

24. *"Mivtsa 'Yonatan' (Entebeh) le-Or ha-Halakhah," Shevilin* 29–30 (1977): 93–102.

another issue.[25] The main focus of the article is on the question of whether a Jew is allowed to violate the Sabbath to rescue another Jew from a danger that is spiritual in nature. Halakhic sources are unequivocal that a Jew is required to save a fellow Jew from a physical danger, even if it means violating the Sabbath. But what if the danger is not physical but spiritual? For example, if one knows of a fellow Jew who is about to abandon his commitment to Judaism, and the only way to save him from spiritual oblivion is to perform an action in violation of the Sabbath, is one allowed to do so?[26]

In the course of dealing with this question, R. Yisraeli once again discusses the obligation of a Jew to risk his life to rescue another individual from a lethal threat that is physical in nature, and it is in this part of the essay that he brings in the issue of war. R. Yisraeli begins this portion of his deliberations by discussing a situation in which a Jew has an opportunity to rescue a fellow Jew from danger but without having to risk his own life. The requirement for a Jew to render assistance in this scenario is explained as follows:

> When one is talking about the rescue of someone in danger, the requirement [to rescue] ... is a special law that removes the [act] of rescue from the parameters of "I—you" and "mine—yours" that exist in other situations. For in this [instance], the boundary between one person and another is nullified. ... One must see things [in this situation] **from the standpoint of the collective**; a person belonging to [the people of] Israel is in danger and there are means by which to save him. For having control over the means [to rescue a fellow Jew] cannot **be a factor** that has any bearing on the act of rescue. Having control [over the means of rescue] is nullified and removed [from the rescuer] when one is talking about a person belonging to [the people of] Israel.[27] This [requirement to rescue] is therefore not a commandment between a person and his fellow human being but is a commandment on **the collective** [people] of Israel and for the sake of rescuing every individual who makes it up.[28]

A Jew is obligated to save his fellow Jew from danger because whenever a Jew is confronted with another Jew whose life is threatened, the individual identities of the rescuer and the rescued, in effect, disappear; both are considered part of the collective of the Jewish nation as a whole. Therefore one must rescue a fellow Jew in such a situation as if one were rescuing oneself. In fact,

25. *"Pikuah Nefesh be-Sakanah Ruhanit,"* Tehumin 2 (1981): 27–34.

26. Ibid., 27–29.

27. R. Yisraeli's point is that the means for rescue in no sense "belong" to that rescuer such that he decides whether to use those means when someone else is in danger because the rescuer and the person in need of rescue are, in effect, one entity, and therefore the means for rescue belong to both parties here.

28. Ibid., 31 (R. Yisraeli's emphasis).

on a metaphysical level, one *is* rescuing oneself because the boundary between "self" and "other" has been erased here. They are one and the same.

In a later passage, R. Yisraeli applies this thinking specifically to a situation in which the rescuer's life is in danger as well. Here, too, the rescuer must act despite the risk because "the boundary between him and his fellow [Jew] disappears." Therefore, one has to "judge this [situation] from the standpoint of the **two** [as a unit]—and [from the standpoint] that the one [person] will definitely die if someone does not save him, while the second [person] is [only in] possible [danger]—and [from the standpoint] that the possible [danger] is overruled by the certain [danger]."[29]

R. Yisraeli, therefore, takes the same position here that we have seen in other writings after the Kibiyeh essay. One is required to endanger one's life to save another from harm, even according to everyday Halakhah. However, R. Yisraeli comes up with a new way of arguing in favor of this ruling. He takes a distinctively theological approach.

R. Yisraeli goes on to argue that his ruling here is supported by both the Jerusalem and Babylonian Talmuds. We have already seen that in the essay in *Erets Hemdah* R. Yisraeli draws on both Talmuds in attempting to establish the notion that a Jew must risk his life to save the life of another Jew, but that in a subsequent essay, he seems to have retreated from that position by asserting that only the Jerusalem Talmud supports his view. In the essay in *Tehumin* that we are now examining, R. Yisraeli appears to return to the first position that both Talmuds, in fact, endorse his view.[30]

R. Yisraeli refers here to the same passages in the Jerusalem Talmud to support his viewpoint that he cited in his previous essays. However, the passage in the Babylonian Talmud he refers to for the same purpose is new to his deliberations, and it brings the subject of war into his discussion. R. Yisraeli does not actually cite the Babylonian Talmud explicitly, but he quotes a ruling in the *Shulhan Arukh* that is clearly based on one of its passages, and it is a passage that we have already encountered in an earlier chapters.[31] In *'Eruvin* 45a, we find a ruling that Jews are required to come to the rescue of a Jewish town that is under siege from non-Jews, even on the Sabbath.[32] R. Yisraeli comments on this ruling as follows:

> It stands to reason that these gentiles [who attack the Jewish city] also have weapons. And when they [i.e., the Jewish rescuers] come to rescue those under siege, there is no guarantee that the gentiles will flee for their lives. It is most likely that they [i.e., the gentiles] will wage war on those who have come to the

---

29. Ibid., 32 (R. Yisraeli's emphasis).
30. Ibid.
31. *Shulhan Arukh, Orah Hayim*, 329:6; above, p. 34.
32. BT *'Eruvin* 45a.

rescue, and that perhaps some of the rescuers will also fall [in battle] in the course of the act of rescue. Nonetheless, they [i.e., the rescuers] are obligated not to refrain from actions of rescue. For that is what Halakhah requires—that [an individual] endanger himself to rescue those under siege, seeing as they are in danger of certain destruction.[33]

According to R. Yisraeli, we can presume that in such a scenario the Jews who take up arms to save their fellow Jews are risking their lives to fulfill their duty, even if the Gemara and the *Shulhan Arukh* do not say this explicitly. Therefore, this passage proves once again that a Jew must endanger himself for the sake of rescuing another Jew from harm.

R. Yisraeli's deliberations here are important for a couple of reason. First, they reinforce the position that we have seen R. Yisraeli develop in his post-Kibiyeh writings, which is that a Jew is required to endanger his life to save others from harm regardless of whether or not the situation is one of war. The only difference is that, while up to now, R. Yisraeli has argued for the existence of this obligation in everyday life and has then applied it to war, here he does the reverse. He adduces the source in *'Eruvin* 45a showing that this obligation must be fulfilled in wartime in order to prove that the same obligation applies in everyday life. This source teaches us that in war Jews are required to aid fellow Jews who have come under attack by non-Jews, and R. Yisraeli presumes that this ruling therefore informs us about how Jews are to behave in non-war situations as well. Second, and more important, R. Yisraeli makes use of the theological reasoning introduced earlier in his essay according to which a Jew must risk his life to save others. When Jews are being threatened, individual identity disappears, and the situation must be viewed from the perspective of the interests of the nation as a whole, as if it were an individual in its own right.

In the essay under examination, R. Yisraeli has thus introduced a new type of argument based on theological considerations to explain why Jews must risk their lives for others in waging a war in response to enemy attack. R. Yisraeli had, in fact, presented a similar theological argument regarding war in the essay in *Erets Hemdah*. There as well, he argued that a Jew was required to risk his life in a war waged in response to enemy attack in order save his fellow Jews from danger because in war the identity of the individual is essentially subsumed within the collective, and therefore it is only the survival of the collective that matters.[34] We passed over this theory in our discussion of the essay because R. Yisraeli eventually rejects it in favor of another position. As we have already seen, R. Yisraeli concludes the essay with the argument

33. *"Pikuah Nefesh be-Sakanah Ruhanit,"* 32.
34. *"Berihah min ha-Arets,"* 50.

that a Jew has a halakhic imperative to save fellow Jews from danger that is directed at the individual qua individual.[35] However, in the *Tehumin* essay, R. Yisraeli resurrects the theological approach suggested in *Erets Hemdah* and uses it to justify the requirement for Jews to risk their lives to save their fellow Jews from danger regardless of whether or not the situation involves war.

The ultimate basis of R. Yisraeli's thinking here may be a passage in the Maharal that we referred to in chapter 6 that addresses the story in Genesis 34 recounting the slaughter of the Shechemites at the hands of Simeon and Levi after the rape of their sister Dinah. The Maharal asked whether the slaughter was justified given that only Shechem himself perpetrated the crime against Dinah. The Maharal answers in affirmative with the claim that Jacob's clan and the Shechemites were essentially two nations at war, and that in war innocent lives can be taken because the individuals in each nation lose their individuality and are considered part of the collective.[36]

But these intricacies should not distract us from the fact that the essential lines of argumentation in R. Yisraeli's thinking have remained fairly consistent in the post-Kibiyeh works we have examined thus far. Once again, a Jew is required to risk his life in war in order to save his fellow Jews from danger because that imperative is operative even in non-war situations. The only variable is how R. Yisraeli justifies his position. He consistently relies on the Jerusalem Talmud as an authoritative source for his views and always cites the same passages from this text to support his views. His reliance on the Babylonian Talmud is more inconsistent; he does not always cite it as a source for his thinking, and when he does, his selection of passages varies. We have also encountered an essay in which R. Yisraeli attempts to bolster his position with reasoning that is theological in nature.

TEHUMIN 10: THE COMMANDMENT TO CONQUER THE LAND OF ISRAEL

The last essay R. Yisraeli wrote that deals with wars waged in response to enemy attack appeared in the journal *Tehumin* in 1989.[37] Its purpose was to respond to the position taken by R. 'Ovadyah Yosef, the leading Sefardic halakhic authority in Israel at the time, regarding relinquishing to the Palestinians territory that had been captured by Israel in the Six Day War. R. Yosef had

---

35. Ibid., 51.
36. Above, pp. 159–60.
37. "*Mesirat Shetahim me-Erets Yisra'el be-Makom Pikuah Nefesh,*" *Tehumin* 10 (1989): 48–61. The essay was reprinted in *Havat Binyamin*, ed. R. Neriyah Gutel (Kefar Darom, Israel: Makhon ha-Torah ve-ha-Arets, 2002), vol. 1, pp. 94–103. The pagination I cite here is from the online version of this reprint, available at Hebrewbooks.org.

taken the position that Jews are permitted to give away territory as part of a peace deal with the Arabs, if it could be shown that such a concession would save Jewish lives.[38] R. Yisraeli's views on this matter went through a number of changes over the course of his career, but when he composed his response to R. Yosef's views in 1989, he was firmly opposed to giving away territory to the Palestinians under any circumstances.[39]

It is in dealing with this issue that R. Yisraeli touches on the question of war waged in response to enemy attack. One of his arguments against R. Yosef's position draws from sources to which we have already alluded. We noted in the previous essay we examined that R. Yisraeli cites a ruling in the *Shulhan Arukh* based on the talmudic passage in *'Eruvin* 45a that requires Jews to take up arms to fight on behalf of a Jewish town that has been besieged by non-Jews, even on the Sabbath. Now the original text in the Gemara upon which this ruling is based also deals with a more specific scenario discussed earlier in this study, in which the Jewish town being besieged is close to the border of the attacking nation. The Gemara tells us that when a town in this location is under siege, Jews are required to come to the town's assistance and to fight on its behalf even on the Sabbath, and even if it is clear that the enemy army is only interested in robbing the Jews of their material goods, not in killing them.[40] The presumption here is that border towns are the first line of defense against enemy incursion and thus critical to the security of the Jewish population in the interior of the country; therefore Jews must go to war to ensure that these towns do not fall into enemy hands. R. Yisraeli makes use of this source to reject R. Yosef's argument that Jews may relinquish territory in a peace deal with the Arabs on the premise that such a concession would save Jewish lives. R. Yisraeli points out that, according to the Gemara in *'Eruvin*, Jews are, in fact, required to risk their lives and go to war rather than allow a hostile enemy to take territory that brings the enemy closer to Jewish population centers in the heart of the country, and that is effectively what a peace deal involving territorial concessions to the Arabs would do. A deal of this sort is therefore forbidden.[41]

---

38. R. 'Ovadyah Yosef, *"Hahzarat ha-Shetahim me-Erets Yisra'el be-Makom Pikuah Nefesh,"* *Torah she-be-'al Peh* 21 (1980): 12–20. The essay was republished in *Tehumin* 10 (1989): 37–47, in the same volume of the journal in which R. Yisraeli published the essay currently under examination.

39. The evolution of R. Yisraeli's thinking on this matter is analyzed in an excellent article by Hayim Burganski, *"Yahaso ha-Hilkhati shel ha-Rav Yisra'eli le-Sugyat Hahzarat ha-Shetahim,"* *Diney Yisra'el* 22 (2003): 241–67. See, however, R. Neryah Gutel, *"Kavim le-Mishnato ha-Sheleimah shel Rabenu,"* *Ga'on ba-Torah u-ve-Midot: Perakim le-Darko ve-li-Demuto shel Maran ha-Ga'on Sha'ul Yisra'eli zts"l,* ed. Yisra'el Sharir (Jerusalem: Erez, 1999), 197. R. Gutel insists that R. Yisraeli's views on this matter did not go through any evolution and that what appear to be changes in his views were not changes at all and can be explained by looking at the contexts in which those views appear.

40. Above, p. 34.

41. *"Mesirat Shetahim,"* 73–75.

R. Yisraeli does not delve into the question of how wars waged in response to enemy attack are justified if Halakhah does not normally require an individual to risk his life to spare others from danger. R. Yisraeli's interests are focused primarily on the issue of relinquishing territory for the sake of peace. However, R. Yisraeli's deliberations here are consistent with the position upheld in his post-Kibiyeh writings that wars waged in response to enemy attack are justified because they are meant to protect Jewish lives, not because they are for the purpose of wreaking revenge.

However, R. Yisraeli's rebuttal of R. Yosef's views is focused mostly on another argument involving war that we have not yet encountered and that requires our attention. R. Yisraeli brings in Nahmanides' position that the imperative to conquer the land of Israel is one of the 613 commandments. R. Yisraeli does not believe that this commandment is applicable nowadays in the sense that Jews must initiate wars to expand the territory of the state of Israel, but he does believe that once Israel captures territory, the commandment still forbids Jews from giving it back and requires them to defend it even at the risk of endangering Jewish lives. In short, the state of Israel is justified in sending its soldiers into battle not just to protect Jewish lives but also to safeguard Jewish sovereignty over the land of Israel. Thus, the land captured in the Six Day War cannot be returned to the Arabs as part of a peace deal, even if Jewish lives will be saved.[42]

Interestingly, R. Yisraeli had entertained this very argument in his earlier essay in *Erets Hemdah* but had rejected it for two reasons. First, he believed that it was not clear that the establishment of the state of Israel was the beginning of the messianic redemption, and therefore there was no requirement for Israel to risk Jewish lives to defend land captured in war. Second, only a Jewish king could lead a Jewish state into war, and while R. Kook had ruled that any Jewish government could function as a substitute for a king, R. Yisraeli believed that there was no agreement among rabbinic authorities on whether this viewpoint applied to the Israeli government.[43] These objections, however, are nowhere mentioned in the later essay currently under discussion.

R. Yisraeli's thinking here echoes that of R. Isaac Herzog and R. Tsevi Yehudah Kook who also attempted to justify defensive wars waged by the state of Israel on the basis of Nahmanides' views.[44] However, R. Yisraeli's interpretation of Nahmanides is, in crucial respects, quite different from that of predecessors. R. Herzog and R. Tsevi Yehudah Kook believed that, according to Nahmanides, the commandment to conquer the land of Israel meant military conquest and that this imperative was very much in force in our day and age. R. Yisraeli does not take this position. According to his reading of

---

42. Ibid., 69–73.
43. "*Berihah min ha-Arets*," 50–51.
44. Above, pp. 87, 112.

Nahmanides, the commandment to conquer the land militarily is no longer in force. Jews fulfill the commandment of conquest by buying property in the land of Israel and settling it. However, when Jews are faced with an enemy that wants to take the land away from them by military force, Jews are required to respond with military force to defend what they already own.[45]

SHEVILIN 29–30: THE ENTEBBE RAID

Let us now examine the essay that we skipped over earlier in our discussion because its views were at odds with those of the other essays we have examined in this chapter. As we have already noted, this essay appeared in *Shevilin* in 1977.[46] Its subject was the Entebbe raid, a military operation that had taken place a year earlier, in which Israeli commandos stormed the Entebbe airport in Uganda and freed a group of Jewish hostages who were being held by hijackers. The hijackers were threatening to kill the hostages if the Israeli government did not release a number of convicted Palestinian terrorists from Israeli jails. R. Yisraeli addresses two questions in this essay. The first is whether, from the standpoint of Halakhah, the Israeli government was justified in negotiating with the hijackers for the release of terrorists. The second is whether Halakhah would approve of the military operation that eventually freed the hostages, given that this operation risked not only the lives of the Israeli commandos but also the lives of the hostages themselves.[47]

It is in dealing with the second question that R. Yisraeli discusses the issue of war waged in response to enemy attack. However, some of his deliberations about the first question are highly significant with respect to this issue as well. Most important is that R. Yisraeli rejects the suggestion that a Jew is required to risk his life to save a fellow Jew from danger. He informs us that the Jerusalem Talmud does indeed take the position that a Jew must subject himself to "possible danger" in order to save a fellow Jew who is in "certain danger," but he finds nothing in the Babylonian Talmud that confirms this obligation, and he therefore concludes that a Jew has no obligation to risk his life to save a fellow Jew from danger, though he may do so voluntarily.[48] R. Yisraeli, in other words, pulls the rug out from under the key point that guided all his other post-Kibiyeh writings on wars waged in response to enemy attack that we have examined thus far. As we have shown, in these works R. Yisraeli argued that Jews were commanded to participate in

---

45. "*Berihah min ha-Arets*," 50–51.
46. See citation p. 177n24. above. I will be citing the pagination of the online reprint of this essay in *Havat Binyamin*, vol. 1, available at Hebrewbooks.org.
47. "*Mivatsa 'Yonatan*'," 91.
48. Ibid., 91–94.

defensive wars, despite the risks involved, because even in non-war situations Jews had a requirement to risk their lives to save fellow Jews from danger. Here this reasoning is implicitly rejected. How this position helps R. Yisraeli answer the first of his questions about whether the state of Israel was allowed to negotiate for the release of convicted terrorists need not preoccupy us here. The important point is that he has now resurrected his opinion in the Kibiyeh essay that one is not required to risk one's life for the sake of others who are in danger.

While dealing with the second question about whether the military operation at Entebbe was allowed according to Halakhah, R. Yisraeli provides an argument for why a Jewish government may force its citizens to fight in a war initiated by an enemy nation, and here as well, he returns in large measure to the approach he took in the Kibiyeh essay. As in that work, R. Yisraeli bases the right of a Jewish government to act in this manner on the biblical narrative regarding the war against the Midianites in the book of Numbers, but he provides a new interpretation of the story to justify this right. In the Kibiyeh essay, R. Yisraeli focused on the imperative to wreak revenge on the Midianites as the reason that all Israelites were required to participate in the war effort. Revenge was taken against the Midianites in response to their spiritual "attack" on the Israelites in tempting them into idol-worship. The notion of revenge therefore served as a basis for the requirement that all Jews participate in subsequent wars initiated by an enemy, physical or spiritual.[49] In the current essay, R. Yisraeli makes no mention of revenge and focuses instead on the imperative of *kidush ha-shem*, "sanctification of the divine name." It is this factor that required all Jews to take up arms in the Midianite war, and it continues to require them to participate in wars waged in response to enemy attack.

The concept of *kidush ha-shem* has a long history, and its meaning in Halakhah varies from source to source, but here R. Yisraeli equates it with martyrdom, one of its common usages, especially in the medieval period.[50] R. Yisraeli illustrates its meaning by citing a halakhic ruling, originating in the Talmud and endorsed by a number of later authorities, that when a non-Jewish tyrant orders his Jewish subjects to transgress the divine commandments for the expressed purpose of destroying the Jewish religion, Jews are required to submit to death rather than obey the tyrant's orders, even for the most minor of transgressions.[51] According to R. Yisraeli, this act of martyrdom

---

49. Above, pp. 143–47.

50. For an insightful discussion of the history of this concept and how it has been used by religious Zionist thinkers, see Ronen Lubits, "Ha-Musagim 'Kidush ha-Shem' ve-'Hilul ha-Shem' be-Hagut ha-Tsiyonut ha-Datit," *Sha'anan* 16 (2011): 113–45.

51. BT *Sanhedrin* 74a. R. Yisraeli cites *Hiddushey ha-Ran* on the relevant talmudic passage s. v. "*aval bi-she'at ha-gezerah*." A similar ruling can be found in MT *Yesodey ha-Torah* 5:3.

is a "sanctification of the divine name" because it brings honor to the God of Israel by demonstrating the strength of conviction that Jews have in the truth of His Torah and the depth of their dedication to His commandments. Moreover, Jews are God's representatives on earth, and therefore any action taken against them is an action taken against God Himself, and it therefore has to be resisted even at the cost of one's life. In R. Yisraeli's opinion, this logic applied to the Midianite war because the attack of the Midianites on the Jewish people in tempting them into idolatry was also an attack on God Himself. The Israelites were therefore required to wage war against them not just for the sake of their own honor but for God's honor as well. The biblical text itself testifies to this interpretation. When God commands Moses to wage the war, He first tells him to "avenge the Israelite people on the Midianites" (Num. 31:2), but shortly afterward, when Moses assembles his army, he commands them to "wreak the Lord's vengeance on Midian" (Num. 31:4). In the biblical text, the need to fight for the honor of the Jewish people is interchangeable with the need to fight for the honor of "the Lord."[52]

The same logic also applies to all subsequent wars waged in response to enemy attack. Whenever an enemy nation initiates a war against the Jewish people, it is an insult against God in being a blatant disregard for the special status that the Jews have as His chosen nation. A war against the Jewish people is a war against God. In a war of this kind, all Jews must therefore go into battle despite the risk to their own lives because the honor of God is at stake.[53]

R. Yisraeli also applies this way of thinking to the Entebbe raid. He reasons that even though this operation was not really a battle in a formally declared war, the imperative of *kidush ha-shem* was appropriate. The hijackers divided the Jews from the non-Jewish passengers, freed the latter, and held the Jews as hostages. R. Yisraeli declares that there is no greater "desecration of the divine name" (*hilul ha-shem*) than these actions, for in singling out the Jews, the hijackers were publically targeting the Jewish people and thus targeting God as well. Thus, here too, the sending of commandos to free the hostages was warranted because of *kidush ha-shem,* despite the risk not only to the lives of the commandos but also to the lives of the hostages themselves.[54]

R. Yisraeli's views are nicely summarized in the following passage:

In the case of an enemy [nation] that attacks [the people] of Israel **because they are [the people] of Israel**—as in the case [of gentiles] "who have attacked **Israelite** cities,"[55] and as in our case in which they [i.e., the hijackers]

52. *"Mivtsa 'Yonatan',"* 95–96.
53. Ibid.
54. Ibid.
55. BT *'Eruvin* 45a.

deliberately separated the Jews from the members of others nations and were careful to specifically set aside just Jews and Israeli citizens—if their schemes succeed, there is no greater desecration of the divine name than this. Therefore, a war against them [i.e., a nation that attacks the people of Israel] is in the category of *kidush ha-shem*. Similarly, in the case of the war in Midian, from which we learn, as noted above, the principle of mandatory war in [a situation] of "saving Israel from the clutches of an enemy"—God said to Moses "avenge the Israelite people on the Midianites ..." (Num. 31:2), while Moses said [to the Israelites] "to wreak the Lord's vengeance on Midian" (Num. 31:4). Rashi on this passage says that one who stands against Israel, stands, as it were, against God. Thus, a war for the sake of the honor of Israel is akin to *kidush ha-shem*.[56]

Here, R. Yisraeli applies the notion of *kidush ha-shem* to the Midianite war, all subsequent wars initiated by enemy nations, and the Entebbe situation.

We have examined R. Yisraeli's views on wars in his writings after the Kibiyeh essay, specifically those focused on war waged in response to enemy attack, and we have found that in a number respects he departs from the approach to this type of war presented in the Kibiyeh essay. First, R. Yisraeli's focus of interest has narrowed. In the Kibiyeh essay, he was concerned with moral challenges presented by conscription and the killing of enemy noncombatants, but in the later writings, only the former issue concerns him. Second, and more important, in his treatment of the question of conscription, R. Yisraeli argues in most of his later essays that there is no distinction between war and everyday life. A Jew must risk his life to save others from harm according to wartime Halakhah because the same obligation applies in everyday Halakhah.

This second observation deserves special attention. Up this point in our study, we have not seen an approach to conscription quite like the one R. Yisraeli offers here. R. Kook assumed a clear distinction between wartime Halakhah and everyday Halakhah, and conscription was a good illustration of this division; it could be justified only according to wartime Halakhah. R. Herzog largely followed R. Kook on this point. He does open up the door to justifying conscription according to everyday Halakhah by expressing support for the position of the Jerusalem Talmud according to which an individual is, in fact, required to risk his life to save others from harm. However, R. Herzog acknowledges that this opinion is a minority viewpoint and therefore lacks authority. He approves of conscription in the 1948 war within the parameters of everyday Halakhah only because of the unique challenges facing the Jewish

---

56. Ibid., 95 (my emphasis).

people at the time this war was waged. R. Waldenberg also took R. Kook's line that conscription in war is permitted because the laws of war are different from those of the everyday. Like R. Herzog, he opens the door to the possibility that conscription can be justified according to everyday Halakhah when he co-opts the views of the *Shem Aryeh* into his thinking. But he seems to have been unaware of the implications of the *Shem Aryeh*'s views, and therefore we cannot say that R. Waldenberg consciously questioned the distinction between wartime Halakhah and everyday Halakhah when it came to the issue of conscription. Finally, R. Yisraeli himself, in his essay on Kibiyeh, saw conscription as justifiable only in accordance with wartime Halakhah, not with everyday Halakhah.

Yet, in his later writings, R. Yisraeli argues that when it comes to conscription, there is no distinction between war and everyday life. In defensive wars, Jews are required to risk their lives to defend others because of a similar obligation in non-war situations. This position is argued repeatedly and explicitly in several essays, and it is not specific to any particular defensive war, as was the case with R. Herzog; it is meant to apply to any and all wars waged in response to enemy attack.

We might also note the resemblance between R. Yisraeli's views here and those of R. Shlomo Zalman Pines, whom R. Kook debated on matters of war. R. Pines also claimed that the requirement of Jews to risk their lives in war could be justified within the framework of everyday Halakhah. I am not suggesting that R. Yisraeli was influenced by R. Pines's viewpoint. We have no evidence that he was acquainted with R. Pines's end of the correspondence with R. Kook. However, R. Yisraeli certainly takes an approach to war that is reminiscent of R. Pines's thinking.

We also noted in our chapter on R. Kook that R. Pines's views on conscription found precedent in the commentary of R. David Frankel on the Jerusalem Talmud, *Shiyarey Korban*, and it is perhaps more likely that R. Yisraeli was familiar with R. Frankel's views than he was with those of R. Pines, given that the *Shiyarey Korban* appears in standard editions of the Jerusalem Talmud. However, once again, we cannot be sure of a direct influence here because R. Yisraeli does not cite R. Frankel's commentary explicitly.

Why the change in direction for R. Yisraeli? We can only speculate. It may be that he was attempting to bring his views on war more into line with his overall approach to other political issues. We noted in chapter 6 that R. Yisraeli was a pioneer in attempting to create a body of Halakhah on political matters in the state of Israel in the spirit of R. Kook's notion of "the Torah of the land of the Israel," and that R. Yisraeli's rulings on these issues were often characterized by a desire to enhance the public welfare. We also noted that in his essay on Kibiyeh, R. Yisraeli's views on war were somewhat inconsistent with this thrust because here the protection of communal interests was not paramount. In mandatory wars waged in response to enemy attack, revenge was the motive for war, not the protection of the public from harm.[57] It is perhaps for this reason that in his later writings, R. Yisraeli adopted the position that wars waged in response to enemy attack are indeed waged for the sake of defending the nation. This approach brought his views on wars of this kind into harmony with his other political rulings because the new approach made the public welfare the primary focus of this type of war.

A consequence of this change in direction is that in one respect it brings R. Yisraeli's thinking on war closer to that of R. Kook than was the case in the Kibiyeh essay. R. Kook held that war, whether mandatory or discretionary, was meant to promote the public good, and R. Yisraeli seems now to be saying the very same thing. In R. Yisraeli's later writings, mandatory wars responding to enemy attack are no less concerned with the public welfare. However, in another respect, R. Yisraeli has distanced himself from his predecessor. While R. Kook believed that the laws of war were different in kind from those governing everyday life, R. Yisraeli is now claiming that there is no such difference, at least with respect to one important issue: the conscription of soldiers to fight in wars waged in response to enemy attack.[58]

Another consideration that helps explain R. Yisraeli's position on conscription in his later writings is that he was attempting to appeal to the ultra-Orthodox community to defend the Jewish state. That community could not easily sanction the notion that wars in the formal halakhic sense could be fought in our day and age because it believed that it was forbidden to wage war in the absence of the proper political institutions that would be re-established only with the coming of the messiah—that is, Davidic kingship and the Sanhedrin. R. Yisraeli may have therefore felt the need to justify conscription on the basis of arguments that had nothing to do with political institutions. Hence the claim that a Jew had an obligation to risk his life for a fellow Jew who was in danger, even in non-war situations. Such an argument, if correct, would obligate those who rejected the legitimacy of the political structures of the Jewish state to participate in defensive wars as much as those who accepted them.

One very puzzling feature of R. Yisraeli's writings on war after Kibiyeh still needs to be explained. Why does R. Yisraeli, in his analysis of the Entebbe operation, choose to return to an approach similar to the one he took in the Kibiyeh essay? This shift in thinking is even more perplexing because it turns out to be temporary. In R. Yisraeli's writings on war subsequent to the

---

57. Above, pp. 165–66.

58. In the essays that we have examined in this chapter, R. Yisraeli discusses the views of only one of his three predecessors examined in this study. He briefly engages R. Kook's ideas on war in Halakhah on two occasions. However, in neither instance does he adopt R. Kook's views. The first instance can be found in R. Yisraeli's essay on Rashi's views regarding discretionary war, and as we have shown, the views depicted in this essay are ultimately not R. Yisraeli's own. See "Milhemet Reshut u-Gedareha," 155 (section 4). The second instance can be found in R. Yisraeli's essay on the Entebbe raid where R. Yisraeli adduces R. Kook's views in order to criticize them. His comments here are part of a discussion of a theory a war that he eventually rejects. See "Mivtsa 'Yonatan'," 94–95.

Entebbe essay, the approach of the Kibiyeh essay never appears again; in these writings, he continues the line of thinking we saw him developing before the publication of the essay on Entebbe.

To be more precise about the difficulty here, we analyzed six essays that R. Yisraeli composed after the essay on Kibiyeh, and in these works he was fairly consistent in basing the requirement for Jews to participate in wars responding to enemy attack on the premise that even in non-war situations a Jew must risk his life to save a fellow Jew from danger. The essay on Entebbe appeared chronologically as the fourth of these six essays, and it clearly departs from those written before and after it. It returned to the position in the Kibiyeh essay according to which the imperative to participate in a war initiated by an enemy has nothing to do with an everyday duty to save Jewish lives but instead is based on an obligation drawn from the Midianite episode and unique to wartime. Now, in the essay on Kibiyeh, that obligation was for the purpose of revenge against those who have dared to harm the Jewish people, while in the Entebbe essay it is for the sake of *kidush ha-shem*. Nonetheless, the basic structure of thinking in both essays is the same in its reliance on the biblical narrative about the Midianites and in drawing a sharp distinction between wartime Halakhah and everyday Halakhah.

A number of explanations are possible for R. Yisraeli's brief return to the thinking of the Kibiyeh essay. One is that he was predisposed to approve the Entebbe operation but could not easily justify it on the premise that the raid was akin to a defensive war in which Jews had an obligation to risk their lives to save others. That is because he had doubts about whether, in the Entebbe situation, military action was the best way to safeguard other Jews from harm. As R. Yisraeli points out in his essay, in the case of Entebbe, the Israeli government had the option to accede to the demands of the hijackers and release Palestinian terrorists from Israeli jails, and, in fact, there were arguments to be made in favor of this option from a halakhic standpoint. This move would have saved the lives of the hostages, and while it would have entailed some risk to the Israeli population because the freed terrorists could threaten Israeli citizens in the future, this risk was not nearly as serious as the one the hostages faced when the Israeli commandos stormed the Entebbe airport.[59] Therefore, if R. Yisraeli was going to find a way to approve of the raid, he had to find it in an approach that did not focus on seeing the military operation as a defensive war meant to save Jewish lives. He did so by going back in large part to the approach he used in the Kibiyeh essay. This approach focused on the Midianite war which taught the notion that all Jews must participate in wars waged in response to enemy attack because of the principle of *kidush ha-shem*. The purpose of such wars was not to save Jews but to defend God's honor, and it is this purpose that obligates Jews to risk their lives for the war

59. *"Mivtsa 'Yonatan',"* 94–95.

effort. For the same reason, the Israeli government was fully justified in send-ing commandos to Entebbe to rescue the hostages despite the danger to Israeli soldiers and hostages alike. Here, too, God's honor needed to be safeguarded, even at the cost of Jewish life.

Another consideration is that it is perhaps no coincidence that in the two essays in which R. Yisraeli used the Midianite episode to justify wars respond-ing to enemy attack, he was focused on cases involving terrorism. R. Yisraeli may have felt that in such instances the obligation of Jews to rescue each other from danger was not strong enough to deal with terrorism. More was at stake here than just saving Jewish lives. Terrorism often arouses strong feelings of revulsion because it deliberately targets unarmed civilians, and R. Yisraeli may have been affected by emotions of this kind as well. Therefore, in the Kibiyeh essay, R. Yisraeli advocated revenge as the key reason for requiring Jews to fight their enemies, while in the Entebbe essay, the principle of *kidush ha-shem* served that role. However, when R. Yisraeli dealt with more conventional war-fare in his other essays, neither of these suggestions seems to have had a last-ing impact on his thinking. In all of these works, the cause of saving Jewish lives seems to have sufficed as a reason for sending Jews into battle.[60]

One may also wonder why R. Yisraeli interpreted the Midianite episode somewhat differently in the Entebbe essay than he did in the essay on Kibiyeh. Why the change of focus from the theme of revenge to *kidush ha-shem*? Once again, R. Yisraeli does not give us explicit guidance here. However, it is pos-sible that he preferred the theme of *kidush ha-shem* to revenge because the former notion had a more positive valence than the latter one. Revenge is a concept with violent overtones, and, as we have seen, its use by R. Yisraeli has drawn criticism for this reason; *kidush ha-shem*, by contrast, has a more posi-tive ring to it in being focused on the lofty spiritual goal of sanctifying God's name. R. Yisraeli may have also been influenced by the fact that the biblical text does indeed describe the Midianite war as being for the sake of God's honor. Therefore, exegetical motives may have played a role in R. Yisraeli's change of emphasis when he returned to the Midianite episode in his essay on Entebbe.

60. We may also speculate that R. Yisraeli was concerned that the new approach he espoused in his later writings suggesting that wars waged in response to enemy attack were defensive in nature, did not rest on solid ground. That approach was based on the notion that in everyday Halakhah there was a requirement for a Jew to risk his life to save another individual from harm, and this obligation was clearly endorsed only by the Jerusalem Talmud, not the more authoritative Babylonian Talmud, nor the major-ity of later halakhic authorities. R. Yisraeli attempted to bring the Babylonian Talmud into line with his thinking in some of his essays. In one essay, he also gave a theological justification for his thinking with the claim that when Jewish life was in danger, the distinction between the individual Jew and the collective disappeared in a metaphysi-cal sense. Yet, R. Yisraeli may still have had doubts about this whole approach, and he may have therefore returned in the essay on Entebbe to reconsider the approach taken in the Kibiyeh essay.

Still, these observations should not distract us from the main point that comes out of this chapter. In almost all of R. Yisraeli's other essays after Kibiyeh, he formulated a new and innovative approach to conscription for defensive wars, one which depended on erasing the distinction between wartime Halakhah and everyday Halakhah. The essay on Entebbe was the lone exception. Only in this work did he revert to the paradigm of the Kibiyeh essay.

Table 7.1. R. YISRAELI'S ESSAYS IN WHICH WARS WAGED IN RESPONSE TO ENEMY ATTACK ARE WARS OF DEFENSE

	Essay Title				
	Erets Hemdah I, Chapter 11 (1957)	*'Amud ha-Yemini,* Chapter 14 (1966)	*Torah she-be-'al Peh* 10 (1968)	*Tehumin* 2 (1981)	*Tehumin* 10 (1989)
1. Defense of What?	lives	lives	lives	lives	1. lives 2. land
2. Individual or Collective Obligation?	individual	collective	individual	individual	no statement
3. Primary Halakhic Sources	JT, BT, MT	Rashi on the Midianite narrative	JT, MT	JT, BT, MT	1. BT, MT 2. Nahmanides

Table 7.2. R. YISRAELI'S ESSAYS IN WHICH WARS WAGED IN RESPONSE TO ENEMY ATTACK ARE *NOT* DEFENSIVE WARS

	Essay Title	
	Ha-Torah ve-ha-Medinah 5–6 (1953–4) (Kibiyeh)	*Shevilin* 29–30: (1977) (Entebbe)
1. Reason for War	revenge, punishment	*kiddush ha-shem*
2. Individual or Collective Obligation?	individual and collective[a]	individual and collective[b]
3. Primary Halakhic Sources	Midianite narrative, MT	Midianite narrative

[a]The obligation is "individual and collective" here because the imperative to take revenge is applicable only in situations in which the entire Jewish nation has been attacked by an enemy nation, but the individual still has an obligation qua individual to fight in such a war.
[b]My observations in note a above apply here as well, except that the motivation for going to war is *kidush ha-shem.*

CHAPTER 8

✧

R. Shlomo Goren

Rabbi Shlomo Goren (1918–94) is distinguished from the other figures examined in this study in at least two ways. First, none of the figures we have looked at thus far actually served in the military. R. Goren not only did military service but turned it into a distinguished career. He joined the Haganah in 1947, fought in Israel's War of Independence in 1948, and in that same year was named the first Chief Rabbi of the Israeli Defense Forces, a position he held for twenty-three years. R. Goren's second distinction among the figures we are exploring is that he is the most prolific author on the subject of war in Halakhah. One of R. Goren's central missions in life was to provide the Israeli army with comprehensive halakhic guidelines on all matters pertaining to military life, and his efforts in this area produced an immense body of writings.[1]

R. Goren was born Shlomo Goronchik in Zambrow, Poland. His family moved to Warsaw in 1921 when he was three, but R. Goren's parents were strong Zionists, and therefore, in 1925, they relocated the family to Palestine. R. Goren's father, upon his arrival, cofounded the settlement of Kefar Hasidim near Haifa, but the hardships of establishing a new community in the Palestinian countryside were too great for the Goronchik family, and in 1928 they moved to Jerusalem. R. Goren, now age ten, attended yeshiva and

---

1. The best source for R. Goren's biography is Shifrah Mishlov, "Be-'Ein ha-Se'arah: Demuto ha-Tsiburit ve-Yetsirato ha-Toranit shel ha-Rav Shelomoh Goren ba-Shanim 1948-1994" (PhD diss., Bar-Ilan University, 2010), chapter 1. Also helpful is Avi'ad Yehi'el Hollander, "Deyokano ha-Hilkhati shel ha-Rav Shelomoh Goren: 'Iyunim be-Shikuley ha-Pesikah ve-Darkey ha-Bisus be-Ma'amarav ha-Hilkhatiyim" (PhD diss., Bar-Ilan University, 2011), 1–21. A number of book-length biographies of R. Goren have been published, but they are not scholarly. A list of these books is found in Mishlov, 1n3. Mishlov also lists other works on various aspects of Goren's life, 1–2.

was soon recognized as a prodigy in traditional Talmud study. At age twelve, he was accepted as a student in the prestigious Hebron Yeshiva, which had moved from Hebron to Jerusalem after the 1929 massacre of the Jewish community in Hebron. During these years, R. Goren also became enamored of the writings of R. Abraham Isaac Kook and adopted the latter's version of religious Zionism, an ideology that would guide him for the rest of his life. In addition to his yeshiva studies, in these years R. Goren also had interests in academic learning, and took courses in philosophy, mathematics, and classics at the Hebrew University.

R. Goren's military career began during the Arab uprising of 1936–39 when he volunteered to help defend the Jewish community. As already noted, he subsequently joined the Haganah in 1947 and fought in the 1948 war. His accession to the position of Chief Rabbi of the Israeli army in the same year was on account of his prodigious Jewish learning and his courage in warfare, an unusual combination of talents at the time. R. Goren served in that capacity until 1971. One year later, he became Ashkenazi Chief Rabbi of Israel, a position he held until 1983. He continued an active public life until his death in 1994.

R. Goren wrote a great deal on political theology, and we therefore have a good idea of what his beliefs were regarding the establishment of a modern Jewish state. In his early writings, he viewed the state through a religious lens heavily tinted by the theology of R. Kook. He saw it as representing an intermediate phase between the period of the exile and the messianic era but was unsure about whether it would evolve to play a direct role in the messianic redemption. The future of the Jewish state as a messianic entity depended on whether the state and its people would adopt a life based on Torah. However, after the stunning Israeli victory in the Six Day War and the capture of large areas of land viewed by Jewish tradition as belonging to the future messianic kingdom, R. Goren began to talk openly about the state of Israel as *athalta di-ge'ulah*, the beginning of the messianic redemption.[2]

In conjunction with this perspective, R. Goren developed positions on the relationship between religion and state in the new Jewish polity. He proposed that the state create two court systems: one governed by Halakhah for observant Jews and another based on secular law for nonobservant Jews. The first court system would be responsible for dealing with the many halakhic challenges posed by the existence of a Jewish state that was a potential precursor to a messianic one. R. Goren believed that even though Halakhah did not have a sufficient body of laws to deal with a premessianic Jewish state, Halakhah

---

2. Mishlov, "*Be-'Ein ha-Se'arah*," 69–70, 74–76; idem, "*Hashkafato ha-Tsiyonit shel ha-Rav Shelomoh Goren*," *Yisra'el* 20 (2012): 81–106.

had within it the capacity to develop these laws because of its dynamism and flexibility.

R. Goren also had an idea about the overall direction that Halakhah should take in the new circumstances. He stated quite openly that a conscious effort should be made by rabbinic authorities to come up with halakhic positions that would be acceptable to the secular population in Israel. The goal was to demonstrate to the secular public how attractive Halakhah was as a way of life so that secular Jews would be encouraged to return to traditional Judaism. Their return to religion was, after all, an important feature of the messianic era. In the meantime, secular Jews could avail themselves of the secular courts. Once these Jews returned to religion in the messianic period, such courts would no longer be needed, but they would still be relevant for non-Jews living in the Jewish state.

It is important to understand that R. Goren was not advocating that rabbinic authorities simply invent halakhic positions to accommodate the secular population. His view was that Halakhah had a wide range of opinions on just about every matter it touched; therefore one should be able to find authoritative views to formulate rulings acceptable to secular Jews, even if in some instances, it meant favoring minority opinions. R. Goren also believed that throughout the centuries the rabbis had always been creative interpreters in dealing with the ever-changing historical circumstances of the Jewish people, and it was their responsibility to do so again in light of the new political reality. Therefore, for R. Goren, halakhic rulings in the Jewish state still had to be based on prior sources and precedent, and while he exerted every effort to find positions appealing to the secular public, that did not mean a wholesale rethinking of halakhic practice. Still, R. Goren's views on Halakhah and its role in the state allowed for unusually innovative thinking on a range of issues compared to that of his more traditional Orthodox colleagues.[3]

By the late 1970s, R. Goren had become disillusioned with his messianic vision. The nation did not seem any closer to becoming halakhically observant than it had been at its inception. The 1973 Yom Kippur War was also disheartening for R. Goren because he had hoped that the Six Day War would be the last war Israel would fight before the messianic redemption. Even more disheartening was the signing of the Oslo Accords in 1993, which raised the prospect that the territorial gains of the Six Day War would be reversed. In 1994, the final year of his life, R. Goren sadly declared that the state of Israel could no longer be regarded as the beginning of the messianic redemption.[4]

---

3. Hollander, "*Deyokano*," chapter 13, focuses on R. Goren's views about the role of Halakhah in the state of Israel. Hollander's dissertation, in general, is devoted to exploring R. Goren's halakhic method in light of that relationship.

4. Mishlov, "*Be-'Ein ha-Se'arah*," 77–79.

Yet, the twists and turns in R. Goren's theology of the Jewish state did not affect his determination to provide a comprehensive body of Halakhah for dealing with military life. Even when disillusionment set in regarding the messianic import of the Jewish state, R. Goren continued to produce a steady stream of writings on military matters in Halakhah. R. Goren's writings on this topic initially took the form of articles that appeared in various journals and newspapers, most notably *Mahanayim*, a rabbinic journal devoted to issues pertaining to the Israeli army, and *Ha-Tsofeh*, a religious Zionist newspaper. In R. Goren's later years, many of these articles were edited into collections, the most important of which was *Meshiv Milhamah*, a four-volume work devoted exclusively to military matters. Other collections contained essays on military issues as well, most notably, *Torat ha-Shabbat ve-ha-Mo'ed*, *Torat ha-Medinah*, and *Mishnat ha-Medinah*.[5]

Surprisingly, academic scholarship on R. Goren has only just begun to appear. At the forefront of this trend are several doctoral dissertations on his life and work that have recently been completed. However, few studies have been devoted exclusively to R. Goren's treatment of war in Halakhah. We therefore have much work to do in this chapter to map out his views on the questions that are of interest to us.

Many of R. Goren's essays on war in Halakhah are written in order to provide guidance to soldiers and army commanders about how to act in accordance with Halakhah in specific situations. These writings are therefore composed in the style of the responsa literature (*she'elot u-teshuvot*) that has been produced by rabbis over the centuries.[6] However, a number of R. Goren's essays on war are more theoretical in nature. They are concerned with exploring Halakhah in order to define a range of positions on a given matter and refine our understanding of the distinctions between those positions. They are not necessarily concerned with determining which position is correct or giving practical guidance on how to act in a given circumstance. These essays are written in the spirit of the literature of novellae (*hidushim*) that have also been produced by rabbis over the centuries.[7] The following discussion cites essays of both types,

---

5. *Meshiv Milhamah: She'elot u-Teshuvot be-'Inyaney Tsava, Milhamah, u-Bitahon*, (Jerusalem: Ha-Idra Rabbah, 1982–1991) 4 vols.; *Torat ha-Shabbat ve-ha-Mo'ed* (Alon Shevut, Israel: Yad Shapira, 1982); *Torat ha-Medinah: Mehkar Hilkhati Histori be-Nos'im ha-'Omdim be-Rumah shel Medinat Yisra'el me'az Tekumatah*, ed. Yisra'el Tamari (Jerusalem: Ha-Idra Rabah, 1999); *Mishnat ha-Medinah: Mehkar Hilkhati Histori be-Nos'im ha-'Omdim be-Rumah shel Medinat Yisra'el me'az Tekumatah*, ed. R. Mikhah Halevi (Jerusalem: Ha-Idra Rabah, 1999).

6. See, for example, "*Ha-Matsor 'al Beirut le-Or ha-Halakhah*," in *Meshiv Milhamah*, 3:239–65, which dealt with whether the Israeli army was required, according to Halakhah, to leave an escape route for civilians during its siege of Beirut in the first Lebanon War. We will be discussing this essay later.

7. See, for example, "*Milhemet Mitsvah ve-Milhemet Reshut*," in *Meshiv Milhamah*, 3:351–68, originally published in *Mahanayim* 69 (1962): 5–15. This essay attempts to understand the various positions on the differences between mandatory war and

but we will be primarily interested in those in the first group. Our focus in this study is on how Halakhah is actually enacted in war, and for this purpose R. Goren's responsa will be most helpful.

THE THEOLOGICAL BACKGROUND

Before we deal with R. Goren's halakhic views on war, I would like to explore what is perhaps R. Goren's most important theological essay on war, "Spirit and Power in the Teachings of Judaism." This essay appeared in 1966, and it gives critical insight into R. Goren's views on the broad issue of military power and its place in Judaism. It will therefore provide a theological framework for understanding R. Goren's views on the more practical concerns of war in Halakhah.[8]

R. Goren opens the essay by entertaining the hypothesis that Judaism favors a life of spirituality over one focused on physical might. The entire history of Judaism, it would seem, is a story of survival predicated on this emphasis, for in cultivating a way of life centered on spirituality, Jews have consistently been able to deal with the adversity that has characterized most of their history. R. Goren, however, rejects this way of thinking. Physical might is no less important in Judaism than spiritual strength. In the Bible, God's plan for the Jewish people includes the exercise of military power. At critical junctures in the biblical history, God commands the Jews to wage war against other nations, most notably against the Canaanite nations, wars that allow the Israelites to take possession of the land of Israel in fulfillment of God's covenant. And even though God helps bring victory in such military campaigns, this assistance in no way precludes the need for Israel to fight wars as any other nation would. Moreover, while in the messianic era peace will reign, that peace will come about only after the Jews have waged war against their enemies to reclaim their homeland. Prophecies about this era in the Bible, such as those concerned with the war of Gog and Magog, attest to this prediction.[9]

---

discretionary war that are found in the Babylonian and Jerusalem Talmuds, as well as later medieval halakhic literature. It also delves into the debate between Nahmanides and Maimonides on whether there is a commandment to conquer the land of Israel. However, at no point in this essay does R. Goren decide which positions are correct on these matters. He is solely interested in defining what those positions are.

8. "Ha-Ruah ve-ha-Koah be-Mishnat ha-Yahadut," Mahanayim 100 (1966): 5–16. I cite the reprint of this article in Torat ha-Shabbat ve-ha-Mo'ed, 303–23. An excellent discussion of this essay can be found in Aryeh Edrei, "Divine Spirit and Physical Power: Rabbi Shlomo Goren and the Military Ethic of the Israel Defense Forces," Theoretical Inquiries in Law 7, no. 1 (2006): 278–82.

9. "Ha-Ruah ve-ha-Koah," 303–15.

But R. Goren warns that there is danger in detaching physical power from the realm of the spiritual. This uncoupling can lead to wanton violence that knows no bounds and is highly destructive.

[T]he Torah of Israel teaches us, and its prophets inculcate in us, that we do not separate between those who carry the flag of morality and spirit and those who carry the flag of physical liberation, even by means of war and conquest. All the great ones of Israel, its teachers, and its spiritual leaders in ancient times, integrated in their souls power and spirit together. The men of spirit also provided an example of independent courage in fighting on the battlefields against the enemies of Israel and its oppressors. This integration of the sword and the book is a continuous thread in Jewish history not just in the period of the Bible, but also afterwards in the period of the Hasmoneans and after the destruction of the Second Temple in the period of the Second revolt in the days of Bar Kokhba, R. Akiva, R. Simeon bar Yohai and his friends.[10]

R. Goren seems to assume that it is in the realm of the spirit that moral values originate, and therefore the realm of physical power, left on its own, can easily lead to brutality. That is why we are warned in a number of biblical passages not to place trust in our own strength but in God alone. The right path is one that combines the spiritual and the physical, or as R. Goren puts it, "the sword and the book."[11]

R. Goren's essay has a polemical element in it. He directs some of his remarks to secular Jews, whom he criticizes for placing exclusive emphasis on the moral dimension of Judaism and insisting that Judaism is a religion focused entirely on peace. R. Goren does not deny that peace is the ultimate goal for which all Jews must strive. The messianic era, after all, will culminate in an everlasting peace for all nations. However, R. Goren insists that physical might has always been central to the Jewish ethos, and that its use is necessary for achieving the longed-for messianic peace at the end of history.[12] Yet, one suspects that R. Goren's remarks are also directed against the ultra-Orthodox community, even though he does not mention this audience in the essay. This community took a pacifist position on the conflict with Arabs as part of an overall rejection of Zionism, and it is likely that R. Goren had them in mind here as well in his criticism of Jews who reject the importance of physical power.

R. Goren's desire to give equal emphasis to spirit and physical power characterizes the rest of his writings on war. He constantly strives to find a balance between the need to wage war and the goal of seeking peace, between the

10. "*Ha-Ruah ve-ha-Koah*," 316.
11. "*Ha-Ruah ve-ha-Koah*," 315–23.
12. "*Ha-Ruah ve-ha-Koah*," 318–19.

imperative to defeat Israel's enemies and the obligation to be sensitive to the moral dilemmas war raises. R. Goren is often able to find harmony between these aims, but we will also see instances in which they are in tension.

THE METHODOLOGY OF WARTIME HALAKHAH

Let us now move on to R. Goren's treatment of war in Halakhah. The best place to begin is with his preface to the first volume of *Meshiv Milhamah*, in which he spells out the challenges the subject presents and the methodology needed to deal with them. R. Goren begins with the admission that Halakhah does not provide adequate guidance on matters relating to war because Jews have had neither political sovereignty nor an army for close to two thousand years. Indeed, there are halakhic sources in which the laws of war are discussed, but they are intended for the messianic era (*hilkheta de-meshiha*) and are too sparse to provide comprehensive guidance in a premessianic world. Even Maimonides' discussion of laws of war in his *Mishneh Torah* belongs in this category. R. Goren therefore declares his intention to develop a comprehensive body of laws on war that will be able to guide a Jewish state prior to the messianic era. For this purpose, he will probe biblical and rabbinic literature on the premise that it contains fragments of a comprehensive body of halakhic material on war that existed when Jews last had political power. According to R. Goren, the laws of war can be resurrected by assembling these fragments and filling in the gaps with creative interpretation. R. Goren informs us that for this purpose he will also explore historical sources not normally consulted by rabbinic authorities, such as the books of the Maccabees and the writings of Josephus.[13]

The use of the latter sources is unusual for an Orthodox halakhic authority given that they are not normally considered canonical texts in rabbinic tradition. Aryeh Edrei has argued that R. Goren made use of such sources for polemical reasons. Secular Zionists had rejected rabbinic literature in formulating their views on political matters, including war, because this literature, most notably the Babylonian Talmud, had been produced primarily by Jews living in exile. An authentic Jewish approach to such issues had to be based either on the biblical text or on such sources as Maccabees and Josephus because these works had been composed in the land of Israel. David Ben Gurion, who was a friend of R. Goren, was a leading representative of this approach. R. Goren, not surprisingly, rejected this way of thinking and claimed that rabbinic literature had to be the primary resource for any investigation into political matters in Judaism. Yet, he also demonstrated a willingness to make a concession

13. Preface to *Meshiv Milhamah*, 1:9–12.

to Ben Gurion and other secular Zionists by utilizing the sources revered by
them for the treatment of political issues. This explains R. Goren's intention
to draw upon Maccabees and Josephus when dealing with matters of wars. It
also explains a tendency one sees throughout his writing to base his positions
directly on the biblical text, a method that is also unusual for an Orthodox
rabbi. In traditional halakhic discourse, the Bible is authoritative only when
coupled with its interpretation in classical rabbinic literature.[14]

Avi'ad Hollander, however, has argued that R. Goren's innovation here is
not as radical as it might seem. Hollander demonstrates that in instances in
which R. Goren directly engages the biblical text or consults such sources as
Maccabees and Josephus, he always takes a position that is, in fact, in line
with positions found in classical rabbinic literature, even if they are minority
ones. Thus, his concession to Ben Gurion and company is perhaps more sym-
bolic than substantive.[15]

WHICH WARS ARE PERMISSIBLE FOR
THE STATE OF ISRAEL?

Let us now delve into R. Goren's halakhic rulings on war. I begin by looking
at R. Goren's opinions on which wars are permissible for the state of Israel.
R. Goren addresses this issue in a number of places in his writings, but one
of his introductory essays in the first volume of *Meshiv Milhamah*, "The Wars
of Israel in Our Time in Light of Halakhah," is devoted specifically to this
question, and we will therefore use it as a basis for exploring this matter. We
will also consult other works by R. Goren to clarify and expand on individual
points in this essay.[16]

Defensive War

As has almost every figure we have examined thus far, R. Goren informs us
in this essay that the state of Israel may wage wars of self-defense to protect
itself from its enemies.[17] The permissibility of this type of war is rooted in
two basic halakhic principles that are applicable in all places and times. One
is the right of self-defense that each and every individual possesses and is

---

14. Edrei, "Divne Spirit," 268–70.
15. Hollander, "*Deyokano*," 34–64.
16. "*Milhamot Yisra'el bi-Zeman ha-zeh le-Or ha-Halakhah*," *Meshiv Milhamah*,
1:110–38.
17. The only exception is R. Yisraeli who in his Kibiyeh essay argues that wars waged
in response to enemy attack are for the purpose of seeking revenge, not self-defense.

encapsulated in the talmudic dictum that "if someone comes to slay you, slay him first."[18] The second is the biblical commandment in Leviticus 19:16, "do not stand idly by the blood of your neighbor," which requires that a person come to the aid of another individual who is in harm's way.[19] While the first source allows one to use lethal force to protect oneself from harm, the second requires an individual to protect his fellow human beings from harm.[20]

R. Goren's choice of Leviticus 19:16 as the biblical source for the imperative to rescue others from harm deserves comment. R. Goren calls on this verse repeatedly throughout his writings to anchor the obligation of all Jews to participate in defensive wars, and his choice of this verse is noteworthy because according to the Talmud, it authorizes an individual to rescue someone from harm, such as a person who is drowning or being robbed by criminals, but it does not necessarily permit an individual to kill a pursuer for that purpose. For the latter dispensation, the Talmud turns to the case of the betrothed young woman discussed in Deuteronomy 22:5–9, which R. Goren does not mention.[21] Thus it would seem that R. Goren does not see the obligation to participate in defensive war as an application of the law of the pursuer. Rather, what is operative in this type of war is the more general commandment to rescue individuals whose lives are in danger.

Why R. Goren sees things this way is not clear. By killing enemy soldiers in war, is one not, in effect, killing "pursuers" threatening the lives of one's own kinsmen? It may be that R. Goren did not believe that the paradigm of the pursuer was useful for defensive war because it applied in specific circumstances in which an attacker was clearly out to kill a particular individual, while in war, soldiers do not necessarily target particular individuals on the enemy side in this manner. Armies fight armies in a more collective manner. R. Goren may have therefore felt that the more general imperative to safeguard others from harm was more apt for defensive war.

R. Goren goes on to find proof that defensive war is still permissible in our time by citing two passages in Maimonides. Maimonides, in his introduction to his Sefer ha-Mitsvot, explicitly rules out the possibility of waging discretionary war after the destruction of the Second Temple,[22] but he says nothing about mandatory war. R. Goren infers from Maimonides' silence that mandatory war is still permissible. And since the mandatory wars against the Canaanites and the Amalekites are no longer possible given that neither of these nations still exists, the implication that mandatory war is still operative must refer to the only remaining type of war in this category: war of self-defense. The

18. Above, pp. 43–44.
19. Above, pp. 44–45.
20. "Milhamot Yisra'el," 111, 115.
21. Above, p. 45.
22. Sefer ha-Mitsvot, introduction, shoresh 14.

second source in Maimonides that R. Goren refers to as evidence that defensive wars are still allowed is the *Mishneh Torah*. As we have seen repeatedly in this study, such wars are referred to in the *Mishneh Torah* as wars initiated to "save Israel from the clutches of the enemy," *'ezrat yisra'el mi-yad tsar*.[23]

An intriguing feature of R. Goren's interpretation of Maimonides is his insistence that when Maimonides permitted defensive war even after the exile, he could not have been referring to wars initiated only by the enemy; he must have had preemptive wars in mind as well:

> The words of Maimonides [in *Sefer ha-Mitsvot*] clearly reject only discretionary war in the present time ... which means that mandatory war is [still] customary in the present time. It goes without saying [that this permission includes] mandatory war of "saving Israel from the clutches of the enemy" (*'ezrat yisra'el mi-yad tsar*), which is the third type of [mandatory war] explicated in Maimonides' *Hilkhot Melakhim* 5:1—i.e., actual defensive war. For if we are attacked by an enemy, there is certainly no need for any authority to respond with war that has arisen in order to defend ourselves, nor is it about this matter that there is a need to prove that it [i.e., defensive war] is in effect also in the present time, for the Torah story has said, "if someone comes to slay you, slay him first" (*Berakhot* 58 and parallel sources). And the Torah did not differentiate between the time of the Temple and the present time, nor between saving many people and saving the individual, for whoever can save [another] must save [him] because of "do not stand idly by the blood of your fellow," as we have explained several times in these responsa. However, the intention [of Maimonides in allowing defensive war in our time] is certainly addressed to the category of defensive war that is preemptive, when we initiate an attack on an enemy to preempt an attack initiated by him on us, [a war] that is also called mandatory war of the variety of "saving Israel from the clutches of the enemy," and it too [i.e., preemptive war] is customary in our time.[24]

R. Goren reasons that permission to wage war against an enemy that has initiated hostilities is so obvious that Maimonides did not have to state it explicitly because the sources mentioned above regarding the individual's right to self-defense and the imperative to rescue others from harm make that permission abundantly clear. Thus, in stating that wars of self-defense are permitted, Maimonides must have intended to allude to wars of the preemptive variety as well—that is, wars in which Jews initiate hostilities in order to prevent an enemy that is about to launch an attack of its own. It is not obvious that such wars were permitted, and therefore Maimonides' intention was to make clear

23. MT *Melakhim* 5:1; "*Milhamot Yisra'el*," 111, 115–16, 137.
24. "*Milhamot Yisra'el*," 115–16.

that they were. R. Goren goes on to claim later in his discussion that the same position is held by a number of medieval halakhic authorities: the Rif, the Rosh, and the *Tur*.[25]

What is perplexing about these comments is that permission to wage defensive war has not been at all obvious to the figures we have examined thus far in our study. After all, our entire discussion has been premised on the fact that Halakhah presents formidable obstacles to the waging of war of any kind, including the prohibition against forcing someone to risk his life for others and the taking of innocent life. Therefore, an explanation is required for R. Goren's insistence that the permission to wage defensive war is so obvious that Maimonides, in allowing this type of war, must have been concerned primarily with war that is preemptive in nature.

We may gain insight into R. Goren's position here by noting that he himself participated in a preemptive war that had an enormous impact on the state of Israel and marked a turning point both in the development of religious Zionism and in R. Goren's own theology. I am referring, of course, to the Six Day War in which Israel initiated hostilities when it became clear that the surrounding Arab nations were planning an attack on the Jewish state. R. Goren was the Chief Rabbi of the Israeli Defense Forces at the time. One of the most iconic images we have from that war is R. Goren standing at the Western Wall holding a Torah scroll and blowing a ram's horn just after the old city of Jerusalem had been captured. Moreover, as we noted earlier, the Six Day War was of such momentous significance to R. Goren, that it convinced him that the establishment of the state of Israel was, in fact, the beginning of the messianic redemption. It is therefore no surprise that R. Goren would insist that preemptive war must have been included in Maimonides' position permitting wars of self-defense. The Israeli military victory in 1967 had to be based on firm halakhic footing.

While these observations make R. Goren's position more understandable, they do not solve the halakhic difficulties posed by it. He must still deal with the halakhic obstacles to waging war that have troubled every figure we have analyzed in this study. R. Goren was not unaware of these difficulties, and as we shall see, he does address them. But I will hold off treatment of these issues for later discussion. The important point for us thus far is that for R. Goren defensive wars are permitted in our time, and they include preemptive wars as well.

25. Rif, *Shabbat* 7b, *'Eruvin* 5a; Rosh, *Shabbat* 19a; *Tur, Orah Hayim* 158, 249. "*Milhamot Yisra'el*," 135–36. Rif is the acronym for R. Isaac ben Jacob Alfasi ha-Cohen (1013–1103), who composed one of the earliest authoritative works on the Talmud. Rosh is the acronym for R. Asher ben Yehiel (1250 or 1259–1327), and the *Tur* refers to the halakhic work, *Arba'ah Turim*, which was composed by the Rosh's son, R. Jacob ben Asher (1269–1343).

One challenge that R. Goren is easily able to solve in the essay we are examining is the problem of legitimate authority in waging defensive war.[26] According to Maimonides' *Mishneh Torah*, wars of self-defense have to be initiated by a king, but this office no longer exists. R. Goren deals with this problem in the same way that most of the other figures in our study have: he adopts R. Kook's notion that in the absence of a king, any government representing the Jewish people assumes the king's political authority. In fact, in R. Goren's opinion, Maimonides himself implies support for this idea.[27] That, of course, means that the Israeli government, as a democratically elected body, fills the role of the king and therefore has the right to wage wars. Thus, the absence of a king presents no problem for waging defensive wars in our time.[28]

R. Goren takes this position in other places in his writings,[29] but in one passage he places particular emphasis on the notion of the social contract as a basis for legitimate government. Instead of relying on R. Kook, he cites a source in the biblical book of Joshua in which it is stated that Joshua received his authority as leader of the Israelite nation from the Jewish people itself. R. Goren also notes that R. Moses Schreiber (1762–1839), better known as the *Hatam Sofer*, endorsed this conception of authority as well.[30] Still, R. Goren's reasoning here reflects the same basic line of thinking regarding legitimate authority that we find in other passages in his writings: any Jewish government supported by the people has the same authority as a king, and this includes the right to initiate wars of self-defense.

Discretionary War

In the essay currently being explored, R. Goren also takes up the question of whether discretionary war may be conducted in our time. On this issue, R. Goren follows the general consensus of most contemporary halakhic authorities that discretionary war may not be initiated nowadays due to the lack of a Sanhedrin. While a king may be replaced with any legitimate Jewish government, there is no authority that can serve in place of the Sanhedrin, and this body will not be revived until the messianic period. According to

---

26. The stated purpose of the essay under examination here is, in fact, to explore the issue of authority ("*Milhamot Yisra'el*," 110). However, as we have seen, this essay deals with a wide range of other issues as well.

27. MT *Sanehdrin* 14:13.

28. "*Milhamot Yisra'el*," 114–15; Above, pp. 70–71.

29. "*Milhemet Shelom ha-Galil le-fi ha-Halakhah*," *Meshiv Milhamah*, 3:267–68; "*Ha-Mitsvot she-bein Adam la-Medinah*," *Torat ha-Shabbat ve-ha-Mo'ed*, 451–52. The first essay originally appeared in *Ha-Tsofeh*, 27 *Tammuz*, 1983, p. 5; 5 *Av*, 1983, p. 5.

30. *Hatam Sofer, Orah Hayim* 208; "*Ma'amad ha-Shilton lefi ha-Halakhah*," *Torat ha-Medinah*, 24–25.

R. Goren, the Sanhedrin is consulted in discretionary war for two reasons: it is the highest authority on interpreting the Torah and its laws, and it represents the will of the people, who must agree to a discretionary war before it can be initiated. R. Goren also notes that according to Maimonides' *Sefer ha-Mitsvot*, the waging of discretionary war requires consultation with the *urim ve-tumim*, the oracle on the breast-plate of the High Priest, and this, too, is unavailable to us nowadays.[31]

Yet, R. Goren provides a number of tantalizing hints that discretionary war may be conducted again in the near future, even before the arrival of the messianic era. In the same passage in which R. Goren rules out the waging of discretionary war in our day, he also raises the possibility that the Sanhedrin may soon be reconstituted. As he puts it, "[T]here is a fundamental possibility of establishing the Sanhedrin in the present time.[32] The prerequisite for having a Sanhedrin would be a revival of the form of rabbinic ordination that was practiced when the Sanhedrin existed and was required for all rabbis who served on it.[33] This type of ordination had not been practiced for centuries, but passages in Maimonides' writings suggest that its revival is indeed possible in the period of exile.[34] R. Goren is by no means the first halakhic authority to have noticed these passages in Maimonides. These sources led to periodic attempts by several prominent rabbis since Maimonides' time to bring back classical rabbinic ordination and reestablish the Sanhedrin, though none of these attempts was successful.[35] R. Goren's claim that the Sanhedrin may be reconstituted before the messianic period is therefore not unprecedented. But most important for our purposes is that in raising this issue in the context of a discussion about discretionary war, R. Goren is clearly implying that a path exists for the state of Israel to wage wars of this kind.[36]

Later on in the essay, R. Goren again takes up the question of discretionary war, and here, too, we find hints regarding the possibility of waging

31. Maimonides, *Sefer ha-Mitsvot*, introduction, *shoresh* 14; "*Milhamot Yisra'el*," 110–15, 137; "*Tsava u-Bitahon*," *Meshiv Milhamah*, 3:374–75.
32. "*Milhamot Yisra'el*," 112.
33. "*Milhamot Yisra'el*," 112–13.
34. Maimonides, MT *Sanhedrin* 4:11; and *Peirush ha-Mishnah*, *Sanhedrin* 1:3.
35. Jacob Katz, "Rabbinical Authority and Authorization in the Middle Ages," *Studies in Medieval Jewish History and Literature*, ed. Isadore Twersky (Cambridge, Mass: Harvard University Press, 1979), 1:41–56; idem, "The Dispute between Jacob Berab and Levi ben Habib Over Renewing Ordination," in *Binah: Studies in Jewish History, Thought, and Culture*, ed. Joseph Dan (New York: Praeger,1989), 1:119–41.
36. See Mishlov, "*Be-'Ein ha-Se'arah*," 43, who notes that when R. Goren became Chief Ashkenazi Rabbi of Israel, he referred to the office of the chief rabbinate as "*Sanhedrin she-ba-derekh*," "a Sanhedrin in the making." With this in mind, R. Goren worked to strengthen the authority and stature of the office, but had great difficulty doing so because of opposition from a number of quarters, most notably the ultra-Orthodox community.

this type of war in the near future. R. Goren claims that statements in the *Sefer ha-Hinukh* imply this possibility. R. Goren notes that in a couple of passages in which the *Sefer ha-Hinukh* discusses the laws of war, we are told that these laws, including those governing discretionary war, will be reinstituted at a time when the Jewish people is once again "in its land" and "settled" (*'al adamto, be-yishuvah*).[37] According to R. Goren, there is no suggestion here that this period is one in which the Temple will be rebuilt or the messiah will have arrived, and he infers from this observation that the *Sefer ha-Hinukh* could very well be speaking about a Jewish state established before the advent of the messianic period.[38] R. Goren also finds support for his position in the Rif, Rosh, and *Tur*, all of whom discuss discretionary war but without seeming to limit it to the time in which Jews have a temple in Jerusalem, either in the ancient past or the messianic future. Moreover, the entire agenda of the *Tur* is to discuss only those laws that are still applicable during the period of the exile, and thus the fact that he deals quite explicitly with laws of discretionary war indicates again that this form of war is by no mean defunct.[39] R. Goren, however, admits to some doubt about whether the Rif, Rosh, and *Tur* support the revival of discretionary war prior to the messiah because, he notes, they do not take up the question of reinstituting classical rabbinic ordination or the Sanhedrin, which would be necessary for waging this type of war.[40]

The reader may find R. Goren's inferences from the authorities he cites here to be even weaker than he himself admits. He argues primarily on the basis of what the texts he cites do *not* say rather than what they *do* say. However, this observation does not take away from our main point, which is that R. Goren evidently has a desire to reinstitute discretionary war, and his determination to do so is manifest in the way he struggles to justify that possibility through the inferences he draws.

R. Goren must also deal with the role that the *urim ve-tumim* play in discretionary war. A number of authoritative halakhic sources require that this oracle be consulted before discretionary war is initiated, and the essay we are examining contains a lengthy and complex treatment of this question. R. Goren's main concern seems to be that Maimonides' position on this issue is inconsistent. In his *Sefer ha-Mitsvot*, Maimonides takes the view that the *urim ve-tumim* are needed for waging discretionary war, while in the *Mishneh Torah* there is no

---

37. *Sefer ha-Hinukh, halakhot,* 525–57. *Sefer ha-Hinukh* is of unknown authorship. It was composed in thirteenth-century Spain, and it provides a systematic explication of the 613 commandments in accordance with Maimonides' enumeration of the commandments in *Sefer ha-Mitsvot*.

38. "*Milhamot Yisra'el,*" 135, 137.

39. Rif, *Shabbat* 7b, '*Eruvin* 5a; Rosh, *Shabbat* 19a; *Tur, Orah Hayim* 158, 249; "*Milhamot Yisra'el,*" 136, 137–38.

40. "*Milhamot Yisra'el,*" 136–37, 137–88.

such stipulation.[41] R. Goren seems to settle the matter by claiming that in the *Sefer ha-Mitsvot* Maimonides rules in accordance with the Babylonian Talmud that sees the *urim ve-tumim* as necessary for all discretionary wars, while in the *Mishneh Torah*, he adopts the position of the Jerusalem Talmud, according to which the use of the *urim ve-tumim* in this type of war is optional.[42] R. Goren leaves us with no decision about which view is correct. However, in light of the foregoing discussion about R. Goren's desire to bring back the institution of discretionary war, one suspects that he was more favorable to the view expressed in the *Mishneh Torah*. The *urim ve-tumim* are, after all, no longer in existence, and therefore the position of the *Mishneh Torah*, which does not require them, would allow this type of war to proceed in their absence. We can also assume that R. Goren would have viewed the position of the *Mishneh Torah* as decisive, given its much greater stature as an authoritative halakhic source.

Mandatory War in *Sefer ha-Mitsvot*

The mention of *Sefer ha-Mitsvot* here provides a transition to an issue that crops up in a number of places in R. Goren's writings when he deals with the question of which types of wars are permitted in our time. We noted earlier that R. Goren cites a passage in the introduction to *Sefer ha-Mitsvot* stating that discretionary wars can no longer be waged nowadays, and he infers from the absence of any mention of mandatory wars here that the latter type of war is still permissible. However, R. Goren notes that manuscripts of the *Sefer ha-Mitsvot* contain a different version of this passage. In the standard printed editions, the text reads as follows:

> All positive or negative commandments that are tied to the sacrifices, or the temple rituals, or the death penalty, or the Sanhedrin, or the prophet and king, *or discretionary war*—I do not have to say about them "this is obligatory only in the presence of the Temple," since it is obvious.[43]

However, in the manuscripts, one finds a crucial change:

> All positive or negative commandments that are tied to the sacrifices, or the temple rituals, or the death penalty, or the Sanhedrin, or the prophet and king, *or mandatory war, or discretionary war*—I do not have to say about them "this is obligatory only in the presence of the Temple," since it is obvious.[44]

41. *Sefer ha-Mitsvot*, introduction, *shoresh* 14; MT *Melakhim* 5:2.
42. "*Milhamot Yisra'el*," 116–34, 137.
43. *Sefer ha-Mitsvot*, introduction, *shoresh* 14 (my emphasis).
44. As cited by R. Goren in "*Milhamot Yisra'el*," 110–11 (my emphasis).

R. Goren regards this latter reading as the authentic version, but the difficulty is that it states quite clearly that after the destruction of the Temple, Jews must abstain from waging not just discretionary war but mandatory war as well. Thus, Maimonides appears to be telling us that no war of any kind may be waged until the messianic age, including wars of self-defense. The correct reading of the passage in *Sefer ha-Mitsvot* therefore goes against one of R. Goren's most basic premises regarding war, which is that the state of Israel may wage wars of self-defense against its enemies.

In the essay we are looking at, R. Goren makes no attempt to resolve this problem; however, in other essays written in the same period, he does. In an article composed in 1982 dealing with the Israeli army's siege of Beirut during the first Lebanon War, R. Goren argues that when Maimonides rules out waging mandatory wars until the messianic period in the *Sefer ha-Mitsvot*, he must have been referring only to wars initiated by Jews for the purpose of "conquest" or "revenge." Maimonides could not have possibly had defensive wars in mind here, seeing as Jews are required to obey the commandment "do not stand idly by the blood of your fellow," in all places and times.[45] R. Goren makes a similar argument in an essay written a year later, in which he claims that Maimonides' refusal to sanction mandatory wars until the messianic period in the *Sefer ha-Mitsvot* was only in reference to wars against the Canaanites and Amalekites. Once again, according to R. Goren, Maimonides could not have possibly ruled out wars of self-defense even in the period of the exile, seeing as the commandment not to stand idly by the blood of one's fellow is still very much in effect. R. Goren also notes that the *Tur* and *Shulhan Arukh* both speak about the permissibility of defensive wars, and neither of these works could have considered this type of war to be defunct because they were written for the purpose of providing guidance only on halakhic matters applicable after the destruction of the Second Temple.[46]

War for Conquering the Land of Israel

An important issue raised by R. Goren in the essay we have been analyzing is whether Jews have an ongoing commandment to conquer the land of Israel. As we have seen in earlier discussions in this study, Nahmanides championed the affirmative position on this matter, while Maimonides appears to have ignored the issue altogether. Great effort has been expended by religious Zionist rabbis, including some in our study, to prove that Maimonides' viewpoint was identical to that of Nahmanides, but R. Goren does not go along with this effort. He

45. "*Ha-Matsor 'al Beirut*," 241–42.
46. "*Milhemet Shelom ha-Galil*," 279–80.

sees the two great medieval halakhists as having two fundamentally different positions. Nahmanides clearly supports the notion that Jews have a commandment to conquer the land of Israel, and that commandment is ongoing, while Maimonides does not.[47] In fact, according to R. Goren's position, Maimonides' view is that Jews have never had such a commandment. Maimonides speaks of there having been a commandment in the time of Joshua instructing the Israelites to wipe out the Canaanite nations, but there was no commandment focused specifically on conquering the land of Israel per se.[48]

The question of whether Jews have such a commandment occupies R. Goren even more in some of his later writings, particularly in several essays in which he discusses whether the state of Israel has a halakhic status of the kind that Jewish kingdoms had in the time of the First and Second Temple. Not surprisingly, R. Goren claims that in Nahmanides' opinion, Israel would have such a status, whereas for Maimonides, it would not. Since Nahmanides' view is that Jews have an eternal commandment to conquer the land of Israel, clearly a Jewish state set up in the wake of such a conquest has legitimate halakhic status.[49] Maimonides, by contrast, would not see the modern state of Israel as a halakhically sanctioned entity, because he does not support the notion that there is a commandment to conquer the land; therefore a state that emerges as a consequence of such a conquest is at best neutral in its halakhic status.[50] Evidence that this is Maimonides' position is a statement in the *Mishneh Torah* in which Maimonides says explicitly that one of the chief tasks of the messiah is to establish a sovereign Jewish state. The implication here is that this action cannot be taken prior to the messiah's arrival.[51]

47. "*Milhamot Yisra'el*," 110–11; Maimonides, *Peirush ha-Mishnah, Sotah* 8:7, MT *Melakhim* 5:1.

48. Above, pp. 37–38. According to R. Goren, that is why Maimonides, when discussing the conquest of the land, cites the biblical commandments in Deut. 20:17, "you must utterly destroy them"—that is, the Canaanites. In Maimonides' thinking, the essential imperative to the Israelites when Joshua led them into the land of Israel was not to capture land per se, but to annihilate the Canaanite nations who lived in the land.

49. "*Ma'amad ha-Shilton*," 21–22; "*Sheleimut ha-Arets lefi ha-Halakhah*," *Torat ha-Medinah*, 97; "*Ma'amadam ha-Hilkhati shel Yehudah ve-Shomron ve-Hevel 'Azah*," *Torat ha-Medinah*, 117–18. In one of his later essays, R. Goren also claims that Nahmanides' position regarding the imperative of conquering the land has precedent in a passage in the Jerusalem Talmud predicting that Jews will rebuild the Temple before the arrival of the messiah. R. Goren reasons that this source must have presumed that Jews would also conquer the land of Israel before the messianic period because they would have to have sovereignty there in order to rebuild the Temple. This source therefore takes for granted that a conquest of the land is in accordance with God's will, and Nahmanides, in affirming that conquering the land of Israel is an ongoing imperative, is merely endorsing this early rabbinic view. See JT *Ma'aser Sheni* 5:2; "*Ma'amad ha-Shilton*," 21–22.

50. "*Sheleimut ha-Arets*," 91–94, 96–97; "*Ma'amadam ha-Hilkhati*," 118.

51. "*Sheleimut ha-Arets*," 96–97; "*Ma'amadam ha-Hilkhati*," 118. In the latter passage, R. Goren reiterates his view that, according to Maimonides, we have no commandment to conquer the land of Israel. However, the proof that is offered here by R. Goren

In his later essays, R. Goren marshals support for his view that Maimonides did not see the conquest of the land of Israel as a commandment by adducing the passage in the introduction to Maimonides' *Sefer ha-Mitsvot* that we discussed earlier. As we have seen, the correct reading of that passage precludes the possibility that Jews may fight wars of any kind before the messianic period, including mandatory wars. R. Goren argues that this prohibition clearly rules out wars for the purpose of conquering the land of Israel as well. It also confirms that a Jewish state built as a result of such a conquest would not have halakhic status of the kind accorded to Jewish states prior to the destruction of the second Temple.[52] Of course, R. Goren once again must confront the difficulty that if, as this source tells us, all mandatory wars are prohibited until the messianic period, the ban would include defensive wars as well. His response to this problem is similar to that which we saw in earlier essays. He argues that Maimonides' prohibition against waging mandatory wars does not extend to wars of self-defense; these are still permitted.[53]

R. Goren also takes up the issue of the status of land conquered in Israel's wars in 1948 and 1967. According to R. Goren, there is no question that Nahmanides would confer Jewish sovereignty over this land, seeing as it was taken in the course of fulfilling a divine commandment. But what is most interesting is R. Goren's claim that Maimonides would take the same position. For, even if, according to Maimonides' position, the wars of 1948 and 1967 are regarded as wars of straight conquest and thus forbidden, it is inconceivable that he would deny Jewish sovereignty over territory taken in these wars, seeing as a legitimately constituted government representing the Jewish people initiated them and the territory captured is in the land of Israel promised by God to the Jews. Maimonides would certainly confer de facto recognition on a conquest of this type. Moreover, R. Goren claims that the argument can easily be made that the wars of 1948 and 1967 were not wars of conquest but wars of self-defense, because they were foisted on Israel by their Arab enemies, and in that case, the argument that Maimonides would uphold Jewish sovereignty over the conquered land is even stronger. In light of the fact that Maimonides

---

to support this reading of Maimonides comes from *Megilat Ester*, a medieval commentary on *Sefer ha-Mitsvot*, ascribed to the fifteenth-century Spanish figure, R. Isaac de Leon. This commentary claims that Maimonides' position is based on the talmudic and midrashic tradition of the three oaths which forbids Jews to take the land of Israel by force after the exile (*Megilat Ester* on Nahmanides' addenda to the *Sefer ha-Mitsvot*, positive commandment #4; chapter 2, above pp. 40–41). Yet, the implication of this interpretation of Maimonides is that the commandment to conquer the land existed from the time of Joshua to the destruction of the Second Temple, a position that contradicts R. Goren's assertion in other places that, according to Maimonides, there was no commandment to conquer the land to begin with, only a commandment to annihilate the Canaanites. R. Goren does not seem to have been aware of the inconsistency.

52. "*Ma'amad ha-Shilton*," 19–21; "*Sheleimut ha-Arets*," 93–94, 96–97.
53. "*Ma'amad ha-Shilton*," 23–24.

supports waging wars of self-defense in the *Mishneh Torah* without any apparent qualification, he would undoubtedly rule that any territory in the land of
Israel taken by Jews in a war of this kind, fully belongs to them.[54]

Incidentally, R. Goren also concludes from these insights that neither
Nahmanides nor Maimonides would approve of the state of Israel returning
land to its Arab enemies in order to make peace, even if it can be shown that
it would save Jewish lives in the long run. Nahmanides' view that Jews must
wage war to conquer the land of Israel presumes that Jewish lives may be lost
in a war of this kind, and it therefore stands to reason that Jews would have to
accept the loss of lives in order to retain control over that territory even after
the war was over. Therefore, the sparing of Jewish lives cannot be a reason
to surrender territory. Maimonides would come to the same conclusion, for
even if he does not believe that there is a commandment to conquer the land,
he rules in the *Mishneh Torah* that Jews may not allow non-Jews to live in the
land of Israel when Jews have sovereignty.[55] This position implies a conclusion similar to that inferred from Nahmanides' viewpoint, for if Jews must
exercise full control over their land, they must also use force, if necessary, to
maintain that control, and this use of force brings with it the possibility of
losing Jewish lives, whether in war or in peacetime. R. Goren also argues that
the same conclusion may be drawn about Maimonides' views on relinquishing
land, if one assumes, as R. Goren does, that Maimonides endorses the right of
the state of Israel to wage wars of self-defense. This right would include permission to initiate wars to defend territory that Israel had captured in earlier
defensive wars, and again it would imply permission to sacrifice Jewish lives
to maintain control of that territory, even in times of peace.[56]

To sum up our discussion thus far, R. Goren's views on which types of war
are permitted in our day seem to reflect his belief that Judaism has always
attempted to strike a balance between "spirit" and "power," between a life in
which Jews emphasize moral values and one in which they use brute force to

---

54. "*Ma'amad ha-Shilton*," 23–24; "*Ma'amadam ha-Hilkhati*," 118. Hollander, "*Deyokano*,"
134, argues that R. Goren regarded Maimonides' *Sefer ha-Mitsvot* as having less authority
than his *Mishneh Torah*. However, that does not seem to be the case with respect to the
topic that we have been examining thus far—i.e., the types of war that are halakhically
permitted in the present era. As we have seen, in discussing this matter, R. Goren cites the
Sefer ha-Mitsvot perhaps as frequently as he does the *Mishneh Torah*.

55. MT *'Akum* 10:6.

56. "*Admat ha-Kodesh ve-Pikuah Nefesh mi-Nekudat Mabat ha-Halakhah*," *Torat ha-
Medinah*, 33–35. This essay was originally published in *Ha-Tsofeh*, 29 *Elul*, 1989. It was
also published in *Tehumin* 15 (1995): 11–22. A similar position to the one described
here is taken by R. Goren in "*Ma'amadam ha-Hilkhati*," 119–20. For a more thorough
discussion of R. Goren's views on territorial concessions, see Shifrah Mishlov, "'*Emdato
shel ha-Rav Goren bi-Devar Mesirat ha-Shetahim Temurat Shalom*," *Mehkerey Yehudah ve-
Shomron* 22 (2013): 243–59.

achieve their goals. On the side of spirit, R. Goren informs us that wars of self-defense are the only wars permitted nowadays, a position that exhibits a degree of antipathy to the use of physical power. However, an emphasis on physical power seems to emerge in R. Goren's suggestions that the waging of discretionary wars is also a possibility if Jews are able to revive the Sanhedrin.

R. Goren's attempt to balance spirit and physical power is perhaps most evident in his discussion of whether Jews have a commandment to conquer the land of Israel. On the one hand, the spiritual factor seems to come to the fore in R. Goren's view that the dispute between Nahmanides and Maimonides on this issue is unresolved and that therefore the state of Israel may not initiate wars for the sole purpose of fulfilling this commandment. On the other hand, the value of physical power asserts itself in R. Goren's belief that if the state of Israel does go to war, it does not have to relinquish any territory it conquers as a result, especially if the war was waged in self-defense. Wars of aggression are therefore not encouraged by R. Goren, but he is happy to confer his blessing on any territorial gains achieved when wars are waged for other purposes.

CONSCRIPTION

We are now ready to take a look at how R. Goren deals with the more specific question of conscription. If the only wars that the state of Israel may wage are wars of self-defense, how does one justify forcing soldiers to risk their lives for the sake of the nation? In everyday Halakhah, one may not require an individual to sacrifice his life to save someone else from harm.

R. Goren deals with this issue in the introductory essays to the first volume of *Meshiv Milhamah*. In the first of these, entitled "The Morality of Warfare in Light of Halakhah," he cites two sources that prove that sending soldiers into battle at the risk of their lives is permissible in Halakhah, and both are familiar to us from previous chapters. The first is the talmudic statement in *Shevu'ot* 35b, in which we are told that a king may kill up to "one-sixth." R. Goren adopts the view of *Tosafot* that this rule refers to the permission given to a king to sacrifice up to one-sixth of his own population when waging discretionary war. R. Goren infers from *Tosafot*'s position that the same principle would govern defensive war, seeing as an even stronger case can be made for the sacrifice of life in wars of this kind. The second source supporting the requirement for Jews to fight in wars of self-defense despite the risks involved is the *Minhat Hinukh*, which argues that in Halakhah the waging of war is predicated on the expectation that the lives of Jewish soldiers will be lost because we are told in the Talmud that Jews may not depend on miraculous divine intervention to save them from harm.[57]

---

57. "*Musar ha-Lehimah le-Or ha-Halakhah*," "*Musar ha-Lehimah le-Or ha-Halakhah*," *Meshiv Milhamah*, 1:12–13; *Minhat Hinukh* 425, 504; above, pp. 64–65, 122.

Yet an in-depth discussion of conscription and the problem it raises is reserved for the second introductory essay in *Meshiv Milhamah*, "The Wars of Israel in Our Time in Light of Halakhah," a piece we are already familiar with from an earlier discussion in this chapter. As we have already noted, in this essay R. Goren bases the imperative that Jews participate in wars of self-defense on the biblical commandment, "do not stand idly by the blood of your fellow." While one has the right to defend oneself from an assailant according to the dictum "if someone comes to slay you, slay him first," the requirement that one must also save others from their attackers is encapsulated in that biblical verse.[58] Thus, while the first essay in *Meshiv Milhamah* grounds the right of the king to send soldiers into battle in rabbinic sources, it is the second essay that informs us about the ultimate biblical basis of that norm.

What is important to note here is that the requirement to fight in defensive wars is part of everyday Halakhah and is not specific to wartime. After all, as R. Goren notes, the imperative not to stand idly by the blood of one's fellow is operative in all places and times. This point is made by R. Goren in a passage we have already cited, and it deserves a second look:

> For if we are attacked by an enemy, there is certainly no need for any authority (*samkhut*) to respond with war that has arisen in order to defend ourselves, nor is it about this matter that there is a need to prove that it [i.e., defensive war] is in effect also in the present time, for the Torah story has said, "if someone comes to slay you, slay him first" (*Berakhot* 58 and parallel sources). And the Torah did not differentiate between the time of the Temple and the present time, nor between saving many people and saving the individual, for whoever can save [another] must save [him] because of "do not stand idly by the blood of your fellow," as we have explained several times in these responsa.[59]

R. Goren tells us here that the obligation to fight in defense of the nation is not dependent on the call of any "authority," presumably a reference to halakhic or political authority. In this type of war, each and every individual Jew has the both right to defend himself and the obligation to defend others from violence, just as he would in any non-war situation. In fact, as we saw earlier, it was this point that prompted R. Goren to declare elsewhere in the same essay that when Maimonides grants permission to wage defensive war, he cannot be referring to defensive war in the simplest sense. Instead, Maimonides must be alluding to preemptive war because the permission to wage defensive war against an enemy that has already attacked is so plainly obvious in light of the

---

58. *"Milhamot Yisra'el,"* 111, 115; above, pp. 200–201.
59. *"Milhamot Yisra'el,"* 115; above, p. 202.

commandment to not stand idly by the blood of one's fellow that Maimonides would not need to tell us that a simple defensive war is permitted.[60]

Similar statements are found elsewhere in R. Goren's writings. In a passage in another essay addressing Maimonides' views on war, R. Goren says:

> [W]ould it occur to us that the prohibition of "do not stand idly by the blood of your fellow," is operative only during the time of the Temple? [When] a Jewish town is being attacked and is in danger in our time, [is it possible that] we would not have the obligation and imperative to save it because there is no king or High Priest? Behold that from the words of Maimonides in chapter 1 of *Hilkhot Rotseah u-Shemirat ha-Nefesh*, halakhah 10, it is clear that the prohibition, "do not stand idly by the blood of your fellow," is operative in all times, as he writes there: "everyone who is able to save [others] and does not save [them], transgresses [the commandment], 'do not stand idly by the blood of your fellow.'"[61]

Here, too, R. Goren bases the imperative of Jews to fight in wars of self-defense on the biblical commandment to save others from harm, and he emphasizes that this commandment is directed to the individual in all places and times, regardless of whether or not the situation is one of war. Thus the absence of a king or High Priest has no effect on the requirement to take up arms against the enemy. Nor does there appear to be a need for a Jewish government of any kind. The obligation to fight is based solely on the biblical commandment not to stand idly by the blood of one's fellow.

In yet another essay, "Army and Security in Light of Halakhah," R. Goren makes a similar statement by informing us that the requirement to participate in defensive wars is included in the commandment not to stand idly by the blood of one's fellow, a commandment that "foists the obligation of saving [others] by means of self-sacrifice, on every man in Israel."[62] Here, too, R. Goren emphasizes that in war, this commandment is directed at the individual *qua* individual in the same way that it would be in non-war situations.

One difficulty here is that if R. Goren treats the imperative that all Jews participate in wars of self-defense as a requirement independent of the initiative of any political authority, he appears to contradict a basic premise in his views on war, which is that a king must lead the nation into war, and if there is no king, a Jewish government that has the support of the people must do so. My guess is that R. Goren would respond to this problem by reiterating that a properly constituted Jewish government must lead the nation to war, but that the quintessential obligation for each Jew to fight in such a war is rooted in

60. Above, pp. 202–203.
61. *"Sheleimut ha-Arets,"* 94.
62. *"Tsava u-Bitahon,"* 372.

the separate norm that one must not stand idly by the blood of one's fellow, for again, this imperative is operative in all places and times. That is, fighting a defensive war does not require justification by a political authority, but it is the political authority that is charged with organizing the military campaign and executing it.[63]

A more serious difficulty in the texts cited thus far is that R. Goren has not really dealt with the fact that it is highly problematic to apply the everyday halakhic imperative to rescue others from harm to wartime situations, for while in everyday Halakhah, a Jew is not required to save others if he must put himself in danger, in war that requirement is taken for granted. R. Goren handles this problem in a number of passages by simply stating that in war the imperative to defend other Jews "overrides" (doheh) the right to refuse assisting others out of fear for one's own safety.[64] R. Goren therefore acknowledges that while the obligation to participate in defensive wars is rooted in everyday Halakhah, war does, in fact, affect the way in which that imperative is applied. R. Goren, therefore, appears to take a middle position on whether wartime Halakhah is separate from everyday Halakhah when it comes to the issue of conscription. On the one hand, there is no distinction between the two spheres because the commandment not to stand idly by the blood of one's fellow is operative for the individual in war in the same way it is in non-war situations. An individual Jew must always come to the rescue of other Jews who are in harm's way. On the other hand, in wartime, the right everyday Halakhah confers on the individual to set aside a commandment when his own life is endangered is nullified.

The most thorough treatment of this whole issue is contained in an essay that R. Goren composed in 1983, a year after the conclusion of the first Lebanon War, in which he assessed whether the war had been permissible according to Halakhah.[65] At the beginning of the essay, R. Goren notes that some rabbinic authorities had been opposed to the war because it was waged to protect communities in the Galilee region that were subject to rocket attacks from Palestinian militant groups in southern Lebanon, and, according to these authorities, the attacks were neither frequent enough nor sufficiently lethal to justify a wholesale war in which a large number of innocent Lebanese lives would be lost.[66]

---

63. According to R. Goren, would the same thinking apply to a discretionary war? It is not clear. On the one hand, discretionary wars are not initiated for defensive purposes. However, as we note below, in R. Goren's thinking, these wars become defensive once they are initiated. Therefore, my guess is that R. Goren would say that the initial decision to wage discretionary war would indeed require a political authority, but once the war was underway, no political authority would be needed for Jews to be obligated to fight, seeing as the commandment not to stand idly by the blood of one's fellow would come into effect.

64. "Musar ha-Lehimah," 13; "Tsava u-Bitahon," 371.

65. "Milhemet Shelom ha-Galil," 267–83.

66. "Milhemet Shelom ha-Galil," 267–68.

These observations prompt R. Goren to provide an in-depth analysis of the circumstances under which a defensive war may be waged, and it begins with an examination of the obligation of a Jew to save someone else from harm. Here, R. Goren goes over ground familiar to us from previous chapters in this study. He informs us that while there is unanimity among rabbinic authorities that no one is required to give up his life to save another person from danger, there is a division of opinion with regard to situations in which the would-be rescuer faces only possible danger (*safek sakanah*), while the individual in need of rescue is threatened by danger that is certain (*vaday sakanah*). Most authorities rule that in situations of this kind, the rescuer still has a right to abstain from rendering assistance, but a minority opinion holds the view that because the level of risk faced by the potential rescuer is lower than that faced by the person in need, the former is obligated to help the latter despite the risks involved.[67] However, R. Goren reiterates his position that there is no doubt that in war Jews must enter situations of possible danger to save others from certain danger because in wartime the right to refrain from rescuing others out of fear for one's own safety is set aside in light of the fact that the nation as a whole is at risk.

Thus, once again, we see R. Goren taking a middle position on the distinction between everyday Halakhah and wartime Halakhah. He sees no distinction between the two spheres when it comes to the basic requirement to fight in defensive wars. He emphasizes that this imperative is based on the commandment "do not stand idly by the blood of your fellow," which is applicable in all places and times, everyday situations as well as in wartime. As R. Goren puts it, this imperative is "foisted on each and every individual,"[68] and is "not dependent on any time period, and is not conditioned on any provisos."[69] However, R. Goren also informs us that a distinction between everyday Halakhah and wartime Halakhah does exist when it comes to the question of the danger to which the individual must expose himself when going to war, for "when one has the problem of safeguarding the life of the individual [i.e., the rescuer himself] alongside safeguarding the life of the collective, concerns about the life of the individual are set aside in favor of [concerns about] the survival of the collective."[70]

Incidentally, R. Goren also explains here why it is that Jews must risk their lives to participate in discretionary war. While the initial cause of the war may not be defensive in nature, the war automatically becomes a defensive

67. "*Milhemet Shelom ha-Galil*," 268–69.
68. "*Milhemet Shelom ha-Galil*," 278.
69. "*Milhemet Shelom ha-Galil*," 274.
70. "*Milhemet Shelom ha-Galil*," 274. Cf. Edrei, "Divine Spirit," 271, who says that R. Goren treated war as a normative category separate from everyday Halakhah. Our observations here indicate that the matter is more ambiguous than Edrei suggests.

one once it has been started because at this point, the nation of Israel is in the same danger it would encounter in the latter type of war. Thus here, too, Jewish soldiers must be prepared to risk their lives.[71]

Later on in the essay on the Lebanon War, the tensions we see in R. Goren's views on conscription are evident once again in a discussion that identifies a number of biblical verses as sources for the requirement that Jews fight in wars of self-defense. Once again, R. Goren looks to the biblical commandment not to stand idly by the blood of one's fellow as his main prooftext for this obligation. However, he now invokes other biblical sources for the same purpose that were not adduced in any of his writings that we have examined thus far. He cites Deuteronomy 22:2, which instructs Jews to return a lost object to its owner. The reason this verse is significant for R. Goren is that the Talmud uses it as an alternative prooftext for the notion that one must save a fellow Jew from harm. The premise here is that the object being returned to the owner in this instance is the body of the individual facing danger, which will be lost if he is not rescued![72] R. Goren also cites as proof that Jews must fight in defensive wars an imperative in Deuteronomy 20:3 in which soldiers who are about to enter combat are commanded not to be "fainted-hearted." This charge, which is uttered by a priest who is given the task of rallying the troops before a war begins, is regarded by R. Goren as inclusive of the commandment requiring Jewish soldiers to go into battle despite these risks, for the whole point of the priest's words is to ensure that the soldiers will fight despite the risks involved and the fear they engender. Finally, R. Goren cites Joshua 1:18 as support for the obligation to participate in defensive wars, a verse in which the Israelites agree to be obedient to Joshua as their new leader on pain of death. R. Goren takes this verse as an ongoing commandment requiring Jews in any place or time to obey their king, or any legitimate political body that takes his place, and the commandment includes the requirement to follow the king's orders to go to war.[73]

What is significant for our purposes about this list of prooftexts is that here, too, R. Goren gives mixed signals about whether the imperative to risk one's life to fight in defensive wars is rooted in everyday Halakhah or distinct from it. The first two prooftexts are verses that specify commandments applicable to everyday life. One has an obligation not to stand idly by the blood of one's fellow and to "return" a person's body to him regardless of whether or not the situation is one of war. However, the last two prooftexts are meaningful only in wartime. These verses refer to commandments not to be fearful in battle and to obey a king when he commands us to go to war. The

71. "*Milhemet Shelom ha-Galil,*" 274.
72. BT *Sanhedrin* 73a.
73. "*Milhemet Shelom ha-Galil,*" 276–77.

latter commandment is particularly significant because it seems to contradict R. Goren's tendency in other passages we have seen, to detach the commandment to fight in defensive wars from political authority altogether. Here, it is the authority of the king or his political equivalent that requires a soldier to go into battle to defend the nation, despite the risks involved.[74]

Although we have gleaned from R. Goren's essay on the first Lebanon war what we need for our present discussion, we should report his conclusion regarding the halakhic status of that war. The essay, after all, was devoted to determining whether it was halakhically permissible. R. Goren's assessment is that it most definitely was. Toward the end of the essay, he describes the dangers the communities in the Galilee experienced as a result of the Palestinian rocket attacks, and he concludes that the war to stop those attacks fell under the rubric of defensive war. As support for his position, he also cites the talmudic passage in 'Eruvin 45a that allows Jews to go to war even on the Sabbath to protect border towns from enemy attack. In effect, the towns in the Galilee targeted by the Palestinian rockets were in this category, seeing as most of them were in reasonably close proximity to the Lebanese border, and therefore Israel had every right to go to war to ensure that the attacks on those towns cease.[75]

What emerges from our exploration of R. Goren's views on conscription is that his thinking on the issue is quite complex. That complexity is best appreciated by comparing R. Goren's views on conscription with those of the other halakhic authorities examined in this study. R. Kook, R. Herzog, R. Waldenberg, and R. Yisraeli in his essay on Kibiyeh, all took the position that the requirement that Jews risk their lives by participating in defensive wars is an obligation unique to wartime Halakhah. However, R. Yisraeli, in a number of his later writings, departed from this approach by claiming that the requirement that soldiers go into battle is governed by the same norms that govern everyday life. An individual must risk his life to save others from danger in non-war situations, and a soldier must therefore do so the same in war.

74. We see the same tension between these two alternatives in R. Goren's essay "Tsava u-Bitahon." R. Goren at first argues that it is incumbent on every individual to participate in wars of self-defense because of the imperative not to stand idly by the blood of one's fellow (pp. 370–71, 372). Yet, R. Goren then tells us that the obligation to fight in wars of this kind is based on the authority of the king who can force his subjects to serve (p. 374). Here too, R. Goren cites Josh. 1:18, as support for this latter point. He also cites Maimonides' MT Melakhim 3:5 which states that a king is permitted to kill anybody who disobeys him, even over trivial matters, a source that again indicates that the king has the authority to force his subjects to go to war. Bolstering the same point is MT Melakhim 4:10, in which Maimonides lays down the principle that the king's job is centered on two obligations: to create a just society and to wage wars. The latter obligation again implies that the king has a right to send soldiers into battle despite the risks involved.

75. "Milhemet Shelom ha-Galil," 277–78.

R. Goren's views on conscription appear to stake out a position between the two approaches just outlined. He adopts the approach of the later R. Yisraeli according to which the requirement to participate in defensive wars follows from the prescription in everyday Halakhah about rescuing others from danger. At the same time, R. Goren acknowledges that the requirement of Jews to fight in defensive wars is different from that of everyday life because in these wars one must be willing to endanger oneself for others. On this point, R. Goren's thinking is more akin to that of R. Kook, R. Herzog, R. Waldenberg, and R. Yisraeli in the Kibiyeh essay.

R. GOREN'S RIGHT TURN

Thus far in our discussion, R. Goren has emerged as a strong Jewish nationalist, but it is also clear that he resists adopting nationalism in its most extreme form. While R. Goren believes that Jews may hold on to territory captured from their Arab enemies in defensive wars and opposes giving it back as part of a peace settlement, he does not take the position, as some religious Zionist rabbis have, that Jews may wage unprovoked war in order to conquer land God promised to Abraham in the original covenant. As we have seen, in R. Goren's thinking there is an unresolved dispute between Nahmanides and Maimonides on whether a commandment to conquer the land of Israel exists; therefore R. Goren tends to shy away from any suggestion that Jews may initiate war for this purpose.

R. Goren's position on conscription provides another example of the same tendencies. The nationalist dimension of R. Goren's thinking is evident in his belief that Jews must be prepared to give up their lives by going to war for the sake of defending the nation. At the same time, that imperative is primarily based on a norm in everyday Halakhah directed at the individual *qua* individual, which is not to stand idly by the blood of one's fellow. There is no suggestion on R. Goren's part that the life of the individual has meaning only in subordination to the nation, as we find in extreme expressions of nationalism.

R. Goren's desire to protect the individual against the interests of the state is, in fact, expressed quite explicitly in his work *Torat ha-Filosofiyah*, in which he compares Aristotle's view of the state to that of Judaism. R. Goren tells us that for Aristotle, "the purpose of the individual is subservient to the idea of the telos, which is the state," while in Judaism it is the reverse: "[T]he state is not the goal and the telos but rather the means to serve the individual and the citizen and to guarantee his life and rights."[76]

---

76. *Torat ha-Filosofiyah: Leket Hartsa'ot be-Filosofiyah Yehudit* (Jerusalem: Ha-ʿIdra Rabbah, 1998), 21; Mishlov, *"Be-ʿEin ha-Seʿarah,"* 70.

Yet, there is one essay in R. Goren's corpus of writings in which the nationalistic dimension of his thinking is far more pronounced than it is in the writings we have looked at, and it deserves our attention. The essay is entitled "The Commandments Between Man and the State," and in it, R. Goren posits the existence of three categories into which the 613 commandments can be divided.[77] R. Goren acknowledges that his tripartite scheme is unusual. The first two categories are well-known to anyone familiar with rabbinic and medieval Judaism; they consist of commandments governing the relationship between a Jew and God, and commandments governing the relationship between a Jew and his fellow human beings. The third category, however, is not identified in any rabbinic source, and it consists of commandments regulating the relationship between a Jew and the political state, which includes a Jew's relationship to the Jewish people and the land of Israel in which it resides.

R. Goren goes on to argue that this last category of commandments, while unacknowledged by previous commentators, is, in some respects, more important than the other two. A Jew does not have to perform any of the commandments in the first two categories if their fulfillment endangers his life. The only exceptions to this principle are the prohibitions against idolatry, murder, and the most grievous of sexual offenses, as well as the imperative to die as a martyr, which applies in highly specific circumstances.[78] By contrast, most laws concerning the relationship of the Jew to the state do, in fact, require the individual to sacrifice his life for the sake of their fulfillment. That is because these commandments are concerned with the survival of the Jewish people as a whole and the defense of its land:

> [W]ith respect to everything that pertains to this third category—the majority of the commandments between a person and the people, the land, and the state, override [concerns about] saving [one's own] life, and one must also fulfill them at the price of self-endangerment. This principle is valid for positive commandments and negative commandments [in this third category] because performing them or not performing them touches on the endurance of the nation and the liberation and defense of the land of Israel or a portion of it, which according to Halakhah, override [concerns about] saving the life of the individual, as will be explained later: for at any moment that we have before us a decision between saving the nation and saving the life of the individual, or between the defense of the land of the forefathers or a portion of it, and saving the lives of individuals—[concern about] saving the lives of individuals is overridden in favor of defending the nation or the land.[79]

77. "*Ha-Mitsvot bein Adam la-Medinah,*" *Torat ha-Shabbat ve-ha-Mo'ed*, 447–57.
78. BT *Sanhedrin* 74a; MT *Yesodey ha-Torah* 5:2.
79. "*Ha-Mitsvot bein Adam la-Medinah,*" 447–48.

As R. Goren's discussion proceeds, it becomes clear that the third category of commandments consists largely of those concerned with war:

> These positive commandments that override [concerns about] saving lives, are tied to mandatory wars and discretionary wars, as Maimonides enumerates them in his *Sefer ha-Mitsvot* and *Mishneh Torah*, positive commandments 187 and 190. And the same [goes] for the ongoing commandment to liberate the land of Israel and defend it, about which it is written "go and inherit" (Deuteronomy 1:21), as Nahmanides posits in his glosses on *Sefer ha-Mitsvot*; and with respect to negative commandments, [the same goes for] everything pertaining to our being commanded that our soldiers not be fearful and not be frightened by their enemies in the time of war, as it says "do not stand in dread of them" (Deuteronomy 7:21), [commandments] that Maimonides adduced in *Hilkhot Melakhim*, chapter 7 halakhah 15.
>
> Also the negative commandment 297 in the *Sefer ha-Mitsvot*, not to stand idly by the blood [of one's fellow], as it says, "do not stand idly by the blood of your fellow" (Leviticus 19:16), also concerns the obligations of a person toward the nation and the public, as Maimonides adduces in the first chapter of *Hilkhot Rotseah u-Shemirat ha-Nefesh*, halakhah 14.[80]

All of R. Goren's examples here have to do with war: the laws of war discussed by Maimonides in his *Sefer ha-Mitsvot* and *Mishneh Torah*; the imperative to go to war in order to liberate and defend the land of Israel, as specified by Nahmanides; the commandment not to be fearful in war that is found in Maimonides' *Mishneh Torah*; and the commandment not to stand idly by the blood of one's fellow which can be applied to war as well, as we have already seen.

R. Goren concludes the essay by explaining why the three oaths mentioned in the Talmud that would seem to preclude Jewish military activity after the destruction of the Temple, have no relevance for the state of Israel. First, R. Goren cites a Kabbalistic source claiming that the oaths were meant to be in effect only for a thousand years, and they are therefore no longer valid. Second, even if one insists that the oaths are still in effect, they have been nullified because one of the oaths was taken by the non-Jewish nations which promised not to oppress the Jewish people more than necessary, and that promise has clearly been violated, thereby canceling the other two oaths as well. Third, the oath taken by the Jews specified that they not take back the land of Israel by "going up in a wall"—that is, by means of violent rebellion— and Jews did not do so; the Zionist movement settled the land in a gradual peaceful fashion. Finally, it could be argued that the Jews' oath has not been

---

80. *"Ha-Mitsvot bein Adam la-Medinah,"* 449.

violated because it was the United Nations that created the state of Israel, and therefore the Jews did not take the land of Israel by force.[81]

A number of points are striking in this essay. First, R. Goren supports Nahmanides' position that Jews have a commandment to conquer the land of Israel. While in his other writings, R. Goren consistently balances Nahmanides' view against that of Maimonides who, in R. Goren's thinking, does not recognize the existence of such a commandment, here Nahmanides' view is allowed to stand unchallenged. We therefore see a more potent religious nationalism here than we do in R. Goren's other works.

The nationalist bent of R. Goren's essay is perhaps even more evident in the very suggestion of a special category of commandments concerned solely with the political state, a category that, R. Goren acknowledges, has never been posited in any previous Jewish source. The nationalist emphasis is further accentuated by R. Goren's argument that the third category of commandments is more important than the other two because Jews must sacrifice their lives in fulfilling them. What is striking is not that R. Goren has introduced here for the first time the notion of giving up one's life for the Jewish state; we have seen R. Goren often insist that Jews must make this sacrifice by participating in wars of self-defense. It is that in his other discussions on war, the most commonly cited reason that Jews must participate in defensive wars is the commandment not to stand idly by the blood of one's fellow, while the issue of risking one's life and the halakhic problems it raises, is a secondary concern. In the essay under examination, the issue of self-sacrifice for the state takes center stage. It is for this reason that halakhic norms governing the individual's relationship to the state are distinct from all other halakhic prescriptions.

How marked the contrast is between R. Goren's thinking in this essay with the statement just cited in *Torat ha-Filosofiyah*! According to the latter the state serves the individual. Here, however, it would seem that the individual serves the state.

CIVILIAN CASUALTIES

Let us now move on to the question of killing enemy noncombatants. R. Goren gives this issue more attention do than any of the other figures examined in our study. Most significant is an essay in the first volume of *Meshiv Milhamah*, entitled "Combat Morality in Light of Jewish Law,"[82] which is devoted mostly

81. "*Ha-Mitsvot bein Adam la-Medinah*," 452–57.
82. "*Musar ha-Lehimah le-Or ha-Halakhah*," *Meshiv Milhamah*, 1:3–40. This essay originally appeared in *Ha-Tsofeh*, 28 *Shevat*, p. 5; 12 *Adar*, p. 5. It is discussed in Edrei, "Divine Power," 282–87; idem, "Law, Interpretation, and Ideology: The Renewal

to this issue. R. Goren opens the essay with a discourse on the sacredness of all human life, including non-Jewish life. He begins by focusing on the well-known statement in the Mishnah in *Sanhedrin* that God created the human race by starting with a single individual in order to teach that "anyone who destroys a single life in Israel, Scripture regards it as if he has destroyed the entire world."[83] This statement, which appears in traditional printed editions of the Mishnah, seems to give value only to Jewish lives. However, R. Goren points to manuscripts of the Mishnah for evidence that the original text had a more universalistic message. According to this version, the text should read that "anyone who destroys a single life, Scripture regards him as if he has destroyed the entire world," with the critical phrase "in Israel" missing. The principle, therefore, applies to Jews and non-Jews alike.[84]

In his next set of observations about the passage in Mishnah *Sanhedrin*, R. Goren notes that Maimonides, in one place in the *Mishneh Torah*, cites the formulation of the source as it appears in the manuscripts, according to which all human life is valued.[85] However, in another passage in the *Mishneh Torah*, Maimonides cites the formulation as it appears in the printed texts, according to which it is only Jewish life that is valued.[86] R. Goren explains the discrepancy by arguing that the first citation was meant to refer to "the world that will be renewed in the future" (*'olam he-'atid le-hithadesh*),[87] in obvious reference to the messianic world, while the second citation alludes to the present world which was created for the sake of the Jewish people. That is, in the world in which we currently live, only Jewish life has ultimate value, but when the messianic period arrives, the lives of non-Jews will be similarly valued, presumably because they will all recognize the God of Israel as the true God.[88]

R. Goren's reading of Maimonides is strikingly at odds with the universalism that he espouses in the rest of his essay. However, it is possible that R. Goren is merely attempting to explain Maimonides' remarks, not endorse them. Still, we must leave open the possibility that R. Goren has injected a particularistic element into his thinking here that is in conflict with the universalism expressed in the rest of his essay.

R. Goren cites other rabbinic sources well-known for their universalism. For instance, he refers to the early rabbinic debate between R. Akiva and Ben

of Jewish Laws of War in the State of Israel," *Cordozo Law Review* 28, no. 1 (2006): 218–25; "*Mi-Kibiyeh 'ad Beirut: Tehiyatam shel Diney ha-Milhamah ha-Hilkahatiyim bi-Medinat Yisra'el*," *Yosef Da'at* (2010), 118–26.

83. M *Sanhedrin* 4:5.
84. "*Musar ha-Lehimah*," 3–5.
85. MT *Sanhedrin* 12:3.
86. MT *Rotseah* 1:16.
87. "*Musar ha-Lehimah*," 3–4.
88. "*Musar ha-Lehimah*," 3–4.

Azay in a passage in *Sifra* in which R. Akiva extols the verse, "Love your fellow as you love yourself" (Lev. 19:18), as a major principle of the Torah, while Ben Azay insists that the verse, "These are the generations of mankind" (Gen. 5:1), imparts an even greater principle.[89] R. Goren interprets the debate as follows: R. Akiva emphasizes the virtue of loving other Jews; hence the citation of a verse enjoining the love of one's "fellow." Ben Azay, however, insists that it is all human beings that one must love; hence the citation of a verse referring to the generations of "mankind." R. Goren believes that the two positions are not mutually exclusive. Jews must first learn to love other Jews, and on the basis of that love, learn to love all human beings.[90]

Here again, R. Goren's thinking appears to turn in a more particularistic direction. When discussing Ben Azay's viewpoint, R. Goren informs us that Jews should love non-Jews only when the latter have taken on "the yoke of heaven."[91] R. Goren does not clarify what this last phrase means, but in light of his earlier remarks about Maimonides, he may be alluding to the messianic period when non-Jews will recognize the God of Israel. Thus, once again, the imperative for Jews to love all human beings would be reserved only for messianic times when the non-Jewish world will finally adopt the fundamental truths of Judaism. The problem with this reading is similar to the one we encountered earlier with Maimonides' remarks; it goes against the universalistic thrust of R. Goren's essay by assuming that Jews are, not in fact, required to love all human beings in the world as presently constituted.

Yet, the key question is what R. Goren means when he refers to non-Jews taking on the "yoke of heaven." R. Goren may be referring to non-Jews in the present world who are monotheists, or, better yet, observe the Noachide commandments. If that is the case, R. Goren's remarks here would be more in line with the overall universalistic bent of his essay.

In the next portion of his essay, R. Goren applies the notion that all life has value even to Israel's enemies. He adduces rabbinic sources warning Jews not to exult when their enemies have lost their lives. He cites, for instance, yet another well-known rabbinic passage that reports a dialogue between God and his angels after the splitting of the Red Sea in which God forbids the angels to sing songs of praise to Him because the victory of the Israelites has come at the cost of the lives of the Egyptian soldiers.[92] R. Goren concludes that if God does not celebrate the death of Israel's enemies, the Jews should not do so either.[93]

89. *Sifra Kedoshim* 4:12; also cited in JT *Nedarim* 9:4.
90. *"Musar ha-Lehimah,"* 5.
91. *"Musar ha-Lehimah,"* 5–6.
92. BT *Megilah* 6b; *Sanhedrin* 39b.
93. *"Musar ha-Lehimah,"* 6–11.

R. Goren is now ready to speak about the killing of enemy noncombatants, and he tells us that while war inevitably results in the death of noncombatants, one must not kill them intentionally. This position clearly follows from what R. Goren has already said. If all human life is sacred, including that of non-Jews, one must minimize the carnage of war:

> [A]lthough the commandment to go to war is explicitly stated in the Torah, we are also commanded to have compassion on the enemy. We may not kill [the enemy] even in a time of war, except when there is a necessity to defend ourselves [and] for the purpose of conquest and victory. [We also] may not kill women and children who are not participating in war.[94]

The only exception to this rule, R. Goren tells us, was the war against the Canaanites when Joshua led the Israelites into the land. Here the deliberate killing of noncombatants was justified because of the great cruelty of Canaanite culture as a whole.[95]

R. Goren next conducts a lengthy discussion of why King David was not allowed by God to build the Temple and his son Solomon was given that task instead. R. Goren cites the biblical passage in which we are told that God did not choose David because he had blood on his hands, but it is not clear to what action or actions this accusation specifically refers.[96] After much deliberation, R. Goren concludes that David's sin was that he spilled blood needlessly because he waged war outside the land of Israel before completing the conquest of the land of Israel itself. Jewish law requires a king to wage mandatory war to conquer the entirety of the land of Israel promised by God to the Jewish people before waging discretionary war anywhere else.[97] Therefore, David sacrificed Jewish lives without warrant.[98]

R. Goren focuses on one other biblical source to support his point about the need to minimize the carnage of war, which is the story in Genesis 34 in which Simeon and Levi slaughter the males of the city of Shechem in retaliation for the rape of Dinah. This story is particularly appropriate for the question of whether one is allowed to kill noncombatants in war because one could

---

94. "*Musar ha-Lehimah*," 14.

95. "*Musar ha-Lehimah*," 14–17. R. Goren's focus on the cruelty of the Canaanites as an explanation for their annihilation seems to be based on the accusations in the biblical text that the Canaanites indulged in child-sacrifice. See Deut. 4:19; 29:25; 32:8–9. However, the primary reason given by the biblical text for the annihilation of the Canaanites is that the Israelites were in danger of being tempted by their idolatrous religion. See Deut. 7:2–4; 20:16–18. We may note a certain irony in R. Goren's position that the complete destruction of the Canaanites was justified by their cruelty.

96. I Chron. 1:28.

97. MT *Melakhim* 5:1.

98. "*Musar ha-Lehimah*," 16–25.

argue that it was only Shechem—here I am referring to the person, not the city—who was culpable in the rape of Dinah, not the other male inhabitants of the city, and yet they were killed as well. R. Goren claims that Maimonides and Nahmanides render different judgments on the actions of Jacob's sons. Maimonides rules that the killing of the males in the city was justified because they failed to take Shechem—the person—to court and punish him for his crime.[99] Nahmanides concludes that the killing was not justified because even though the city's inhabitants were remiss in not prosecuting Shechem, they did not deserve to die for that infraction.[100] R. Goren believes that both sides have a point. According to the strict letter of the law, Maimonides is correct; the Shechemites deserved the death penalty for their failure to bring their leader's son to justice. However, R. Goren also informs us that Nahmanides' position is correct according to the "teaching of the pietists" (*mishnat hasidim*); Simeon and Levi should have refrained from the killing of the males of the city out of compassion for them. R. Goren's final judgment supports the latter viewpoint. He concludes his analysis by ruling that in matters of life and death, the "teaching of the pietists" is preferable. Mercy should trump a strict application of the law. Therefore, in war the same principle should apply. The lives of noncombatants should be spared whenever possible.[101]

R. Goren's analysis of the Shechem episode is obviously intended to instruct Jews about how they should conduct themselves in their conflict with their enemies, and the general message is that mercy should guide their actions. However, there may be a more specific message here. One of the questions that has been raised in this study and continues to preoccupy Israeli rabbinic authorities, is whether Arab civilians should be held responsible if they do not take their own leaders to task for waging war against Israel. As we have seen, R. Yisraeli was particularly concerned with this question in his essay on Kibiyeh when he asked whether Arab civilians should be accountable if they do not stop terrorists living among them from attacking Jews. R. Goren may have this same question in mind in his analysis of the Shechem episode, even if he does not explicitly say so. After all, in his reading of this story, the main question is whether the male inhabitants of the city should be responsible for not bringing Shechem, the son of their leader, to justice, a question awfully similar to the more contemporary problem of how to treat Arab civilians who may be accused of a similar failure. If that is indeed what R. Goren had in mind here, his remarks on the Shechem episode are quite significant. He would be telling us that from a technical halakhic standpoint, Arab civilians who fail to take their leaders to task for waging war against Israel are culpable for the actions

99. MT *Melakhim* 9:14.
100. Nahmanides, *Peirushy ha-Torah*, Gen. 34:14.
101. *"Musar ha-Lehimah,"* 25–29.

of those leaders, but they should not be legitimate targets in war because Jews must treat their enemies with compassion.

In the last portion of R. Goren's essay on combat morality, he discusses the responsibility of Jewish public officials to keep their constituents safe. These officials must do everything in their power to protect the public from danger. This imperative includes making every effort to safeguard the public even from indirect dangers, such as unsafe roads. The mandate for this obligation comes from the same biblical sources that requires a Jew to save others from harm—most notably, not to stand idly by the blood of one's fellow. R. Goren also points out that the punishment for a public official, who fails to fulfill this obligation vis-à-vis the community, is more severe than it is for the ordinary citizen who is remiss with respect to this obligation in his private life. If an individual does not rise to the occasion to save another person from harm when he is able to, he is "punished by Heaven," not a human court. That is, judgment here is left to God. However, a public official who fails to keep the public safe when it is in his power to do so, is taken to court so that he may be punished immediately. R. Goren extends this principle to military officers. They are held responsible for the safety of their troops and are therefore culpable for any action that may needlessly subject them to danger.[102]

R. Goren does not explain what his remarks here have to do with the theme of his essay, but Aryeh Edrei astutely provides the missing connection. The central point of the essay, according to Edrei, is that in war the loss of life should be minimized, and what R. Goren is telling us in the last section of his essay is that this principle applies to loss of life not just on the enemy side, but on the Jewish side as well. Military officers and public officials must therefore take the safety of Jewish soldiers into account when considering military action.[103]

However, while Edrei is certainly correct, I think it can be argued that here again, R. Goren may be addressing a more specific issue. R. Goren spends a good deal of energy in the essay under examination explaining that when Jews wage war, they should do their best to prevent loss of life among enemy civilians. However, those who deal with war ethics know that when armies attempt to minimize enemy casualties, they often have to confront the dilemma that such action frequently involves subjecting their own soldiers to greater risk. The moral question in such situations is how much risk an army should take on in order to spare enemy civilians.[104] I suspect that it is this problem that motivates R. Goren to discuss the responsibilities that public

---

102. *"Musar ha-Lehimah,"* 29–38.
103. Edrei, "Divine Spirit," 283.
104. In international law, this issue is referred to as "force protection." See Yoram Dinstein, *The Conduct of Hostilities under the International Law of Armed Conflict,* 2nd ed. (New York: Cambridge University Press, 2010), 141–42, 286–87; Gary D. Solis, *The*

officials have toward their own constituents, and he is signaling to us that while Israeli public officials and military officers must do everything they can to minimize fatalities among enemy civilians, they must not forget that they also have responsibilities to protect their troops who are risking their lives by going into battle.

The Siege of Beirut

R. Goren's approach to killing noncombatants went from the realm of theory, in the essay just examined, to practice, in another essay mentioned earlier in this chapter, one that he composed in 1982 during the first Lebanon War when the siege of Beirut was in progress. The war was initiated by Israel in an attempt to uproot the Palestine Liberation Organization from Lebanese territory on account of the threat it posed to Israel. R. Goren's essay discusses whether the Israeli army was required by Halakhah to leave an opening in the siege to allow the inhabitants of the city to flee. It is here, therefore, that R. Goren's views on how to treat enemy civilians in war were tested in a real-life situation.[105]

The question of how the Israeli army should proceed here arose because of a law going back to an early rabbinic source in medieval Halakhah that a Jewish army is not allowed to completely surround a city which it has attacked. The city may be encircled on only three of its four sides in order to allow the inhabitants of the city to flee from the open side. This rule is first mentioned in an early rabbinic midrash and is codified into law by both Maimonides and Nahmanides.[106] There is much debate among halakhic authorities over whether the rule applies to mandatory war, discretionary war, or both.[107] There is also disagreement over the reason for this rule. Maimonides gives none, while Nahmanides suggests that it is for both humanitarian and strategic reasons. The humanitarian reason requires little explanation; leaving the fourth side open allows the city's inhabitants to escape harm. The strategic reason is that if a substantial number of the city's inhabitants flee, those remaining will be disheartened and will be more likely surrender, thereby facilitating victory for the Jewish side.

Law of Armed Conflict: International Humanitarian Law in War (New York: Cambridge University Press, 2010), 263, 284–85.

105. "*Ha-Matsor 'al Beirut le-Or ha-Halakhah*," cited on p. 196n6 above. This essay originally appeared in *Ha-Tsofeh*, 17 Av, 1982, p. 3.

106. *Sifrey ba-Midbar* 157 on Num. 31:7 in a passage that deals with war against the Midianites; MT *Melakhim* 6:7; Nahmanides' addenda to *Sefer ha-Mitsvot*, positive commandment #5.

107. Maimonides gives no indication of his position on this matter, while Nahmanides takes the position that it applies only in discretionary war. See sources in p. 228 above.

It is against this background that R. Goren takes up the question of whether the Israeli army is allowed to surround Beirut on all four sides. After much deliberation, he concludes that the Israeli army is prohibited from doing so; it has to leave an escape route for those wishing to flee. He argues that Maimonides and Nahmanides concur that the rule of leaving open the fourth side applies in defensive wars, and since the Lebanon War is a war of this variety, the rule applies here as well.[108] R. Goren acknowledges that the application of this halakhic requirement may result in some of the PLO fighters escaping the siege along with innocent civilians. Yet, that possibility has no effect on his ruling; the fourth side must still remain open. R. Goren also takes the position that, in general, the obligation to leave an escape route is for humanitarian reasons. He reiterates the belief, emphasized in the previous essay we examined, that Jews must be guided by the principle of mercy when waging war, and he again adduces Nahmanides' interpretation of the Shechem episode as proof for his position. R. Goren also invokes the concept of *kidush ha-shem*, "the sanctification of God's name," to support his viewpoint. Jews must behave with compassion in the war in Lebanon because the eyes of the world are upon the Jewish state and its actions, and it would therefore be a desecration of God's name if Jews were to be seen as killing the innocent alongside the guilty.[109]

The Siege of Tripoli

It would seem, however, that R. Goren takes a different approach toward a similar situation a short year after his composition of the essay on the siege of Beirut. In an essay entitled, "The Removal of the Naval Blockade from the Terrorists in Tripoli," R. Goren addresses whether Israel was justified in allowing Yasser Arafat, head of the Palestinian Liberation Organization at the time, and his fighters, to flee Lebanon in December of 1983. Throughout the fall of that year, Arafat's forces were under attack in northern Lebanon from the Syrian army and Palestinian rebels, and as the year drew to a close, Arafat and his fighters found themselves cornered in Tripoli. Their only escape route was the Mediterranean Sea, but that route was sealed off by the Israeli navy. Under intense international pressure, Israel eventually lifted the blockade and allowed

---

108. *"Ha-Matsor 'al Beirut,"* 245. Even though Nahmanides seems to limit the rule of leaving the fourth side open to discretionary wars, R. Goren believes that Nahmanides extends the rule to defensive wars as well, which is mandatory.

109. *"Ha-Matsor 'al Beirut,"* especially 264–65. R. Goren spends a good portion of his essay refuting the opposing view of R. Yisraeli who argued in an earlier article that, according to Halakhah, the Israeli army was allowed to seal off Beirut on all sides. See *"Ha-Matsor 'al Beirut,"* 249–65.

Arafat and his men safe passage out of Lebanon. R. Goren, along with many Israelis, wondered whether Israel had acted properly here. Were they required to let one of Israel's most notorious enemies flee along with his fighters, or should they have maintained the blockade in order to bring about their demise?[110]

R. Goren begins his deliberations on this question by reiterating his view that in defensive wars, a Jewish army laying siege to a city must leave the fourth side open to allow the enemy to escape. However, R. Goren concludes that in this instance, the Israeli army had no such obligation because the requirement to leave an escape route applies only when a Jewish army has encircled the enemy on the other three sides, and that was not the case here. Arafat and his men were surrounded on three sides by Syrian and Palestinian rebel forces, and the Israeli naval blockade was located only on the remaining fourth side. Therefore, according to Halakhah, the Israeli government had no obligation to lift the blockade and should not have done so.[111]

R. Goren asks whether Israel's actions may have been justified because of the diplomatic pressure it was under. In Halakhah, Jews are sometimes required to transgress a commandment when its fulfillment may inflame hatred against Jews, thereby placing Jews in physical danger. This principle is known as *mishum eivah*, "on account of enmity," because halakhic decisions may be altered to preempt enmity toward Jews that those decisions may create.[112] R. Goren entertains the possibility that this principle applied in this situation. Had Israel refused to let Arafat go, enmity against the Jewish state on the part of the non-Jewish world would have certainly increased, and its relationship to other nations in the international community might have been jeopardized as well. However, R. Goren concludes that in this instance, no such reasoning applies. Allowing Arafat and his fighters to leave Lebanon put Jewish lives at risk because he and his men were going to continue attacking Jews in Israel and elsewhere after being let go, and the principle of *mishum eivah* does not override the imperative of *pikuah nefesh* which dictates that Jews must save lives whenever possible. In essence, R. Goren was arguing that letting Arafat and his men go posed a greater threat to Israel than any ill-will that would have been aroused in the international community if Israel had refused to comply with its demands. Therefore, Israel should have maintained the blockade.[113]

110. "*Hasarat ha-Matsor ha-Yami me-'al ha-Mehablim be-Tripoli*," *Meshiv Milhamah*, 3:283–303. This essay originally appeared in *Ha-Tsofeh*, 24 *Tevet*, 1983; p. 5; 2 *Shevat*, 1983, p. 5.

111. "*Hasarat ha-Matsor*," 286–88.

112. A discussion of this principle can be found in *Entsiklopediyah Talmudit*, eds. R. Me'ir Bar Ilan and R. Shelomoh Yosef Zevin (Jerusalem: Mosad ha-Rav Kuk, 1947–), vol. 1, 229–30.

113. "*Hasarat ha-Matsor*," 299–302.

R. Goren also claims that the principle of *mishum eivah* does not apply in instances when one is required to punish transgressors for their crimes. It therefore does not matter what the non-Jewish world thinks when dealing with the likes of Arafat. Israel's enemies must not only be stopped from doing harm to its citizens; they must also be punished for what they have done, regardless of the enmity such action may inspire. R. Goren supports his position here by invoking the Shechem episode once again. Maimonides, who believes that Simeon and Levi were justified in killing the entire male population of the city, shows no concern about the two brothers inspiring hatred among the local population on account of their actions, even though they should have foreseen such a consequence. Thus, Maimonides clearly does not feel that the principle of *mishum eivah* has to be taken into account when meting out punishment to those deserving it. Of course, Nahmanides objects to the actions of Simeon and Levi, but R. Goren surmises that Nahmanides' judgment against Simeon and Levi is only with respect to their killing the men of the city who had no direct involvement in the rape of Dinah. In R. Goren's opinion, Nahmanides—even though he does not say so explicitly—would agree with Maimonides that Shechem, the individual who actually committed the crime, deserved to die for his actions, and that Simeon and Levi were therefore justified in killing him. Moreover, Nahmanides does not mention any concern for the enmity that the killing of Shechem would have likely aroused among the local population. Therefore, Nahmanides would agree with Maimonides that the principle of *mishum eivah* should not be considered when punishing those who are directly involved in violence against Jews.[114]

It would seem that R. Goren's second essay on the Lebanon War is inconsistent with the first, for a number of reasons. In the first essay, the emphasis is on mercy toward the enemy. R. Goren argues that not only must the Israeli army leave an open side in its siege of Beirut to allow civilians to flee, it must do so even if it means some of the PLO fighters will escape as well. Yet, in the second essay, on the siege of Tripoli, R. Goren insists that a similar concession should not have been made to Arafat and his men; the naval blockade should have been maintained. R. Goren may be justified in arguing that, in the latter instance, the rule about leaving the fourth side open does not apply in light of the fact that the Israeli army had not encircled Arafat and his men on the other three sides. However, it would seem that mercy has no place in his deliberations here in the way that it does in the first essay. R. Goren seems happy to exploit a technical loophole in Halakhah in order to argue that Israel made a mistake in letting Arafat and his men go free. A second inconsistency between the two essays is that in the first essay on Beirut, R. Goren bases his ruling about leaving the fourth side open, in part, on how Israel's actions

---

114. *"Hasarat ha-Matsor,"* 300–301.

would be perceived by the outside world. Israel must act so as to bring honor to God's name, and that means having mercy on those who wish to flee the fighting. However, in the second essay on Tripoli, R. Goren explicitly rules out taking world opinion into account. Arafat and his men should have been punished for their crimes, and what the rest of the world thought about Jews as a result of such action should not have been a concern. Finally, in the first essay, R. Goren makes use of the Shechem story in the Bible to underscore the need for mercy when dealing with Israel's enemies, while in the second essay the same story is used to demonstrate that Jews must use the principle of strict justice in such situations.

However, upon closer examination, the inconsistencies here are only apparent. The situations in Beirut and Tripoli were quite different and therefore elicited different responses from R. Goren. When R. Goren wrote his essay on Beirut, the question was whether to allow civilians to flee, even if it meant allowing some of the PLO fighters to escape as well. However, when R. Goren addressed the situation in Tripoli, the only people that needed to flee were PLO fighters, not civilians. The difference appears to have been crucial to his deliberations. In the essay on Beirut, R. Goren seemed to have been willing to take the element of mercy into account for the sake of the civilians involved, and he therefore ruled that the fourth side be left open so that they could escape. Yet in the essay on Tripoli, he saw no need to invoke such a consideration, seeing as there *were* no civilians. He was therefore happy to invoke a technicality in the law to argue that the fourth side should have remained sealed.

The same distinction appears to have influenced R. Goren's judgment about whether international pressure should be taken into account in the two situations. Because civilians were involved in the siege of Beirut, R. Goren insists that Israel leave an escape route, lest the nations of the world see Jews as lacking compassion toward the innocent. However, in Tripoli, the only people needing to flee were Arafat and his fighters whom R. Goren regarded as hardened killers bent on the destruction of the Jewish state and who therefore deserved no compassion whatsoever. Thus, in this instance, international pressure to open the fourth side did not have to be taken into account.

Our observations also help make sense of how R. Goren uses the Shechem story in the two essays. Because R. Goren is concerned in the Beirut essay with the treatment of enemy civilians who were not directly involved in the fighting, he focuses on the men of the city of Shechem who had no direct role in the crime against Dinah that was committed and were, at worst, negligent in not bringing the perpetrator to justice. The question is whether Simeon and Levi were justified in killing these people, and R. Goren states his preference for Nahmanides' viewpoint that they should have been spared. Thus, R. Goren rules, the civilians in Beirut who had no direct involvement in the war against Israel, should be allowed to flee. However, in the Tripoli essay,

R. Goren refers to the Shechem episode to answer a completely different question. Here his interest is not in how to treat enemy civilians, but how to treat enemy combatants who have been engaged in direct military action against Israel and whether that treatment should depend on world opinion. R. Goren therefore invokes the Shechem story in order to focus on Shechem son of Hamor, the individual who actually committed the crime against Dinah, and he surmises that not only would Maimonides support his killing, so would Nahmanides. Furthermore, according to R. Goren, neither of these halakhic authorities seems to have been concerned about the reaction that the killing of Shechem would elicit from the local population surrounding the city of Shechem. Hence, R. Goren concludes, Israel should not have let Arafat and his fighters go, given their crimes against the Jewish people, even in the face of international opinion to the contrary.[115]

What emerges here is that when it comes to actual wars, the theoretical approach that R. Goren established regarding noncombatants in his first essay of *Meshiv Milhamah* is largely maintained. In that essay, R. Goren took the position that while war inevitably results in casualties among enemy civilians, the latter group should not be directly targeted by Israeli forces. Mercy and compassion must dictate how one treats this sector of the enemy population. That is why R. Goren takes a lenient position on the siege of Beirut. Civilians are involved here, and he therefore applies the rule of leaving the fourth side open to allow them to escape harm, even if it means that some combatants will escape as well. However, situations which involve only enemy combatants are a completely different matter. Fighters sworn to the destruction of the Jewish state should elicit no mercy or compassion whatsoever and should be treated with the strictest of justice. It is for this reason that R. Goren criticizes the Israeli government for lifting the naval blockade against Arafat and his fighters in Tripoli. No civilians were present here, only people who had actually fought against Israel and deserved to be punished for their crimes.

These conclusions help explain other rulings by R. Goren. In another essay, he supports the death penalty for terrorists.[116] In yet another essay, R. Goren argues that children who throw stones at Israelis are to be treated in accordance with the law of the pursuer (*rodef*), which means that one may injure them in order to stop the stone-throwing, or even kill them, if there is no other alternative.[117] Once again, a firm line is to be drawn between those in the enemy population who take violent action against Jews and those who do

---

115. See Hollander, "*Deyokano*," 41–42, who offers a different explanation for the difference between the two essays with respect to the Shechem episode.

116. "*Hatalat 'Onesh Mavet 'al Mehablim le-Or ha-Halakhah*," *Meshiv Milhamah*, 3:305–27.

117. "*Netuney Petihah be-Esh Lefi ha-Halakhah*," *Mishnat ha-Medinah*, 71–72.

not. The latter are to be treated with mercy and compassion, while the former are to be punished.

We began our discussion in this chapter by looking at an essay in which R. Goren argued that the Jewish approach to war is defined by two opposing values: "spirit" and "power." It is perhaps in his deliberations on enemy noncombatants that we see most clearly R. Goren's attempt to balance the two principles. On the one hand, spirit, which is the source of our moral values, must govern the interactions with this sector of the enemy population in that their lives must be spared to the extent possible. However, wars are waged to be won, and therefore physical power dictates that it is permissible to kill enemy civilians when it is necessary to achieve victory. Moreover, at the moment that a civilian has chosen to become a combatant against the Jewish state, that individual must be judged by standards of strict justice, standards that are also rooted in the value of physical might.

R. Goren has bequeathed to us a large body of rich material on war in Halakhah. In the first part of this chapter, we looked at how R. Goren treats the various types of war and which of these he deems halakhically permissible in our era. Not surprisingly, he agrees with all the other thinkers in our study that the state of Israel is allowed to wage defensive war. Also not surprising is his insistence that the permission to conduct this type of war includes the right to initiate preemptive war. After all, the Six Day War was a war of this variety. R. Goren was Chief Rabbi of the Israel Defense Forces when it was waged, and the Israeli victory had a big impact on R. Goren's messianic theology. He therefore had very good reason to give preemptive war halakhic legitimacy.

When it comes to discretionary war, R. Goren also takes the same position that most modern halakhic authorities do, which is that this form of war can no longer be conducted because of the absence of a Sanhedrin. However, R. Goren's discussions of discretionary war contain a number of tantalizing hints that this form of war may be revived prior to the messianic period because the reconstitution of the Sanhedrin is not out of the question before that era arrives. No other thinker examined in this study takes such a position.

R. Goren also addresses Nahmanides' view that Jews are commanded to wage war to conquer the land of Israel and that this imperative is an eternal one that is in effect even in the period of the exile. R. Goren has reservations about Nahmanides' position because Maimonides does not recognize any such commandment. Therefore, in R. Goren's view, Israel may not initiate wars for the sole purpose of capturing territory promised to the Israelites in the Bible in preparation for the messianic era. However, that does not stop R. Goren from arguing that when land is taken by Israel in defensive wars, it should remain in Jewish hands, and on this point, he claims that Maimonides would concur with Nahmanides.

In all these reflections, R. Goren's concern for balancing the values of "spirit" and "power" is evident. For instance, the emphasis on spirit, which is the basis of our moral values, comes through in R. Goren's insistence that the only wars Jews may fight nowadays are defensive wars. However, the value of physical might emerges in R. Goren's willingness to entertain the possibility of reviving the more aggressive institution of discretionary war before the messianic period, as well as in his ruling that all land captured by Israel must remain under Jewish sovereignty.

Some of R. Goren's most interesting reflections on war are found in his treatment of conscription. Here, R. Goren takes a position somewhere between the view that the obligation to fight in defensive wars is continuous with obligations in everyday Halakhah, and the view that it is distinct from them. On the one hand, R. Goren speaks about continuity between the two realms in passages in which he argues that the requirement for soldiers to go to war is based on the commandment not to stand idly by the blood of one's fellow, a halakhic norm applicable in everyday life. On the other hand, R. Goren acknowledges a disjunction between everyday Halakhah and wartime Halakhah in his claim that the waging of war requires soldiers to risk their lives for others and that everyday Halakhah cannot account for this obligation. The same disjunction is also implied in R. Goren's attempt to ground the requirement to defend the nation in a commandment not concerned with everyday life but specifically with war: the biblical injunction that Jews not be "faint-hearted" when engaging in battle. R. Goren also claims that the requirement for Jews to participate in wars may be justified on the basis of yet another biblical source that obligates Jews to obey the king, who is charged with initiating wars. This argument again assumes that the imperative to participate in wars is rooted not in the obligations of the individual in everyday life, but in those concerned with the welfare of the nation as a collective.

When it comes to the killing of noncombatants, R. Goren gives us less guidance than he does on the other matters we have discussed, but here too, R. Goren has a good deal to say. His basic position is that one may kill enemy civilians in war, but one must not do so intentionally. This position is predicated on the sanctity of all human life. However, R. Goren also insists that one must not forget that Jewish life is sanctified as well, and he therefore tells us that Israeli public officials and army commanders have a responsibility to safeguard the lives of their own citizens, including soldiers. In his insistence on this point, R. Goren seems to show an awareness that many of the moral conundrums that arise in war regarding enemy civilian casualties often involve questions about making trade-offs between the lives of a nation's own soldiers and the lives of enemy noncombatants.

We would have benefited if R. Goren had said more about this thorny issue. His discussion remains in the realm of general principles rather than specifics.

Then again, R. Goren may have resisted saying more about this question out of recognition that this matter cannot easily be dealt with by laying down hard and fast rules. How much risk a commander is willing to subject his soldiers to when faced with the prospect of killing enemy civilians, is a question that, one could argue, is highly dependent on context. The ethic here is therefore a situational one that resists neat moral formulations.

We saw how R. Goren applied his theoretical positions on noncombatants to actual wartime situations when we looked at his treatment of the sieges of Beirut and Tripoli. What we discovered is that R. Goren's rulings in dealing with these events are fairly consistent with his theoretical formulations. Noncombatants have to be treated with mercy, even if it means that combatants will benefit as well. For this reason, R. Goren insists that the Israeli army not encircle Beirut on all four sides so as to allow those who wished to leave to escape harm. When it comes to situations involving only combatants, R. Goren is harsher. Thus, with respect to the siege of Tripoli, R. Goren feels that no mercy should have been shown to Arafat and his men who were cornered by Syrian and rebel Palestinian forces, and Israel should not have allowed them to escape harm. Here, there are no considerations of mercy as there were in the Beirut situation. R. Goren likewise takes tough positions on the death penalty for terrorists and Palestinian children throwing stones at Israeli soldiers. Anyone actively involved in attacking Jews is to be dealt with in accordance with the principle of strict justice.

Once again, we see here how the opposing values of "spirit" and "power" are balanced against each other. R. Goren goes to great lengths to ensure that the moral values rooted in the realm of spirit guide the actions of the Israeli army when dealing with enemy noncombatants, even those with negative sentiment toward Israel. However, he is just as quick to invoke the value of physical might when addressing the question of enemy combatants who actively seek to destroy the Jewish state.

We have seen that on the issue of conscription, R. Goren fashioned a position that vacillated between opposing values of another kind: the desire to make wartime Halakhah continuous with everyday Halakhah and the desire to keep them distinct. What about his views on the killing of enemy noncombatants? Do we see something similar? My sense is that we do. R. Goren's position on how Jewish soldiers should treat enemy civilians in war assumes that the morality expected of Jews in the realm of the everyday extends to war as well. Jewish soldiers are to be guided by such overarching principles as the sanctity of human life and the obligation to treat others with mercy and compassion, values that Jews must uphold whether or not they are at war. It is because of these values that a Jewish army is required to spare the lives of enemy civilians to the extent possible. However, R. Goren recognizes that when it comes to this sector of the enemy population, war is also different from the everyday in one crucial respect: Jews are, in fact, allowed to kill enemy civilians if they cannot achieve victory otherwise.

R. Goren's vacillation on whether wartime Halakhah is continuous with everyday Halakhah or distinct from it, is evident in his halakhic deliberations on one more topic: Sabbath law in the military. An analysis of how R. Goren approaches this subject falls outside the purview of our study, given our primary focus on moral issues. However, it is instructive to look briefly at how R. Goren deals with laws of the Sabbath in war because we will see how his attempt to balance continuity and disjunction in the relationship between everyday Halakhah and wartime Halakhah is pervasive in his thinking. We would also be remiss in ending this chapter without any mention of R. Goren's views on Sabbath law in the military because he regards this sector of Halakhah as the greatest challenge that rabbinic authorities face in dealing with Jewish life in the military in general.[118] Moreover, his halakhic rulings on this issue are strikingly original.

At first glance, it would seem that R. Goren's thinking on Sabbath law in the military finds only disjunction between everyday Halakhah and wartime Halakhah.[119] All rabbinic authorities agree that in everyday life the requirement to save lives "overrides" (doheh) the restrictions of Sabbath law. That is, if someone's life is in danger on the Sabbath, these restrictions are suspended so that the necessary life-saving procedures may be performed. Most rabbinic authorities also take this position when it comes to war. The waging of war involves the saving of lives as well because nations fight wars to protect their citizens from danger, and therefore, here too, all Sabbath restrictions are suspended so that soldiers can perform the essential duties needed to achieve victory. However, R. Goren takes the unusual position that the requirement to perform military duties on the Sabbath does not merely suspend Sabbath prohibitions, they "permit" (matir) them. That is, the prohibitions of Sabbath law are not merely put in abeyance here, they are completely set aside. R. Goren bases his position on the minority opinion of Shammai who, in a tannaitic source cited in the Talmud, says that Jews are allowed to continue the siege of a city on the Sabbath because the Torah tells us that Jews may extend such a siege "until it [i.e., city] has been vanquished" ('ad ridetah).[120] Shammai's invocation of this phrase is taken by R. Goren to mean that permission to violate Sabbath law when performing military duties is of a completely different order from the permission to do so in everyday life.

118. Preface to Meshiv Milhamah, 1:11.

119. "Lehimah be-Shabbat be-Askpeklaryah shel ha-Halakhah," Meshiv Milhamah, 1:41–109. This essay originally appeared in R. Yehudah Leib ha-Kohen Maimon, ed., Sinai: Sefer Yovel (Jerusalem: Mosad ha-Rav Kuk, 1949), 148–88. In the discussion that follows, I am greatly indebted to Hollander's treatment of R. Goren's views on Sabbath law in the military, "Deyokano," 216–54.

120. Deut. 20:20; BT Shabbat 19a; Hollander, "Deyokano," 217.

The debate here may seem focused on mere semantics, but the issue goes deeper. If Sabbath law is merely "overridden" to save lives, one would have to attempt to minimize Sabbath violations while performing the life-saving actions, and limit the transgressions to rabbinic decrees, not biblical ones, to the extent possible. Yet, if activities normally restricted on the Sabbath are "permitted," as R. Goren claims they are for military duties, these considerations would not have to be taken into account, and one would be allowed to perform a much greater range of activities normally forbidden on the Sabbath.[121]

R. Goren created controversy in the Orthodox rabbinic world by taking this position.[122] However, he felt that widening the scope of military activities that could be performed on the Sabbath was critical because of what was at stake: maintaining Jewish sovereignty over the land of Israel, and ensuring that the state of Israel be able to protect itself from its enemies. Therefore, it was not good enough to say that one could violate the Sabbath for military purposes as a concession; such violations had to be fully permitted to begin with.[123]

Thus far, R. Goren's treatment of Sabbath law in the military emphasizes the distinction between wartime Halakhah and everyday Halakhah. However, Avi'ad Hollander has shown in an insightful analysis that the opposite tendency is also evident in his thinking. In a number of instances, R. Goren restricts activities by army personnel on the Sabbath that should have been permitted according to the approach just outlined.[124] In these instances,

---

121. Hollander, "*Deyokano*," 218. Hollander also shows that, in some instances, R. Goren even applied this approach to military activities that were not connected to war, or preparedness for war. Thus, R. Goren ruled that soldiers could evacuate army bases in the Sinai on the Sabbath after the 1956 war because of diplomatic pressures on Ben Gurion to do so. Here the impetus for lenience on Sabbath law was the need for Israel to maintain good standing among its friends in the international community (pp. 220–21).

122. R. Goren's position was severely criticized by R. Moshe Tsevi Neryah, as discussed by Hollander, "*Deyokano*," chapter 2.

123. Hollander, "*Deyokano*," 218, 225–26. See also, Hollander's discussion, 347–49, which demonstrates that R. Goren's approach to Sabbath law in the military is an excellent example of his approach to religion and state in general. As we have already noted at the beginning of this chapter, R. Goren believed that Halakhah could accommodate the new reality of the Jewish state if halakhic authorities were willing to make use of the full range of opinions in halakhic literature, including minority ones. R. Goren made use of this technique in his approach toward Sabbath law in the military, for, as we have seen, he made it possible for soldiers to fulfill their military duties, despite the restrictions of the Sabbath by supporting the minority tannaitic view of Shammai.

124. Hollander, "*Deyokano*," 222–24. For instance, R. Goren prohibited soldiers from cleaning and oiling their guns on the Sabbath, even though this activity should have been allowed according to R. Goren's overall approach toward Sabbath law in the military. In another instance, R. Goren ruled that when a soldier needs to write down something for military purposes, he should do so with an "alteration" (*shinuy*)—that

R. Goren seems to concede that military activities in violation of the Sabbath are not always treated differently from activities in everyday life. Hollander claims that there are several reasons why R. Goren issued rulings of this kind. They include a desire to preserve the religious identity of Orthodox soldiers; a desire to safeguard the Jewish character of the Israeli army; a belief that soldiers should adhere to a stricter interpretation of Jewish law when it is easy to do so and it poses no threat to life; uncertainty on R. Goren's part in some instances about whether he was correct in formulating his controversial approach to Sabbath law in war; a belief that, as a government official, he was obligated to come up with halakhic decisions that were not too innovative so that they would be acceptable to other rabbinic authorities; and a simple wish to stand by what is customary in Halakhah.[125] But what is most important for our concerns here is that regardless of R. Goren's motivations, many of his rulings on Sabbath law in the military reflect a desire to establish a certain degree of continuity between everyday Halakhah and wartime Halakhah, even though his overall approach to this issue was designed to create a disjunction between the two.

What emerges here is that in more than one area R. Goren vacillated between treating wartime Halakhah as continuous with everyday Halakhah, and treating the two areas of Halakhah as distinct. Such vacillation could be construed as evidence of confusion on R. Goren's part, as an indication that he had not entirely figured out how the two spheres should relate to each other. However, I prefer a more generous reading of R. Goren's approach. I believe that more than any other figure in our study, R. Goren appreciated the complexity of the question of how military Halakhah should be dealt with. As I pointed out at the beginning of our study, all ethicists who deal with war, Jewish and non-Jewish, struggle with how the ethics of war relate to that of the everyday. On the one hand, war seems to require an ethics different from that of ordinary life. On the other hand, the ethics of war cannot be so completely detached from that of the everyday that it bears no relation to the ethical standards by which we normally live. It would appear that R. Goren struggled with the same problem within the realm of Halakhah, and the result was a constant effort on his part to balance the need to separate military Halakhah from everyday Halakhah so that wars could be fought and won, against the desire to ensure that military Halakhah stayed connected enough to everyday Halakhah to guarantee that the latter would have some influence on the way war was conducted.

---

is, he should write in a manner that is, in some way or other, different from his normal habit. Here, too, R. Goren's approach to Sabbath law in the military should have allowed soldiers to perform this activity without the added encumbrance.

125. Hollander, *"Deyokano,"* 222–57.

In conclusion, it would seem that R. Goren, more than any other figure in this study, appreciated the tensions endemic to the subject of war, and he dealt with them through a constant effort to create delicate balances and subtle compromises between extremes. That tendency was evident when we looked at the theological underpinnings of R. Goren's views on war at the beginning of the chapter. According to R. Goren, the Jewish approach to war must be grounded in an attempt to balance the value of spirit with that of physical power. In our ensuing discussion, the same approach underlay R. Goren's views on war in Halakhah. Wartime Halakhah and everyday Halakhah were neither completely congruent with each other, nor completely separate.

CHAPTER 9

⊂∿⊃

Summary and Conclusions

At the beginning of our study, we identified several major halakhic obstacles that the religious Zionist movement had to confront regarding wars
waged by the state of Israel, and we resolved to explore how five leading rabbis
in that camp attempted to overcome them. Our analysis was focused primarily
on issues that were connected to the moral sphere. We are now in a position to
provide an assessment of what we have discovered in our investigation, and it
is to that end that this final chapter is devoted.

A RECAP OF THE MAJOR QUESTIONS

But before we embark on that task, let us first be reminded of the halakhic
difficulties that our five rabbis had to address. The first and most general
question was determining which types of war the state of Israel could wage.
Medieval Halakhah allowed for the waging of mandatory wars and discretionary wars, and each of these categories, in turn, contained several sub-
categories of wars. Our rabbis therefore had to ask which of these types of
war, if any, could be conducted by a modern Jewish state. This question was
in turn dependent on the issue of whether a modern Jewish state had legitimate authority for waging war. What was one to do about the provision in
Halakhah that a mandatory war could be initiated only by a Jewish king?
What about the additional provisions in discretionary war of securing the
approval of the Sanhedrin and possibly the *urim ve-tumim*? In our era, none
of these institutions exist.

The second challenge was concerned with assembling an army. Was conscription allowed, and if so, why? Halakhah permitted a king to draft soldiers for both mandatory and discretionary wars but said little about an obvious halakhic difficulty that conscription entailed: an individual was not normally required to fulfill a divine commandment if it endangered his life; yet that was precisely what conscription involved. How, then, could one justify conscription for wars fought by the state of Israel?

Finally, there was the challenge of killing in war. Wars cannot easily be won without killing innocent civilians; yet, it was not clear why Halakhah would allow this type of killing, even in the context of war. In halakhic sources, one can certainly kill an individual who is directly threatening one's life or the life of another person, and therefore killing enemy combatants in the heat of battle requires no special dispensation. However, Halakhah does not normally allow the killing of innocent individuals, even for defensive purposes. Thus, if one's life is threatened by another person, one may not kill the assailant if innocent bystanders will be killed as well—even if it means dying at the hands of the assailant. Applied to war, this principle would make the waging of it virtually impossible. One could not attack an enemy army that had initiated hostilities against a Jewish state if there were any chance that innocent civilians would be harmed. How, then, in Halakhah, could one conduct a war of any type?

PERMITTED WARS AND LEGITIMATE AUTHORITY

Let us now look at how each of these challenges was dealt with by our rabbis. On the question of which types of wars the state of Israel was permitted to wage, most of our rabbis strongly believed that Israel was allowed to conduct mandatory wars of self-defense. These wars fell under Maimonides' rubric of 'ezrat yisra'el mi-yad tsar—"saving Israel from the clutches of the enemy." An exception here, of course, was R. Kook, who died before the founding of the state and therefore could make no pronouncement on this matter. Another exception was R. Yisraeli, who, in his essay on Kibiyeh, supported Maimonides' conception of 'ezrat yisra'el mi-yad tsar, but gave it a meaning entirely different from that upheld by the other figures in our study. R. Yisraeli insisted that there really was no such thing as a Jewish war of self-defense because of the conscription issue; one could not demand that Jewish soldiers risk their lives for the sake of protecting others. Therefore R. Yisraeli proposed that a Jewish state could respond to wars initiated by an enemy and could draft soldiers for that purpose only because of the imperative to wreak revenge on the hostile nation. It was to this type of war that Maimonides was referring when he spoke of 'ezrat yisra'el mi-yad tsar. The precedent for wars of this kind was the war of the Israelites against the Midianites, which was initiated by a divine command, and revenge was its prime motive. In one of his later essays, R. Yisraeli continued the line of thinking in the Kibiyeh essay, but with a different twist. In a piece written in response to the Entebbe raid, R. Yisraeli again argued that there were no wars of self-defense in Halakhah, and here too, he focused on the Midianite war as inspiration for his view. But in this instance, he focused not on revenge as the motivation for waging war initiated by an enemy, but on *kidush ha-shem*, "the sanctification of God's name." Yet, in all his other later essays, R. Yisraeli's thinking underwent a dramatic shift away from that of the earlier one on Kibiyeh. In these works, he now fell in line with the other figures in our study and understood *'ezrat yisra'el mi-yad tsar* as referring to wars of self-defense, plain and simple.

R. Yisraeli's notion of wars of revenge brings us to the question of what our rabbis had to say about wars waged for aggressive purposes—that is, wars that had no defensive value and were conducted with other goals in mind. R. Yisraeli's concept of wars of revenge was, for the most part, his own original construction, but there were other forms of aggressive war that were sanctioned in medieval Halakhah, such as discretionary war and wars waged to conquer the land of Israel, and therefore the rabbis in our study had to grapple with these types of war in addition to those waged in self-defense. We found less consensus among our rabbis regarding wars of this variety than we did with defensive wars. Moreover, the same rabbi sometimes offered divergent views regarding wars of this kind in different writings. The lack of consistency here is perhaps understandable in light of the moral challenges these forms of war raised. The rabbis in our study at times seemed torn between the feeling that aggressive warfare was perfectly acceptable—given that biblical and rabbinic sources sanctioned this type of activity—and the sense that Jews should model behavior in which aggression should be kept in check.

These observations can be illustrated by looking at how our rabbis dealt with discretionary war. This type of war was problematic for our rabbis not only because of its aggressive character, but also because it required the approval of a Sanhedrin before it could be waged. Three of our five rabbis discussed discretionary war, and the three who dealt with it had widely different positions on what its precise purpose was and whether it could still be conducted.

R. Kook lived before the founding of the state of Israel, but his ruminations on discretionary war highlighted the problems that this form of war raised for modern halakhic authorities. R. Kook seemed uneasy about discretionary war, an uneasiness that was probably connected to his reservations about war in general. It was perhaps for this reason that R. Kook gave us an inconsistent picture of what discretionary war was intended to accomplish. He seemed to acknowledge its aggressive character in one passage, when he cited the view of the Talmud and Maimonides that this form of war could be waged for the expansion of territory, but in another passage he also appeared to make an attempt to give this type of war a purpose that was more acceptable from a moral standpoint by claiming that it served quasi-defensive purposes; it could be waged because of *hora'at sha'ah*, an emergency measure, when the Jewish people faced a physical or spiritual crisis of some sort. But what R. Kook meant here was not explained, nor was how the aggressive and defensive elements of discretionary war were compatible with each other.

R. Kook's unease with discretionary war also seemed to come through in his insistence that only a Jewish king could wage this type of war and that no political authority standing in place of the king could do so. This position was inconsistent with R. Kook's view that any Jewish political authority supported by the people could substitute for the king. Yet, the inconsistency here was, again, understandable in light of R. Kook's discomfort with discretionary war. The limitation he placed on legitimate authority in waging this form of war seemed designed to ensure that its practice would not be revived any time soon.

R. Yisraeli provided us with the most innovative understanding of discretionary war in our study. He was the only thinker we encountered who believed that discretionary war could still be conducted. However, in his view, this form of war and the permission to wage it were not unique to the Jewish people. Discretionary war referred to all wars that nations were permitted to fight according to international law and custom, including those for non-defensive purposes. Such wars were allowed in Halakhah because of the principle of *dina de-malkhuta dina*, "the law of the kingdom is the law," which dictated that what was customary among the nations in the international sphere had the approval of Halakhah as well. Therefore, as long as the nations of the world recognized war, whether it be defensive or aggressive, as a legitimate feature of international relations, Halakhah would follow suit. R. Yisraeli circumvented the problem that Jews needed a Sanhedrin to wage this type of war by arguing that the approval of this body was not required when Jews had no king and the popular will was in favor of war. But it was not clear what implications this had for the state of Israel.

Yet, despite R. Yisraeli's willingness to accept discretionary war as a legitimate feature of international relations, there was also some discomfort on his part regarding this form of war. R. Yisraeli openly acknowledged the moral challenges discretionary war presented and seemed genuinely distressed by them. How is it, he asked, that Halakhah accepted wars that had no defensive value and might lead to enormous loss of life? R. Yisraeli expended a great deal of effort attempting to solve this problem, and he finally arrived at the rather odd theory that the carnage of discretionary war was permitted because non-Jews were, in a metaphysical sense, in possession of their souls in the way that Jews were not, and they could therefore waive their right to life if they so chose. That is what they effectively did when waging discretionary war against each other. It was not clear, however, what implications this position had for a nation being dragged into a war against its will, as often happens.

The only figure in our study who seemed to have had an unequivocally positive view of discretionary war was R. Goren. He did not believe that this form of war could be waged in our day and age, but he seemed quite open to the possibility that it could be revived in the near future, and he appeared to look forward to that prospect. The only obstacle was the absence of a Sanhedrin, but R. Goren believed that Halakhah allowed for the reconstitution of this body before the messianic era, and it seemed, in his thinking, that the existence of a modern Jewish state presented an opportunity for such an event to take place.

Another aggressive form of war that a number of our rabbis dealt with was war waged for the purpose of conquering the land of Israel. Nahmanides was the source of the view that initiating this type of war was a biblical commandment and that this imperative was eternally in force, and because of Nahmanides' immense stature in Halakhah, the rabbis in our study had to address his position. Yet as with discretionary war, we saw a fair amount of inconsistency among our rabbis regarding this type of war, and here too, one suspects that the inconsistency was, at least in part, due to the serious moral questions that this form of war raised.

R. Herzog was the first to deal with Nahmanides' viewpoint. He identified several reasons why the 1948 war was a mandatory war, and one of them was that this war was meant to fulfill the imperative to conquer the land of Israel as specified by Nahmanides. In one responsum, R. Herzog also added that the 1948 war had messianic meaning. A Jewish victory would move the messianic process forward by convincing the world that the Jewish God was the one true God. Thus, in R. Herzog's thinking, the commandment to conquer the land, according to Nahmanides' reasoning, was alive and well and was applicable in the state of Israel's first war.

However, R. Herzog backed away somewhat from his commitment to Nahmanides' position after R. Meshulam Roth's criticisms of his views. R. Roth expressed strong doubts that the 1948 war was a mandatory war of any kind, and he was not at all convinced that it fulfilled the commandment to conquer the land as Nahmanides conceived of it. In response to R. Roth's critique, R. Herzog claimed that the primary reason for identifying the 1948 war as mandatory was that it was a war of self-defense and that his reference to Nahmanides' view was secondary to that main point. However, R. Herzog was clearly backtracking here. His original communication to R. Roth did not suggest any such distinction.

Greater ambivalence toward Nahmanides' viewpoint was evident in R. Yisraeli's writings. He addressed the position of Nahmanides in his later essays. In these writings, R. Yisraeli claimed that the commandment to conquer land was applicable during the biblical period but was no longer in force, and the state of Israel, therefore, could not wage wars for this purpose. However, R. Yisraeli also argued that the commandment to conquer the land was still applicable in one respect. If territory in the land of Israel had been captured in wars waged for defensive purposes, it could not be relinquished even for the purpose of making peace because the imperative of conquering the land implied that Jews had an obligation to retain sovereignty over whatever territory they had in their possession.

R. Goren's views on Nahmanides' notion of waging war to conquer the land were similar to those of R. Yisraeli. R. Goren also believed that wars could not be initiated by the state of Israel for the sole purpose of conquering territory, though in R. Goren's thinking, that was not because the commandment to do so was no longer in effect, as R. Yisraeli believed, but because Nahmanides' opinion was opposed by Maimonides who held that Jews never had a commandment to conquer the land in the first place. Still, on the question of relinquishing land that had been captured in wars waged for other purposes, R. Goren echoed R. Yisraeli's sentiments. Such land could not be given up, even for the sake of making peace. R. Goren believed that Nahmanides would certainly have taken such a position given his belief that there was a commandment to conquer the land in the first place, but in R. Goren's thinking, even Maimonides would have gone along with this ruling, as well.

We also found that one of R. Goren's essays presented a viewpoint on Nahmanides that was inconsistent with his positions elsewhere. In this essay, R. Goren came out as a strong religious nationalist and abandoned his ambivalence toward Nahmanides' notion that the commandment to conquer the land was eternal. Here, R. Goren voiced strong support for that view.

What about legitimate authority in waging war? How did our rabbis circumvent the difficulties that Halakhah presented on this issue? Of all the problems our rabbis faced in dealing with war, this one elicited the least amount of commentary. All of the rabbis after R. Kook adopted his position that any Jewish government with the backing of the people whom they govern possessed the same political authority as a king. The government of Israel could therefore wage wars falling under the category of "saving Israel from the clutches of the enemy" because no political authority other than the king was needed to initiate a mandatory war.

Discretionary war presented unique problems when it came to political authority. Here, the approval of a Sanhedrin was required. Most of the rabbis in our study did not believe that there was a substitute for this body in our time, and therefore, they did not see discretionary war as an immediate possibility. The exception was R. Yisraeli in his essay on Kibiyeh, and we have already summarized how he was able to support the waging of discretionary war despite the lack of a Sanhedrin. We have also noted that R. Goren, while agreeing that discretionary war could not be waged at present, held out hope that the Sanhedrin would soon be revived, and with it, the capacity to wage discretionary war.

CONSCRIPTION

Of all the issues we analyzed, it was the question of conscription that inspired the most interesting and provocative reflections on the part of our five rabbis. This issue was taken up by R. Kook in his debate with R. Pines about when a Jew was required to endanger his life for the sake of others, and even though the debate took place well before the founding of the Jewish state and R. Kook did not discuss the conscription issue at any length, his statements on the matter had an enormous influence on how it would be handled by halakhic authorities after the state was founded. R. Kook argued that a king had a right to draft soldiers and send them into battle, despite the risks involved, because the laws of war were different in kind from those of everyday Halakhah. The laws of war belonged to a special sector of Halakhah that was the preroga- tive of the king and allowed him to do whatever was necessary to protect and enhance the welfare of the nation, even in violation of norms of every- day Halakhah. Forcing soldiers to endanger themselves to protect the nation was but one example of this prerogative. R. Pines disagreed and claimed that the obligation for Jews to participate in wars could be justified perfectly well within the bounds of everyday Halakhah.

R. Herzog's views on conscription were largely an application of R. Kook's position to the 1948 war. R. Herzog saw this war as a mandatory war of the defensive variety, and all Jews were required to take up arms to fight at the risk of their lives because wartime Halakhah was fundamentally different from that of the everyday. However, R. Herzog seemed to drop R. Kook's view that the laws of war were distinctive because they belonged to a larger group of laws concerned with communal welfare. For R. Herzog, only the laws of war appeared to be distinctive from everyday Halakhah.

Most intriguing was R. Herzog's attempt to present arguments for con- scription that would also satisfy those who did not regard the 1948 war as a halakhically sanctioned military campaign. Here too, he relied on R. Kook by adopting the latter's ruling that an individual Jew must be willing to sacrifice his life, even in non-war situations, if he is uniquely positioned to save the Jewish people from destruction. R. Herzog's belief was that the 1948 war pre- sented Jews in the newly created state of Israel with a situation of precisely this kind because a defeat would have catastrophic consequences, not just for that community but for the Jewish community worldwide.

R. Waldenberg followed R. Kook's thinking on conscription as well, but he also saw a resonance between R. Kook's view and that of the Netsiv. The Netsiv, like R. Kook, supported the notion that the king could draft soldiers because wartime Halakhah was different from everyday Halakhah, but according to the Netsiv, this prerogative was ultimately grounded in natural law. It took some time for R. Waldenberg to appreciate the differences between the Netsiv's position and that of R. Kook. In *Hilkhot Medinah*, R. Waldenberg believed that

R. Kook's view was identical to that of the Netsiv and that R. Kook also believed that the laws of war were rooted in natural law, but later on, R. Waldenberg came around to the position—the correct one, to my mind—that R. Kook did not invoke natural law to support his position. Instead, R. Kook believed that the difference between wartime Halakhah and everyday Halakhah originated in Halakhah itself. Still, R. Waldenberg was consistent in upholding the basic premise that conscription was justified because the laws of war were different from those of everyday life.

We saw that R. Waldenberg seemed to incorporate into his thinking a viewpoint on conscription that was at odds with this approach when he cited the position of the *Shem Aryeh*. According to the *Shem Aryeh*, conscription was permitted in Halakhah because the dangers of war were akin to the risks people regularly face in their day-to-day lives, and such risks were not seen by Halakhah as obstacles to carrying on with one's ordinary routine. Therefore, one did not have to avoid the dangers of war any more than any of the other dangers one encountered in daily life. Here, conscription was justified with the argument that there was no real distinction between everyday Halakhah and wartime Halakhah, at least on this one issue. However, R. Waldenberg did not appear to be conscious of the implications of the *Shem Aryeh*'s views. R. Waldenberg cited the latter's views because they supported the notion that war was a natural phenomenon and they therefore were in line with the position of the Netsiv. He seemed unaware that those same views also undermined the distinction between wartime Halakhah and everyday Halakhah on the conscription issue.

R. Yisraeli, in his essay on Kibiyeh, also followed R. Kook's thinking by arguing that conscription was permitted for wars initiated by an enemy nation because, again, there was a sharp distinction between wartime Halakhah and everyday Halakhah. However, R. Yisraeli imparted his own innovative spin to this approach by claiming that Jews could be forced into battle in such wars because Jews had a special commandment to wreak revenge on any nation that initiated hostilities against them. In his later essay on the Entebbe raid, R. Yisraeli made a similar argument but claimed that the rationale for conscription was based on the principle of *kidush ha-shem*, sanctifying God's name.[1]

But in most of the essays written after Kibiyeh, R. Yisraeli adopted an entirely different approach to the issue of conscription, one that was at odds with that of R. Kook. He now argued that conscription was allowed in wars initiated by an enemy because, on this issue, there was, in fact, no distinction between wartime Halakhah and everyday Halakhah. R. Yisraeli ruled that in ordinary life, Jews were required to enter situations of potential danger in

---

1. R. Yisraeli seems not to have dealt with this issue in discretionary war, at least with respect to Jews.

order to rescue fellow Jews who were in certain danger, and Jews had an obligation to fight in wars of self-defense because wars of this kind were a prime instance in which this very principle was applicable.

A similar approach to conscription had been entertained by R. Pines in his debate with R. Kook about the circumstances under which a Jew was required to endanger his life for the sake of others. However, it is unlikely that R. Yisraeli was influenced by R. Pines's views. We also raised the possibility that R. Yisraeli's views here were influenced by R. David Frankel, who, in his commentary on the Jerusalem Talmud, *Shiyarey Korban*, also appears to see no distinction between wartime Halakhah and everyday Halakhah when it comes to defending others from harm. However, in the absence of any explicit citation by R. Yisraeli of R. Frankel's views, we could not make a firm determination on this point.

Two other rabbis in our study entertained ideas about conscription that seemed to hint at a position similar to that of R. Yisraeli in his post-Kibiyeh writings. One was R. Herzog who invoked a passage in the Jerusalem Talmud to argue that in the 1948 war Jews had an obligation to fight, even according to the standards of everyday Halakhah. However, R. Herzog did not go as far as R. Yisraeli did. R. Herzog recognized that the opinion of the Jerusalem Talmud could not serve as the basis of his own position because it was not supported by the more authoritative Babylonian Talmud. He therefore had to argue that conscription for the 1948 war could be justified within the parameters of everyday Halakhah, only if one took into account R. Kook's view that a Jew was required to sacrifice his life, even in non-war situations, when the entire Jewish people faced demise and he was in a unique position to avert the disaster. R. Herzog believed that the 1948 war was a scenario of precisely this kind, and thus all Jews were obligated to fight in this instance. The implication here was that the same obligation would not necessarily be applicable in other wars. R. Herzog's argument for justifying conscription within the parameters of everyday Halakhah was therefore of limited significance. As we noted earlier, R. Waldenberg, in citing the *Shem Aryeh*'s views on conscription, also seemed to incorporate into his thinking the notion that conscription was permitted because of considerations contained in everyday Halakhah. However, we also pointed out that R. Waldenberg appeared not to be aware of the implications of the *Shem Aryeh*'s views.

What emerges here, therefore, is that R. Yisraeli's position on conscription in his later writings was unique in our study. His position here was the only instance in which one of our figures was willing to explicitly and consciously erase the distinction between wartime Halakhah and everyday Halakhah when it came to the question of conscription, or any other question for that matter.

R. Goren presented us with the most complex position on conscription by staking out a position that was somewhere between the view that wartime Halakhah was continuous with everyday Halakhah, and the view that it was distinct from it. R. Goren's most common argument for requiring Jews to fight in wars of self-defense was that this obligation emanated from the biblical norm not to stand idly by the blood of one's fellow Jews, a norm that was applicable in everyday life. In a number of passages, R. Goren underscored the everyday nature of this commandment by arguing that when the Jewish nation had to fight a war of self-defense, the obligation of all Jews to participate was so obvious, that no authority, political or halakhic, was required to compel Jews to take up arms. The commandment was in force in all situations in which the lives of fellow Jews were endangered, and therefore no added imperative was needed to apply it in wartime. R. Goren used similar reasoning to argue that the permission granted by Maimonides to conduct wars of self-defense included the right to initiate preemptive wars. According to R. Goren, permission to wage defensive wars was, again, so obvious in light of the commandment not to stand idly by the blood of one's fellow that Maimonides would not have needed to make a special ruling allowing this form of war. That he did so must surely have been due to his desire to grant permission for the waging of preemptive wars as well.

However, R. Goren also acknowledged that the wartime application of the commandment not to stand idly by the blood of one's fellow, differed from that of everyday life in one important respect. While in non-war situations, a Jew was permitted to refrain from rescuing his fellow Jews from danger if the rescuer himself was also endangered, no such dispensation could be granted in war.

We also encountered other passages in which R. Goren treated the obligation of Jews to fight in wars of self-defense as an imperative entirely separate from commandments governing the everyday. In one passage, this requirement was based on the commandment not to be fearful when going to war, a commandment that clearly was applicable only in the context of war. The same requirement was also justified by R. Goren on the basis of the commandment to obey a king's orders, an imperative not unique to war but certainly incumbent on the individual as a member of a political community. This last argument was particularly striking in light of R. Goren's arguments elsewhere that the obligations of Jews to fight on behalf of their nation was based on the commandment not to stand idly by the blood of one's fellow Jew, a commandment that needed no political authority for justification in wartime.

We also saw that in one of his essays, R. Goren justified the obligation to participate in war by postulating that it belonged to a larger category of commandments that was focused on the relationship between a Jew and the state and that was distinct from the rest of the commandments because these political commandments required a Jew to sacrifice his life in their fulfillment.

Here too, there was a sharp distinction between wartime Halakhah and every-day Halakhah.[2]

CIVILIAN CASUALTIES

Only two figures in our study gave significant attention to the last of our challenges: the question of killing enemy civilians. R. Yisraeli and R. Goren both took the position that killing individuals in the enemy population who were uninvolved in the war effort was permitted, but both also felt such individuals should not be deliberately targeted. Casualties among enemy noncombatants were a necessary, though unfortunate, byproduct of war.

Each arrived at this position in a different way. R. Yisraeli first expressed his views on noncombatant casualties in the essay on Kibiyeh when discussing discretionary wars, which for him were all wars waged by the nations in accordance with international law and custom, but he did not say much about the issue of civilian deaths here. He informed us only that in such wars, innocent people could be killed alongside the guilty because that was the nature of war. His reticence here probably stemmed from the fact that he was ultimately less interested in discretionary war than in mandatory war as a model for the type of military raid conducted in Kibiyeh. Thus, when R. Yisraeli finally settled on the notion that mandatory war was, in fact, the preferred paradigm here, he had more to say about noncombatant casualties. Here he informed us that civilians uninvolved in the war effort could be killed in the course of battle but not intentionally. Moreover, instead of speaking only vaguely about the nature of war as the reason that deaths among innocent civilians were tolerated, he now provided a halakhic argument by citing the war of the Israelites against the Midianites as the source of his thinking. R. Yisraeli expressed particular concern about the killing of children in mandatory war, a sector of the enemy population that was always innocent. He pointed out that on this issue, Jews should not follow the conduct of the Israelites in the Midianite war in which children were targeted, because the sin of the Midianites tempting the Israelites into idolatry was far worse than the physical assault of the Arabs against the state of Israel, and, therefore, the latter did not require a response that was as harsh as that enacted against the Midianites.

R. Goren adopted a similar approach to civilian casualties, but his treatment of the issue was more theological than that of R. Yisraeli. The requirement

---

2. R. Goren's position here reminds us of the approach taken by R. Kook who also saw the laws of war as belonging to a larger sector of Halakhah concerned with communal welfare. According to this position, the relevant distinction was not so much between wartime Halakhah and everyday Halakhah, but between communal Halakhah and Halakhah directed at the private individual.

to avoid such casualties to the extent possible was based on the notion that all life was sacred. R. Goren also emphasized the notion that Jewish life was sacred as well, and therefore Jewish political leaders and army commanders had to have the well-being of their own people in mind as well when waging war. Though R. Goren did not say so explicitly, he seemed to have in mind here the inevitable dilemmas that Israeli army commanders had to face between preserving the lives of enemy civilians and doing the same for their soldiers. It is not always possible in war to give both groups equal consideration.

The concrete implications of R. Goren's thinking here came through in his treatment of the siege of Beirut in the first Lebanon War, and the siege of Tripoli a short time later. During the siege of Beirut, R. Goren ruled that one side of the city remain open, as Halakhah dictated in such situations, and he specifically cited a humanitarian motive to explain this halakhic prescription. Civilians had to be allowed to flee during a siege, even if it meant that enemy fighters would escape as well. However, when it came to the siege of Tripoli, R. Goren was happy to exploit a halakhic loophole in order to argue that Israel acted incorrectly in lifting the siege and that the city should have remained sealed. The major difference with the Beirut situation, it seemed, was that the only people wishing to escape Tripoli were not civilians, but Yasser Arafat and his fighters, for whom there should be no mercy because they had taken up arms against Israel and were bent on its destruction.

R. Yisraeli was unique among our rabbis in dealing with the question of how one treats enemy civilians who give material and moral support to fighters attacking the Jewish state. This question was the central problem in R. Yisraeli's essay on Kibiyeh, and he ruled that this sector of the enemy population could be targeted in reprisal for its actions. These civilians were thus, in effect, involved in the war effort and were therefore to be considered combatants.

There was some evidence, however, that R. Goren had a similar issue in mind in his interpretation of the Shechem episode. He informed us in one of his essays that, according to Maimonides, the Shechemites deserved to be killed by Simeon and Levi for failing to hold their leader accountable for the rape of Dinah. However, R. Goren argued that while this ruling was correct according to a strict interpretation of Halakhah, the preferred approach was that of Nahmanides who ruled that Simeon and Levi should have acted in accordance with the principle of mercy and left the Shechemites alone. We surmised that with this reading, R. Goren was perhaps grappling with the question of whether Arab civilians were culpable for supporting their leaders who were committed to Israel's destruction, and that he was signaling to us that Nahmanides' more gentle approach should prevail. If that was the case, R. Goren took a position quite different from that of R. Yisraeli on this matter.

A question one may ask is why the rabbis in our study spent much more energy discussing the risks that Jewish soldiers face when going to war than the risks that threaten enemy civilians. As we have noted, all of our rabbis grappled with the question of conscription and how Jews could be drafted if it forced them to endanger their lives for the sake of the state, and the ways in which our rabbis treated this problem provided us with the most interesting and probing insights of our investigation. Yet, only two of our rabbis dealt with the issue of enemy civilian casualties, and the two who did had far less to say about it than they did about conscription.

The discrepancy here may simply reflect a certain insensitivity on the part of the figures we have examined in our study. People often value the lives of their own group more than the lives of those outside it, and that tendency certainly emerges more strongly in war when the outsider is a lethal threat. And even if the outsider in war is merely a civilian not directly involved in combat, he is often still considered an enemy whose life is of less concern than that of a soldier fighting for one's own side, especially if that civilian supports the enemy's war effort. These considerations would explain why our rabbis were far more interested in the lives of the members of their own community than those of enemy civilians.

Yet, while there may be some truth in these observations, there is another reason that can help us explain why our rabbis were so focused on Jewish soldiers and the dangers they faced in war. We have to keep in mind that the rabbis we have examined were religious Zionists who came of age when the state of Israel was relatively young. This was a time when the religious Zionist camp was small, and it had not yet developed a strong sense of identity. The problem was compounded by the fact that religious Zionism had a huge rival in the ultra-Orthodox community that had predated them in Palestine, rejected the legitimacy of the state of Israel, and forbade its followers from serving in the Israeli army. Therefore, one of the first challenges that the rabbis in our study had to confront when Israel was created and found itself immediately at war, was to come up with convincing arguments that Jews did, in fact, have a halakhic requirement to support the state by fighting for it on the battlefield. It was perhaps for this reason that the conscription issue occupied so much of their attention and forced them to think in highly creative terms to justify it. If these rabbis could not convince their followers—and themselves—that Jewish soldiers had to risk their lives for the sake of the state, they would have been effectively conceding that the state could not exist, seeing as its very survival depended on having an army that was willing to fight.

Another factor that has to be considered here is that the problem of enemy civilian casualties was not a big issue for Israelis until the 1980s because up to that point in time, Israel's wars were primarily conventional military campaigns in which armies fought against armies, and civilian casualties were not a major issue. In the 1980s this changed because Israel began dealing with irregular warfare against guerrilla and terrorist groups that did not fight in a conventional manner, and Israel found itself killing significant numbers of civilians in order to defeat these groups. This issue had been a concern since the founding of the state of Israel because cross-border raids by Palestinian terrorist groups stationed in the surrounding Arab countries began almost immediately after the founding of the state. Yet it began to emerge as a far more significant problem in the first Lebanon War. Up to that point, Israel had dealt with cross-border terrorist activity with limited military operations. The first Lebanon War was the first instance in which Israelis conducted a full-fledged war against a terrorist group, in this case the PLO, that was threatening Israel on its northern border. The same problem occurred twenty years later in the second Lebanon War against Hezbollah, as well as in the recent military campaigns against Hamas in Gaza. The two intifadas could be mentioned here as well, although one might question whether these were wars in any formal sense. In all these conflicts, Israel was criticized by the international community for violating the principle of proportionality. The accusation was that Israel was killing many more civilians than was warranted.

Three of the five rabbis in our study were still alive when the first Lebanon War was waged and the first intifada broke out. However, none were alive for any of the other conflicts just mentioned. Moreover, the first Lebanon War and the first intifada occurred relatively late in the careers of the three rabbis still alive at the time. It is therefore not surprising that the issue of enemy civilian casualties did not grab the attention of our rabbis as much as the problem of fielding a Jewish army. It was the latter issue that was the major challenge because if it were not possible to solve the problem of conscription, the state of Israel would have no way to defend itself. It was therefore left up to a younger generation of rabbis to focus on the issue of enemy civilian casualties in a way that the rabbis in our study did not.

THE RELATIONSHIP OF WARTIME HALAKHAH TO EVERYDAY HALAKHAH

One of the most important questions we asked in chapter 1 concerned the overall relationship between wartime Halakhah and everyday Halakhah. We have touched on this issue in this chapter, but we must now look at it more closely. How did the rabbis we explored in our study envision the relationship between the two spheres of Halakhah? Was wartime Halakhah different from the Halakhah that governed ordinary life, and if so, to what extent? We noted in that introductory chapter that a similar question has often been asked by Western ethicists and legal scholars, for they, too, have had to define the relationship between the rules of war and those of everyday life. We also noted that in grappling with this issue, Western ethicists and legal scholars often recognize that, in some respects, the rules of war are quite different from those that govern non-war situations but also acknowledge that the two spheres must share some commonality. Certainly, in war one must be allowed to violate the laws the norms of society because in order to achieve victory one must be permitted to kill in a way that would usually be forbidden. Yet, one's conduct in war cannot be so completely detached from that of the everyday that there are no restrictions whatsoever on what one may do to win. Without some connection to everyday ethics, war would become a barbarous affair, as it often has been throughout history. How, then, did our five rabbis deal with this issue in the realm of Halakhah? Did they treat wartime Halakhah merely as an extension of everyday Halakhah? Or did they view the two spheres as separate and if so, to what degree?

The question of how wartime Halakhah relates to everyday Halakhah surfaced constantly throughout our study, but our rabbis tended to address it when discussing two topics in particular: conscription and enemy civilian casualties. That these topics inspired our rabbis to wrestle with this issue, is understandable. The questions of conscription and enemy civilian casualties were concerned with the nitty-gritty of war, with war as a life-or-death issue for Jewish soldiers and enemy civilians alike, and the weightiness of such matters seems to have prompted our rabbis to reflect on the fundamental character of wartime Halakhah and its relationship to the rest of the halakhic corpus.

What, then, did the rabbis have to say about this relationship? It would seem that, for the most part, they emphasized the distinction between wartime Halakhah and the Halakhah of everyday life. It was for this reason that conscription was permitted. The majority of our rabbis argued that even though one could not normally force an individual to risk his life for the sake of others, in war a king or his political equivalent was allowed to do so. The same manner of thinking explained why in war one could kill enemy civilians. Killing innocent people was normally forbidden, but our rabbis recognized that in war such killing was unavoidable.

We may also note that R. Kook, who initiated this overall approach to war for the thinkers in our study, saw the laws of war as part of a larger sector of Halakhah that was concerned with communal welfare. Therefore, for R. Kook the distinction was not so much between wartime Halakhah and everyday Halakhah, but between communal Halakhah and Halakhah which pertained to the private individual. However, the rest of our thinkers did not conceive of matters in this way. Wartime Halakhah was mostly treated as a sector of Halakhah sui generis within the halakhic corpus.

None of this means that our rabbis saw wartime Halakhah as divorced from the Halakhah of everyday life altogether. At no point did any of them claim that because wartime Halakhah was distinct from everyday Halakhah, all was permitted in war in order to achieve victory. It was evident that for our rabbis, the general moral concerns that informed Halakhah in general also carried over into the sphere of war in some respects. Discussion of such issues as whether Jewish soldiers could be forced to sacrifice their lives in war, or whether a Jewish army was allowed to kill enemy civilians, were all predicated on moral principles that were basic to Halakhah as a whole. In their treatment of both these questions, the rabbis we examined expressed deep concern about the taking of life, both Jewish and non-Jewish, and they fashioned their positions on these issues in light of this concern. Therefore, our rabbis took an approach similar to that of Western ethicists and legal scholars in maintaining that the rules of war were different from those of everyday life in critical respects while presuming that the two bodies of law were not completely detached from each other.

When our rabbis insisted that wartime Halakhah was indeed different from everyday Halakhah, they were divided on what standards should be used to adjudicate the distinctive laws that applied to war. The most obvious approach was to argue that one could justify the norms of war by adducing biblical and rabbinic sources for a given position, in the same way a halakhic authority would in dealing with any other halakhic issue. That is, wartime Halakhah was distinctive, but the methodology for adjudicating it was not. Thus, for instance, on the issue of conscription, R. Kook and R. Herzog argued that wartime Halakhah differed from everyday Halakhah by relying on a combination of standard talmudic and medieval halakhic sources dealing with war, most notably Maimonides' rulings on war in the *Mishneh Torah*. R. Yisraeli, in his essay on Kibiyeh, took a similar approach in his treatment of mandatory wars waged in response to an enemy attack, wars which he identified as wars of revenge. R. Yisraeli formulated positions both on conscription and the killing of enemy civilians in this type of war that presumed a distinction between wartime Halakhah and everyday Halakhah, and he constructed his views on these matters on the basis of biblical and rabbinic sources. In this instance, R. Yisraeli focused primarily on the story of the Midianite war in the biblical text, as well as a midrashic source that interpreted that story, but he also supported his position with the help of Maimonides' *Mishneh Torah*.

However, there were instances in which our rabbis constructed positions within the distinctive sphere of wartime Halakhah by drawing from sources outside biblical and rabbinic literature. Most important in this regard was R. Yisraeli's treatment of discretionary war in his essay on Kibiyeh, a form of war which for him referred to all armed conflicts waged by the nations in accordance with the laws and customs of the international community. In R. Yisraeli's thinking, Halakhah approved of these wars, but it looked to the laws and customs of the international community for the rules that regulated them. Thus, in this instance, R. Yisrael went outside the realm of Halakhah to anchor the norms that govern war.

Nonetheless, it would be a mistake to conclude that in R. Yisraeli's thinking the rules of discretionary war had no connection to Halakhah whatsoever, as some commentators have assumed. The principle that allowed R. Yisraeli to go outside the realm of Halakhah in this instance was very much part of

Halakhah itself: *dina de-malkhuta dina*, "the law of the kingdom is the law." That is, the source of the laws regulating discretionary war in R. Yisraeli's thinking did indeed come from outside Halakhah, but the principle of *dina de-malkhuta dina* was necessary for allowing those laws to be incorporated into Halakhah in the first place. Thus, on the issue of discretionary war, R. Yisraeli certainly reached outside of Halakhah in a manner that was bold and innovative, but the connection with Halakhah was not entirely lost.

R. Waldenberg provided yet another example of how the distinctive laws of war were anchored in a sphere outside Halakhah but he based much of his thinking on war on the view of the Netsiv, according to whom war was permitted because of natural law.[3] But R. Waldenberg did not develop his views here in any detail. He provided no discussion about how the sphere outside of Halakhah regulating war—in this case, natural law—was connected to Halakhah itself.

Yet, while the predominant view among our rabbis was that wartime Halakhah was distinct from everyday Halakhah on the critical issues of conscription and the killing of civilians, there were some notable exceptions. Most significant in this regard was R. Yisraeli's position on the conscription issue in his post-Kibiyeh writings, where he argued that the obligation of Jewish soldiers to participate in defensive wars was a mere extension of prescriptions found in everyday Halakhah. As we noted earlier, R. Yisraeli's views on conscription in his later writings were unique in our study. None of the other four figures we explored consciously and explicitly removed the distinction between wartime Halakhah and everyday Halakhah with regard to this issue in the way that R. Yisraeli did in his later works. In fact, R. Yisraeli's views on conscription here were the only instance in which a figure in our study consciously and explicitly denied that distinction on any major halakhic issue regarding war.

However, we must keep in mind that R. Yisraeli took this approach only in the writings composed after the Kibiyeh essay. Moreover, among these writings was the essay on Entebbe in which R. Yisraeli strayed from the position just outlined and reverted to the position in the Kibiyeh essay according to which Jews are required to participate in defensive wars because wartime Halakhah was fundamentally different from everyday Halakhah. We must also keep in mind that R. Yisraeli did not extend his later approach to conscription to other areas in war. Thus, when it came to the issue of enemy civilian

---

3. As we noted earlier, R. Waldenberg eventually argued that R. Kook presented an alternative position to that of the Netsiv, according to which, war was permitted only because Halakhah gave sanction to it, not because of natural law, but R. Waldenberg never rejected the views of the Netsiv, and in supporting the Nestiv's views as one possible approach to war, R. Waldenberg implied that wartime Halakhah could be justified as different from everyday Halakhah because it was rooted in the law of nature.

casualties, R. Yisraeli at no point in his post-Kibiyeh writings suggested that here too wartime Halakhah was an extension of everyday Halakhah, as he did with conscription. In fact, such a suggestion would have been unthinkable. The killing of innocent people was clearly prohibited in everyday Halakhah, and if this norm were applied to war, the waging of war of any kind would have been impossible since innocent people are always killed in the course of war.

Why R. Yisraeli came to treat conscription as an exception in this regard can be explained by observations we made earlier. R. Yisraeli may have been addressing the ultra-Orthodox community, which refused to recognize the legitimacy of the Jewish state or its army. Perhaps it was for this reason that he came around to the view that the obligation to defend the Jewish state had nothing to do with war per se. That obligation was an extension of norms that were grounded in everyday Halakhah that all Jews had to observe regardless of their feelings about the state of Israel.

R. Goren's views on conscription also proved to be an exception when it came to the relationship of wartime Halakhah to everyday Halakhah. R. Goren's complex position on this issue lay somewhere between the view that wartime Halakhah was an extension of everyday Halakhah and the view that the two realms were separate. Therefore R. Goren, like R. Yisraeli in his later writings, broke ranks with the other rabbis in our study who emphasized the difference between wartime Halakhah and everyday Halakhah when it came to the question of conscription. Yet, unlike R. Yisraeli, R. Goren did not erase that distinction entirely.

It is possible that R. Goren's motivations in formulating his approach to the conscription issue were influenced by considerations similar to those that may have inspired R. Yisraeli to take the stand he did on that question. R. Goren, like R. Yisraeli, may have also been concerned about demonstrating to the ultra-Orthodox community that serving in the Israeli army was not necessarily connected to the state per se. He therefore argued that it was grounded, at least in part, on a commandment that was applicable in everyday life: "Do not stand idly by the blood of your fellow."

If R. Yisraeli and R. Goren formulated their views on conscription with the ultra-Orthodox community in mind, we should be reminded that Kalman Neuman suggested a similar reading for R. Herzog's reflections on that issue as it pertained to Israel's War of Independence in 1948.[4] R. Herzog consistently maintained the distinction between wartime Halakhah and everyday Halakhah when discussing conscription, but he tried to show that fighting in the 1948 war was an obligation on all Jews even according to the latter category because of the unique circumstances of the war. It is therefore possible that up to three of our five rabbis—R. Herzog, R. Yisraeli, and R. Goren—at

4. Above, pp. 95–6.

one time or another formulated positions on conscription that were specifically designed to appeal to the ultra-Orthodox community.

That all three addressed the ultra-Orthodox community on this issue of conscription, is perhaps an odd suggestion given that none of them formally belonged to that camp or had any real standing in it. The inclusion of R. Goren in this group may seem particularly odd because his relationship with the ultra-Orthodox community was deeply troubled throughout his public career. Many ultra-Orthodox Jews regarded R. Goren as a traitor for taking positions on halakhic matters they considered unacceptable.[5] However, I think an argument can still be made that all three rabbis had the ultra-Orthodox community in mind when speaking about conscription. All of them had grown up in that community and received their rabbinic training in it, and just because they no longer belonged to it in any formal sense, it does not mean that they no longer cared about it or about what its constituents thought. When one leaves a community in which one has been brought up, it is often difficult to sever all ties. And even when one does so externally, the psychological connection often remains. That connection may also manifest itself in the form of polemic or aggression. It is not uncommon for an individual who has left a particular community to continue shadow-boxing with that community for the rest of his life. It may have therefore meant something to R. Herzog, R. Yisraeli, and R. Goren to make a case for conscription to the ultra-Orthodox community, even if they knew it was unlikely to be accepted.

Moreover, conscription was not just any issue. It divided—and still divides—the ultra-Orthodox community from the rest of Israeli society perhaps more than any other issue that separates them. Ultra-Orthodox Jews have steadfastly refused to serve in the Israeli army since its creation, and their unwillingness to do so has aroused great bitterness in the rest of Israeli society. Therefore, if R. Herzog, R. Yisraeli, and R. Goren were going to address their former community—or shadow-box with them—about any matter, it would have been this one.

We also have to keep in mind the complex nature of the relationship that religious Zionists in general have always had with the ultra-Orthodox community in Israel. As we noted earlier, though religious Zionists had an affinity with secular Zionists because of the common commitment to Zionism, they also retained an affinity with the ultra-Orthodox community that was absent in their relationship with secular Zionists because of the commitment of ultra-Orthodox Jews to traditional Judaism and a halakhic way of life.[6] This background may also help explain why R. Herzog, R. Yisraeli, and R. Goren constructed arguments for conscription that would make sense within an

5. This issue is discussed throughout Mishlov's *"Be-'Ein ha-Se'arah."*
6. Above, pp. 17–18.

ultra-Orthodox worldview. Despite the differences these rabbis had with this community, they, like many other religious Zionists, still had fundamental commonalities with them on some level.

HALAKHAH VERSUS INTERNATIONAL LAW

As I pointed out in chapter 1, my intent in this study was to focus primarily on the moral challenges presented by war, even though much of the discussion of military issues in recent halakhic literature has been devoted to ritual matters. I chose to concentrate mainly on moral and political issues in Halakhah for a number reasons, one of which was that these issues lend themselves to comparisons with other moral and political systems. I would therefore like to offer some insights on how the thinking of the rabbis examined in this study compare with treatments of war in Western ethics.

Discussions of war in Western ethics tend to take place in two spheres: just war theory and international law. The first refers to a tradition of thought that began with Augustine, evolved throughout the medieval and early modern periods, and continues to be developed in the modern era. It accepts war as morally justified under certain conditions, and it spells out what those conditions are. Prior to the early modern period, the just war tradition was closely tied to Christian ethics, but in that period, a secular version of it began to emerge. Nowadays, we have just war theorists in both camps, those who are committed Christians and deal with war from a religious perspective, and those who are secular in orientation. As its name suggests, just war theory tends to be theoretical and philosophical in its methodology. That is, it attempts to arrive at norms that govern war by arguing from general ethical principles.

International law, the second major sphere of Western ethics dealing with war, gradually grew out of the just war tradition in the early modern period and has become consolidated in the past 150 years. Specialists in this area of law treat it in the same way legal analysts treat any other area of law. The methodology is hermeneutic in focus. These specialists spend their energy probing and interpreting the rules of war laid down in international treaties regarding the use of military force, as well as the rules of war dictated by customary international law that is unwritten but nonetheless authoritative because it reflects the long-standing behavior of nations.

A full treatment of how the views of the rabbis we have examined compare with these two traditions is beyond the scope of our study. Both traditions are rich and ramified, and on any one aspect of war, both provide a considerable range of opinions. A comprehensive comparison would therefore require a good deal of preliminary discussion of how just war theory and international law deal with war, and this task could easily occupy a number of chapters.

I therefore concentrate my efforts on one of these two spheres, that of international law, because the material in this discipline more closely resembles the material on war that we have examined in this study than that which is found in just war theory. Halakhah is, after all, a body of law as well. Moreover, international law is my preferred choice because it is more influential than just war theory on the actual conduct of war in today's world. Army manuals in individual countries are generally based on the former rather than the latter.

I will make this discussion manageable by limiting my analysis to issues that are sufficiently broad that we avoid becoming entangled in the complex debates about the details of international law on war. My intent here is to provide only preliminary insights for further research.

But before we begin this analysis, we must respond to a potential objection. One may question whether a comparison between Halakhah—at least as it is understood by the figures in our study—and international law is at all appropriate. Our rabbis view Halakhah as a body of religious law, the authority of which ultimately rests on sources believed to be revealed by God. These sources consist of both the written Torah and the oral Torah that is embodied in rabbinic tradition and literature. International law, by contrast, is secular in its orientation.

However, one must keep in mind that international law is an expression of Western ethics, a tradition that is based, at least in part, on Christian morality, which, in turn, has roots in the Hebrew Bible. Therefore, Jewish morality has certainly had influence on international law. International law is, therefore, not entirely secular. Conversely, we can also presume that the rabbis examined in our study were aware of, and in some instances influenced by, the secular ethical currents in the non-Jewish world that inform international law, even when they did not explicitly acknowledge it. Almost all of our rabbis had some connection to the world of Western learning. R. Kook was, of course, famous for incorporating Western thinking on a wide range of matters into this thought system. R. Herzog received a doctorate from the Sorbonne. R. Yisraeli, in his essay on Kibiyeh, displayed some knowledge of international law when he openly accepted it as a source for halakhic norms governing discretionary war. R. Goren pursued secular studies in the university as well. Only R. Waldenberg did not appear to have a connection with the world of secular learning. We may also make the general observation that the boundaries between the Orthodox Jewish world and the outside world are more porous than is often assumed. Therefore, with all these considerations in mind, we can conclude that the positions of the rabbis in our study and the prescriptions found in international law, while based on different premises, are not entirely alien to each other. International law has ties to Jewish ethics, and the rabbis in our study were certainly aware, on some level, of the ethics of the Western world that inform international law.

Let us, then, proceed with our comparison. We will begin by looking at how the views of our rabbis compare to international law on the question of which kinds of war may be fought. International law permits war only for the sake of self-defense. The first multilateral treaty that set forth this rule was the Kellogg-Briand Pact of 1928 that was signed by sixty-three states, but the rule was not sufficiently clarified until the United Nations Charter of 1945. The key provision was article 4.2 of the charter. Most of the states of the world are signatories to the UN Charter and must therefore adhere to this provision, but states that are not signatories are still obligated by international law to refrain from war for purposes other than self-defense because the ban on aggressive warfare now has the status of customary international law and is therefore binding on all states.[7]

All the rabbis in our study certainly permitted the waging of defensive war. In fact, this notion was one of the few ideas on which they all agreed. R. Yisraeli's essay on Kibiyeh was perhaps an exception. In it, R. Yisraeli effectively ruled out self-defense as a reason for waging war. However, he did permit the waging of war in response to hostilities initiated by an enemy nation for the purpose of retaliation, and though he did not call this type of war a war of self-defense, one could argue that the difference was perhaps more semantic than substantive. R. Yisraeli believed that the intention of wars of retaliation was different from that of other wars but that the rules governing them were the same. Moreover, in most of his writings after the Kibiyeh essay, R. Yisraeli came around to the view that wars waged in response to enemy attack were indeed justified on the basis of the principle of self-defense.

Where our rabbis clearly part company with international law is in supporting forms of war that are non-defensive in nature. All of them believed that discretionary wars were permitted when the Jewish monarchy was in power and that wars of this type included those specified by Maimonides in his *Mishneh Torah*: wars to expand the borders of the Jewish state and wars meant to elevate the prestige of the king. However, as noted earlier, it was only R. Goren who seemed to have an unequivocally positive view of these wars and was eager to see them revived in his own time. R. Yisraeli in his Kibiyeh essay believed that discretionary war could still be waged because he defined these wars as those which were waged with the approval of international law or custom, but he was clearly troubled by the fact these wars were often aggressive in nature and took innocent lives. And if R. Yisraeli had known more about international law at the time of the writing of his essay, he would have had to concede that, in fact, only wars of self-defense were permitted. Therefore, while all of the rabbis in our study supported discretionary war

---

7. Solis, *Law of Armed Conflict*, 77; Dinstein, *War*, 85–101.

from a theoretical standpoint, only R. Goren seems to have desired to see it resurrected in the aggressive form defined by medieval Halakhah.

An equally serious challenge to international law is the notion that a Jewish state may wage war in accordance with Nahmanides' notion that Jews have an ongoing commandment to conquer the land of Israel. That a state would wage war for a religious motive such as this one has no place in international law. Yet only two of our rabbis supported Nahmanides' position explicitly and their support was somewhat soft. R. Herzog initially incorporated Nahmanides' view into his thinking about Israel's War of Independence in 1948, but he backed away from that position to some degree under pressure from R. Roth. R. Goren upheld Nahmanides' view in one of his essays, but elsewhere he did not commit to it because of the opposing view of Maimonides. R. Yisraeli took Nahmanides' view into account but only when it came to the issue of giving back land Israel had conquered in war for the sake of making peace. According to R. Yisraeli, the imperative to conquer the land of Israel required that once sovereignty had been achieved over any portion of the land, it could not be relinquished.

What comes out of all this is that the rabbis in our study did indeed go beyond the boundaries set by international law when it came to the reasons for waging war. Yet, for all practical purposes, their transgressions of those boundaries were, for the most part, neither frequent nor extreme. They generally saw war as an instrument for defending the Jewish state from attack, a position very much in line with international law.

Yet most of the prescriptions about war in international law are focused on how armies should conduct themselves once war has been waged—that is, *jus in bello*, as opposed to *jus ad bellum*. The body of law that deals with such behavior is referred to as the "international law of armed conflict," or "international humanitarian law," though the first designation is more common. The underlying principle of the international law of armed conflict (henceforth LOAC) is that when armies conduct military operations in war, they must strive to find the proper balance between doing what is necessary to achieve victory and minimizing loss of life on the enemy side. Put succinctly, the goal is to find an equilibrium between military necessity and humanitarian considerations.[8]

In the LOAC, the imperative to minimize loss of life in the enemy population is, in turn, mostly focused on civilian casualties, seeing as they are generally regarded as the ultimate victims of war.[9] International law recognizes that because of military necessity, civilian casualties in war are unavoidable and that armies cannot achieve victory without their occurrence.[10] But to

---

8. Dinstein, *Conduct*, 4–8
9. The points made in this paragraph repeat some of the observations that were made in our discussion of R. Yisraeli's essay on Kibiyeh. See above, pp. 154–56.
10. Dinstein, *Conduct*, 123–24.

minimize the loss of civilian lives, two rules must be obeyed: armies are forbidden to target civilians intentionally, and they must conduct their operation with the principle of proportionality in mind. The first rule, remarkably, did not find explicit expression in international law until relatively recently. The blanket protection of civilians from deliberate attack was considered part of international customary law throughout the better part of the twentieth century, and the Geneva Conventions of 1949 touch on it as well by protecting certain groups of civilians. Yet, only with the signing of Additional Protocol I in 1977 was the protection of civilians made explicit in a multilateral treaty.[11] The principle of proportionality is tricky to define and implement. It requires that in any given military operation, the number of civilian deaths is not excessive in relation to the military advantage achieved by that operation. The problem is that there is no easy way to make the required calculation. How does one gauge military advantage, an idea that cannot easily be quantified? And even if one could, how does one determine how many civilian deaths are allowed per "unit" of military advantage?[12]

As we have noted, only two figures in our study dealt with the issue of enemy civilian casualties in any detail. The most thorough discussion was that of R. Goren, and his thinking here is certainly resonant with international law. According to R. Goren, civilian deaths were a part of war, but one could not target civilians deliberately, just as international law specifies. Much of his discussion was taken up with citations from biblical and rabbinic sources that underscored the sacredness of life and the need to preserve it as much as possible even in situations of war.

We have already discussed how R. Yisraeli's views regarding civilian casualties in the Kibiyeh essay compare to those found in international law in chapter six. In some respects, his views fell in line with those of international law. According to R. Yisraeli, enemy civilians who were innocent should not be targeted. However, R. Yisraeli diverged from international law in his assessment of who was regarded as "innocent." Only the children of Kibiyeh deserved this designation. The adults of the village were legitimate targets because of their support for the terrorists who had attacked Jewish villages in Israel. These civilians therefore deserved to be punished. International law, by contrast, does not sanction the targeting of civilians unless their role in the war effort is more direct than was the case with the residents of Kibiyeh. Moreover, civilians are culpable only if they are caught in the act of performing military activities, and that was not the case in Kibiyeh. Moreover, international law would certainly not support R. Yisraeli's notion that retaliation is a legitimate reason

---

11. Additional Protocol I, art. 48, 51.1, 51.2; Solis, *Law of Armed Conflict*, 232–34, 251–58; Dinstein, *Conduct*, 8, 89, 121, 124.

12. Additional Protocol I, arts. 51.5(b), 57.2(b); Solis, *Law of Armed Conflict*, 272–85; Dinstein, *Conduct*, 128–34.

for attacking civilians.[13] However, we also argued that while R. Yisraeli's position here is inimical to international law as it is currently understood, that assessment was less true at the time that he composed his essay. Laws regarding the treatment of civilians in war had not yet taken precise shape.[14]

As we have already noted, the issue of conscription elicited perhaps the most interesting insights from our rabbis on the subject of war. However, this issue is the only major one we have explored that does not lend itself to a comparison between the views of our rabbis and those of international law. That is because laws of conscription are not, for the most part, an international matter; each state has its own body of laws governing the drafting of soldiers, and they are all different. Nonetheless, one finds reflection on conscription from a more theoretical and hence universal standpoint in another Western academic discipline: political thought. Moreover, studies by a handful of academic scholars have analyzed how Western political philosophers treat this issue. The methodology here is, of course, philosophical rather than legal in its orientation. Still, it is instructive to take a brief look at how the views of our rabbis compare to those found in philosophical treatments of this topic.

The first important study of Western philosophers on this issue was a thoughtful essay written by Michael Walzer in 1970 entitled, "The Obligation to Die for the State."[15] Walzer asks whether the citizen is required to lay down his life for the political community and if so, under what circumstances. For instance, if a prisoner has been sentenced to death, does he have the right to escape his confinement in order to save his life, or is he required to submit passively to his punishment? Walzer has in mind here the famous account of Socrates, who after being sentenced to death by the Athenian courts, chooses to die rather than consider escape. Another example Walzer's essay takes up is conscription. What gives the state the right to send soldiers off to war, with all the risk that entails? May a soldier legitimately refuse to serve? Here, the state is not necessarily requiring the citizen to die for its sake because not all soldiers are killed in battle. Nonetheless, for Walzer the dangers of war are sufficient that this question is relevant to the overall issue he is considering.[16]

Walzer juxtaposes two opposing responses in the Western political tradition to the general question posed here. The first is that of Thomas Hobbes (1588–1679), who takes the position that one does not, in fact, have an obligation to die for the state. For Hobbes, the whole point of establishing a political

---

13. Additional Protocol I, art. 51.3, with further clarification in a report by the International Commission of the Red Cross in 2009. See Solis, *Law of Armed Conflict*, 202–6, 252–53, 539, 543–44; Dinstein, *Conduct*, 146–52.

14. Above, pp. 154–56.

15. Michael Walzer, "The Obligation to Die for the State," in *Essays on Disobedience, War, and Citizenship* (Cambridge, Mass.: Harvard University Press, 1970), 77–98.

16. Walzer, "Obligation to Die," 77–80.

community is for individuals to achieve physical security that they would not otherwise have in the state of nature. Therefore, it makes no sense for the individual to willingly give up his life for the state. For Hobbes, a prisoner sentenced to death thus has every right to escape, though the state also has every right to prevent him from doing so in order that the punishment may be carried out. When it comes to wars of self-defense, Hobbes does require citizens of a state to take up arms to defend it, even at the risk of their lives, because if the state serves the function of giving its citizens security, the individual should be motivated to defend its existence from enemies seeking to destroy it. Walzer, however, devotes a good deal of discussion to Hobbes's treatment of conscription and concludes that, for a number of reasons, Hobbes's position is problematic.[17] The second approach, according to Walzer, is that of Jean Jacques Rousseau (1712–78) who believes that one must indeed lay down one's life for the state. For Rousseau, the state is created to represent the shared values of its constituents, an arrangement that is concretized in the social contract, and therefore it is assumed that the individual should be willing to sacrifice his life for its sake. According to this approach, the prisoner sentenced to death is required to accept execution, and the citizen who is drafted must go to war at the behest of the state despite the risks involved.[18]

Walzer's essay inspired another study composed by Geoffrey B. Levey in 1987, entitled "Judaism and the Obligation to Die for the State," which discusses what the stance of Judaism would be regarding the issues raised by Walzer.[19] Levey focuses in particular on how biblical and medieval rabbinic law approach the question of conscription. Does a Jewish state have a right to force its citizens to participate in wars despite the dangers involved, and if so why? That is, Levey's analysis focuses squarely on the major question that preoccupied the rabbis in our study regarding conscription.

But before responding to this question, Levey notes that the difficulty in comparing ideas in modern Western political thought with those found in Judaism is that in Judaism the social contract is not between the people and the sovereign, but between the people and God to whom they demonstrate their obedience by observing His commandments. Therefore, in Judaism the state is only a means for allowing Jews to fulfill their obligations to God and is not an end in itself. If that is the case, Jews have no obligation to die for the state per se.[20] Still, Levey believes that a comparison here is meaningful, even

17. Walzer, "Obligation to Die," 80–89
18. Walzer, "Obligation to Die," 89–98.
19. Geoffrey B. Levey, "Judaism and the Obligation to Die for the State," *AJS Review* 12, no. 2 (1987): 175–203. This article was reprinted in Michael Walzer, ed., *Law, Politics, and Morality in Judaism* (Princeton, N.J.: Princeton University Press, 2006), 182–208. Page numbers are from the Princeton University Press edition.
20. Levey, "Judaism," 84–85.

if in Judaism the state is conceived only as a means to another end. I might also interject here that even Western political philosophers do not necessarily see the state as an end in itself. It often serves a higher end that transcends the state. Therefore, the gap between Judaism and Western political thinking is not as great as Levey suggests. Moreover, obedience to God requires observing commandments that are very much concerned with matters of this world, including commandments that focus on one's obligations to the political community. According to Halakhah, the Jew is therefore required to obey the sovereign. The only exception is when a sovereign issues orders directly contrary to Halakhah. Thus, for the most part, obligations to God and obligations to the state are not mutually exclusive.

But the central issue that Levey tries to tackle is what biblical and medieval rabbinic law have to say about the question of conscription and whether the individual has an obligation to risk his life by going to war. According to Levey, the matter is complicated. When it comes to discretionary war, rabbinic sources generally agree that a Jew may be called on to serve, but he may also avoid going into battle by invoking the military exemptions spelled out in Deuteronomy 20:1–8. Thus, as we have already observed, a man does not have to fight if he has just been married, has built a new home, or has planted a new vineyard.[21] Levey is particularly intrigued by the last of the exemptions, which specifies that even a person who is fearful of war may refrain from going into battle.[22] That such a provision exists indicates to Levey that, in discretionary war, one does not have an obligation to risk one's life for the state. After all, anyone can say they are fearful, and, presumably, they have to be believed. Therefore, all potential soldiers have easy means to escape military duty if they want to. Consequently, it would seem that in discretionary war, Hobbes's approach holds sway.[23] Yet, when it comes to mandatory war, according to Levey, things are different. Here, according to most rabbinic sources, the military exemptions do not apply. All able-bodied adults must go to war. In this instance, therefore, it would seem that Rousseau's view has the upper hand.[24]

Levey raises a question about defensive wars, in particular, that is all too familiar to us. Defensive wars are mandatory, and yet, according to Halakhah, a Jew cannot be required to sacrifice his life to protect others from harm. How then can the state impose that requirement in war? According to Levey, this question does not arise in the other forms of mandatory war—that is, wars against the Canaanites and Amalekites—because these wars are commanded

21. Deut. 20:5–7. Above, p. 32.
22. Deut. 20:8.
23. Levey, "Judaism," 186–92.
24. Levey, "Judaism," 192. Levey admits that some rabbinic authorities extend the exemptions to mandatory war as well, but in the rest of his discussion he assumes that the majority view restricts the exemptions to discretionary war.

directly by God.[25] Levey responds by citing one contemporary halakhic authority who claims that the requirement of Jews to participate in defensive wars derives from the special authority of the king.[26] Levey also entertains the possibility that, according to Halakhah, the state needs no justification to send men to battle in defensive wars because the obligation to defend the state is axiomatic. That is why Maimonides in his *Mishneh Torah* provides no biblical or rabbinic sources to support the king's permission to wage wars of this type.[27]

How would the rabbis in our analysis respond to Levey's assessment? Since none of the rabbis in our study considered discretionary war to be a viable option at present, let us focus on defensive war, which is the type of war about which they are most concerned. Would our rabbis agree that in such wars the individual is required to risk his life for the state, as Rousseau believed?

Some certainly would. R. Kook most clearly saw the obligation to risk one's life for the state as a political matter. The king's law gave the monarch the right to send soldiers into battle to safeguard the well-being of the state. R. Herzog largely followed R. Kook's thinking. He did not adopt R. Kook's concept of the king's law; nonetheless, he believed that the individual had to sacrifice his life in defensive wars for the sake of the Jewish community. The Jewish community here, however, encompassed more than the politically organized community in the land of Israel and included world Jewry as a whole. Thus, for R. Herzog, the Jewish political state is less the focus than the Jewish people in general. R. Waldenberg also followed R. Kook, but supplemented the latter's views with those of the Netsiv. Still, with respect to the issue at hand, the results were the same; the king had the right to draft soldiers and send them into battle with all the dangers that war entails.

R. Yisraeli, however, would not agree with Levey's formulation. In his essay on Kibiyeh, R. Yisraeli argued that the obligation to fight against an enemy nation that had initiated hostilities was not based on a requirement to defend the state but was due to an imperative to punish the enemy. Preserving the state was therefore not the central issue here so much as retaliation against another state that had committed a wrong. In his later writings, R. Yisraeli adopted an entirely different approach, according to which the requirement to wage war against an enemy that had initiated a war was indeed for the purpose of self-defense, but here too the state was not the focus. R. Yisraeli now claimed that the obligation of Jews to participate in wars of this kind was based on an imperative to enter a situation of possible danger in order to rescue a fellow Jew who was in certain danger. One was therefore required to

25. Levey, "Judaism," 193.

26. J. David Bleich, "Preemptive War in Jewish Law," *Contemporary Halakhic Problems* (New York: Ktav, 1989), 3:282–83.

27. Levey, "Judaism," 193–95.

defend the individual fellow Jew, not the state per se. When the state went to war to defend itself, it merely enforced an obligation on individuals that they had prior to the waging of war. Thus, in his Kibiyeh essay and his later writings, R. Yisraeli takes a position at odds with the early rabbinic tradition as interpreted by Levey.

R. Goren's thinking fits into Levey's assessment but only in part. On the one hand, R. Goren based the requirement to fight in wars of self-defense on the commandment not to stand idly by the blood of one's brother, a commandment directed at the individual. Here too, the obligation to risk one's life in war did not concern the state. In addition, we cited a passage in which R. Goren explicitly put the rights of the individual above that of the state. However, we also saw that in some passages R. Goren adduced reasons for the obligation of the individual to go to war that were indeed based on his obligation to the state, such as the commandment to obey the orders of a king.[28]

Levey does not touch on the issue of mandatory war waged for the purpose of conquering the land of Israel in accordance with Nahmanides' view. We saw that R. Herzog and R. Goren entertained the possibility that Israel may wage war to fulfill this goal. Would this imperative then be another instance of the individual being obligated to risk his life for the state? We cannot provide a clear answer to this question on behalf of R. Herzog or R. Goren because it was unclear how committed either of them was to Nahmanides' position.[29]

---

28. We might also note that even those rabbis in our study who believed that the individual had an obligation to endanger his life to defend the state may not have seen things in quite the same way Levey has suggested. Every one of our thinkers asked the question how it was possible for the state to send its men to war given that Halakhah did not require an individual to endanger his life for others, and the very question, as well as the prodigious efforts on the part of our rabbis to answer it, indicate they did not believe that the right of the state to send men into battle, even for the sake of self-defense, was at all obvious. Thus, while a number of our rabbis believed that the rights of the state ultimately predominate over those of the individual when it comes to wars of self-defense, the rights of the individual were not easily dismissed. In other words, while the rabbis in our study ultimately sided with a position similar to that of Rousseau, they did not entirely let go of considerations similar to those that motivated Hobbes's thinking.

29. But even if we assume that they were indeed committed to it, the role that the state plays in Nahmanides' viewpoint is not clear. One difficulty is that Nahmanides seems to have had in mind a war to conquer the land for the purpose of *establishing* a Jewish state. Therefore, the war being waged here takes place before there is even a state to speak of. For this reason, it is hard to say whether, in Nahmanides' mind, going to war to conquer the land is really focused on sacrificing one's life for the state. On the one hand, there is obviously no state to obligate anyone in such a war. On the other hand, one might argue that if the purpose of conquest of land is to build a Jewish state, the state does, in some sense, have obligatory power in an indirect manner. Another complication here is that a number of commentators have interpreted Nahmanides to be saying that the commandment to conquer the land has two aspects. One is a collective obligation on the Jewish people as a whole to wage war in order to take control of the land, while the second is an individual obligation on each and every Jew to

I would like to share one more series of observations that bring us back to a comparison between the views of the rabbis we have examined and those found in international law. Perhaps the most fundamental question we have attempted to tackle in this study is to define the overall relationship between wartime Halakhah and everyday Halakhah. We showed earlier in this chapter that our rabbis lean toward the view that the two realms are distinct from each other. However, we also saw notable exceptions in R. Yisraeli's views on conscription in his later writings, and to some extent, R. Goren's views on this matter as well. Scholars of international law ask a similar question about the relationship of laws of war with the rest of international law: are the two realms of law distinct and if so, to what extent? This issue has engendered a good deal of debate. In general, the argument is cast in terms of the relationship between human rights law (henceforth, HRL), and LOAC. HRL is a branch of international law that took shape after World War II and is designed to protect the fundamental rights of all individuals against the encroachments by their own governments or by other actors in the international community. These rights were first brought to the fore and solidified in international law with the UN Charter and were further developed in such conventions as the Universal Declaration of Human Rights, in 1948, and the International Covenant on Civil and Political Rights, in 1966. The key question is whether HRL continues to function in wartime. Frequently, HRL and LOAC are in harmony with each other, but there are instances in which they clash. Examples include such issues as the detention and internment of prisoners, security restrictions imposed on civilians, and use of torture. In these instances, commentators have asked which body of law takes priority. The European approach tends to favor HRL over LOAC when there is a conflict, whereas the American approach tends to favor LOAC over HRL. Therefore, when dealing with war, the Europeans tend to favor the body of human rights law that governs non-war situations over that which governs wartime; for US analysts, it is the reverse.[30]

purchase a parcel of land and settle it. See, for example, R. Ya'akov Ari'el, "*Ha-Hebetim ha-Hilkhatiyim shel Ba'ayat ha-Nesigah me-Heveley Erets Yisra'el*," *Be-Ohalah shel Torah* (Kefar Darom, Israel: Makhon ha-Torah ve-ha-Arets, 2003), 91–92; Hayim Burganski, "*Yahaso ha-Hikahati shel ha-Rav Yisra'eli le-Sugyat Hahzarat ha-Shetahim*, 245. While the first aspect of the commandment to conquer the land may involve the Jewish community as a politically organized entity, the second would not.

Levey, "Judaism," 192–93, notes that a number of halakhic authorities view the commandment to wage war against the Canaanites as having the same duality. On the basis of a careful reading of Maimonides' wording regarding this commandment, they conclude that the commandment is directed both to the community of Israel and to the individual. The commandments to fight other types of wars do not have this feature.

30. Solis, *Law of Armed Conflict*, 24–26; Dinstein tends to assume that the American approach is correct. See *Conduct*, 19–26.

It is the American position that is analogous to that taken by most of the thinkers in our study. The point becomes clear when we look at the following statement of one American analyst:

> [It] has become common in some quarters to conflate human rights and the laws of war. ... Nevertheless ... significant differences remain. Unlike human rights law, the law of war allows ... the killing and wounding of innocent human beings not directly participating in an armed conflict, such as civilian victims of lawful collateral damage. ... As long as rules of the game are observed, it is permissible [in armed conflict] to cause suffering, deprivation of freedom, and death.[31]

What this commentator is saying is that the laws of war are, in some respects, fundamentally different from those that govern everyday life, and when war is waged, wartime laws take priority. Those who followed R. Kook's example in our study—and they were the majority—made a similar argument about the relationship of wartime Halakhah to everyday Halakhah. In war situations, the first has priority over the second.

However, we did see exceptions to this approach among our rabbis. Once again, R. Yisraeli in his later writings saw conscription as imperative in defensive wars because of laws found in everyday Halakhah, and R. Goren, at least in part, followed in R. Yisraeli's footsteps on this point. Therefore, in this instance, both R. Yisraeli and R. Goren take a path that is perhaps more consistent with the European approach in international law than the American one.

In our attempt to compare laws of war in Halakhah with those found in international law, we have grazed only the surface. Much more could be said about each of the issues raised in connection with this comparison. A more thorough treatment, however, will have to wait for another occasion.

I would like to conclude by emphasizing that the five rabbis we have examined in this study by no means represent the sum total of what modern Halakhah has to say about the justification of war from a moral standpoint. As rabbis of great stature, their influence on the halakhic authorities in their own time regarding questions of war, as well as subsequent halakhic authorities who have dealt with this issue, has been substantial. Yet, I hope this study has provided important insights that will serve as a foundation for further research into the way in which Halakhah deals with one of the most pressing issues of our time.

---

31. Theodor Meron, "The Humanization of Humanitarian Law," *American Journal of International Law* 94, no. 2 (2000): 239–40, cited in Solis, *Law of Armed Conflict*, 25.

WORKS CITED

Ahituv, Yosef. "*Milhamot Yisra'el u-Kedushat ha-Hayim.*" In *Kedushat ha-Hayim ve-Heruf ha-Nefesh*, edited by Aviezer Ravitzky and Isaiah Gafni, 255–76. Jerusalem: Merkaz Zalman Shazar, 2003.

———. "*Min ha-Sefer el ha-Sayif: 'Al Demuto ha-Hazuyah shel ha-Tsava ha-Yisra'eli 'al pi ha-Torah ba-Shanim ha-Rishonot le-Kum ha-Medinah.*" In *Sheney 'Evrey ha-Gesher: Dat u-Medinah be-Reshit Darkah shel Yisra'el*, edited by Mordekhai Bar-On and Tsevi Tsameret, 414–44. Jerusalem: Yad Yitshak ben Tsevi, 2002.

Alfasi, R. Isaac ben Jacob. *Sefer ha-Halakhot*. In Babylonian Talmud, standard edition.

Amital, R. Yehudah. "*Milhamot Yisra'el 'al pi ha-Rambam.*" *Tehumin* 8 (1987): 454–61.

Aran, Gideon. "*Bein Halutsiyut le-Limud Torah: Ha-Reka' le-Ge'ut ha-Datit Le'umit.*" In *Me'ah Shanot Tsiyonut Datit: Heibetim Ra'ayoniyim*, edited by Avi Sagi and Dov Schwartz, vol. 3, 31–72. Ramat Gan: Bar-Ilan University Press, 2004.

Ari'el, R. Ya'akov. *Be-Oholah shel Torah*. 5 vols. Kefar Darom, Israel: Makhon ha-Torah ve-ha-Arets, 2003.

Ari'el, R. Yig'al. "*Mesirut Nefesh 'avur ha-Kelal.*" In *Berurim be-Hilkhot ha-Re'iyah*, edited by R. Moshe Tsevi Neryah, R. Aryeh Shtern, and R. Neryah Gutel, 73–89. Jerusalem: Beit ha-Rav, 1992.

Artson, Bradley Shavit. *Love Peace and Pursue Peace: A Jewish Response to War and Nuclear Annihilation*. New York: United Synagogue of America, 1988.

Avidor, Shmu'el. *Yahid be-Doro: Megilat Hayav shel ha-Ga'on Rabi Yitshak Aizik ha-Levi Hertsog, Rosh Rabbaney Yisra'el*. Jerusalem: Keter, 1980.

Aviner, R. Shlomo. "*Korot Rabeinu 'al Giyus Talmidey Yeshivot.*" *Iturey Yerushalayim* 85 (Elul, 5773 [2013]): 3–12.

Avineri, Shlomo. *The Making of Modern Zionism: The Intellectual Origins of the Jewish State*. New York: Basic Books, 1981.

———. "Zionism and Jewish Religious Tradition: The Dialectics of Redemption and Secularization." In *Zionism and Religion*, edited by Shmuel Almog, Jehuda Reinharz, and Anita Shapira, 1–9. Hanover, N.H.: University of New England Press, 1998.

Babad, R. Joseph. *Minhat Hinukh*. Jerusalem: Jerusalem Institute, 1998.

Babylonian Talmud, standard edition.

Ba-Midbar Rabbah. In *Midrash Rabbah*, standard edition.

Ben-Artsi, Hagi. *Ha-Hadash Yitkadesh: Ha-Rav Kuk ke-Posek Mehadesh*. Tel Aviv: Yedi'ot Ahronot and Sifrey Hemed, 2010.

Berger, Michael S. "Taming the Beast: Rabbinic Pacification of Second-Century Jewish Nationalism." In *Belief and Bloodshed: Religion and Violence across Time and Tradition*, edited by James K. Wellman Jr., 47–62. Lanham, Md.: Rowman and Littlefield, 2007.

Berlin, R. Naftali Tsevi Yehudah. *Ha'amek Davar*. 5 vols. Jerusalem: Yeshivat Volozhin, 1998.

Blau, R. Yitzchak. "Biblical Narratives and the Status of Enemy Civilians in Wartime." *Tradition* 39, no. 4 (2006): 8–28.

Bleich, J. David. "Preemptive War in Jewish Law." In *Contemporary Halakhic Problems*, vol. 3, 251–92. New York: Ktav, 1989.

Blidstein, Gerald J. "The State and the Legitimate Use of Coercion in Modern Halakhic Thought." *Studies in Contemporary Jewry* 18 (2002): 3–22.

———. *"Torat ha-Medinah be-Mishnat ha-Rav Sha'ul Yisra'eli."* In *Sheney 'Evrey ha-Gesher*, edited by Mordekhai Bar On and Tsevi Tsameret, 350–63. Jerusalem: Yad Yitshak ben Tsevi, 2002.

———. "The Treatment of Hostile Civilian Populations: The Contemporary Halakhic Discussion in Israel." *Israel Studies* 1, no. 2 (1996): 27–45.

Broyde, Michael J. "Just Wars, Just Battles and Just Conduct in Jewish Law: Jewish Law Is Not a Suicide Pact!" In *War and Peace in the Jewish Tradition*, edited by Lawrence Schiffman and Joel B. Wolowelsky, 1–44. New York: Yeshiva University Press, 2007.

Burganski, Hayim. *"Kehilah ve-Mamlakhah: Yahasam ha-Hilkhati shel ha-Rav Y"A Hertsog ve-ha-Rav Sha'ul Yisra'eli li-Medinat Yisra'el."* In Dat u-Medinah be-Hagut ha-Yahadut be-Me'ah ha-'Esrim, edited by Aviezer Ravitzky, 267–94. Jerusalem: Ha-Makhon ha-Yisra'eli le-Demokratyah, 2005.

———. *"Yahaso ha-Hilkhati shel ha-Rav Yisra'eli le-Sugyat Hahzarat ha-Shetahim."* Diney Yisra'el 22 (2003): 241–67.

Cohen, Asher. *Ha-Talit ve-ha-Degel: Ha-Tsiyonut ha-Datit ve-Hazon Medinat ha-Torah Bi-Yemey Reshit ha-Medinah*. Jerusalem: Yad Yitshak ben Tsevi, 1998.

Cohen, Stuart A. "Dilemmas of Military Service in Israel: The Religious Dimension." In *War and Peace in the Jewish Tradition*, edited by Lawrence Schiffman and Joel B. Wolowelsky, 313–40. New York: Yeshiva University Press, 2007.

———."The Quest for a Corpus of Jewish Military Ethics." *Journal of Israeli History* 26, no. 1 (2007): 35–66.

———. "The Re-Discovery of Orthodox Jewish Laws relating to the Military and War (*Hilkhot Tzavah U-Milchamah*) in Contemporary Israel: Trends and Implications." *Israel Studies* 12, no. 2 (2007): 1–28.

———. *"Sifra ve-Sayfa u-mah she-Beinehem: 'Itsuv Hilkhot Tsava u-Milhamah be-Yisra'el."* 'Iyunim bi-Tekumat Yisra'el 15 (2005): 237–49.

Cohn, Haim H. "Extraordinary Remedies." In *The Principles of Jewish Law*, edited by Menachem Elon, 552. Jerusalem: Keter, 1974.

De Boton, R. Abraham. *Lehem Mishneh*. In *Mishneh Torah*, standard edition.

Devarim Rabbah. In *Midrash Rabbah*, standard edition.

Dinstein, Yoram. *The Conduct of Hostilities under the International Law of Armed Conflict*. 2nd ed. New York: Cambridge University Press, 2010.

———. *War, Aggression, and Self-Defence*. 4th ed. New York: Cambridge University Press, 2005.

Don-Yehiya, Eliezer. *"Dat ve-Teror Politi: Ha-Yahadut ha-Datit u-Pe'ulot ha-Gemul bi-Tekufat 'Ha-Me'ora'ot.'"* Ha-Tsiyonut 17 (1993): 155–90.

Dorff, Elliot N. *To Do the Right and the Good: A Jewish Approach to Modern Social Ethics*. Philadelphia: Jewish Publication Society of America, 2002.

Edrei, Aryeh. "Divine Spirit and Physical Power: Rabbi Shlomo Goren and the Military Ethic of the Israel Defense Forces." *Theoretical Inquiries in Law* 7, no. 1 (2006): 257–99.

————. "Law, Interpretation, and Ideology: The Renewal of the Jewish Laws of War in the State of Israel." *Cardozo Law Review* 28 (October 2006): 187–227.

————. *"Mi-Kibiyeh 'ad Beirut: Tehiyatan shel Diney ha-Milhamah ha-Hilkhatiyim bi-Medinat Yisra'el."* In *Yosef Da'at: Mehkarim be-Historiyah Yehudit Modernit Mugashim le-Prof. Yosef Salmon le-Hag Yovlo*, edited by Yossi Goldshtein, 95–127. Be'er Sheva: Ben Gurion University Press, 2010.

Eidels, R. Samuel. *Hidushey Halakhot ve-Aggadot*. In Babylonian Tamud, standard edition.

Eisen, Robert. *The Peace and Violence of Judaism: From the Bible to Modern Zionism*. New York: Oxford University Press, 2011.

————. "R. Abraham Isaac Kook on War in Jewish Law." *Modern Judaism* 33, no. 1 (2013): 24–44.

————. "Rabbi Eliezer Yehudah Waldenberg on the Justification of War." *Torah U-Madda Journal* (forthcoming).

————. "War, Revenge, and Jewish Ethics: Rabbi Shaul Yisraeli's Essay on Kibiyeh Revisited." *AJS Review* 36, no. 1 (2012): 141–63.

Elon, Menachem. Introduction to *The Principles of Jewish Law*, edited by Menachem Elon, 6–46. Jerusalem: Keter, 1974.

————. "On Power and Authority: Halachic Stance of the Traditional Community and Its Contemporary Implications." In *Kinship and Consent: The Jewish Political Tradition and Its Contemporary Uses*, edited by Daniel J. Elazar, 183–216. Lanham, Md.: University Press of America, 1983.

————. "Public Authority and Administrative Law." In *The Principles of Jewish Law*, edited by Menachem Elon, 645–54. Jerusalem: Keter, 1974.

Entsiklopediyah Talmudit, edited by R. Me'ir Berlin and R. Shelomoh Yosef Zevin. Jerusalem: Yad ha-Rav Hertsog, 1947–.

Epshtein, R. Yehi'el Mikhal. *Arukh ha-Shulhan*. New York: Oz Vehadar, 2006.

Falk, R. Joshua. *Sefer Me'irat 'Einayim*. In *Shulhan Arukh: Hoshen Mishpat*, standard edition.

Finkelman, Yoel. "On the Irrelevance of Religious Zionism." *Tradition* 39, no. 1 (2005): 21–44.

Firestone, Reuven. *Holy War in Judaism: The Fall and Rise of a Controversial Idea*. New York: Oxford University Press, 2012.

Fishman, Aryeh. *Bein Dat le-Idiologiyah: Yahadut ve-Modernizatsyah be-Kibutz ha-Dati*. Jerusalem: Yad Yitshak ben Tsevi, 1990.

Frankel, R. David. *Korban ha-'Eidah*. In the Jerusalem Talmud, standard edition.

————. *Shiyarey Korban*. In the Jerusalem Talmud, standard edition.

Fruman, R. Menahem. *"Le-'Inyan Mesirut Nefesh 'avur ha-Kelal."* In *Berurim be-Hilkhot ha-Re'iyah*, edited by R. Moshe Tsevi Neryah, R. Aryeh Shtern, and R. Neryah Gutel, 121–46. Jerusalem: Beit ha-Rav, 1992.

Gellman, Ezra, ed. *Essays on the Thought and Philosophy of Rabbi Kook*. Rutherford, N.J.: Fairleigh Dickinson University Press, 1991.

Gerondi, R. Nissim ben Re'uven (Ran). Commentary on R. Isaac Alfasi's *Halakhot*. In the Babylonian Talmud, standard edition.

Goren, R. Shlomo. *"Admat ha-Kodesh ve-Pikuah Nefesh mi-Nekudat Mabat ha-Halakhah."* In *Torat ha-Medinah: Mehkar Hilkhati Histori be-Nos'im ha-'Omdim be-Rumah shel Medinat Yisra'el me'az Tekumatah,"* edited by Yisra'el Tamari, 28–42. Jerusalem: Ha-Idra Rabah, 1999.

————. "Ha-Matsor 'al Beirut le-Or ha-Halakhah." In *Meshiv Milhamah: She'elot u-Teshuvot be-'Inyaney Tsava, Milhamah, u-Bitahon*, vol. 3, 239–654. Jerusalem: Ha-Idra Rabbah, 1982–1991.

————. "Ha-Mitsvot she-bein Adam la-Medinah." In *Torat ha-Shabbat ve-ha-Mo'ed*, 447–57. Alon Shevut, Israel: Yad Shapira, 1982.

————. "Ha-Ruah ve-ha-Koah be-Mishnat ha-Yahadut." *Mahanayim* 100 (1966): 5–16.

————. "Hasarat ha-Matsor ha-Yami me-'al ha-Mehablim be-Tripoli." In *Meshiv Milhamah: She'elot u-Teshuvot be-'Inyaney Tsava, Milhamah, u-Bitahon*, vol. 3, 283–303. Jerusalem: Ha-Idra Rabbah, 1982–1991.

————. "Hatalat 'Onesh Mavet 'al Mehablim le-Or ha-Halakhah." In *Meshiv Milhamah: She'elot u-Teshuvot be-'Inyaney Tsava, Milhamah, u-Bitahon*, vol. 3, 305–27. Jerusalem: Ha-Idra Rabbah, 1982–1991.

————. "Lehimah be-Shabbat be-Askpeklaryah shel ha-Halakhah." In *Sinai: Sefer Yovel*, edited by R. Yehudah Leib ha-Kohen Maimon, 148–88. Jerusalem: Mosad ha-Rav Kuk, 1949; reprinted in *Meshiv Milhamah: She'elot u-Teshuvot be-'Inyaney Tsava, Milhamah, u-Bitahon*, vol. 1, 41–109. Jerusalem: Ha-Idra Rabbah, 1982–1991.

————. "Ma'amadam ha-Hilkhati shel Yehudah ve-Shomron ve-Hevel 'Azah." In *Torat ha-Medinah: Mehkar Hilkhati Histori be-Nos'im ha-'Omdim be-Rumah shel Medinat Yisra'el me'az Tekumatah*, edited by Yisra'el Tamari, 114–34. Jerusalem: Ha-Idra Rabah, 1999.

————. "Ma'amad ha-Shilton lefi ha-Halakhah." In *Torat ha-Medinah: Mehkar Hilkhati Histori be-Nos'im ha-'Omdim be-Rumah shel Medinat Yisra'el me'az Tekumatah*, edited by Yisra'el Tamari, 18–27. Jerusalem: Ha-Idra Rabah, 1999.

————. "Milhamot Yisra'el bi-Zeman ha-zeh le-Or ha-Halakhah." In *Meshiv Milhamah: She'elot u-Teshuvot be-'Inyaney Tsava, Milhamah, u-Bitahon*, vol. 1, 110–38. Jerusalem: Ha-Idra Rabbah, 1982–1991.

————. "Milhemet Mitsvah ve-Milhemet Reshut." In *Meshiv Milhamah: She'elot u-Teshuvot be-'Inyaney Tsava, Milhamah, u-Bitahon*, vol. 3, 351–68. Jerusalem: Ha-Idra Rabbah, 1982–1991.

————. "Milhemet Shelom ha-Galil le-fi ha-Halakhah." In *Meshiv Milhamah: She'elot u-Teshuvot be-'Inyaney Tsava, Milhamah, u-Bitahon*, vol. 3, pp. 267–83. Jerusalem: Ha-Idra Rabbah, 1982–1991.

————. "Musar ha-Lehimah le-Or ha-Halakhah." In *Meshiv Milhamah: She'elot u-Teshuvot be-'Inyaney Tsava, Milhamah, u-Bitahon*, vol. 1, 3–40. Jerusalem: Ha-Idra Rabbah, 1982–1991.

————. "Netuney Petihah be-Esh Lefi ha-Halakhah." In *Mishnat ha-Medinah: Mehkar Hilkhati Histori be-Nos'im ha-'Omdim be-Rumah shel Medinat Yisra'el me'az Tekumatah*, edited by R. Mikhah Halevi, 67–74. Jerusalem: Ha-Idra Rabah, 1999.

————. "Sheleimut ha-Arets lefi ha-Halakhah." In *Torat ha-Medinah: Mehkar Hilkhati Histori be-Nos'im ha-'Omdim be-Rumah shel Medinat Yisra'el me'az Tekumatah*, edited by Yisra'el Tamari, 68–102. Jerusalem: Ha-Idra Rabah, 1999.

————. *Torat ha-Filosofiyah: Leket Hartsa'ot be-Filosofiyah Yehudit*. Jerusalem: Ha-Idrah Rabah, 1998.

Gorny, Yosef. *Zionism and the Arabs, 1882–1948: A Study of Ideology*. Oxford: Oxford University Press, 1987.

Gutel, R. Neryah. *Hadashim gam Yeshanim: Bi-Netivey Mishnato ha-Hilkhatit Hagutit shel ha-Rav Kuk*. Jerusalem: Magnes Press, 2005.

————. "Hagdaratan ha-Hilkhatit shel Milhamot Yisra'el be-Mishnat ha-Rav Hertsog." In *Masu'ah le-Yitshak*, edited by R. Shelomit Eli'ash, R. Itamar Varhaftig, and R. Uri Dasberg, vol. 2, pp. 311–22. Jerusalem: Yad ha-Rav Hertsog, 1989.

————. "'Hufshah Li-Veney Yeshivateinu 'o Mitsvat Giyus: 'Al Igeret ha-R'YH Kuk ve-Pulmus Parshanutah." In *'Amadot: 'Am—Medinah—Torah*, edited by Moshe Rahimi, vol. 1, pp. 25–40. Elkanah / Rehovot, Israel: Mikhlelet Orot Yisra'el, 2010.

———. "*Kavim le-Mishnato ha-Sheleimah shel Rabenu.*" In *Ga'on ba-Torah u-ve-Midot: Perakim le-Darko ve-li-Demuto shel Maran ha-Ga'on Sha'ul Yisra'eli zts"l*, edited by Yisra'el Sharir, 197–222. Jerusalem: Erez, 1999.

———. "*Lehimah be-Shetah Ravey Ukhlosiyah Ezrahit.*" In *Ha-Milhamah ba-Teror*, edited by Ya'ir Halevi, 43–106. Kiryat Arba: Makhon Le-Rabaney Yishuvim, 2006.

———. "*Samkhuyot Manhigey Yisra'el.*" In *Berurim be-Hilkhot ha-Re'iyah*, edited by R. Moshe Tsevi Neryah, R. Aryeh Shtern, and R. Neryah Gutel, 107–20. Jerusalem: Beit ha-Rav, 1992.

Ha-Kohen, R. Shabbetai ben Me'ir. Commentary on *Shulhan 'Arukh*, standard edition.

Hertzberg, Arthur. *The Zionist Idea: A Historical Analysis and Reader*. Philadelphia: Jewish Publication Society of America, 1997.

Herzog, R. Isaac Halevi. *Peskaim u-Khetavim be-Diney Orah Hayim*. Edited by Shlomo Shapira. Jerusalem: Mosad ha-Rav Kuk, 1989.

Hollander, Avi'ad Yehi'el. "*Deyokano ha-Hilkhati shel ha-Rav Shelomoh Goren: 'Iyunim be-Shikuley ha-Pesikah ve-Darkey ha-Bisus be-Ma'amarav ha-Hilkhatiyim.*" PhD diss., Bar-Ilan University, 2011.

Holtser, Eli. *Herev Pipiyot be-Yadam: Activizm Tseva'i be-Hagutah shel ha-Tsiyonut ha-Datit*. Jerusalem: Hartman Institute, 2009.

Ibn Zimra, R. David ben Solomon. *Teshuvot Radbaz*. 6 vols. Jerusalem: Yerid Sefarim, 2003.

Inbari, Motti. *Messianic Religious Zionism Confronts Territorial Compromises*. Cambridge: Cambridge University Press, 2012.

Ish-Shalom, Benjamin. *Rav Avraham Itzhak HaCohen Kook: Between Rationalism and Mysticism*. Translated by Ora Wiskind-Elper. Albany: State University of New York Press, 1993.

Ish Shalom, Benjamin, and Shalom Rosenberg, eds. *The World of Rav Kook's Thought*. Translated by Shalom Carmy and Bernard Casper. Avi Chai Foundation, 1991.

Isserlein, R. Israel ben Petahiah. *Terumat ha-Deshen*. New York: Y. Volf, 1958.

Jerusalem Talmud, standard edition.

Kagan, R. Israel Meir. *Sefer Mahaneh Yisra'el*. Beney Berak, Israel: Torah va-Da'at, 1967.

Kaplan, Lawrence J., and David Shatz, eds. *Rabbi Abraham Isaac Kook and Jewish Spirituality*. New York: New York University Press, 1995.

Karo, R. Joseph. *Beit Yosef*. In *Arba'ah Turim*, standard edition

———. *Kesef Mishneh*. In *Mishneh Torah*, standard edition.

Katz, Jacob. "The Dispute between Jacob Berab and Levi ben Habib over Renewing Ordination." In *Binah: Studies in Jewish History, Thought, and Culture*, edited by by Joseph Dan, vol. 1, pp. 119–41. New York: Praeger, 1989.

———. "Rabbinical Authority and Authorization in the Middle Ages." In *Studies in Medieval Jewish History and Literature*, edited by Isadore Twersky, vol. 1, pp. 41–56. Cambridge, Mass: Harvard University Press, 1979.

Kimelman, Reuven. "The Ethics of National Power: Government and War from the Sources of Judaism." In *Authority, Power, and Leadership in the Jewish Polity*, edited by Daniel Elazar, 247–94. Lanham, Md.: University Press of America, 1991.

Kofman, Yitshak. "*'Et Milhamah ve-'Et Shalom 'al pi ha-Nestiv.*" *Merhavim* 6 (1997): 285–97.

Kook, R. Abraham Isaac. *Igrot ha-Re'iyah*. 3 vols. Jerusalem: Mosad ha-Rav Kuk, 1985.

———. *Mishpat Kohen*. Jerusalem: Mosad ha-Rav Kuk, 1966.

———. *Orot*. Jerusalem: Mosad ha-Rav Kuk, 1982.

Kook, R. Tsevi Yehudah. *Li-Netivot Yisra'el*. 2 vols. Beit El, Israel: Mei-Avney ha-Makom, 2003.

Landes, Daniel, ed. *Omnicide: Jewish Reflections on Weapons of Mass Destruction.* Northvale, N.J.: Jason Aronson, 1991.

Levey, Geoffrey B. "Judaism and the Obligation to Die for the State." *AJS Review* 12, no. 2 (Fall 1987): 175–203; reprinted in *Law, Politics, and Morality in Judaism*, edited by Michael Walzer, 182–308. Princeton, N.J.: Princeton University Press, 2006.

Levin, Yigal, and Amnon Shapira, eds. *War and Peace in the Jewish Tradition: From the Biblical World to the Present.* London: Routledge, 2012.

Lifshits, R. Aryeh Leib ben Elijah. *She'elot u-Teshuvot Shem Aryeh.* Vilnius: Rom Family, 1874.

Loew, R. Judah ben Betsal'el. *Gur Aryeh.* Tel Aviv: Pardes, 1956.

Lubits, Roncn. *"Ha-Musagim 'Kidush ha-Shem' ve-'Hilul ha-Shem' be-Hagut ha-Tsiyonut ha-Datit."* *Sha'anan* 16 (2011): 113–45.

Luz, Ehud. *Religion and Nationalism in Early Zionist Thought (1882–1904).* Translated by Lenn J. Schram. Philadelphia: Jewish Publication Society of America, 1988.

———. *Wrestling with an Angel: Power, Morality, and Jewish Identity.* Translated by Michael Swirsky. New Haven, Conn: Yale University Press, 2003.

Maimonides. *Mishneh Torah*, standard edition.

———. *Peirush ha-Mishnah.* Edited by R. Joseph Kafih. Jerusalem: Mosad ha-Rav Kuk, 1963.

Meiri, R. Menahem. *Beit ha-Behirah: Sanhedrin.* Edited by Avraham Sofer. New York, 1962.

Meizlish, Sha'ul. *Rabbanut bi-Se'arat ha-Yamim: Hayav u-Mishnato shel ha-Rav Aizik ha-Levi Hertsog, ha-Rav ha-Rashi le-Yisra'el.* Tel Aviv: Merhav, 1991.

Meron, Theodor. "The Humanization of Humanitarian Law." *American Journal of International Law* 94, no. 2 (2000): 239–78.

Mirsky, Yehudah. *Rav Kook: Mystic in a Time of Revolution.* New Haven, Conn: Yale University Press, 2014.

Mishlov, Shifrah. *"Be-'Ein ha-Se'arah: Demuto ha-Tsiburit ve-Yetsirato ha-Toranit shel ha-Rav Shelomoh Goren ba-Shanim 1948-1994."* PhD diss., Bar-Ilan University, 2010.

———. *"Hashkafato ha-Tsiyonit shel ha-Rav Shelomoh Goren."* *Yisra'el* 20 (2012): 81–106.

———. *"'Emdato shel ha-Rav Goren bi-Devar Mesirat ha-Shetahim Temurat Shalom."* *Mehkerey Yehudah ve-Shomron* 22 (2013): 243–59.

Mishnah. In Babylonian Talmud, standard edition.

Morris, Benny. *Milhamot ha-Gevul shel Yisra'el: 1949–1956.* Tel Aviv: 'Am 'Oved, 1996.

Myers, Jody. "The Messianic Idea and Zionist Ideologies." In *Studies in Contemporary Jewry VII: Jews and Messianism in the Modern Era: Metaphor and Meaning*, edited by Jonathan Frankel, 3–13. New York: Oxford University Press, 1991.

Nahmanides. "Addenda to Positive and Negative Commandments." In Maimonides' *Sefer ha-Mitsvot*, standard edition.

———. *Peirushey ha-Torah.* Edited by C. Chavel. 2 vols. Jerusalem: Mosad ha-Rav Kuk, 1975.

Neuman, Kalman. "The Law of Obligatory War and Israeli Reality." In *War and Peace in Jewish Tradition: From the Biblical World to the Present*, edited by Yigal Levin and Amnon Shapira, 186–200. London: Routledge, 2012.

Nozick, Robert. *Philosophical Explanations.* Cambridge, Mass.: Harvard University Press, 1981.

Peels, H. G. L. *The Vengeance of God.* Leiden: E. J. Brill, 1995.

Penslar, Derek. *Jews and the Military: A History.* Princeton. N.J.: Princeton University Press, 2013.

Rakover, Nahum. *Mesirut Nefesh: Hakravat ha-Yahid le-Hatsalat ha-Rabim.* Jerusalem: Moreshet ha-Mishpat le-Yisra'el, 2000.

Rashi. *Perush 'al ha-Torah.* Standard edition in rabbinic Bibles.

Ravitzky, Aviezer. *Messianism, Zionism, and Jewish Religious Radicalism.* Translated by Michael Swirsky and Jonathan Chipman. Chicago: University of Chicago Press, 1996.

Rekhnits, 'Ido, and El'azar Goldshtein. *Etikah Tseva'it Yehudit.* Tel Aviv: Yedi'ot Sefarim, 2013.

Roness, Yitzcahk Avi. *"'Al Musariyutah shel ha-Milhamah be-Sifrut ha-Halakhah be-Me'ah ha-'Esrim."* In *'Amadot: 'Am—Medinah—Torah,* vol. 1, edited by Moshe Rahimi, 193–214. Elkanah / Rehovot, Israel: Mikhlelet Orot Yisra'el, 2010.

———. "Halakhah, Ideology, and Interpretation: Rabbi Shaul Yisraeli on the Status of Defensive War." *Jewish Law Association Studies* 20 (2010): 184–95.

———. *"Medinat Yisra'el be-Mishnato ha-Hilkhatit shel ha-Rav Hertsog."* MA thesis, Touro College, Jerusalem, 2005.

———. *"Milhamot Yisra'el—Halakhah ve-Idi'ologiyah be-Mishnat ha-RY' Hertsog."* In *Masu'ah le-Yitshak,* edited by R. Shelomit Eli'ash, R. Itamar Varhaftig, and R. Uri Dasberg, vol. 1, pp. 451–72. Jerusalem: Yad ha-Rav Hertsog, 1989.

———. *"Mishnato ha-Hilkhatit shel ha-Rav Sha'ul Yisra'eli."* PhD diss., Bar-Ilan University, Israel, 2012.

Rosenak, Avinoam. *A. I. Kook.* Jerusalem: Merkaz Zalman Shazar, 2006.

———. "The Conquest of the Land of Israel and Associated Moral Questions in the Teachings of Rabbi Kook and His Disciples: Thoughts in Light of the Book, *Herev Pipiyot be-Yadam."* In *The Gift of the Land and the Fate of the Canaanites in Jewish Thought,* edited by Katel Berthelot, Joseph E. David, and Marc Hirshman, 399–428. New York: Oxford University Press, 2014.

———. *Ha-Halakhah ha-Nevu'it: Ha-Filosopiyah shel ha-Halakhah be-Mishnt ha-R"YH Kuk.* Jerusalem: Magnes Press, 2007.

———. *"Musar, Milhamah, ve-Shalom be-Mishnat ha-Rav Kuk ve-Talmidav: Ha-Mifgash bein Utopiyah le-Metsi'ut."* Mayim mi-Dalyo 25–26 (2014–15): 235–62.

Roth, R. Meshulam. *Kol Mevaser.* Jerusalem: Mosad ha-Rav Kuk, 1955.

Sagi, Avi, and Dov Schwartz. *"Bein Halutsiyut le-Limud Torah: Zavit Aheret."* In *Me'ah Shanot Tsiyonut Datit: Heibetim Ra'ayoniyim,* edited by Avi Sagi and Dov Schwartz, vol. 3, pp. 73–76. Ramat Gan: Bar-Ilan University Press, 2004.

Salmon, Yosef. *Dat ve-Tisyonut: 'Imutim Rishonim.* Jerusalem: Magnes Press, 2001.

———. *Im Ta'iru ve-Im Tit'oreru: Ortodoxiyah be-Metsarey ha-Le'umiyut.* Jerusalem: Zalman Shazar Center, 2006.

Schreiber, R. Moses. *She'elot u-Teshuvot Hatam Sofer.* Bratislava, 1912.

Schwartz, Dov. *Erets Mamashut ve-Dimyon: Ma'amdah shel Erets Yisra'el be-Hagut ha-Tsiyonut ha-Datit.* Tel Aviv: 'Am 'Oved Publishers, 1997.

———. *Etgar u-Mashber be-Hug ha-Rav Kuk.* Tel Aviv: 'Am 'Oved Publishers, 2001.

———. *Faith at the Crossroads: A Theological Profile of Religious Zionism.* Translated by by Batya Stein. Leiden: E. J. Brill, 2002.

———. *Ha-Tsiyonut ha-Datit: Bein Higayon le-Meshihiyut.* Tel Aviv: 'Am 'Oved Publishers, 1999.

———. *Religious Zionism,* 2nd ed. Brighton, Mass.: Academic Studies Press, 2012.

Sefer ha-Hinukh. Jerusalem: Mekhon Yerushalayim, 1991.

Shakh, R. El'azar Menahem Man. *Be-Zot Ani Boteah: Igrot u-Ma'amarim 'al Tekufat ha-Yamim u-Me'ora'oteha.* Bney Berak: n.p., 1998.

Shapira, Anita. *Land and Power: The Zionist Resort to Force, 1881–1948*. Translated by William Templer. New York: Oxford University Press, 1992.

———. "The Religious Motifs of the Labor Movement," *Zionism and Religion*, edited by Shmuel Almog, Jehuda Reinharz, and Anita Shapira, 251–72. Hanover, N.H.: University of New England Press, 1998.

Shapira, Yosef. *Hagut, Halakhah, ve-Tsiyonut: 'Al 'Olamo ha-Ruhani shel ha-Rav Yitshak Ya'akov Reines*. Tel Aviv: Ha-Kibuts ha-Me'uhad, 2002.

Sharir, Yisra'el. *"Ish Emet ve-'Anavah—Pirkey Hayim."* In *Ga'on ba-Torah u-ve-Midot: Perakim le-Darko ve-li-Demuto shel Maran ha-Ga'on Sha'ul Yisra'eli zts"l*, edited by Yisra'el Sharir, 11–97. Jerusalem: Erez, 1999.

Shaviv, R. Yehudah. *"Le-Mi Mishpat ha-Melukhah?"* In *Berurim be-Hilkhot ha-Re'iyah*, edited by R. Moshe Tsevi Neryah, R. Aryeh Shtern, R. Neryah Gutel, 147–54. Jerusalem: Beit ha-Rav, 1992.

Shiloh, Shmu'el. *Dina de-Malkhuta Dina*. Jerusalem: Jerusalem Academic Press, 1974.

Shimoni, Gideon. *The Zionist Ideology*. Waltham, Mass.: Brandeis University Press, 1995.

Shir ha-Shirim Rabbah. In *Midrash Rabbah*, standard edition.

Shmerlovski, R. Menashe. *"Milhemet Mitsvah ve-Milhemet Reshut."* In *Sefer Har'el*, edited by R. Eliezer Hayim Shenvald, 47–87. Hispin, Israel: Ha-Golan, 1999.

Shteiner, R. Hayim Yisra'el. *"Malkhut Hashmona'im le-Or Tefisat Rabeinu be-*Mishpat Kohen *Siman 144 ve-ha-Hashlakhah le-Yameinu."* In *Berurim be-Hilkhot ha-Re'iyah*, edited by R. Moshe Tsevi Neryah, R. Aryeh Shtern, and R. Neryah Gutel, 155–82. Jerusalem: Beit ha-Rav, 1992.

Shulhan Arukh, standard edition.

Sifre: A Tannaitic Commentary on the Book of Numbers. Translated by Reuven Hammer. New Haven, Conn: Yale University Press, 1987.

Sifrey ba-Midbar. Edited by H. S. Horovitz. Jerusalem: Shalem, 1992.

Sifrey Devarim. Edited by Louis Finkelstein. New York: Jewish Theological Seminary Press, 1969.

Solis, Gary D. *The Law of Armed Conflict: International Humanitarian Law in War*. New York: Cambridge University Press, 2010.

Sprinzak, Ehud. *The Ascendance of Israel's Radical Right*. New York: Oxford University Press, 1991.

Tanhuma. Jersalem: Eshkol, 1972.

Teitelbaum, R. Yoel. *'Al ha-Ge'ulah ve-'al ha-Temurah*. Brooklyn: Sander Deitsh, 1967.

———. *Va-Yo'el Moshe*. Brooklyn: Jerusalem Publishing, 1961.

Te'omim, R. Joseph ben Meir. *Peri Megadim*. In *Shulhan Arukh: Orah Hayim*, standard edition.

Tosefta. In Babylonian Talmud, standard edition.

Waldenberg, R. Eliezer Yehudah. *Sefer Hilkhot Medinah*. 3 vols. Jerusalem: 1951.

———. *Tsits Eli'ezer*. 22 vols. Jerusalem, 1945–1994.

Walzer, Michael. *Just and Unjust Wars: A Moral Argument with Historical Illustrations*. 4th ed. New York: Basic Books, 2006.

———. "The Obligation to Die for the State." In *Essays on Disobedience, War, and Citizenship*, 77–98. Cambridge, Mass.: Harvard University Press, 1970.

Walzer, Michael, Menachem Lorberbaum, and Noam J. Zohar, eds. *The Jewish Political Tradition*. 2 vols. New Haven, Conn: Yale University, 2000.

Wanefsky, Joseph. *Rabbi Isaac Jacob Reines: His Life and Thought*. New York: Philosophical Library, 1970.

Waxman, Chaim Isaac Waxman. Edited by *Religious Zionism Post-Disengagement: Future Directions*. New York: Yeshiva University Press, 2008.

Yisraeli, R. Sha'ul. "*Berihah min ha-Arets bi-She'at Sakanah.*" In *Erets Hemdah be-Hilkhot Erets Yisra'el*, vol. 1, pp. 49–52. Jerusalem: Mosad ha-Rav Kuk, 1989.

———. *Havat Binyanim.* 2 vols. Edited by R. Neryah Gutel. Kefar Darom, Israel: Makhon ha-Torah ve-ha-Arets, 1991.

———. "*Mesirat Shetahim me-Erets Yisra'el be-Makom Pikuah Nefesh.*" *Tehumin* 10 (1989): 48–61; reprinted in *Havat Binyamin*, edited by R. Neriyah Gutel, vol. 1, 94–103. Kefar Darom, Israel: Makhon ha-Torah ve-ha-Arets, 2002; (available online at Hebrewbooks.org)

———. "*Milhemet Mitsvah ve-Milhemet Reshut.*" *Torah she-be-'al Peh* 10 (1968): 46–50.

———. "*Milhemet Reshut u-Gedareha.*" In *'Amud ha-Yemini*, 153–60. Tel Aviv: Moreshet, 1966.

———. "*Mivtsa 'Yonatan' (Entebeh) le-Or ha-Halakhah.*" *Shevilin* 29–30 (1977): 93–102; reprinted in *Be-Tsomet ha-Torah ve-ha-Medinah*, 253–89. Alon Shevut, Israel: Tsomet, 1991.

———. "*Pe'ulot Tseva'iyot le-Haganat ha-Medinah.*" In *'Amud ha-Yemini*, 168–205. Tel Aviv: Moreshet, 1966.

———. "*Pikuah Nefesh be-Sakanah Ruhanit.*" *Tehumin* 2 (1981): 27–34.

———. "*Takrit Kibiyeh le-Or ha-Halakhah.*" *Ha-Torah ve-ha-Medinah* 5–6 (1953–54): 71–113.

Yosef, R. 'Ovadyah. "*Hahzarat ha-Shetahim me-Erets Yisra'el be-Makom Pikuah Nefesh.*" *Torah she-be-'al Peh* 21 (1980): 12–20.

Yost, Ari'av. "*Me'afyeney ha-Pesikah ha-Tsiburt be-Mishnato ha-Hilkhatit shel ha-Rav Sha'ul Yisra'eli: Haf'alat ha-Mishtarah be-Shabbat ke-Mivhan.*" *Diney Yisra'el* 28 (2011): 145–85.

———. "*Pesikat ha-Halakhah shel ha-Rav Sha'ul Yisra'eli, Nokhah Etgar ha-Ribonut ha-Yehudit be-Me'ah ha-'Esrim.* MA thesis, Tel Aviv University, 2010.

INDEX LOCORUM

GENERAL INDEX